Living in God's Providence

Living in God's Providence

*History of the Congregation of
Divine Providence of San Antonio, Texas
1943-2000*

Mary Christine Morkovsky, CDP

To order additional copies of this book, contact:
Xlibris Corporation
1-888-795-4274
www.Xlibris.com
Orders@Xlibris.com
53330

CONTENTS

"This volume tackles the challenging task of interpreting the story of the enormous transitions in the life of American women religious in the rapidly shifting social and ecclesiastical context since 1943. The author considers the CDPs 'well situated to embrace the shifting demands of religious mission because their very heritage was grounded in ongoing transformations . . . played out on a highly charged stage of oppression concerning multi-racial relationships.' This book provides an invaluable insiders' look at the increasingly varied ministries and changes in community life that have equipped a dedicated group of women religious to continue to serve Divine Providence in the 21st century."

Rev. Robert E. Wright, OMI

Professor of U.S. Religious History,
Oblate School of Theology
Executive Board member,
Commission for the Study of Church
History in Latin America

ACKNOWLEDGEMENTS

For the Congregation of Divine Providence of San Antonio, Texas,[1] the approach of a new millennium seemed an appropriate time to update its history. *Memoirs of 50 Years* by Sister Mary Joseph Neeb covered the years 1866 to 1916. *The History of the Sisters of Divine Providence, San Antonio, Texas,* by Sister Mary Generosa Callahan began with the cultural backgrounds of the Congregation, founded in France in 1762, and detailed its years in Texas from the arrival of the Sisters in 1866 until 1943, the year the first U.S.-born superior was elected. This book covers the history of the Congregation from 1943 until 2000.[2] It is a history of the Sisters rather than of successive administrations, so in addition to facts it contains the Sisters' reactions to events.

To Sister Elizabeth McCullough, who was convinced of the necessity for this book and supported every step taken to bring it to completion, the Congregation owes an immense debt of gratitude. Every Sister of Divine Providence who was interviewed contributed to this book by her willingness and her honesty in expressing her remembrances and opinions. More than 30 Sisters cheerfully conducted interviews.[3] Sisters Leola Ann Doerfler, Clemence Ribitzki, and María

---

[1] This history will sometimes use the acronym CDP for this Congregation. CDP can also refer to an individual Sister while CDPs refers to all the Sisters of this Congregation.

[2] In rare cases, pertinent information from a later date is included.

[3] Besides members of the CDP history committee, the following Sisters conducted interviews: Sisters Ann Linda Bell, Elise Bengfort, Theresa Anne Billeaud, Angelina Breaux, Constance Christopher, Jane Coles, Virginia Clare Duncan, Marietta Fischer, María Guerra, Teresa Pauline Hereford, Joyce Jilek, Rosalie Karstedt, Kathryn Keefe, Jackie Kingsbury, Marian Frances Margo, Margaret Clare Mathews, Imelda Maurer, Laverne Mettlach, Madlyn Pape, Frederick Joseph Pirotina, Annalee Prather, María Cristina Ruelas, Madonna Sangalli, Jane Ann Slater, Michael Rose Stanzel, Elizabeth Anne Sueltenfuss, Patricia Ann Sullivan, and Alexia Vinklarek.

Esther Guerra were among those who offered office supplies and assistance. Without patient transcribers, the Sisters' views would be harder to access. Thanks are extended to Mrs. Lisa Roberts, who transcribed the majority of the interviews from cassette tapes, and Sister Madeleine Zimmerer, another faithful scribe. Mrs. Julia Lusk, Sister Eileen (M. Florian) Klein and Sister Alma Rose Booty also helped. Sister Agnes Marie Marusak plied her computer skills to bring all the footnotes into standard form and Sister L. Suzanne Dancer her expertise in statistics to shape tables in the Appendices. Cathy Maule and Associate Kimberly Gibson supplied invaluable technical assistance. Sisters Margaret Riché and Charlotte Kitowski, successive directors of the CDP Archives, spent many hours locating materials and verifying information. Sister Jane Coles donated many weeks to editing, and Sisters Margeta Krchnak and Agnes Marie Marusak helped to compile the indexes. Dr. Anne M. Butler, Sister Martine Hundelt, SSSF, and Sister Marion Verhaalen, SSSF, critiqued the whole manuscript.

All the members of the CDP history committee—Sisters María Carolina Flores, Rose Marie Gallatin, Charlotte Kitowski, Elizabeth McCullough, Mary Christine Morkovsky (chair), Angelina Murphy, Margit Maria Nagy, and Margaret Riché—were generous with their time and energy. Sisters Marian Angela Aguilar, Janet Griffin, Diane Langford, and Mary Paul Valdez also served on the committee for a time. Sister María Carolina Flores deserves special credit for organizing the interview process. She and another historian, Sister Margit Mária Nagy, patiently critiqued several drafts.

The use and development of personal gifts is helped or hindered by the organization to which an individual belongs, and this is especially the case for a woman religious who finds her deepest identity in her religious congregation. We share much in common with other communities of women, but we also possess unique qualities and characteristics as individuals and as a community. This history is part of the process of learning who we are in order better to serve the world we inhabit. The first audience for this book is the community, that is, the members of this Congregation. We invite others to enter our story and share our ongoing journey. Readers will learn how our core belief in Providence has at times impelled us and at times compelled us to respond to the signs of the times. Often this trust meant beginning anew with few resources and with no guarantee of ultimate success.

INTRODUCTION

In 1943 the bell attached to a rope on both floors of a plain box-like convent in Houston, Texas, rang at 5 a.m. The nine Sisters of Divine Providence stationed at the grade school arose, reciting aloud the traditional prayer that began "Live, Jesus, in my heart! My God, I give you my heart. Mercifully deign to receive it and grant that no creature shall possess it but Thou alone." Continuing to pray aloud for five more minutes, the Sisters who shared small bedrooms began to dress. All had developed in their novitiate a rhythm for this process, which launched each day in a uniform way.

Over 20 items of dress had to be donned in a certain order. Before Morning Prayer at 5:25 in the small chapel on the first floor, the Sisters also stripped their single beds, flipped the thin mattresses, and replaced the bed linens, trying not to invade a companion's limited space. Usually it was still dark outside when they started to recite morning prayers unique to the Congregation. This was followed by chanting in Latin on one tone Matins, Lauds, Prime, Tierce, Sext, and None from the Little Office of the Blessed Virgin Mary. Then the superior read aloud some points for reflection, and the Sisters meditated in silence for half an hour. This was the first time of the day they had some relatively unstructured time, and they sometimes experienced "distractions." Perhaps they planned how to teach something better or recalled problematic students.

At 6:30 one of the parish priests offered Mass, which was followed by breakfast. The Sisters ate in silence while one of them read passages from the *Imitation of Christ*. By 8 a.m. they were leading their pupils across the playground to the children's daily Mass in the parish church.

In sharp contrast, in 1990 Sister Mary Walter Gutowski, CDP, one of two Sisters living in a small apartment, was the administrator of Our Lady of Guadalupe clinic for low income Latinos and African Americans in Rosenberg, Texas. Sister Walter, who was credited with having delivered more than 3,000 babies under difficult rural circumstances, once remarked, "When someone knocks at my door in the middle of the night, I get dressed in two minutes flat because I never know what will be waiting for me outside."[1]

What explains this dramatic change of style and ritual in the routines of Catholic Sisters living in mission houses? How did the Sisters move from cloisters to apartments? How did the rigid routines of the nine Sisters of 1943 transmute into the singular and unstructured life of Sister Mary Walter? What are the connections between the bell that rang at five in the morning and the one that sounded at any hour?

This study examines the period of 1943 to 2000, an era during which the Sisters of Divine Providence redefined their perspective and practices within the context of a changing American Catholic church. It demonstrates that the Sisters were well situated to embrace the shifting demands of religious mission because their very heritage was grounded in ongoing transformations. Those transformations were played out on a highly charged stage of oppression concerning multi-racial relationships, one that further prepared the Sisters for the intense dynamics of modern church life.

---

[1] Article by Stephen Johnson, *The Houston Chronicle*, March 24, 1980, Sec. 3, p. 3, located in the archives of the Congregation of Divine Providence at Our Lady of the Lake Convent in San Antonio, Texas. Henceforth, CDPA.

CHAPTER 1

RESPONDING TO PARADIGM SHIFTS

In 1943 the Sisters of Divine Providence had been in Texas and surrounding states for 77 years. They had survived conflict with a bishop, received new members from Europe and the U.S., and become known as competent and forward-looking educators. As they held their General Chapter, which convened every six years, they could not foresee the social and economic changes World War II would precipitate, the influence of the Second Vatican Council on the whole church, or the resulting paradigm shifts which would affect the Congregation's membership and ministries. The post-war population boom and increased prosperity for Catholics, a larger Hispanic presence in the Southwest, and the strong leadership of a new archbishop would be among the external influences. Meanwhile, the Congregation's interior life would be affected by directives from the Vatican, greater unity among U.S. women religious, and local needs for new services.

In the summer of 1943, 66 Sisters returned to the motherhouse at Our Lady of the Lake Convent in San Antonio earlier than the rest of their community because they were delegates[1] to the General Chapter which would elect general superiors and take up "the most important affairs of the Congregation." These affairs largely concerned the "secondary end" of the Congregation, which was "the Christian education and instruction of children and young ladies and the care of the sick."[2]

---

[1] Some capitulars (members of the chapter) took their place "of right": the Mother General and her Council, former Mothers General, the Secretary General, and the Treasurer General. Others were delegates elected by the Sisters. All delegates were capitulars, but not all capitulars were delegates (See "Constitutions of the Sisters of Divine Providence, San Antonio, Texas, U.S.A.," # 188). This booklet was published by Mission Press, S.V.D., Techny, Illinois, 1927 and re-published by the Seraphic Press, Milwaukee, Wisconsin, 1947. Hereafter, Constitutions.

[2] Constitutions, # 2 and # 186.

The two ends of the Congregation account for a kind of dichotomy between the private and public lives of its members. On the one hand, the Sisters had a special duty "to practice in their conventual life all the virtues of the most fervent and regular communities" so the Congregation could achieve its primary end, "the sanctification of its members." This was interpreted to mean daily communal prayers, silence except during daily recreation together and for necessary practical communication, and readiness to obey authorities. On the other hand, they were "to impart to children and young girls instruction suitable to their position in society; and, above all, to give them a religious education."[3] To do this, they had to study and obtain certification, usually at the college the Congregation staffed and maintained next to the motherhouse, and keep up with the best contemporary educational content and methods.

The General Chapter of 1943

The delegates represented the ethnicity and age of the Congregation's membership of about 680 Sisters. Thirty-seven percent of them were born in Europe.[4] Of the 28 delegates born in the U.S., more than half (15) were from Texas.[5] The oldest Chapter member was Mother Florence Walter,[6] 85, who took her place by right since she was the second Superior General of the Congregation. The youngest Chapter delegate was 33, and the average age of the Chapter members was 58. Comparing the lists of Chapter delegates of the previous Chapter of 1937 and the subsequent Chapter of 1949 reveals continuity in leadership and a very similar proportion of Europeans and North Americans, even though the Congregation had not "recruited" Sisters overseas for more than 40 years.

Mother M. Philothea Thiry, the third Superior General, had served three terms, so it was not surprising that her Assistant, Mother Angelique Ayres, was elected on 2 June 1943 on the first ballot by an absolute majority of votes.[7]

---

[3] Constitutions # 2.

[4] Seventeen were born in Ireland, 15 in Germany, two in France, and one each in Belgium, Czechoslovakia, and Switzerland. One delegate was born in Hull, Ottawa, Canada.

[5] Three were born in Louisiana, three in Oklahoma, and one each in Illinois, Iowa, Kansas, Kentucky, Mississippi, New York, and South Dakota.

[6] See *Mother Florence, a Biographical History*, by Sister Angelina Murphy (Smithtown, New York: Exposition Press, 1980).

[7] Not all future elections would be as predictable. Mother Angelique's successor was elected in 1955 on the third ballot with 36 out of 68 votes, and in 1986 the Superior General was elected on the fourth ballot with 17out of 32 votes. See Appendix I.

Archbishop Robert E. Lucey, who presided at the election, was the dynamic head of the Archdiocese of San Antonio and was becoming known for his interest in social work, catechetics, and ministry to Hispanics. He praised the outgoing Superior General for training Mother Angelique "just as Pope Pius XI trained Pius XII."[8] Also elected on the first ballot were the four General Councilors: Mothers Philothea Thiry, Assistant; Antoinette Loth (re-elected until 1949); Eugenia Kaiser (re-elected until 1955)—all natives of Alsace; and Mother Antonina Quinn, born in Iowa. When Mother Philothea became ill three years later, she was replaced by Mother Angelica O'Neill, a native of Ireland, who had been selected to complete the term of General Councilor Mother Vitalis Tracey in 1933 and would continue to be re-elected until 1955. Sister Gonzaga Menger remained the Secretary General, and Sister Constantine Braun, who had been the Procurator General since 1919, retained this office. The ethnic mix of Sisters from Alsace, Ireland, and the U.S. was to remain the case during both of Mother Angelique's terms as Superior General.[9] The practice of the general councilors' holding administrative positions such as Superior of a local community, Superior of the Motherhouse or the College, or Business Manager also continued.

The three Commissions elected by the chapter delegates made no major recommendations. They did consider a request made by Archbishop Lucey through his Vicar for Religious, Rev. Joseph C. Ei, SM, that the new administration seriously consider "a more just representation for the large communities of the College and the Convent, a fairer proportion between the number of Sisters in these houses and their representatives at the General Chapter. 'Their rules should be made democratic so that all of the Sisters will have fair representation.'"[10] The delegates, however, agreed with the Vicar that the Constitutions already expressed the mind of the church. Before adjourning on 4 June, the Chapter unanimously approved three resolutions that (1) re-emphasized the decisions of previous chapters, (2) called for especially conscientious observance of poverty, and (3) recommended that all pray to the Holy Spirit for divine guidance and blessings on the new administration.

Except for Mother Angelique and Sister Gonzaga, the other administrators elected in 1943 were born in Europe. Their first language was not English, and they had spent their youth in a Roman Catholic atmosphere. But from the beginning English was the language used in the Texas Congregation because it was considered the language of the country and because many of the Sisters came

---

[8] Sister Mary Generosa Callahan, CDP, *The History of the Sisters of Divine Providence, San Antonio, Texas* (Milwaukee: Bruce, 1954) 279. Sister Generosa worked very closely with Mother Angelique for five years to prepare this history.

[9] Appendix II shows the geographical areas from which CDPs have entered.

[10] Rev. Joseph C. Ei, SM, to Mother Philothea Thiry, 1 May 1943.

from Ireland in the early days. Mother Angelique related easily to the Europeans even though her family was Protestant and she was educated in U.S. public grade schools. She entered the convent less than five months after the return from exile of the Texas foundress, Mother St. Andrew Feltin. When she was received on 16 March 1901 the second Superior General, Mother Florence Walter, welcomed her. Her predecessor, the third Superior General, Mother Philothea Thiry, was her Mistress of Postulants and Novices. Since her entrance into the convent Mother Angelique had willingly accepted Mother Philothea's mentoring.

The First U.S.-Born Superior General

Born in Mississippi in 1882 into a family of Protestant immigrants from Europe, Sister Mary Angelique Ayres became the fourth Superior General of the Congregation. She converted to Catholicism in 1897 while attending an academy taught by Sisters of the Holy Cross in Austin, Texas; and four years later she entered the Congregation of Divine Providence.[11] Her many talents were always recognized and appreciated. Even before she made her first religious vows, she taught music at Our Lady of the Lake Academy, a private high school. Less than 10 years after entering the convent, she "was third in rank, although not that in age or in years in the religious life"[12] in the large community stationed at the college. She also taught mathematics, physics, English, and other courses. She was both author and editor in several convent and college publications. She became the registrar of Our Lady of the Lake College[13] in 1913 and helped prepare the college for affiliation with the Catholic University in Washington, D.C. in 1913 and for official approval by the state of Texas in 1919. In 1925 she became Academic Dean of OLLU and was elected to the Executive Committee of the Southern Association of Women's Colleges in 1934.

A dreamer and planner, Mother Angelique nevertheless was not a detached administrator. She looked after details, and her influence on the institution as well as on individuals was strong and lasting. A report of a diocesan canonical visitation of the San Antonio convent in 1911 contains the opinion of Rev. Louis A. Tragresser, SM, that "there is a tendency to cater too much to the worldly spirit

---

[11] The Superior General and her four Councilors all had the title "Mother." In 1961, it was reserved for the Superior General alone. When Sister Elizabeth McCullough was elected Superior General in 1967, "the first thing she did was to get rid of the title 'Mother'" (Sister Benilde Broussard, oral interview, 23 Oct. 2000, CDPA).

[12] Sister Generosa Callahan, *Mother Angelique Ayres, Dreamer and Builder of Our Lady of the Lake University* (Austin: Pemberton Press, 1981) 51. On August 14, 1909, she earned a permanent certificate to teach in any white public school in Texas.

[13] Hereafter referred to as OLLC or more often as OLLU, Our Lady of the Lake University, its name since 1975.

and a diminution of the genuine Catholic spirit of the Church, manifested in the fact that the Academy of Our Lady of the Lake has been affiliated to the State University."[14] Rev. H. H. Hume, chancellor of the diocese, "placed much of the blame for the spirit of worldliness on Sister Angelique which he said was very clear in her opinions."[15] Apparently Sister Angelique's liveliness and intelligence had not been stifled in the convent.

The work of the Sisters also showed the influence of both Europe and the United States. They had the reputation of being fine teachers after the model of their predecessors in the Congregation who were trained abroad, but they were also known for utilizing the latest U.S. pedagogy. Their religious formation and practices remained very similar to those of the motherhouse at St. Jean de Bassel, France; and Mother Angelique saw no need to change them. But in the field of education she realized the necessity of keeping abreast of the latest developments.

Instead of being responsible for the academic life of about 400 women in college, as Superior General Mother Angelique would lead almost 700 Sisters who served over 23,000 people, mostly as teachers but also as domestic workers, catechists, and health care workers.[16] The majority of people she led would no longer be young women preparing to be homemakers or professionals but women religious of all ages. How they were deployed would influence education in Texas and neighboring states for years to come.

The European majority of the general administrators reflected the makeup of the Congregation in the 1940s. A large number of the Sisters born in Ireland and Germany had responded to a call for missionaries issued by Sisters who went from Texas to recruit abroad. The Sisters from Germany were now concerned about their relatives in war-torn Europe, trying to communicate with them, sending them clothing and other necessities, and sometimes selling candy to their students during recess to fund these care packages. Some non-German Sisters were a little resentful of what they perceived as favoritism, or as a little bending of the strict rules on contacts with relatives.

For over 50 years teachers, mostly lay men and women, at the college had in the summertime instructed CDPs[17] as well as Sisters from other Congregations, many of whom taught in small public schools. As Superior General, Mother Angelique continued to encourage improvement at the college by assigning well-educated Sister-teachers, encouraging changes and additions

---

[14] Canonical Visitation report, April 1911, quoted in Callahan, *Mother Angelique* 67.

[15] Callahan, *Mother Angelique* 67.

[16] In 1946 there were 683 Sisters of whom 463 taught in schools in Texas, Oklahoma, Arkansas, New Mexico, and California. See Appendix III for the number of Sisters in the Congregation in subsequent administrations.

[17] This acronym will be used to designate Sisters of the Congregation of Divine Providence.

to the curriculum, and constructing new buildings. By 1946 the 410 college students hailed from 20 states and four foreign countries.[18] *Good Housekeeping* magazine listed OLLC as one of the 50 best small colleges in America. Its music department was particularly strong. With more than 200 music students enrolled, there was no place for practice pianos, so ground was broken for a new fine arts building. Trees were felled, hedges uprooted, and the bath-house building was torn down; but the work proceeded slowly because of "lack of essential steel."[19] Rapid growth led to organizational changes. Preliminary to securing a government loan to build Pacelli Residence Hall, the College was incorporated separately from the Congregation on 16 April 1957.[20] By 1969 all departments were co-educational, and in 1975 the College was re-named Our Lady of the Lake University of San Antonio.

When Mother Angelique died in 1968, undergraduate enrollment (full-time equivalent) was 978; by 1980 it was 2,168. Graduate school enrollment also increased. In 1968, 114 master's degrees were awarded; in 1980, 500 were awarded. While morality, religion, and Catholic identity had been emphasized when she was dean, after 1942 the stated purposes of the college gradually changed. Increased emphasis was put not only on intellectual development but also on professional preparation, which by 1960 was on a par with liberal arts education.[21] In March 1973, the Sisters working at OLLU for the first time gathered "as one group to discuss various aspects of this apostolate of the Congregation." A short time later, Sister Mary Margaret (Emella) Hughes, ninth Superior General and former dean of students at OLL, noted that "CDPs today form a small percentage of the student body and the majority of administrators and faculty are lay people."[22]

In a Country at War

What was going on in the "outside world" as the Sisters devoted their attention to the affairs of the Congregation? They were not accustomed to reading secular newspapers or magazines, but they were made aware of war conditions every day. Their relatives were joining or being drafted into the military; their friends, relatives, and former students were fighting and sometimes dying

---

[18] Family Circular, duplicated CDP newsletter (Hereafter FC), Oct. 1946: 9, CDPA.

[19] FC, April, 1946: 130, CDPA.

[20] GC minutes, 29 Apr. 1975, CDPA.

[21] Sister Virginia Clare Duncan, CDP, "An Analysis of the Evolution of the Purposes of Our Lady of the Lake College," diss., University of Texas at Austin, 1967, 296-297.

[22] *CDP News*, 5 April 1973: 1, CDPA.

overseas. Everyone's diet was more frugal and less varied because of shortages; the motherhouse had a "victory garden." Sister Joan of Arc Heinrich, who taught German at the college, followed closely the career of Admiral Chester Nimitz, gathering material for the biography, *My Name is Nimitz*, which she wrote and published in 1948. The seeds for numerous, dramatic changes that would accelerate during the remainder of the twentieth century were being sown at this very time. Most citizens, however, could not even begin to imagine what changes the war was to precipitate not only in the economy but also in their daily lives as well as in the status of women and educational institutions. The Ford Motor Company, for example, would not only become a multinational corporation, but the Ford Foundation would also provide millions for post-war education projects.

The composition and power of the labor force was changing because of the draft. The new battle cry was "The more women at work, the sooner we will win the war."

In Church news, Pope Pius XII exhorted belligerents to respect the laws of humanity in aerial war. Speaking at the Ex-Students' Association banquet at St. Mary's University the evening of 31 May 1943, Archbishop Lucey said the U.S. Senate was the most potentially dangerous body in the world because 33 Senators "could nullify all the blood, sweat, and tears that will go into the victory of the UN, if they fail to ratify the treaty that will give us peace after this war."[23]

The war affected faculty and students at OLLU in many ways. Lay faculty were drafted or volunteered for military service. Sister M. Elaine Gentemann composed patriotic songs. Students conscientiously bought stamps for their war stamp books which, when filled, became savings bonds. One small example of the wartime admonition, "Use it up or wear it out; make it do, or do without" was when St. Joseph's Academy downtown installed new screens; the old shutters were donated to the college to protect the hay fed to the horses used for riding lessons.[24] The Senior Ball in Providence Social Room on 8 May 1943 had a patriotic scheme. Many of the escorts were servicemen from local military bases.

A performance by the music department of OLLU at the Army Y-USO Club prompted a letter from Chaplain (Captain) A. J. O'Reilly of the Second Infantry Division at Fort Sam Houston to the archbishop. The chaplain complained that this activity placed Catholic chaplains in an "embarrassing position" since the "Army Y is a known agency of the Anti-Catholic sects."[25] Archbishop Lucey sent the letter to Mother Philothea and asked for her "reaction to the

---

[23] *The San Antonio Light*, 1 June 1943: B 2.

[24] FC, 1 Oct. 1943: 15, CDPA.

[25] Chaplain O'Reilly to Archbishop Lucey, 11 May 1942, CDPA.

Chaplain's suggestions."[26] Mother Philothea passed the letters on to Sister Mary Amabilis Hanley, director of the music department at OLLC, who wrote an apology to the Archbishop explaining that she thought the program would be "good entertainment for our soldiers, . . . open to all and in no way partaking of sectarianism." Of the 13 girls who performed, seven were non-Catholics; and no Sisters attended.[27]

The war impinged on all the schools taught by the Sisters of Divine Providence, as news items in the Congregation's monthly "Family Circular" attest.[28] Sisters were among civilian corps who made sure neighborhoods were blacked out during practice air raids. Former pupils were among the victims of the war. A scrapbook of activities pertaining to the war effort assembled by Holy Family School in Tulsa, Oklahoma, was one of three forwarded to Washington to be used in a drive for war bonds. At St. Joseph's Academy in San Antonio the Victory Corps staged a formal flag raising each morning after Mass. Pupils of St. John's School in Ennis, Texas, made gifts for homeless or destitute children in Europe as well as fancy tray covers and Christmas cards for servicemen. In Pecos, New Mexico, and Cloutierville, Louisiana, teachers helped in registration drives for ration books. Children at St. Anthony's School in Bunkie, Louisiana, each month supplied 19 copies of Catholic literature to army chaplains for distribution. Schools in Granger and Wallis, Texas, offered a Junior Red Cross Course in First Aid. Most pupils in all the schools took part in the National Scrap Drive and the Schools at War projects.

Being in a country at war affected the daily lives of the Sisters and those whom they served in many ways. When the conflict was over, it was evident that the vision of many citizens of a country that was becoming a superpower had been expanded.

Summer Activities of 1943

Because of the war attention was focused on Europe and the Pacific area, but Latin America was not forgotten. OLLC offered an Inter-American workshop and seminar series 9 June-16 July 1943. Washington, D.C. funded the events as well as scholarships for teachers in both public and private schools who attended. Course subjects included general background in Latin American materials for both elementary and high school teachers, methods and materials

---

[26] Archbishop Lucey to Mother Philothea, 22 May 1941, CDPA.

[27] Sister Amabilis to Archbishop Lucey, n.d, CDPA.

[28] The examples given in this paragraph are all from FC, April 1943:167-170; October 1943: 15, 17, 18; and November 1943: 37, CDPA.

for instructing Spanish-speaking children, and contemporary collaboration between the Americas.[29] The college also hosted the Summer School of Catholic Action (SSCA) attended by more than 1,200 young people.[30] Lectures on human rights and other social issues formed a large part of the week's curriculum.

The motherhouse was as usual the focus of intense activity as the Sisters returned from their assigned missions during June and July to study and make their annual retreats before returning to work in early August. Immediately after the first summer school session the annual retreat, which lasted seven full days, began. Everyone kept silence during that time and attended conferences preached by a priest three times a day. Among the Sisters who could not make the retreat in 1943 were those who were "going off to study" at universities, usually because they were destined to teach at the college. In 1943, for example, Mother Angelique obtained the archbishop's permission to send seven Sisters for graduate studies at four institutions: Chicago University, Chicago Art Institute, Columbia University, and the Catholic University in Washington, D.C.

Sister-teachers usually could take college courses only in the summertime, and sometimes they missed the first week or more of classes because they were assigned to teach catechism in vacation schools. Others taught catechism in July and August after the annual retreat.[31] In 1942 Sister Generosa Callahan had become the first member of the Congregation to enroll full-time at a secular university for the regular semesters. For the next three years, she returned from her studies at the University of Texas in Austin to the motherhouse one weekend every month to make sure she retained her religious identity and fervor.[32]

After the annual retreat, it was time for the year's assignments. The Superior General and her Council, especially the Mistress of Studies, decided where each Sister was needed. When her name appeared on the blackboard near the Secretary General's office, the Sister—sometimes with trepidation—came to the Superior General's Office to receive her assignment, called her "obedience," for the year. By the middle of August, most of the Sisters had received their obediences and departed for their missions. Except for necessities and emergencies, there would be little contact between them until the following summer.

The group of women religious Mother Angelique would lead for the next 12 years was held together by a strong idealism, a shared sense that their lives as individuals and as a community had meaning. A few of the pioneer Sisters were still living and reminded them of their history of surviving obstacles

---

[29] *Southern Messenger*, 20 May 1943: 9.

[30] *Southern Messenger*, 24 June and 29 July 1943 and *Alamo Messenger*, 6 August 1943.

[31] Sister Aquilina Martínez remembered that one summer she taught three religious vacation schools (oral interview, 26 Jan. 2000, CDPA).

[32] Callahan, *Mother Angelique* 99.

and continually increasing numbers. They believed that their services would contribute to their personal salvation and that of others. The familiar rituals of the Roman Catholic Church as well as those unique to the Congregation that had grown up over the years, including the annual summer gathering for study and retreat at the motherhouse, gave a sense of stability and predictability. The Congregation was solidly established and recognized for the professional qualification of its members and their excellent institutions. The Sisters were neither revolutionaries nor traditionalists. Although their bonds were not predominantly blood ties, friendships, or loyalty to a charismatic leader, they were a united group facing the future with confidence. This unity and trust, as well as the leadership of risk-taking individual Sisters, were a source of strength as they ventured into different types of ministries in the coming decades.

Mother Angelique Ayres,
Golden Jubilee, 1954
(CDP Archives)

CONGREGATIONS OF SISTERS OF PROVIDENCE
ISSUED FROM THE CHARISM
OF BLESSED JEAN MARTIN MOYE

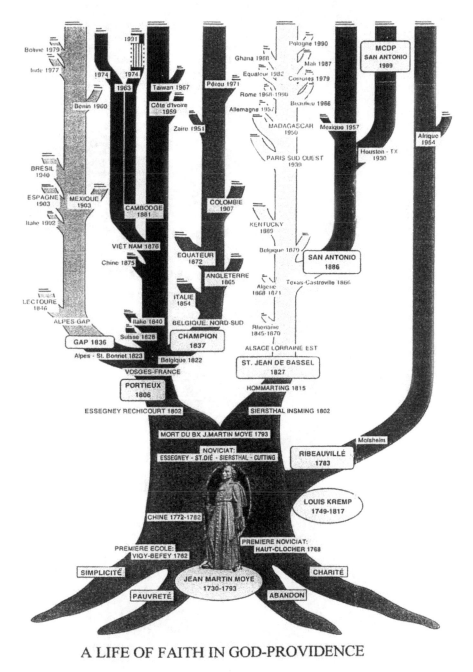

A LIFE OF FAITH IN GOD-PROVIDENCE

First Communion class,
Immaculate Heart of Mary parish,
San Antonio, Texas
1945

CHAPTER 2

SEEING EDUCATIONAL NEEDS
AND TAKING RISKS

Sister Jane (Alice Ann) Coles' first assignment was to the new Providence High
School in San Antonio. She recalled that the pioneer Sister faculty had the sense
of togetherness furthering the educational mission of the Congregation.

> I was excited about being on the faculty at this new school. There was
> a wonderful spirit in the community stemming greatly, I think, from
> the fact that we were a charter faculty. We were about 20 Sisters living
> in local community there, and almost half of us were annual professed.
> I found the students were cooperative and eager to learn. I think the
> easiest part of that first assignment was living in community and working
> with such a spiritually oriented and professionally capable group.[1]

When Sister Bernadette (Margaret Ann) Bezner two decades later taught
in an inner city public school, she found herself alone in a very different
environment.

> I would come back to school on a Monday, and there would be
> tempera paint all over the floor with glue poured on it and the

---

[1] Oral interview, 17 Jan. 2000, CDPA. The description of the early days of PHS given here is from oral interviews with
the pioneer Sisters. The Sisters' work loads were heavy. Sister Mary Elizabeth (Liberta) Jupe, for example, "taught nutrition,
foods, child development, and religion, helped with the Sodality of the Blessed Virgin Mary, and sponsored the Future
Homemakers of America. During these years I also got my Masters at Texas Women's University by studying in the summer"
(oral interview, 11 March, 2000, CDPA).

windows broken out because my classroom had been vandalized. The children were all over the learning scale, from the slow to the exceptional. I had five reading groups. I did home visits when my pupils missed a lot. I found out that often it was because somebody had been shot. The families had so many survival issues that they couldn't value education. It was just a really violent culture and neighborhood.[2]

Like other pioneers, the Sisters did what they needed to do to accomplish their mission. This character still marks their culture—when a need arises, they do what they need to do and they do it well. When one strategy seems ineffective, they try another. When none seems to work, they leave to serve God's family elsewhere. The Sisters are more task-oriented than reflective in their orientation toward life.[3] Some initiatives undertaken in the next few decades may seem small, such as going into a new ministry—prison chaplaincy, executive secretary for a bishop, counselor of drug addicts, or teacher in a school for the deaf. Others involved winning the support of a group—launching a school for licensed vocational nurses (LVNs), getting funding for a school lunch program, or putting on a parish Christmas pageant. Others grew into large enterprises—the Missionary Catechists of Divine Providence, the Sisters of Divine Providence of Mexico, Stella Maris Clinic, and the Providence Home for Children with AIDS. These ventures will be treated later in this book. This chapter will discuss some measures the Sisters took because they detected new educational needs.

As Superior General, Mother Angelique had a wider field in which to detect needs and marshal means to meet them, but support for Our Lady of the Lake College remained a priority. Her dreams for its future were evident in a letter she wrote seven months after her election to Leo M. J. Dielmann, architect for the Sacred Heart Chapel. "I like your optimism and share it to a certain extent, but we are not so sure what effect this aeronautical age is going to have on the dollar after the close of the war. However, we are air-castle minded, and are talking of

---

[2] Oral interview, 17 Sept. 2000, CDPA. Sister Constance Christopher faced similar problems when she served as home school coordinator for the Harlandale School District in San Antonio from 1975 to 1985.

Sister Janez (Rosemary) Schonfeld remembered that when she was stationed at St. Michael's on the near east side of San Antonio in 1956, "many of our students came from Victoria Courts. We were told not to keep the students after school, especially the girls, because if they didn't go home in a group, they could be molested. All the sixth, seventh, and eighth grade girls would carry knives in their socks, simply as protection for themselves" (oral interview, 25 March 2000, CDPA).

[3] Center for Applied Research in the Apostolate (CARA), "Planning for Retirement and Mission: A Best Practices Study" conducted by Mary E. Bendyna, RSM, and Mary L. Gautier, May 2003, revised August 2003: 259. Hereafter, CARA report.

a possible Library building, Fine Arts building, and Social Science building."[4] The college started a fund drive; the Congregation borrowed money and used some of the Sisters' patrimony as well as the chapel fund. Four years later two new buildings were dedicated.

While the Congregation was spending over $600,000 on its college buildings, it was also preparing to build a large new high school in San Antonio. Why was the Congregation willing to undertake another large project before paying for the first one? Fundamentally, because there was a need and the time seemed right. Trust in a Provident God is an essential element of the Congregation's identity. When all signs indicate it is time to start something, hesitation could be a sign of lack of trust in God as well as in people.

The five schools staffed by CDPs near the center of San Antonio originated to meet the educational needs of Irish, German, Polish, and Mexican immigrants. By the late 1940's neighborhoods were becoming more mixed as Roman Catholics became prosperous and assimilated into mainstream U.S. society. The need for ethnic parishes was beginning to be questioned, and correspondingly financial support for their schools was weakening. Although many inner city schools were to close in the later 1960s, in the late 1940s their viability was not seriously doubted.[5] Some of the buildings were old and in need of expensive repairs. Sister Miriam Fidelis Mellein remembered, for example, that St. Mary's School was not fireproof, and conditions were sometimes unsanitary. "The river was not beautiful like it is now. The rats used to come into the school and sometimes come upstairs where we were having teachers' meetings or community prayers. We didn't have much room. There were four or five beds on the porch, which got cold in the wintertime."[6] The pastor took seriously the fact that the street crossing a half-block north of the school had been named as a most likely target for an atomic attack.[7]

All grade schools were becoming overcrowded as the post-war population of the city was growing, indicating a need to prepare for future increased high school enrollment. Teachers in a larger, centrally located school could have larger classes and better equipment. In 1949 Providence Academy in Alexandria, Louisiana, was closed in order to form with other Catholic secondary schools of the city a

[4] Mother Angelique to Leo Dielmann, 15 Jan. 1944, CDPA.

[5] National Catholic school enrollment reached an all-time high of 5.6 million pupils in 1965-66, but Catholic families were rapidly moving to the suburbs. Most of the 452 Catholic schools that closed in 1966-67 were in inner cities. See Mary A. Grant and Thomas C. Hunt, *Catholic School Education in the United States: Development and Current Concerns* (New York: Garland, 1992) 162 and 167.

[6] Sister Miriam Fidelis Mellein, oral interview, 13 June 2000, CDPA.

[7] FC, Nov. 1950: 17, CDPA.

consolidated Providence Central High School.[8] Was it time for a similar joining in San Antonio? None of the private Catholic high schools in San Antonio staffed by different religious congregations was interested in consolidation. Each was more intent on maintaining its uniqueness and traditional clientele.

Considerable diplomacy was exercised to bring pastors to close their high schools and send their students outside the parish to a school owned by the Congregation. In June 1951, the five high schools near the center of San Antonio staffed by Sisters of Divine Providence were notified that Providence High School (PHS) would open 4 September 1951. Four closed right away; the fifth closed three years later. The elementary schools associated with them also eventually closed. The consolidations and closings anticipated the hard choices that continued to present themselves throughout the country in the next decade when financial and personnel problems often made it impossible to maintain both elementary and secondary schools at one site.[9]

Providence High School

A site for the proposed new high school became available only nine blocks from downtown San Antonio. The twelve-room colonial Drought mansion constructed in the late nineteenth century was located next to Central Catholic High School for boys, owned and staffed by the Society of Mary. Mother Angelique thought that the Drought House location was advantageous for a girls' school because it "might bring the right people together."[10] For $110,000 the Congregation bought the homestead in 1950 from Henry Patrick Drought Jr., chairman of the Board of Trustees of OLLC, and began to build the school on the spot where the Drought stables once stood.[11] One year later a long, two-story school of cream brick became a reality. The two and a half story chocolate and vanilla-colored mansion with its columned porches became the home of the Sister-teachers and the location of the music department. The regal porte-cochere

---

[8] FC, Dec., 1949: 34, CDPA.

[9] See Sister Ann Virginia, "The Cruel Choice Facing Catholic Education," *The Catholic World* 195 (Sept., 1962): 343-349.

[10] Not everyone regarded this proximity of teen-aged boys and girls as an advantage, however. Florence Carvajal, the first lay director of the CDP Associates, was enrolled in Ursuline High School a few blocks away on St. Mary's Street because her father did not want her so near to the boys' school (oral interview, 26 Feb. 2002, CDPA).

[11] *Memoirs, a Centennial Project,* 1966, Vol. II, 303-319, CDPA, hereafter cited as *Memoirs,* CDPA. It is interesting to note that Marguerite Lecomte, the first Providence Sister in France, lived and taught in a stable. The village was too small and poor to provide more suitable quarters. See Sister Mary Generosa Callahan, CDP, *The Life of Blessed John Martin Moye* (Milwaukee: Bruce Press, 1964) 27.

sheltered a maroon, wood-paneled station wagon, for this community was the second one in the Congregation to have its own automobile.[12]

Archbishop Lucey was well aware that "to build a large, modern high school, heavy assessments would have to be placed on parishes already burdened with debt." The archbishop was thankful that he did not have to face this prospect since the "Sisters of Divine Providence generously offered to erect a centrally located girls' high school." To secure their good will, he invited 45 priests as well as Brother Henry Ringkamp, SM, principal of Central Catholic High School, to a luncheon at the St. Anthony Hotel on 6 November 1950, "to enlist their support for the school."[13] At the Mass of the Holy Spirit on the opening day of classes at the new school, 4 September 1951, the archbishop paid tribute to the Congregation, saying, "The Sisters have relieved us of a great school problem in this city."

The Sisters provided the "relief" at considerable financial risk and without financial help from the archdiocese. Sister Modesta Boerner, who was the General Treasurer from 1946 to 1970, said the Congregation's hardest financial times were between 1950 and 1955. Schools needed repairs, the Sisters' salaries were low, and the Congregation was constantly borrowing money.[14] The Community Services Bureau of Dallas was hired early in 1951 to raise $500,000 for the proposed new school. They were to receive $36,000 for carrying out the drive.[15] Their campaign flyer stated that the "Sisters of Divine Providence, who have never before asked for public financial support in San Antonio, will make up the difference."

Mother Angelique was an assiduous fund-raiser because she was "very completely convinced that Providence High School for Girls is the most promising venture on the secondary school level the Sisters of Divine Providence have undertaken."[16] "The school is unique, and we hope it may be a pattern for many other such schools in the Southwest."[17]

Despite all efforts, the campaign brought in only $100,000 rather than $500,000; and its downtown headquarters closed 15 May 1951. Although PHS would have well-equipped classrooms, it could not afford to have its own gymnasium or chapel.

---

[12] The station wagon was a gift of Hannah Deutchmann Gaines to Mother Angelique, who wrote to her, "I am going so completely 'all out' for Providence High that we are letting them have the station wagon . . . They do need it." Mother Angelique to Mrs. Arthur Gaines, 28 Aug. 1951, OLLUA.

[13] Archbishop Lucey to Mother Angelique, 30 Oct. 1950, CDPA.

[14] Interview by Sister Angelina Murphy, 1983, CDPA.

[15] GC minutes, 21 Oct. 1950, CDPA.

[16] Mother Angelique to Mr. and Mrs. Meredith Tatton, 30 March 1951, CDPA.

[17] Mother Angelique to Mr. and Mrs. Chas. A. Breitung, 30 March 1951, CDPA.

According to a 1951 letter from the Sisters to the first PHS students, the Christian Family Living program (CFL) was the "center of the entire school curriculum which aims to promote better standards of Christian living and to assist you in equipping yourself to share the responsibilities of a Catholic home." Elementary schools of the Congregation for several years had been following a curriculum stressing family values, and CFL had been introduced at the Congregation's high school in Alexandria, Louisiana, in 1950.[18] CFL concepts were also part of the curriculum at OLLU. The strong home economics department, headed by Sister Providentia Srader, had high enrollments.

The first PHS students could choose from three fields: academic or college preparatory, business, and "a home economics program for those who are interested principally in homemaking, dietetics, or interior decoration."[19] All three fields met the Texas requirements for high school graduation and college entrance. Later a scientific field was added for those who intended to be nurses or technicians.

The PHS campaign newsletter gave another reason for supporting this new school born soon after the atomic bomb was developed and deployed and the Soviet Union took over several countries in Eastern Europe.

> In this period of world crisis, therefore, we must prepare for the future while resisting the onslaughts of world Communism—that evil force which seeks to uproot the influence of the family. . . . Providence School will be a monument to the preservation of Christian family life and a bulwark against the Communist enemies of freedom.[20]

The threat of Communism in Europe that later spread to Cuba was cause for alarm, and McCarthy witch-hunts against suspected Communists were not unusual when PHS came into being. After Fidel Castro seized power in Cuba in 1959, Brother John Totten, SM, of St. Mary's University was giving talks on the philosophy of Communism. At OLL his views "started a crusade among the Sisters and students."[21] Two PHS Sister faculty members formed an anti-Communist club with sophomore students. On the advice of the Superior General, they discontinued it after they received unfavorable publicity in the local secular press.

---

[18] FC, Nov. 1950: 19, CDPA.

[19] 1951 letter from the Sisters to the first PHS students.

[20] Providence High School Campaign newsletter, CDPA.

[21] *News Flashes*, First Edition, 1961: 16, CDPA. "Due to the unsettled conditions in Mexico, arising from the spread of communism," the General Council even considered moving the formation house to San Antonio. (GC minutes, 27 April 1962, CDPA).

The Catholic population was growing; education was a post-war priority; and the archbishop fully supported PHS. On the other hand, the development campaign had not yielded the desired funds. Whether girls from the closed high schools would enroll in the new one was uncertain, and whether the new curriculum would be successful and attractive was unpredictable. But the general administration was convinced that the high school was timely and that the Sisters assigned there would assure its flourishing.

Twenty-one Sisters and five lay teachers formed the first faculty of the school. The Sisters moved into the former Drought mansion only one week before classes began for the first PHS student body of 380 girls. Ten of these Sisters were young, not having yet pronounced their perpetual vows. Madlyn Jo Pape, who later entered the Congregation, came to Providence as a freshman. "It was a new school, and it was a new venture for the Congregation. Some of the best and brightest were there. I was so struck because the Sisters seemed happy, and they seemed to like each other and have fun with each other. My whole concept of religious life was broadened. It was attractive to me."[22]

Another memory of the first days was vivid for Sister Thérèse Pousson, the local superior. "The first week of school we had no janitor, and Sister Maureen [Glahn, the principal] and I did most of the cleaning of the school because the other Sisters had more class preparation to do than we did. There was no air-conditioning whatsoever, not in the house or in the school. That made things doubly hard."[23]

Sister Joan Michele Rake also remembered spending every Saturday morning boiling buckets of long oily dust mops in the basement boiler room of the school while the other Sisters did their housecleaning chores at the convent. By Monday morning the mops were clean, dry, and ready for the custodian to use them on the long terrazzo corridors and asphalt-tiled classrooms.

Tuition was set at $5 a month "to make the advantages of a Catholic education possible to those of moderate means."[24] The faculty was top notch; and the new building had sturdy, serviceable classrooms, laboratories, a library, and a cafeteria. PHS was not able to afford a gymnasium auditorium until 1966, and it constantly struggled to pay off the school's debt to the Congregation. Eighteen

---

[22] Sister Madlyn (Mary Albert) Pape, oral interview. Sister Rose Corrine Medica had similar memories of Providence Academy in Alexandria, Louisiana. "We had a group of very young Sisters who always seemed so joyful. We would visit them and help out in the classroom. I guess that was part of what helped us decide to become religious. A few of us would talk about it every day" (oral interview, 21 Dec. 2000, CDPA).

[23] Oral interview, 10 Dec. 1999, CDPA.

[24] *Memoirs*, II, 308, CDPA.

years later, in 1984, the Congregation forgave the $78,000 debt remaining from the $420,000 cost of the gym.

In the first year of its existence PHS established its identity and already began to acquire a reputation for excellence in education; in its second year it achieved official affiliation with the Southern Association and the Texas Education Agency (TEA). The graduation class grew from 67 in 1952 to 144 in 1960, when around 60 qualified students had to be turned away for lack of space. By 1966, 86% of the graduates were entering college. By 1967 PHS was the largest non-resident all girls' school in the Southwest.

PHS always supported women's issues and religious formation while collaborating with the boys' high school next door. Thousands of students profited from the benefits of single-gender education coupled with the opportunity to take some classes at a boys' school. Cooperation took on different forms over the years. The co-ed band begun in 1975 was the longest standing joint program.

Providence students were for the most part from lower and middle class families of the area who valued education as a means to a better future. In the beginning approximately a third of the students were Mexican-American. By 2000, they were 85% of the student body. The number of African American and Asian American students also grew with time. The financial sacrifices entailed in attending a private school did bear fruit, for PHS girls were not only well-prepared for college but equipped and ready to enter professions opening up to women. For example: Denise Fitzsimon Williams (1977), pediatrician and Professor of Pediatrics at Texas A&M College of Medicine; Christine Hernandez (1969), State Representative; Tish Hinojosa (1974), popular singer and songwriter; and Dora Menchaca (1973) research epidemiologist.[25] A very large number of graduates became superb mothers and homemakers, and a growing number serve the Church in parishes and dioceses in fields such as education

---

[25] Dora died on American flight 77 which crashed into the Pentagon on September 11, 2001. Other outstanding alumnae included: Arlene Seidman Morgan (1952) whose painting hangs in the Texas Governor's office; Katherine Fisher Greco (1959), owner of Greco Construction Company in San Antonio; María Antonietta Rodriguez Berriozabal (1959), city councilwoman; Joan Rauschuber Braden (1963), a Professional Clown for Ministry under the name "Nutme"; Judith Gutierrez Loredo (1964), Dean of Academic Affairs at Huston-Tillotson College in Austin; Berta Mejía (1967), presiding court judge in Houston; Cassandra Franklin-Barbajosa (1973), writer-editor for the *National Geographic* magazine's on-line edition; Maria Lopez Howell (1975), Associate Professor at the Dental School of the University of Texas Health Science Center in San Antonio and national television spokesperson for The American Dental Association; Rebecca Villarreal (1975), who was blind and Director of Ministry to the Handicapped for the Archdiocese of San Antonio; Mary Theresa Cano (1977), structural engineer for the Texas Department of Transportation in Austin; Martha Jimenez (1979), attorney with the Mexican American Legal Defense Fund; Cynthia Saenz (1980), senior editor/writer for *People's* magazine; and Yvette Rogers Johnson (1982) published poet.

and music ministry. Seven or more PHS alumnae are professed religious Sisters in several different congregations.[26]

Sister Margaret Ellen Gallatin, an English teacher at PHS, once pinpointed "the only reason for Catholic schools" and described their faculties. In her view, schools like PHS instill solid values, which are the necessary underpinnings for novelty and originality. She wrote,

> While I assume that academic excellence is still one of our chief goals and innovation is justifiably a top priority, I am convinced that these professional advancements, as necessary as they are, will justify the Catholic school only if those schools are staffed by teachers who themselves possess a spiritual value system that can show students of the twentieth century that God is important in their lives, . . . the joyful, genuine, living testimony of teachers who know what it means to let the Holy Spirit really "take over" in their lives and who have a strong spirit of prayer. This kind of spirituality embodied in an emotionally whole and mature person can be the best lesson of what it means to live in freedom, real freedom of spirit because of one's conviction that God is real in his [sic] life.[27]

Sister Margaret Ellen put into words what many students felt but could not express, partly because the Sisters themselves were not prone to speak about their deepest motivations and educational ideals. If they did, it might be considered "preachy," and they preferred to let their lives and actions be their testimony. In Sister Margaret Ellen's words, "While this kind of witness is not the prerogative of Catholic schools alone, it seems to me at present that this is the best opportunity we have in which to establish consistently an atmosphere that can help students to develop the spirituality that is their right and their need."[28]

Laypeople who joined the Sisters at PHS promoted the goal of helping each student develop as fully as possible as a person and a scholar and also served as role models. Five lay teachers were on the faculty when the school opened, and their number increased almost every year. Ms. Liz Smith taught physical education and courses on the arts and culture from 1964 to 1999. Religious icon artist G. E. (Buddy) Mullan and theologian-activist Robert O'Connor were faculty members. The school was able to take advantage of the fact that many persons who received military training in San Antonio and had assignments

---

[26] Judith Varga (Sister Hildegard, OSB) [1964], for example, was Vice-Chancellor/Archivist for the Diocese of Amarillo, Texas.

[27] "Innovation is Not Enough," *Nunspeak*, June 1971: 12, CDPA.

[28] *Nunspeak*, June 1971: 12, CDPA.

throughout the world decided to retire in the city. For twenty years one couple shared their wisdom at PHS. Retired Air Force Colonel Paul Hass taught mathematics and served as vice-principal while his wife, Margaret, a registered nurse, headed the PHS infirmary and started an AIDS support group. Seven PHS lay faculty members were retirees from the armed forces in 2000. By this time CDPs were a minority at PHS. Even though several Sisters were on the staff, Sister Jane Ann Slater, who had been the ninth CDP Superior General, was the only Sister-teacher.

The PHS Marian Choristers made their school visible through performances on radio and television and special civic events. They sang for visits by foreign ambassadors and church dignitaries as well as for pre-Christmas *posadas* and concerts in businesses such as bank foyers and on the San Antonio Riverwalk. Chapter 123 of the Modern Music Masters, an international music honor society, was chartered in 1955. This group annually helped organize and manage a music festival at OLLC.

Many teachers used their talents for communities outside the classroom. Former Sister Jan Maria Wozniak served on the 15-member Texas History Education Advisory Committee sponsored by the Texas Education Association and the Texas State Historical Association.[29] She also involved PHS students in projects at Mission San José, where she served as a consultant at the time it was a Texas state park. Sister Marian Maurer, accompanied by Sister Catherine (Catherine Henry) Fuhrmann, helped once a week after school at the Women's Shelter of San Antonio.[30] Sister Rosamunda Kadura became a Eucharistic minister.

Three full-time PHS teachers moved into Villa Veramendi Courts, a federal low-cost housing project on the west side of San Antonio, becoming involved in various neighborhood projects in the early 1970s. Sister María Esther (M. Goretti) Guerra taught catechism to youth in St. Timothy's parish and worked with the summer remedial reading program at Guadalupe Recreation Center. Sister Elsa Mary (Eloise) Bennett taught beginners' swimming and was a tennis instructor at the YWCA. Every Wednesday night she rehearsed on her French horn with the 50 member Beethoven Maennerchor Hall Band, which enhanced numerous celebrations. Sister Margit Maria Nagy worked with Senior Community Services to provide programs for senior citizens at the Rex Apartments and Villa Hermosa. In the summer of 1968 she taught for six weeks with four Presentation Sisters in Project REACH on the East side of San Antonio, offering special help in reading and arithmetic to African American children in

---

[29] *Nunspeak*, June 1970: 10, CDPA.

[30] *CDP Times*, 1, 4 (Jan. 1981): 4, CDPA.

grades one to six.[31] During the racial tensions in Crystal City, Texas, in 1969 she was part of a team of teachers led by State Senator Joe J. Bernal who went there over the Christmas holidays to help public school students make up for instruction they had missed.[32]

Financial struggles were almost continuous at Providence High School. In 1968 its future was questionable because of a proposed expressway.[33] The expressway plans were changed, and in 1971 the General Council asked the Sisters at PHS to take the initiative in raising $24,000 to amortize the school's debt. Sister Margaret (Bernard Joseph) Riché (1982-1986) began to develop a Board of Directors. PHS was separately incorporated in 1991 when Sister Alma Rose Booty was principal (1986-1992) and the property was transferred to the corporate Board of Directors. Tuition rose gradually from the original $5 to $383.27 a month in 2000. In 2000 the school hired its first lay principal, Ms. Anne Bristol, who administered a budget of over 2.6 million dollars and supervised a faculty of 35 and a staff of 16 serving 477 students.

Sensitivity and adaptation to social and demographic changes, as well as the willingness of the teachers to try new things, led successive principals to change scheduling methods six times during the first 50 years at PHS.[34] At the opening Mass of the PHS Golden Jubilee in 2001 Sister Antoinette Billeaud, Superior General of the Congregation and former PHS principal (1976-1982), summarized:

> With the changes, we have kept the vision: educating young women
> to their full potential to take an active role in home, church, and
> society and to be aware of their responsibility to make the world
> better for the next generation, with a sense of obligation for the
> care of the earth, the dignity and strength of women, and a strong
> social consciousness. The means and methods have changed but the
> vision remains.[35]

---

[31] "CDP Summer News Bulletin," 16 June 1969: 5, CDPA.

[32] Sister Margit Maria Nagy, communication to Sister Mary Christine (Theresa Clare) Morkovsky, 3 Mar. 2003. (Hereafter, communication to the author.)

[33] GC minutes, 29 March 1968, CDPA.

[34] The types of scheduling were: Traditional (1951-1966), Block (1966-1969), Modular (1969-1972), Scheduling by Appointment (1972-1979), Modular (1979-1981), Traditional (1981-1992), and Block (1992 to date). In Scheduling by Appointment, for example, students progressed at their own rate of speed, so teachers prepared learning activity packages (LAPS) every six weeks. Sister Margeta (Rosello) Krchnak remembered, they also "had to have three different versions of the tests, and we spent every summer preparing them. We couldn't buy them on the market" (oral interview, 6 Dec. 1999, CDPA).

[35] *Movements of Providence*, Fall/Winter 2001: 11, CDPA. Published twice a year for members and friends of the Congregation, this publication will be cited hereafter as *Movements*.

Besides changed means and methods, the Congregation was willing to serve in high schools it did not own which had different types of organization and administration. These high schools opened by the Congregation after 1950 were either diocesan (Holy Savior Menard Central in Alexandria, Louisiana; Teurlings in Lafayette, Louisiana[36]; Central Co-Institutional in Abilene, Texas; Bishop Forest in Schulenburg, Texas; Bishop Kelley in Tulsa, Oklahoma) or a cooperative venture of several religious congregations (Notre Dame in Crowley, Louisiana). A high school for girls who expressed a desire to become Sisters was also opened at the former Moye Military School in Castroville, Texas. Of these schools, only Holy Savior Menard Central and Bishop Kelley remained open in 2000.

Before considering in more detail some of these schools, it is instructive to regard the history of one of the public high schools in which the Sisters taught in the mid-twentieth century when the separation of church and state began to affect U.S. education. Although the reasons for staying in or departing from each school varied, it serves as an example of how the political climate in the U.S. at this time was a relevant consideration in every school.

Public School in Pecos, New Mexico

As ground was broken for Providence High School in 1951, the Sisters were leaving a public school in Pecos, near Santa Fe, New Mexico, after almost thirty years of service. Events indicated that it was time to go, with sadness but without regret. How and when does the call of Providence, which can also be called the will of God, become clear enough for such a decisive move?

Four Sisters first made the long trip by train and bus to the Penitentes region of New Mexico in 1920. The school was a public school, and most of the students in attendance were Roman Catholic. At an attractive salary of $125 a month for the principal and $100 a month apiece for the teachers, the Sisters began classes in a hay barn because repairs to "the old school house" were not complete.[37] By 1941 there was evidence of the Sisters' reputation for excellence in the Pecos public grade school and high school. Laura C. Bailey, teacher in the Demonstration Library at New Mexico Normal University in Las Vegas, New Mexico, praised her students: Sisters Georgia Samland, Richard Culhane, and Geralda Podesva. She wrote, "I find the work of the Sisters so much superior to that of the usual public school. And I have found no one so thoroughly familiar

---

[36] Hospitality to innovation was also evident in this school. In 1968-79, the principal, Sister (Alphonsine) Julie McDougall, initiated team teaching on a small scale. In 1969-70 the school used modular or flexible scheduling ("News Bulletin" sponsored by the Eastern Region, May, 1969: 6, CDPA).

[37] Rev. Edward Paulhan to Mother Florence, 4 Aug. 1920, CDPA.

with the need for a wide use of books by young people such as the school library is organized to provide."[38]

Rev. William Bickhaus, pastor, in 1947 noticed "marked improvement in the life of the people of Pecos. I believe that a great deal of good has been done during the past 20 years and I attribute this in no small measure to the zealous work of the Sisters."[39]

In 1948 ground was broken for two new high school classrooms. This meant that goats from the nearby pasture would no longer wander into the chemistry class.[40] On 17 August 1948, Sister Bibiana Pahlsmeier wrote to Rev. Mother Angelique about a new curtain for the chapel in St. Joan of Arc Convent and said there was no other "big news."[41] But even quiet Pecos was soon caught up in current events involving religion and schools in the U.S.

On 8 December 1947, the U.S. Supreme Court reviewed McCollum v. Board of Education, 333 U.S. 203, referred from Champaign, Illinois. On 8 March 1948, the Supreme Court ruled that the Illinois provision allowing religious instruction in public schools violated the Establishment Clause.[42] Concern about the separation of church and state, fueled by anti-Catholic prejudice, was making its way westward. Clouds were gathering in the clear New Mexico sky in the form of "the Zeller suit" (or "the Dixon Case"), which ended a long-standing practice and influences Catholic education in New Mexico to this day.

On 16 September 1948, Mrs. Lydia Zeller, along with another woman and two Protestant ministers from Dixon, New Mexico, 100 miles away, drove up and asked to see the two public school buildings in Pecos. Sister Bibiana politely showed them around. They went into "every corner, scaled up and down the walls to examine every picture, etc." They took notes and photographs but refused an invitation to come to the convent for refreshments. At noon the lawyer for the Catholic Church's side of the case arrived and said "School affairs in this State are drifting more and more into politics."[43] The Attorney General's office requested that a Sister be interviewed. Sister Rose of Lima Pousson was chosen because she would be "calm enough."

---

[38] Laura C. Bailey to Mother Philothea, 29 March 1941, CDPA.

[39] Rev. William Bickhaus to Mother Angelique, 1 April 1947, CDPA.

[40] FC, Oct. 1945: 15, CDPA.

[41] Sister Bibiana to Mother Angelique, 17 Aug. 1948, CDPA.

[42] In 1952, however, the Supreme Court upheld Zorach v. Clauson, 343 U.S. 306, permitting "release time" for students to attend religion classes off school grounds during the school day.

[43] Sister Bibiana to Mother Angelique, 16 Sept. 1948, CDPA. The previous year religious Sisters and Brothers who taught in New Mexico, including three CDPs who were no longer stationed in Pecos, had to fill out a questionnaire and get it notarized.

The court case of Zeller et al v. Huff et al, #22178, Santa Fe County, was set to begin Monday, 27 September. The plaintiffs charged that religious instruction was given during school hours and paid out of tax funds; the pupils were taught religion and recited Catholic prayers during school hours; public funds for transportation and books were used to disseminate Catholic doctrine; and New Mexico had adopted a line of books for Catholic students only.

Sister Rose of Lima wrote to Reverend Mother that the lawyer phoned at 11:30 a.m. and told her to appear in court at 1:30 p.m. on Thursday, 30 September.

> We kept on teaching till 12:00, then we took a hasty lunch and started out for Santa Fe. Mr. Harry L. Bigbee, the attorney for the plaintiffs, must have asked over a hundred questions. I felt that the Holy Ghost was helping me. I didn't feel nervous, confused, or upset. I am willing to suffer and to go through something—if only we win the case. I feel for those thousands of Catholic children in public schools who would be deprived of all religious education if the Sisters had to give up the public schools. In general, these people are too poor to finance a private school.[44]

Sister Bibiana and Sister Irma Clark, who had been teaching in Pecos since 1936 and was at that time the clerk for the Pecos School Board, also took the witness stand. The prosecutor produced a photo of religious books on a shelf in the library; the Sisters provided records showing that only 2% of the library books were on religion, which was in compliance with the specifications of the Regional Association. He also tried to prove that the Superior General of the Sisters' Congregation managed the Pecos public school, but the Sisters showed that the school board appointed the Sisters as well as the lay teachers.[45] The court case dragged on. By December the Sisters stopped teaching catechism after school. Instead they held eight classes on Sundays from 2 to 3 p.m.[46] After New Year's Day, 1949, they moved into the new school building. Sister Bibiana was pleased, but not completely at ease. "The rooms are modern in every respect [but] Mr. Rivera, the main member of our School Board, died last week. . . . There'll be elections here next month for three new Board members. There are lots of things I would like to tell you about, but must wait till next summer. I rather not put them on paper."[47] Apparently, Sister Bibiana did not communicate by

---

[44] Sister Rose of Lima to Reverend Mother, 1 Oct.1948, CDPA.

[45] Sister Bibiana to Reverend Mother, 4 Oct. 1948, CDPA.

[46] FC, Dec. 1948: 6, CDPA.

[47] Sister Bibiana to Reverend Mother, 18 Jan. 1949, CDPA.

telephone with the motherhouse. Some reasons could well be that telephones were on party lines and long distance calls had to be placed through a local operator, making this means of communication inappropriate for transmitting confidential or sensitive material.

Her apprehension increased a month later when someone forced open the doors and lockers of the high school, taking nothing, but scattering school papers all over the floor. Concern about the safety of the pupils began to arise. "The Department of Education too is very much concerned about the incident because just the Tuesday before someone burned down the school in Mora during the early morning hours. . . . 500 children were without a school at Mora. . . . [O]ur people here are good people, not like Mora or Dixon or Holman."[48] To add to the Sisters' worries, their pastor became ill and had to be replaced.

On 12 March the Sisters found out about the court decision in favor of Dixon from a special edition of the Santa Fe newspaper. Sister Bibiana was stunned. "This is something no one expected. The way he [the prosecuting attorney] interprets it, there isn't such a thing as hours after school. The decision was made known yesterday noon, just as the Legislature closed officially so there is no chance for them to interfere. We do not know what will be done about it."[49]

At the beginning of the following school year, a Santa Fe newspaper carried the headline, "Protestants Will Appeal Dixon School Suit Ruling. Plaintiffs Say Order is not Broad Enough," according to Lawyer Bigbee, "to effectuate the doctrine of separation of church and state." Mrs. Zeller sought "the disqualification of all Catholic nuns and brothers, as a class, as public school teachers. . . . [because their] vows require their allegiance first, to the church, and then to temporal authority. The decision does not permit removal of religious influence from the public school classroom."[50] Thirteen religious congregations discontinued their work and left New Mexico after the Zeller suit.

Seven Sisters remained in Pecos for the 1949-1950 school year, teaching 231 elementary and 89 high school students. They did not return for what would have been the Congregation's 30th year of continuous presence in Pecos. Laws and legislatures had prevailed over the desires of the local pastor and people.

Diocesan Co-educational High Schools

Within the next decade, the Congregation accepted invitations to teach at two newly constructed diocesan high schools, Bishop Forest High School

---

[48] Sister Bibiana to Reverend Mother, 20 Feb. 1949, CDPA.

[49] Sister Bibiana to Reverend Mother, 13 March 1949, CDPA.

[50] *Santa Fe New Mexican*, 20 Sept. 1949, CDPA.

(BFHS) in Schulenburg, Texas (1956), and Bishop Kelley High School (BKHS) in Tulsa, Oklahoma (1960). BFHS lasted 23 years; BKHS continues to function. Archbishop Robert E. Lucey in May, 1954 announced plans for a central Catholic high school to serve twelve rural parishes within the Weimar deanery. Named after John Anthony Forest, the third bishop of San Antonio (1895-1911), the school was the first of four archdiocesan high schools started by Archbishop Lucey.[51] Schulenburg was well located on a major highway mid-way between San Antonio and Houston, and Sisters of Divine Providence had staffed St. Rose Elementary School there since 1890. From 1934 to 1937 St. Rose, the only parish in Schulenburg, also had a high school which the pastor, Rev. Victor Goertz, closed for financial reasons.

> The new school, although having such disadvantages as transportation and financial problems, would offer the student the advantages of religious education and a broader, less provincial, cultural prospective through association with students of other towns. In addition, modern educational facilities could be provided more easily.[52]

The Congregation was willing to provide teachers, trusting that others would be willing to secure the finances and public support. The designated parishes were taxed to pay for operational costs of BFHS, ten dollars a month for each child eligible to attend, whether or not they actually attended. The pastors paid the general administrator of the school who collected five dollars monthly tuition per child, with a reduction for more than one child from a family. The school also paid all transportation expenses. The Bishop Forest Parent-teacher Club raised thousands of dollars over the years.

Classes began on 4 September 1956, and the new pastor, Rev. Eustace A. Hermes, bent all his efforts to secure a broad base of support for the school, but he was under no illusions. "[T]here is much opposition to a Catholic high school here. . . . [T]he Sisters will have more than the ordinary problems to cope with and I am sure that you will agree that it will require someone with almost superhuman stamina and tact to survive."[53]

Mother Angelique was confident that she had such Sisters. Sister Illuminata Petrek was the principal and sophomore homeroom sponsor; Sister Adrienne Marie Schmidtzinsky was the freshman sponsor; Sister Patricia (M. Philomene) Kimball taught music; and Father Hermes taught religion. Mother Adelaide Marie Heyman, Director of Studies for the Congregation, filled in until Sister

---

[51] The other three were high schools for boys in San Antonio: Holy Cross, 1957; La Salle, 1957; and Antonian, 1964.

[52] *Memoirs*, II, 325, CDPA.

[53] Rev. Eustace A. Hermes to Mother Angelique, 1 Feb. 1955, CDPA.

M. Aline Hrncir arrived on 24 September to teach some English and history classes. Sister Patricia was in her first year of teaching, and her impression of the parishioners was very positive. "The people were very generous with their time, making sure the Sisters had what they needed. I don't recall that we ever purchased any big items of food. They were always there with something for us. Nothing was too good for the Sisters; they were number one. The people loved the Sisters."[54]

Sister Maxelinda Lemoine taught at BFHS from 1966 to 1969. She always taught math and loved doing so. Shortly after her arrival, a student announced to her: "Sister, no one has ever been able to teach us math." "Well, we'll see," she responded. She did succeed in teaching them, and the student later analyzed the reason why. "Our other teachers never explained it the way you did."[55]

Sister Rose (Mary Mark) Kruppa, one of four BFHS graduates who later became Sisters of Divine Providence, explained:

> When I was at Bishop Forest in the early sixties, the CDPs who were in that school were outstanding teachers. They were young. They were enthusiastic. They were vibrant. All of the Sisters were very intent on giving us country kids a real push at having our sights set on more than where we came from. They were very understanding of the fact that we were farm kids and that we had little time to study. But they did not give us any slack on not meeting high expectations.[56]

It may seem contradictory to say that the Sisters were well-prepared teachers and at the same time show that sometimes a Sister was asked to teach a subject for which she did not feel prepared. Sister Aida Fleischmann, for example, taught religion, history, and English and took care of the library at BFHS. One day one of the girls asked her for help with an Algebra problem. "Don't ask me about algebra," Sister told the student. "I don't know anything about it." Then the very next year she had to teach Algebra II, and that same student was in the class. The student had either forgotten the incident from the year before or she thought it wiser not to comment. Sister Aida elaborated on the experience of many CDPs. "No one asked if you could teach math or science or whatever. You were told to learn it and teach it, and the miracle was that you taught fairly well and the students learned."[57]

---

[54] Sister Patricia Kimball, oral interview, 21 July 2000, CDPA.

[55] *CDP Times*, 11, 6 (Feb. 1991): 12, CDPA.

[56] Oral interview, 27 July 2000, CDPA. Sister Rose remembered in particular Sisters Agnes Ann Dobrowolski, Marian Maurer, Adrienne Marie Schmidtzinsky, and former Sister Sylvia Schmidt.

[57] *CDP Times* 14, 8 (April 1994): 14, CDPA.

Actually, such unexpected but successful assignments support several facts: (1) Each Sister had a good liberal arts background since, almost without exception, the Sisters received more than two years of college education before they went into the classroom. Therefore, they had a basic knowledge of most subjects in the elementary and high school curriculum. (2) The Superiors had a good idea of each Sister's abilities and therefore knew who could learn new material quickly and teach it well. (3) Sisters living in the same community or a nearby community shared their knowledge and helped one another acquire new skills. For example, only a few Sisters took speech and drama courses from Sister Mary of Lourdes Murphy at OLLC. But since everyone in a school was involved when it was time to present a play, everyone learned by watching and imitating. Thus they could learn from a Sister who had been Sister Mary of Lourdes' student the best way to block scenes, prompt actors, design costumes, or paint scenery. Sister Marcia Havlak recalled single-handedly painting a flower garden on a large stage curtain in Norman, Oklahoma.[58] Receptions and "open house" times furnished opportunities to learn from other Sisters how to design invitations, decorate, arrange space for crowds, and serve different kinds of food. Almost every large celebration in the school or church challenged the Sisters' imaginations, logistics skills, and ability to create much with few resources. With this college background, a teacher's manual, and help from seasoned teachers in her community, no Sister was entirely unprepared to teach a subject in a new field.

Sister Rose Kruppa also remembered that when she was a student at BFHS,

> the Sisters still had a little rule. They should not be out at nighttime with the public. The Sisters at Bishop Forest came early to the football stadium, parked on the fifty-yard line, and stayed sitting in their car watching the game. And I think that during half time they would come out and visit with the parents in the stands. They already knew that we were more than students. We were real people, and I think that is what impressed me. I am not sure I would have entered the convent if I didn't know that the Sisters cared about everything about our lives, not just our academics.[59]

Sister Antoinette Billeaud, who became principal of Bishop Forest in 1968, commented from the faculty perspective, "It was the first time I had ever been to a real football game where I knew the players and got involved in all of the

---

[58] Oral interview, 1 Dec. 1999, CDPA.

[59] Oral interview, 27 July 2000, CDPA.

athletics in the school and band. I had played in the band as a high school student but I hadn't been involved in all of that." She summarized, "We had at Bishop Forest a good little school in a town that valued education. It was not hard to be demanding educationally of the students because the parents worked hard for the school."[60]

By the school year 1958-59 Bishop Forest had two priests, six Sisters, and three lay teachers on the faculty. Twenty-four seniors received diplomas. A peak enrollment of 278 was reached in 1964; and by 1966, the school had graduated 410 students. BFHS continued to expand by adding a field house to the football stadium in 1965 and a baseball field in 1970.

But the fate of BFHS did not lie in the hands of the faculty, students, and parents alone. Concerned about expenses, the school board voted 12 to 4 to close Bishop Forest in its sixteenth year at the end of the 1972 spring semester. Archbishop Frances J. Furey was not pleased. He wrote to Dr. J. A. Watzlavick, President of the BFHS Board: "After the *many and varied* efforts I made to save Bishop Forest High School, of, by, and for the people of the Schulenburg Deanery, I see nothing but opposition from *many and varied* sources."[61] The Sisters persevered despite opposition, and the school remained open for 17 additional years.

When the Victoria diocese was established in 1982, BFHS came under the leadership of Bishop Charles Grahmann, who immediately approved construction of an agricultural building and new cafeteria as well as a reconstruction of the gymnasium. But the enrollment had been falling and continued to fall. In April 1988 more than 300 parishioners of the Schulenburg Deanery parishes met in the Bishop Forest gymnasium to hear Brother Peter Pontolillo, SM, Director of Schools of the Archdiocese of San Antonio, present a five point plan to be executed if the school was to remain open: (1) The present enrollment of 42 students must increase to 50 by May 1989 and 80 by 1993. (2) The debt of $500,000 must be systematically reduced and eventually eliminated. (3) The school must operate in the black and provide full benefits to all the teachers. (4) The school must follow the parish and diocesan subsidy formula so as to reduce the financial burden of parishes that have schools. (5) A part-time director of development and a full-time principal must be hired.[62]

The Sisters continued to uphold the educational standards, but efforts at resuscitating BFHS were in vain. Sources for the required funds could not be found, and parents were reluctant to enroll their children in a small school with an uncertain future. Seven seniors received their diplomas on 26 May 1989; and

[60] Oral interview, 1 June 2000, CDPA.

[61] Archbishop Furey to Dr. Watzlavick, 21 March 1972, CDPA.

[62] *The Catholic Lighthouse*, n.d., CDPA.

on June 10 the Archdiocesan School Board announced that the school would close since it had not met the minimum enrollment requirements. "Just after the announcement of the school's closing, Bishop Forest was named the top school in the state in Class A by the Texas Association of Private Schools [on 23 June in Waco, Texas]. . . . The award was given for excellence in athletics, academics, art, and music."[63] In 1997 Blinn Community College of Brenham, Texas, opened an extension in the BFHS buildings. By 2000 it enrolled over 200 students at the site.

In 1960 the Congregation agreed to administer with the Christian Brothers another coeducational high school, Bishop Kelley High School in Tulsa, Oklahoma. Eleven Sisters and 12 Brothers plus lay faculty welcomed 666 students on opening day.[64] The Sister teachers were well-prepared. For example Diane Langford, who later entered the CDP, remembered learning new ways to study the Bible from Sister Charlene Wedelich, who was passing on what she was learning in her summer school classes at St. Mary's near Notre Dame University.[65] At the end of the first year the school was accredited by the Oklahoma State Department of Education; and the following year, 1962, it received accreditation from the North Central Association.

To form BKHS three schools closed and combined their student bodies: Holy Family High School, Marquette High School, and St. Francis Xavier Junior High School. Holy Family High School, staffed by the Sisters of Divine Providence, seemed to have a bright future after World War II and even enrolled eight ex-servicemen in fall, 1946. Fifteen years later it was ready to combine as it became obvious that because of decreasing enrollments none of the three schools would be able to thrive. There were rivalries and factions among the students for a few weeks until the red-letter day that the BKHS football team beat Cascia Hall, the more exclusive high school staffed by the Augustinians since 1926. Victory helped to unite and animate the students of the new school.

Sister Leola Ann (Adeline Clare) Doerfler enjoyed teaching home economics classes in the "wonderfully equipped department" at BKHS. She was a registered dietician who taught full time besides ordering all the food and supervising the cafeteria employees. She was pleased with her two home economics classes of boys who "really wanted to learn," but the cafeteria presented big challenges her first year. She had to organize the cafeteria records, improve the menus, and

---

[63] Diane Prause, "Bishop Forest: Looking Back on 33 Years of Catholic Education," *Schulenburg Sticker*, June 29, 1989: 1 and 12.

[64] One reason the Congregation could supply faculty was that St. Joseph's High School in Abilene was preparing to close and send some of its teachers to a co-institutional high school, Abilene Central High School, which lasted only seven years, 1963-1970.

[65] Oral interview, 4 Nov. 2000, CDPA.

entice the students to choose more healthful food. "I decided to let the football players go first if they would choose one serving of each hot item and encourage the freshmen to do the same. It worked!"[66]

Basic tuition at BKHS the first year was $100 a year; and girls and boys were divided into separate divisions or units with two completely separate faculties, one for the boys and one for the girls. Brother Kilian Bernardine Kuzminski, FSC, was the superintendent responsible for the physical plant, finances, personnel, and general policies. The Sister Principal and the Brother Principal had the same duties, but the fact that each section was operated differently sometimes caused problems. Sister Angelina Murphy, the first principal of the girls' section, looking back on her experience at BKHS observed in 1983 that she soon became dissatisfied. "It had been an understanding from the first that the Brothers would not have more power and influence than the Sisters because of the fact that the Director was a Brother. But the Brothers assumed more and more responsibility and authority in the school until the Sisters, and it was their own fault, gave in more and more."[67] Brother Bernardine requested that Sister Kathleen Bezner become the sole principal in 1970, but the General Council decided she should continue as principal of the girls' section.[68]

Sister Rose Kruppa enjoyed teaching English at BKHS because most of the students were children of college-educated parents. They were motivated to learn, and discipline problems were minimal. The school also accepted students who were less able, however; so teachers created classes that were responsive to their needs such as sports in literature, ethnic literature, and women in literature. Sister Rose "loved doing that. It was the beginning of the Women's Movement, and I was able to pick current short stories and novels to teach."

Her personal satisfaction with the students did not, however, extend to structures and administrators. "At Kelley there was great need for recognizing the contributions of women. Girls were accepted into the pre-calculus class only if they were willing to work on Saturdays and Sundays because they were deficient." Some of the Sisters also felt frustrated when they tried to contribute.

> Sister Suzanne Dancer and I were valued and appreciated because we knew how to change the oil in a car, or change light bulbs or paint the dining room in the Sisters' residence. We were wonderful for being able to do those things; but when it came to curriculum

---

[66] Oral interview, 21 Jan. 2000, CDPA. Later Sister Leola Ann was assigned to PHS in San Antonio and Bishop Forest High School in Schulenburg, where the cafeterias had similar problems. She successfully repeated her techniques.

[67] Written communication, 1983, CDPA.

[68] Sister Henrietta Schroeder to Brother Bernardine, 30 June 1970, CDPA.

changes in school, all of a sudden we were just too uppity. We were pushing too hard.[69]

The unequal treatment of women teachers by male administrators extended to opportunities available to women students. "The boys had a really strong sports program, and the girls had practically nothing. So a laywoman who taught math and I coached a softball team for the girls. The men got paid; the women were volunteers. But we believed in it so strongly that we were willing to make it happen."[70] The Sisters at Kelley felt that the school's administration, in contrast to that of the Congregation's PHS in San Antonio, did not support their efforts to further equal opportunities for women.

Sister Sylvia Schmidt, head of the BKHS theology department in the early 1970s, also helped in the diocesan religious education office by setting up and carrying out projects for Catholic high school students attending public schools. She decided to leave BKHS because she felt manipulated.[71] The Superior General explained to Brother Bernardine why the General Council approved Sister Sylvia's decision to leave BKHS to counsel runaways and young people on drugs and give "Thrust" weekend retreats: "The salary that Sister will get from her work will balance out the low salary and the lack of hospitalization premiums (approximately one-third) given the Sisters at Bishop Kelley."[72]

Relations between the school and the Congregation were beginning to be strained. The Congregation's general administration noted that "Bishop Kelley High School is dragging its feet in the academic program. It seems no progress is made by consulting Brother Bernardine; so we must contact the General Administration of the Christian Brothers and ask what direction Bishop Kelley will take in the future so we will know where we stand in the school."[73] The Sisters withdrew from Bishop Kelley High School in 1982. Shortage of personnel, especially in secondary education, was the reason for withdrawal given in a letter of the Superior General to Bishop Eusebius J. Beltran.[74] An additional unstated reason for leaving may have been a desire to direct their energies to projects that promoted women's equality instead of engaging in what seemed to be a constant uphill battle with little positive change. The Sisters preferred a more collaborative style of administration and wanted to serve without compromising their ideals.

---

[69] Sister Rose Kruppa, oral interview, 27 July 2000, CDPA.

[70] Sister Rose Kruppa, oral interview, 27 July 2000, CDPA.

[71] Oral interview, 3 Feb. 2003, CDPA.

[72] Sister Elizabeth McCullough to Brother Bernardine, 4 July 1970, CDPA.

[73] GC minutes, 2 Dec. 1974, CDPA.

[74] Sister Mary Margaret Hughes to Bishop Eusebius J. Beltran, 22 Mar. 1982, CDPA.

New Types of Schools

When the Congregation decided to close St. Francis High School in Iota, Louisiana, in 1967,[75] the school took the giant step of consolidating with high schools from Rayne and Crowley on the premises of St. Michael's High School in Crowley, taking the name Notre Dame High School. NDHS was thus an inter-Congregational Catholic high school for the civil parish (called a county in states other than Louisiana) of Acadia. Four communities of Sisters staffed the school and lived in the same house. CDP Sisters Jacqualine (Kenneth Rose) Kingsbury and Frances (John Francis) Klinger were on the faculty, and Sister Frances recalls it as an interesting, positive experience.

> Because the enrollment was larger, we could offer more courses than we were used to providing for our 90 or so students in Iota. The school was integrated, but the African-American enrollment was small because most of the African-American parents were blue-collar workers who could not pay the tuition. It was fabulous to work with the people who appreciated having a good Catholic high school.[76]

The integration at NDHS is noteworthy in view of problems developing at this time in Louisiana private schools. Also of interest is the fact that because they charged tuition most private schools enrolled children from families that could afford such education and thus tended to promote a real, if subtle, racial and class distinction.

Unity High School in Ponca City, Oklahoma, exemplifies a different kind of consolidation. The Congregation began to staff St. Mary's grade school and high school in Ponca City in 1901. Unable to support both schools financially, yet wishing to provide Catholic education, in 1968 Rev. Joseph Mazaika, the pastor, and the Sisters, with the support of parishioners as well as leaders of the civic community, took the daring step of closing the high school and uniting with Angela Hall, which the Felician Sisters built in 1958 as a high school and junior college for members of the order. Mr. Bill Masters, pastor of the First Christian Church, Disciples of Christ, who became President of the Board, recalled the venture as a kind of last resort to boost enrollment.[77] The new school was located on the beautiful grounds of a mansion previously owned by multi-millionaire oilman-philanthropist E. W. Marland, former U.S. congressman and Oklahoma governor. The mansion was serving as the

---

[75] GC minutes, 29 Oct. 1966, CDPA.

[76] Sister Frances Klinger, oral interview, 20 June 2000, CDPA.

[77] Rev. Bill Masters, telephone communication to the author, 21 Jan. 2003.

Felician Sisters' motherhouse. St. Mary's parish built a new gymnasium on the property for Unity High School.

Dedicating the school on Sunday, 29 December 1968, Bishop Victor J. Reed of Oklahoma City-Tulsa reminded his listeners that it was a time of change in every field of endeavor with new values and new ways opening up to attain these values.

> This means a great adjustment must be made by all persons living today. I feel you have in Ponca City a real opportunity to develop a high school that will be truly Christian and an ecumenical experience. I feel you have the material means to accomplish it, and I also feel there are enough people in Ponca City who are interested in the matter of Christian education to make this endeavor a real success.
>
> In addition to that you also have the devotion of two religious orders of women whose lives are devoted principally to the teaching of youth. So I am very hopeful for the future of this school, which seeks to instruct not only by words but by example.[78]

Sister Margaret Ellen Gallatin, CDP, was the principal of this Unity High School, which was interdenominational in student body, administration, and faculty. Fifteen percent of the students were not Catholics; and the 18 member board of governors, which included three students, represented the Roman Catholic, Jewish, Disciples of Christ, Baptist, Presbyterian, Lutheran, and Methodist faiths. The fifteen faculty members included Joe R. Surber, a Presbyterian and former junior high school councilor, two Felician Sisters, and three Sisters of Divine Providence.[79] Sister Agnes Marie Marusak, a math and science teacher at St. Mary's, resumed instruction in math and science at Unity High School.

> My students at Unity were perhaps the best ones I have ever taught. Their parents were professional people; many worked for Conoco Oil Company. The pupils were serious about learning, and the classroom and laboratory arrangement was ideal. Since classes were small, I had the same students over several years, so we could really lay a solid foundation and build on it.[80]

---

[78] *The Ponca City News*, Tues., 31 Dec. 1968, CDPA.

[79] *Oklahoma's Orbit*, 14 March 1971: 6 and 8, CDPA.

[80] Sister Agnes Marie Marusak, communication to the author, 30 Jan. 2003. Sister also noted that there were a few Native Americans but no African American or Mexican students.

Unity High School continued to be short of funds, but no fundraising drive was attempted.[81] Small enrollment forced the school to close in the spring of 1971. Its students enrolled in Ponca City's public high school, which not only offered a good education but also boasted a strong sports program, especially a football team.

Finances continued to be an important factor in choices to open or close schools. Borrowing money had made it possible to add buildings at the Congregation's college and open a new high school in San Antonio in 1951. Twenty years later, the Congregation was still dogged by financial shortfalls yet still determined to continue to support excellence in teacher preparation and classroom performance. Seeing the Congregation's own need, the general administration decided to take the risk of asking Sisters to bring in more money by taking positions with higher salaries in the public schools.[82] Noteworthy is the fact that seven years later even when the income from social security and the investment portfolio was factored in, the income from the Sisters' services, salaries, and stipends was still not sufficient to solve a projected deficit of more than $115,000. The General Council then decided to ask for a higher stipend of $4,300 for the next year and an 8% increase in stipends for the next three years. They also decided to try to increase the number of Sisters on public salaries from 46 to 60.[83]

The Sisters had taught in rural public schools for many years.[84] Deliberately seeking public school posts was, however, a new venture in the Congregation. Some who took this risk discovered they were a minority and not always welcome on the urban scene.

Four Sisters who responded to a call from the Congregation's Central Administration in 1971 for Sisters to take on public school positions with higher pay and benefits chose employment in the public school district in which the Motherhouse was located. They wore veils and usually were allowed to pray with the children in the classroom.[85]

Former Sister Georgia Ann Fucik recalled searching for ways to reach her pupils, many of whom "lived on a level of survival," not only fending for themselves but helping younger siblings. A few had already been in trouble with

---

[81] "CDP News Notes," 1 March 1971: 1, CDPA.

[82] GC minutes, 20 Jan. 1971, CDPA.

[83] GC minutes, 4 Oct. 1978, CDPA. That education of the Sisters remained a priority even in hard financial times is evident, for six Sisters were approved for full-time study for 1979-1980 at the same general council meeting. By 1983 only 37 Sisters earned a salary while 183 were on a stipend and 254 were on social security (GC minutes, 31 Jan. 1983, CDPA).

[84] Sisters Euphrosine Honc, Joyce Jilek, and Rosa (Elvira) Ruiz, for example, were among Sisters who taught at the rural public grade school and high school in Fayetteville, Texas.

[85] Nunspeak, Summer, 1972: 14, CDPA.

the law, and others were convinced they could never learn to read. "I learned that you could make do with very little, and students respond well to the slightest interest in them. They taught me much."[86] She regretfully concluded, however, that she was not going to make a dent in this school system.

Sister Marie Elise Van Dijk admitted that salary was one factor in her going to teach in the Edgewood district, but from her perspective "the main reason was that several CDPs who lived in the housing project were concerned about the low educational level of many teachers in the district. Father Moye would have wanted us to help these needy families get a better education."[87] But she "found ministering in a public school very different—no prayer, no mention of God, weaker discipline, little cooperation from parents. The hardest part was that the rooms looked so unattractive; the desks were scribbled on and damaged; several teachers had absolutely no control." In her ten years at Edgewood, from 1971 to 1981, she learned to be observant, not to say too much at first, and have ideas for improvement ready before making critical comments. She took Spanish courses to be able to talk to the parents of her pupils. "The easiest for me," she said, "was that I had the respect of the faculty and administration, so I was able to assist them often. The most rewarding experience was that so many of my students made great progress once their math level was established and they were grouped by ability levels."[88]

Sister Elsa Mary Bennett contrasted her public school situation with her experiences in private and parochial schools where admissions could be controlled and troublesome students could be dismissed more easily.

> I remember a student who came to our public elementary school because his mother could no longer pay the tuition at the parochial school. It was very difficult for him because of his background of listening and doing what he was told to do. In the public school he found that the pupils did what *they* wanted to do. He wanted to be accepted, but he didn't want to lose the values that he had learned.[89]

Sister Elsa Mary was inclined to place part of the blame on parents who did not make their children do what they were supposed to do. She also recognized,

---

[86] Written interview, 26 Jan. 2004, CDPA.

[87] Communication to the author, 22 May 2003. Sister Charlotte Kitowski, who began teaching at Medina Valley High School in 1968, also remembered that the reason for her move from a private to a public school was not financial. However, her salary "was large enough to pay about one-third of the Sisters' local expenses at Moye Formation Center" (personal communication to the author).

[88] Communication to the author, 22 May 2003.

[89] Oral interview, 28 July 2000, CDPA.

however, that supervision was a problem for parents who worked night shifts or were incarcerated or for grandparents who had already raised a family and might lack motivation and energy to raise another one. After noting differences, Sister finally concluded that she really did not see too much difference between Catholic and public school teaching today.[90]

Occasionally the Sisters felt that they were not accepted because they had more education, degrees, and years of experience than their lay colleagues. Being the minority on a predominantly lay faculty sometimes made them feel they were in the spotlight whereas they just wanted to be good teachers. Their aim was never to proselytize although they did want to be witnesses to the viability of religious life.[91]

Sometimes the Sisters were remembered more for their encouragement than for their instruction. Dr. Regina Cusack, OLLU faculty member, reported meeting a successful professional man who as a child was a neighbor of CDPs living in Mirasol Courts, a San Antonio low income housing project. He remembered that the Sisters encouraged the children to stay in school and sometimes helped them with their lessons. This relieved his mother's stress and helped her deal more patiently and kindly with her family. The Sisters modeled good parenting traits, and one Sister even lent him a car so he could transport his girlfriend on a date. He was grateful for the Sisters' positive role modeling, which boosted his self-esteem and belief in the importance of education.[92]

At a meeting in the summer of 2001, Sisters compared the advantages and disadvantages of teaching in schools owned by the Congregation and in public schools. CDP schools had more freedom to experiment and did not have to answer to a pastor. They tended, however, to be short on finances, so they had to sponsor fundraising events and collect tuition. To be able to send something to the general administration of the Congregation, sometimes the Sisters themselves did janitorial and clerical work.

From 1968 to 1972 Sister Charlotte (M. Linus) Kitowski taught at Medina Valley High School near Castroville and returned to the public school system in 1987 as a librarian at Sinclair Elementary School in San Antonio. Her reflections are representative of the experiences of many Sisters who taught in public schools in urban areas.

> Among the hardest challenges was working with difficult students or some employees who were there just for the paycheck. Probably the most frustrating situations arose from some students' home

---

[90] Sister Elsa Mary Bennett, oral interview, 28 July 2000, CDPA.

[91] Public school teachers' group interview, 18 June 2001, CDPA.

[92] Regina Cusack, e-mail to Sister María Carolina Flores, 2 Apr. 2002.

environments—lack of discipline, of moral teaching, or of support of school efforts. It hurt when my students were killed in drive-by shootings, torn up by sexual abuse, not wanted by anyone in their families, or forced to live out of a station wagon under a bridge.

But satisfying experiences encouraged Sister Charlotte to persevere. She saw students enjoy learning and derived satisfaction from knowing she was able to

support women and minorities—from college bound minorities to African American administrators—to get ahead or make progress in their attempts to survive prejudice. One of the most rewarding experiences was working with so many sincerely dedicated people from many walks of life and religions, all trying very hard to make a real difference in children's lives.[93]

In the twenty-first century, the word "risk" often connotes insurance, lawsuits, or stock market ventures. Taking care of other people's children is considered to be particularly risky, but from its beginnings the Congregation sponsored boarding schools. Even if the Sisters had considered the hazards, they would not have been deterred from providing this needed service. Many of the Sisters agreed with Sister Kathryn Marie (Ancina) Rieger, who said, "I enjoyed the boarders because it seemed like home for me. I had come from a family with younger children, and I liked that. I like children around all the time."[94]

Besides accepting boarders on the elementary, high school, and college level at Our Lady of the Lake, the Sisters teaching in the mid-1950s also cared for resident students at schools in Alexandria, Louisiana; Vinita, Oklahoma; and Abilene, Castroville, and Palestine, Texas, and other schools. The Sisters were with their charges around the clock, kept vigil when they were ill, put up with their pranks, and comforted the homesick. Sisters learned to drive the school bus to take the boarders on outings or were challenged by the responsibility of taking a group into the city or supervising 40 wiggling St. Martin Hall resident students in the OLLU swimming pool. Some students at OLL High School got drunk and sick on a bottle of vanilla. Margaret Luthy Foster told of putting bubble bath in the sugar bowls and pepper into a birthday cake, but she is among the many who credited the Sisters with giving her a value system that proved invaluable in later life.[95]

---

[93] Communication to the author, 16 May 2003.

[94] Oral interview, 21 Feb. 2000, CDPA.

[95] Oral interview, 18 Feb. 2003, CDPA. Some CDPs admitted that when they were college students they stole the sword of St. Joan of Arc from Moye Hall rotunda or smeared cold cream on the Sister prefects' bathroom faucets.

Individual Sisters Who Dared

Trust in a God who would never abandon them was inculcated in all Sisters of Divine Providence and helped to explain why some Sisters took initiatives that required breaking ranks or breaking new ground. True, some people by temperament are more daring than others, but many students and colleagues remember that they could count on support, even for an unexpected request, whenever a CDP was convinced of its value. Their own hesitations were often overcome when they remembered a Sister's example of instigating change and then counting on divine help to persevere in the face of difficulties and obstacles.

Sister Clara (Norbertine) Kliesen was known as an exigent teacher with very high standards who occasionally scolded her students, but two stories reveal another side. While she was teaching at Holy Family High School in Tulsa, Oklahoma, in the late 1940s one of her students tried to pass the GED exam even though he knew he was weak in math. For some reason before the group came to the math part of the test, they were told to go home and come back to take the remainder of the test the following day. He immediately went to Sister Clara, and she tutored him in math late into the night. Next day he passed the test.[96] Sister Clara also taught at Our Lady of the Lake High School in the 1950s and was the principal when it closed in 1966. When senior Dr. Tessa Martínez Pollack, who became president of Our Lady of the Lake University in 2002, submitted a history essay, Sister Clara returned it with a high grade and the comment "You can write." Dr. Martínez Pollack considers this one of her greatest inspirations and certainly a turning point in her life. She went on to work in communications and administration, earning a master's and doctoral degree and serving as president of state junior colleges in Florida and Arizona before becoming the president of OLLU.

Sister Sharon García, while teaching business courses at the parish high school in Ennis, Texas, also taught shorthand two evenings a week to women looking for a refresher course. One weekday night found her teaching knitting to students 10 to 40 years of age. A Congregational publication reports: "It is a drain on someone who has been teaching all day already, but Sister feels that it is worth it. Sister Sharon's night school is an independent, one-man [sic] project. A need existed, and she met it."[97]

Sister Paulette Celis saw the need for a maintenance building for St. Augustine High School and Elementary School in the border town of Laredo,

---

[96] Testimony at Sister Clara's funeral, 2001.

[97] "CDP News Bulletin," Northern Region, Jan. 1969: 7, CDPA. Sister Helen Margaret Schad also remembered Sister Sharon was "a marvelous seamstress" (oral interview, 19 Feb. 2000, CDPA).

Texas. She raised funds through biannual barbecues and a concession stand in the school, recycled unlikely materials, and secured donated construction materials and labor. The building did not compare "in grandeur to the Sistine Chapel, St. Paul's Cathedral, or even the Conventual Chapel at Our Lady of the Lake University," but "it too is a tangible reflection of faith, inspiration, plain old persistence and ingenuity." Sister Maria Cristina (John of the Cross) Ruelas assisted in this five-year project, which was seen as "a monument to inspiration and faith."[98]

Dr. José Roberto Juárez, a retired history professor, credited his teachers at St. Augustine's School in Laredo, Texas, for his professional successes. Sister Sophie Anna (Stephen) Polasek taught him to write term papers and fostered a love for history as well as music. Sister Alban Bezner not only taught typing but also, as moderator for the yearbook, trained the students to solicit advertisements from prominent local people in a professional manner. These skills were invaluable for him in graduate school. Sister Celine Kainer, principal and teacher of algebra and geometry, was instrumental in getting "Beto" a four-year scholarship to St. Edward's University in Austin, Texas. He went on to earn an MA and a PhD from the University of Texas in Austin and was a professor of history for many years.

Dr. Juárez and his wife, María Antonia Martínez Juárez, an OLLU alumna, also appreciated the solid background in all subjects, along with very personal help, the Sisters offered. At St. Augustine's in Laredo, good study habits were inculcated; and mediocre work was not accepted. If the work was inferior, the students might have been kept in from recess to improve it, but they were never physically punished. Looking back, the couple remembered that they heard stories about Purgatory and Hell that may have served as a means to control behavior. However, they quickly pointed out that this was a tool typical of the times; at home, their parents used stories of "La Llorona" and "El Brujo" for the same purpose. As a teacher of Latin American history, Dr. Juárez praised the Sisters in particular for not "anglicizing" the students. For example, the preparation for First Communion included instruction in English in the classroom along with instruction in Spanish from laywomen in the parish church next to the school. Pupils were never made to feel that Spanish was an inferior language.

The Beatitudes were more than a beautiful part of the Gospel at St. Augustine School in Laredo. Students volunteered their services in the community, supported social justice issues, taught catechism in their parishes, and filled their Lenten rice bowls with coins to help the less fortunate. Talents were gifts from God to be used for God's people. Mrs. Juárez saw a strong connection between her education from the Sisters and the fact that after retiring she taught a class

---

[98] Susan Adams, "Building product of faith, ingenuity," *Laredo Morning Times*, 28 June 1990, C1.

for deacon candidates at the Laredo Pastoral Center and a course twice a year in her parish for adults who had not received any Sacraments besides Baptism. The couple felt that their accomplishments were examples of how the good works of the Sisters were extended and multiplied for generations. Dr. Juárez also admired the great spirit of sacrifice of the Sisters.

> They were very poorly paid and sometimes even had to ask friends to obtain little personal items for them. But when they had to move out of the convent next to the international bridge in downtown Laredo, they did not leave the city and all their former students. Rather, they moved with the school to the campus of the former Ursuline School in Laredo, where they continued to teach until the last Sister left in 2001.[99]

Catherine Walter, a graduate of St. Pius Elementary School in Pasadena, Texas, considered the foundation she got there to be more significant than her later high school education for her success in life. Attitudes toward the world and Christian attitudes for living in the world were communicated; and she praised the marriage of belief with action which she observed in the CDPs. Sister Berchmans Fitzpatrick gave "Katy" her first teaching job when Katy was in the fifth grade at St. Pius. Sister Berchmans, who was a very strict teacher, was concerned about several boys who had failed a grade because of poor marks in English and mathematics. Their parents could not afford to send them to summer school for makeup work. Sister Berchmans, along with the other Sisters in the community, left Pasadena for San Antonio every summer. But that year she arranged for these lads to get tutoring in arithmetic and English for several hours a day from Katy Walter at her home. The boys were admitted into the next grade and succeeded.

Catherine Walter has earned a licentiate in French Literature and Linguistics from the Sorbonne in Paris and a doctorate in linguistics from Cambridge University in England. She has published numerous books, one of which earned the Duke of Edinborough Award in 1997. She explicitly links to her association with the Sisters some contributions she has made to society: forging links between EFL teachers' associations in Eastern Europe and other parts of the world, visiting prisoners and serving as a sponsor for released prisoners, and writing letters for Amnesty International.[100]

When Martha Pack Brinkmann paid a visit to the OLL campus in 1955 after her high school graduation, she was impressed with the architecture, especially

---

[99] Dr. José Roberto Juárez, oral interview, 2 June 2002, CDPA.

[100] Catherine Walter, oral interview, 13 Dec. 2001, CDPA.

the rotunda in Moye Hall. Even more memorable, however, was the advice given by her guide, Sister Theresa Joseph Powers, appointed assistant to the academic dean in 1944. "Sister said it was a good idea for students to be involved in several activities—one professional, one social, one spiritual, and one charitable. That chance remark became a lifelong practice for me."[101]

Martha was also impressed by Sister Lourdes Murphy, who "was good enough to teach a special class just for me so I could get the hours I needed to graduate. We met in a basement room of Thiry Auditorium, just Sister and I. I would begin to give one of my brilliant speeches, and she would fall asleep. I remember it was very warm in that room. Just right for a nap."[102] Sister Lourdes recorded speeches on a rather primitive machine and played the record back to give each student a sense of her voice and speaking habits. She also produced a play, "Twelve Angry Women," and another play in which all the actors were supposed to be nuns. Martha was

> especially grateful to Sister Lourdes who probably had more important things to do than to teach one student on hot afternoons in the basement. She allowed me to give a recital of poetry and drama in my senior year. I am now confident in public speaking and used many of the things she taught me about drama when I was teaching school.[103]

Jesse Treviño enrolled at OLL after losing his right forearm in the Vietnam War. He had a good art background, but the trauma left him bitter and discouraged. Sister Tharsilla Fuchs sized up the situation and offered to let him work independently in his studio in downtown San Antonio instead of attending classes. Every three weeks she went to the studio to evaluate his progress.[104] Her trust was amply rewarded. Jesse became an artist of national stature. He received an honorary doctorate of arts and letters from his alma mater, and one of his murals hangs in the Sueltenfuss library on campus.

Sister Tharsilla considered her own "greatest achievement in art" to be the designing of 12 faceted glass windows for St. Timothy's Church located near the CDP motherhouse. They are like "gems in a crown high above the main altar," and each has the symbol of an apostle "integrated in an abstract pattern of a mandala."[105] Sister Tharsilla also designed and began to piece a large appliquéd

---

[101] Oral interview, 7 Sept. 2001, CDPA.

[102] Oral interview, 7 Sept. 2001, CDPA.

[103] Oral interview, 7 Sept. 2001, CDPA.

[104] Videotaped interview, CDPA.

[105] *CDP Times*, 12, 4 (Dec., 1991): 11 and "CDP News Notes," 1 March 1971, n.p., CDPA. Sister Tharsilla also identified a painting of the Immaculate Conception from Mission Concepción, which had been stored at San Fernando Cathedral and

Last Supper, which former pupils completed when a medical condition severely restricted movement in her hands and fingers. This work hangs in the Regan Hall Community Room on the motherhouse campus.

Martha Pack Brinkmann was not an art major, but she learned from Sister Tharsilla's art appreciation course to have a great distaste for artificial flowers, and for many years she had no artificial flowers in her home. "Imagine my surprise when they redid the 'Blue Room' in Providence Hall, and I saw artificial flowers everywhere." For her this epitomized an important aspect of CDP education. "I think that is one of the lessons taught at OLL, as changes come we need to review that change; and if it is good and moral, we should accept it and move on with life."[106]

A CDP author educated by CDPs, Sister Angelina Murphy, was aware of her literary gifts but sometimes experienced obstacles or lack of appreciation rather than support.

> I felt a rhythm inside me, and poetry was a natural expression. This developed into stories, accounts, dramas, and finally into articles for local papers and magazines, and books. So often I felt this call which resulted in something interesting and satisfying that I finally said, "All right, I'll write!" And I kept a pen or pencil handy from then on.[107]

Sister Angelina indeed expressed her thoughts in numerous writings for newspapers and magazines as well as Congregational publications. She obtained permission to write a biographical history of the second Superior General, Mother Mary Florence, but she did not ask for financial or promotional help with her publication. She "was used to doing things on my own. I had saved up some money from my allowance, so I just went ahead. I flew to Europe standby and visited all the places where she had been." After the books were printed, I "loaded boxes of them in a station wagon, gave talks at parish Masses, and had autograph parties all over Oklahoma, Louisiana, and Texas. Later the Generalate asked me to write a biography of Mother Amata, the fifth Superior General."[108] Sister Angelina's unpublished writings include an operetta, a biography of an abused woman, a history of her home parish, and a book of poetry. She also

---

San Fernando Cathedral School from 1794 to 1949, as having been painted before 1745. The painting was restored and later displayed again at Mission Concepción in San Antonio.

[106] Oral interview, 7 Sept. 2001, CDPA.

[107] Oral interview, 4 Apr. 2000, CDPA.

[108] Oral interview, 4 Apr. 2000, CDPA. The biographies are *Mother Florence* (Smithtown, NY: Exposition Press, 1980) and *Green from the Fields* (privately printed, n.d.).

edited a number of Congregational publications and was instrumental in setting up the Congregational archives at the motherhouse.[109]

Some Sisters were concerned about food for the body as well as for the mind. In Cloutierville, Louisiana, the children used to eat outside sitting on a rock until Sister Praxedes Martínez decided, "Something has to be done." She sold snacks until she collected enough money to build a good cafeteria.[110] At St. Henry's School in San Antonio, Texas, Sister George Brossmann, who cooked at the convent and also ran the school cafeteria, served hot cereal to poor children who came to school without breakfast so they could learn better.[111] When Sister Dolores Cárdenas was teaching at St. Patrick's School in Houston, Texas, 1941-1963, she pioneered a school lunch program for 100 children. "I wrote to the Agriculture Department and told them that every child is going to eat lunch, whether they have 10 cents or not. And they helped me."[112] When Archbishop Patricio Flores spoke at Sister Dolores' 100th birthday party, he recalled some lengths to which she went to feed the hungry.

> She would ride to the produce market on Saturday with a parishioner and ask for food they couldn't sell. . . . Someone complained about a nun riding in a truck with a man, so she just took off her veil during the ride. She put it back on at the market, knowing the merchants couldn't say no to a nun. Then she would always spend the whole week giving food to people who needed it.[113]

Sister Joyce (David) Jilek said one of the biggest influences on her faith life was Sister Suzanne Marie Cleaver, whom she considers a mystic who communed directly with God. Sister Suzanne Marie taught her kindergarten pupils to pray with their eyes closed. One little boy went home and told his dad, "Sister talks to God." The dad was not happy to hear this and asked his son, "How do you know? Did she tell you children that?" The little boy answered, "No, I peeked."[114]

Sometimes students also left a lasting impression on their teachers which contributed to their courage in new undertakings. The Congregation had a short-lived house of formation for aspirants (high school students) (1966-1969)

---

[109] These works are titled: "Light on the Mountain, the Story of Our Lady of La Salette" (1954), "The Black Hole," "80 for Those Who Are Strong" (1987) and "Book 7." She also edited *Go Tell It In The Streets*, an autobiography of Bishop Stephen A. Leven (Oklahoma City, 1984).

[110] Sister Jerome Carrión, oral interview, 3 Dec. 1999, CDPA.

[111] Sister Cecile Clare Vanderlick, oral interview, 21 July 2000, CDPA.

[112] Interview by Michele Salcedo, *San Antonio Light*, n.d., CDPA.

[113] Article by J. Michael Parker, *San Antonio Express-News*, 3 Feb. 1991, F: 7-A.

[114] Sister Joyce Jilek, written addendum to oral interview, July 31 2000, CDPA.

in Oklahoma. The aspirants attended diocesan Bishop McGinnis High School in Oklahoma City. Sister Christine (Rose Stephanie) Stephens, who was on the McGinnis faculty at this time, taught an innovative course called "Political Thought," which utilized informal group discussions.[115] Sister Christine recalled that the Oklahoma diocese took very seriously the documents of Vatican II and was very "progressive" in opposing the Vietnam War and segregation. Some of the school's alumni were in Mi Lai in Vietnam and returned to detail their experiences. This atmosphere and exposure as well as interaction with her African American students at McGinnis were among the factors that set her on the path to ministry among African Americans.

> I had gotten very close to a group of African American students who were there at McGinnis High School. It was during the years that Martin Luther King was speaking until he was killed in 1968. They took a lot of time with me and were very patient with me. They told me I taught them some things, but I think they really taught me more things than I taught them. I decided to ask to go into our African American schools.[116]

Sister Christine was preparing to teach African-Americans in Louisiana, but—as will be shown in a later chapter—circumstances were not favorable. In 1978 she definitively left teaching for community organizing ministry.

Noteworthy changes have taken place in education during the past five decades, and most of them have added unprecedented pressures to the life of every educator. On the one hand, national funds and grants for math and science led to better-prepared teachers. On the other hand, colleges put greater pressure on high school graduates by raising entrance requirements. SAT scores were required and competition made it imperative to earn high grades. College admissions officers also began to scrutinize community service points as prerequisites for acceptance. Historical and cultural factors likewise led to challenges that increased stress for teachers. As Sister Charlotte Kitowski stated, "We are patrol officers and psychologists; we have so many roles. We have emotionally disturbed children who are acting out. And the record-keeping! You have to document *everything*."[117] The civil rights movement helped to make students more conscious of their rights and parents more ready to sue. Greater permissiveness in the culture extended to the family and tended to lead to more discipline problems in schools. Sports programs assumed more prominence than heretofore and took more time as well as money. Even the teaching of religion presented added demands. After Vatican II religious education became more ecumenical; teachers had to update

---

[115] *Oklahoma City Times*, 1 Feb. 1970, CDPA.

[116] Sister Christine Stephens, oral interview, 18 June 2000, CDPA.

[117] Oral interview, 13 March 2000, CDPA.

constantly as instruction in other religions became part of the curriculum.[118] As individuals and as a Congregation, the Sisters of Divine Providence met each challenge and adapted with resilience and creativity.

Changes on every level of formal education taking place at this time also impacted the elementary schools, where the majority of CDPs served. Constant updating was a primary concern of their supervisors who dealt with successive trends as well as ever-changing state and Church regulations.

---

[118] CDP high school teachers' oral interview, 17 June 2001, CDPA. Some Sisters were influenced by the ecumenical community of Taizé, France, whose charism was reconciliation, to collaborate with people of different faith traditions. Sister Joyce Jilek, for example, was a charter member of the Christian Women's Association in Columbus, Texas. Sister Angelina Murphy was active in Church Women United.

CHAPTER 3

PROVIDING EDUCATION
FOR THE YOUNG[1]

Sister Rose Marie (M. Constantine) Gallatin, like the majority of Sisters of Divine Providence anywhere in the world, was teaching in an elementary school in 1951. She recalled that the weather in Houston, Texas,

> was so hot and humid the gray cement walls would sweat. The floors were wood saturated with oil. The odors from the Pasadena paper mills and from the bilge in the Houston Ship Channel were so noxious that it was better to keep the windows closed despite the 73 children.

> Not having commercial aids, I made countless teachers' aids and used every inch of available space. I drew and painted clowns along the top border to teach the numbers. Right below were their writing papers. Below that was a seasonal frieze they drew. Under the blackboard, along the chalk ledge, were spelling tablets I made for them.[2]

---

[1] "Nothing is more important than the education of the young; the whole of life depends on youth." *Directory of the Sisters of Providence of Portieux* (Paris: Bray and Retaux, 1874), English translation, 1983, p. 112. This is the opening sentence of Part Two of the *Directory*, which was the best source for the words of their founder available to the Sisters until 2000. He also told them to care for the sick and instruct the village adults in the truths of their religious faith, but the Sisters in France as well as in Texas devoted most of their energy and time to instructing younger children.

[2] Sister Rose Marie Gallatin, communication to the author, 11 Jan. 2002. Sister Florencia Lopez at Our Lady of Guadalupe School across town had 96 little ones in her classroom, and Sister Aquilina Martínez had 116 enrolled with a daily average attendance of 86 (Sister Aquilina Martínez, oral interview, 26 Jan. 2000, CDPA).

Twenty years later in St. Martin Hall, the only elementary school in the San Antonio Archdiocese to be accredited by the Southern Association, classrooms looked very different as the school piloted I.G.E. (Individually Guided Education). Teachers still had to be resourceful, however. Sister Tiolinda (M. Dominic) Marotta recalled:

> We had numerous groupings for our homeroom, and we had to develop stations for the children. The little first graders would get lost as they moved from one station to another. We made huge cardboards with an animal on each of them, and the children had folders with the same animal indicating where they went first. We kept them twenty minutes and gave them individual contracts. They moved along according to their ability.[3]

Sister Rita Louise (Barbara Louise) Petsch found she had to adapt to her pupils.

> The children want action. They have to move. If you try to make them sit at a desk like we did in the early years, you would find that there is no response. My favorite way of teaching now is individualized and contract forms of teaching in which the students are responsible after the material is presented. We certainly have different levels of teaching in each classroom.[4]

Solid, long-term educational goals and a strong support system enabled the Sisters to maintain excellent teaching as times changed. They continued to devote most of their daily time and energy to the progress of their pupils. Their steadfastness along with adaptability will be illustrated in this chapter.

The first women religious invited to teach in Texas belonged to cloistered orders that customarily instructed students inside their convents and in academies which they owned. They were not very much involved in parish or family life. On the other hand, the Sisters of Divine Providence were brought from the Alsace-Lorraine region of France to educate immigrants. As they had done since their inception in 1762, the Sisters went out to the people in small villages and lived among them. In order to obtain pontifical approval for the Congregation, however, in 1912 they had to present *Constitutions* in accordance with Canon Law, which mandated a semi-cloistered way of life even for non-cloistered religious.

---

[3] Sister Tiolinda Marotta, oral interview, 13 June 2000, CDPA. One disadvantage of contract learning was that often the children lacked interaction with one another.

[4] Oral interview, 18 Feb. 2000, CDPA.

Their religious formation inculcated a sense of unchanging basic values as well as a desire to make them attractive and acceptable to people here and now. Adhering to the daily schedule (horarium) was the Sisters' chief way of observing the *Constitutions*. On the one hand, they had a "special duty" to "practice in their conventual life all the virtues of the most fervent and regular communities." This was interpreted to mean daily communal prayers, silence except during daily recreation together and for necessary practical communication, and readiness to obey authorities. On the other hand, they were "to impart to children and young girls instruction suitable to their position in society; and, above all, to give them a religious education."[5] To do this, the Sisters had not only to win their students' confidence but also to study continually and maintain their teacher certification.

Separating the "ends" in this way encouraged distinctions, if not dichotomies, between interior and exterior life, spiritual and apostolic endeavors, and private and public behavior. When the Sisters were not serving in the classroom, office, clinic, or hospital, they were to spend their time with members of their own religious community rather than mingling with laypeople or even members of other congregations. Prayer, study, and household tasks filled the hours outside of the classroom or other workplace. No Sister of this time seriously questioned the need for wearing a cumbersome habit nor the wisdom of accepting so many students. To become a Sister meant to accept assignments and do one's best. Hardships were "offered up" for some good intention such as the conversion of sinners or the release of souls from Purgatory.

The Sisters enjoyed the reputation of being outstanding instructors, responsive to needs, up-to-date in their training, student-centered, and hospitable to new ideas and ways of doing things. Sister Rogata Kalina's experience is typical. She said she never had trouble with her pupils because she was always interested in what they were learning. "I would go to the classroom early in the morning with papers I had checked the night before. If there were problems on the papers, I would call the students individually before class and work with them. I also tutored them after school. I worked so hard with them."[6]

The impact of the Sisters was usually lasting. For example, Harry N. Harper of the Chiropractic Diagnostic Clinic and Acupuncture Research Center in Lawton, Oklahoma, credited Sister Ann Carmel Maggio for his professional success. Calling himself one of her "*delinquent* science students at St. Mary's in 1956," he explained:

> Over the last 20 years I have thought of you many times. Because of your influence in that science class, my life was directed into the

---

[5] Constitutions, # 2.

[6] Sister Rogata Kalina, oral interview, 6 Apr. 2000, CDPA.

healing arts. After many years of hard work, struggling through college and starting a practice, we finally have our feet planted on solid ground. Our blessings have been many, but unfortunately most of us forget sometimes to count them, so I just wanted to say a little "Thank you" for your direction in those *formative* years.[7]

Sister Bernadine (Immaculata) Leonards made a lasting impression on Clara C. Whipp of Lafayette, Louisiana, who wrote about the day she reluctantly started the first grade.

Sister seemed to understand how hard it was for me to leave my mother; perhaps she missed her mother also. She explained that while our mothers cannot be with us always, Mary, our mother in Heaven, is always with us. The year progressed very well. I didn't miss a day of school and I made the honor roll.[8]

Tom Frost, fourth generation overseer of Frost Bank in San Antonio and a lifelong Episcopalian, never forgot his first grade teacher at St. Anthony's School in San Antonio. Sister Dorothy Hunter was in her second year of teaching, and she gave him an unforgettable introduction to the mystery of the Blessed Trinity. "For a person to try to explain to a child who was going on seven what the Father, the Son, and the Holy Ghost were was really kind of daunting. But I can remember to this day that she did a magnificent job. She introduced the concept and the belief and it's been a foundation of my fundamental faith ever since." Tom reminisced that when a fellow classmate burst into tears because he could not read, "Sister Dorothy went straight over there, put her arm around him and said, 'That's exactly why we're here. Now, we're going to teach you how to read.'" She was only 18, but "she demonstrated to me early on that there was nothing wrong with making a mistake or not knowing something. I've never forgotten that."[9]

Tributes to the Sisters' early influence also include the testimony of prominent clerics in San Antonio. Archbishop Patrick Flores credited Sister Benitia Vermeersch with recognizing and supporting his vocation to the priesthood. Monsignor Lawrence Steubben revered his first grade teacher, Sister Aline Hrncir, who recognized his abilities and assigned him to tutor other students.[10] Rev. Virgilio Elizondo, co-founder of the Mexican American

---

[7] Harry N. Harper, D.C. to Sister Ann Carmel Maggio, 14 Oct. 1977, CDPA.

[8] Clara C. Whipp, *Acadiana Catholic*, September, 2002, CDPA.

[9] Article by David Uhler, *San Antonio Express-News*, Oct. 1, 2002: D10.

[10] Sister Aline also prepared him and the future Msgr. Marvin Doerfler for their First Communion. Sister Aline did not remain in the teaching field because she lost her voice as a result of surgery. Her voice did return, however, and she used

Cultural Center and creator of Catholic TV in San Antonio, failed the first grade and made mediocre grades for several years. Then Sister Michael Rose Stanzel, his fifth grade teacher at St. Joseph's Academy, took an interest in him. "I'd always been aware of what I couldn't do, but she made me aware of what I could do," he said. He became a straight-A student, was valedictorian of his high school class, and is considered the father of U.S. Latino theology. According to the testimony of Veronica Perez, he continued to imitate his fifth-grade teacher. "Father is like the Johnny Appleseed of the Hispanic community. He sows seeds, develops these little 'plants,' helps them grow, and lets them develop on their own to become what he and God envision for that person. . . . He helps you see things in yourself that you never imagined and gives you the courage to try."[11]

Sister Jerome Carrión for 17 years taught pre-kindergarten and kindergarten classes at San Juan de los Lagos, a parish of low income families located walking distance from the motherhouse. She witnessed the importance of the first steps in the process of education. "When I meet the adults today whom I trained, giving them a solid beginning on which to build, I am happy. They have done well." And Sister cited statistics to prove her point: "96 of them went to St. Martin Hall [Elementary School], nearly all to high school, 16 to OLL University, and five to Notre Dame University. A number of them had been awarded scholarships. They tell me it was their early beginning that made them able to do what they did later."[12] One of Sister's fondest memories was taking her pupils to dance for Pope John Paul II when he visited San Antonio. He came over and told her "That's a good teacher! I like teachers that know how to dance."[13]

Sometimes the Sisters never had the satisfaction of knowing that projects initiated by them had prospered. An exception was Sister Frederick Joseph Pirotina. In 1990, her last year in D'Hanis, Texas, she staged a live pageant with the children before the Christmas Mass. She did not sense much approval from the pastor at the time; but 11 years later he gave her credit in the Sunday bulletin for starting the presentation, which continues to this day.[14]

Sister Michael Rose Stanzel, a school supervisor, spoke for many CDP teachers when she noted factors that impacted teaching and learning.

---

her business talents for many years in hospitals and at the convent. She also played the organ for funerals and the piano for celebrations in the nursing home in Schulenburg in the 1990s (Sister Aline Hrncir, oral interview, 18 May 2000, CDPA).

[11] Article by J. Michael Parker, *San Antonio Express-News*, Sept. 15, 2002: A18.

[12] Sister Jerome Carrión, oral interview, *CDP Times*, 13, 2 (Oct., 1992): 6, CDPA.

[13] Sister Jerome Carrión, oral interview, 3 Dec. 1999, CDPA. Sister Julianna (Euphrasia) Kozuch coordinated 26 ethnic groups in costume to welcome Pope John Paul II at the beginning of his papal Mass in San Antonio (*Signs of Providence*, October, 1997:10, CDPA).

[14] Sister Frederick Joseph Pirotina, oral interview, 15 Feb. 2000, CDPA.

> In some places the students were already motivated, so we were almost forced to keep up with them. In other places, we were the chief stimulators and motivators. The background of each group of students affected how they appreciated their learning and what opportunities they sensed for their future. Ethnicity, cultural background, and the educational level of parents were other influences.[15]

Sending members throughout the U.S. for higher education was one way the Congregation made sure its teaching cadre kept up with and even stayed ahead of the latest developments in pedagogy as well as in content fields. Sisters with graduate degrees often became instructors in St. Martin Hall, the demonstration school of OLLU begun in 1929, and taught college classes. Sister Eugenia Ann Stell, who served in the Education Department at OLL from 1971 to 1985, recalled teaching "math by discovery" as she had learned it at Columbia University to Sisters in their 60s who wanted to learn about "properties," "sets," and the number system—in other words, to understand mathematical reasoning.[16]

Supervising CDP Teachers

To educate well, the Sisters must themselves be educated, and the *Constitutions* entrusted the supervision of their studies to the Mistress General of Studies. Each General Chapter designated one Sister to supervise all of the Congregation's schools and implement a flexible course of studies first developed after the Chapter of 1907 and continually revised. Mother Adelaide Marie Heyman was the general supervisor from 1946 to 1961. She was the Directress of Studies and Student Teaching from 1961 to 1967 when Sister Marietta Fischer became the general supervisor of all the elementary schools and Sister Lucina Schuler of the high schools.[17] In 1967 Sister Michael Rose Stanzel became the General Director of Studies, but in 1973 the three Regional Coordinators began to visit and supervise the Congregation's schools in their geographical regions.

The Sister-supervisor proposed a degree plan for each Sister that had to be approved by the Mother General and her Council, and she selected the courses the Sister would take. Knowing the tastes, talents, strengths, and weaknesses of the Sisters was necessary in deciding their majors and sometimes spelled the

---

[15] Oral interview, 23 June 2000, CDPA. Sister Michael Rose also attended most of the annual meetings of the National Catholic Education Association for almost 30 years. She said she appreciated them for helping her "see the Church situated in the national picture as well as the universality and trends of Catholic education."

[16] Sister Eugenia Ann Stell, oral interview, 29 March 2000, CDPA.

[17] GC minutes, 26 May 1961, CDPA.

difference between a happy and a disgruntled teacher, not to mention students and parents.

The supervisor was a key advisor to the general administration in deploying the Sisters in a beneficial way. Finding the right "fit" where each Sister could function best was usually more difficult than advising the Sisters of the courses needed for certification. Before the 1950s, the placement system involved positioning flat wooden blocks about the size of dominoes, each representing a Sister. The longer edges of each block were painted red and green, and the Sister's name was printed in elegant Gothic letters on each edge. The name of each mission was printed on gold-colored blocks. Blocks were placed behind the name of each mission, green if the Sister was there the previous year or red if she was newly assigned. Each summer the blocks were shuffled and reshuffled until the best combination was devised. Characteristics of each school also had to be kept in mind—rural or urban; large or small; private, parochial, or public; ethnically Anglo, Hispanic, or Black. The ethnic distinctiveness of the students as well as of the teachers and administrators were also factors to consider.

The supervisor needed to work closely with the college faculty. Sister Frederick Joseph Pirotina recalled an incident that illustrates this. Having obtained her bachelor's degree, she asked to take a summer music course in harmony since she had taught some beginning piano students in Westphalia and was helping with the children's chorus in Texarkana. Sister Adelaide Marie informed her that she would need permission from the college music department to register for the course since it had prerequisites.

> So I went to see Sister Amabilis. She heard my story and then gave me a written note for Sister Adelaide Marie. Without peeking, I took the note back to the convent office, which was crowded with Sisters registering for summer courses. Sister Adelaide Marie opened the note and read it aloud: "Sister Frederick Joseph should not take this course. It would take until Gabriel blows his horn for her to get a music degree." I was really embarrassed when everybody there laughed. Sister Adelaide Marie said, "Oh, don't worry about that. It does take a long time."[18]

Sister Hortensia Gaertner and Sister Henry Ehlen of the OLLU music department tried to persuade Sister Amabilis to change her mind, but she

---

[18] Sister Frederick Joseph, oral interview, 15 Feb. 2000, CDPA. Sister Frederick Joseph enjoyed using her musical talent throughout more than 50 years of classroom teaching. One of the private piano students she taught after school hours, Elmer Hoelscher, directed his own band for many years. Whenever she noticed how exigent music teachers have to be with pupils who don't practice, she was grateful that she was not a full-time music teacher (communication to the author, 8 Jan. 2004).

was adamant, most likely because she wanted only music majors to do music teaching. Sister Adelaide Marie advised Sister Frederick Joseph to start studying for her MEd degree.

The Mistress of Studies was responsible for learning the latest developments in pedagogy and communicating them in meetings she held with different groups of teachers each summer. For example, in 1949 Mother Adelaide Marie Heyman was a "step ahead of the headlines" in preparing the Sisters for the Zaner Bloser handwriting texts.[19] That year she attended a three-day conference of principals and supervisors working on curriculum construction in the elementary schools of Texas. She also read a paper and led a discussion on "Characteristics of a Health Education Program in the Intermediate Grades."[20]

Sister Marietta Fischer kept a diary of her very frequent travels from 1955 to 1967 while she supervised first archdiocesan and then congregational schools. Its pages reveal a busy life that demanded wisdom, organizational skills, and a great deal of stamina. She was aware that school situations were not always ideal. Sisters in schools owned by the Congregation were expected to maintain high standards; but since they were also expected to contribute financially to the Congregation, they were sometimes short of school supplies. Although they had no pastor to obey, they had the responsibility of collecting tuition, raising funds, and sometimes doing janitorial work. Sister Leona Jupe recalled, "On those small missions we had as many as three grades in a room. We had to do our own cooking, washing, and ironing; and we were only three Sisters. The two Sisters with me were always older, so they couldn't do all the chores any more. I think God worked miracles with us."[21]

Besides supervising the Sisters' studies, the Mistress of Studies regularly visited all the schools and spent time in the classrooms. The *Constitutions* (#277) prescribed that the supervisor "should be up to date in the art of teaching, and well acquainted with the latest improvements in school appliances, as well as the new books published." She was also to "take care, nevertheless, that excessive ardor for study does not prejudice the piety of the Sisters."[22] The supervisor stressed the teaching of writing and required the teachers to see that each student wrote one composition a week. The teacher, and then the student, corrected the compositions and collected them in a folder. The supervisor inspected each folder when she came for the annual visitation. After her visits she communicated her recommendations to the principal (usually also the local superior) who was to see that they were put into practice.

---

[19] FC, Dec., 1949: 46, CDPA.

[20] FC, April, 1949: 144, CDPA.

[21] Sister Leona Jupe, oral interview, 14 Apr. 2000, CDPA.

[22] Constitutions, # 266.

Each convent was also a kind of "mini-normal school" in that the Sisters constantly asked for and received advice from one another. True, living with the same Sisters with whom one worked had the danger of limiting everyone's interests to that particular school or hospital, but it also served as a conduit for passing on knowledge that could never be learned in books and courses. Celebrating feasts of the Church year—Advent, Christmas, Lent, Easter—promoted cooperative learning and called forth creativity. Every large celebration in a school or church also challenged the Sisters' imaginations, logistics skills, and ability to create much with few resources.

They also learned much from their pupils. For example, Sister Jane Patricia Coyne, a city girl less than five feet tall, after teaching lower grades in San Antonio for 16 years became directress and eighth grade teacher in a small rural school in Pilot Point, Texas, in 1956. This called for many adjustments. "My students told me about how they planted and introduced me to many farming terms. My pupils' size, their vocabulary, and their ability as farmers indeed made me wonder if the tables were not reversed. I was the learner; they were the teachers."[23]

Feedback from parents was another potential source for improvement. Parent-Teacher Associations, which were a novelty early in the century, became common, especially after the Bicultural Education Act of 1978 required parents to be on advisory councils. These were supplemented by parent-teacher conferences. Parent-teacher relationships were also enhanced by the fact that some mothers volunteered as aides in the classroom. Sister Eugenia Ann Stell noted that in the 1950s, the Sisters interacted mainly with the mothers of the children.

> We never knew their first names, and they didn't know our last names; but whatever we asked them to do, they would do. Twenty years later, there was much more involvement of the dads. People were asked to participate in the planning and to learn what was going on in the school. We asked them for more input, and they were very willing to give it. Also, I involved the parents in decisions being made about their child and the ways of teaching that would work best with them.[24]

Sister Rose Corrine Medica, who taught in southern Louisiana in the 1950s and returned 10 years later, also noted: "We were able to visit families in the

---

[23] Sister Jane Patricia Coyne, oral interview, 7 Oct. 2000, CDPA. Sister went on to say. "Teaching math was my biggest problem, but Sister Basilia Droll was in my community, and she was a wizard at math. She relieved my anxiety by working every problem in the eighth grade math book for me. The whole book!"

[24] Sister Eugenia Ann Stell, oral interview, 29 Aug. 2002, CDPA.

homes, which we did not do before. I noticed the men of the family were more interested and ready to talk about their children."[25]

The Superiors appreciated exposure to diversity that widened horizons and encouraged the Sisters to learn not merely from books but from trips and visits to historical places. Sister Jule Adele Espey remembered that when she was sent to study at Columbia University, Mother Angelique (who had studied there herself) told her, "Get your education from the streets as well as from books." With Sister Jane Marie Barbour as a guide, Sister Jule Adele became very familiar with educational and cultural opportunities in New York City.[26]

The supervisor always encouraged the Sisters to take advantage of workshops and lectures as well as trips that could be educational. Interviewed by a college student when she was in her 80s, Sister Josepha Regan recounted some of her trips.

> While in California she traveled to see Mr. Wrigley's home on Catalina Island. She also traveled to Mt. Wilson and saw all the snow that covered the mountain, leaving no food for the deer and rabbits. "The poor animals were so hungry they would eat bread out of our hands," Sister Josepha told me. Of course she can't forget the passion play against the mountainside or the Boysenberry Farm Restaurant over the inactive volcano. The Boysenberry Farm Restaurant had the best buffalo steak, and they didn't forget the boysenberry dessert. The Sisters also went to San Juan Capistrano. But the best thing in California was watching the sneak previews of the new Walt Disney shows before they were released to the public.[27]

In 1979 Sister Virginia Clare Duncan began an "extra-curricular project" organizing tours in the U.S. and Europe so that Sisters could see and experience the places about which they taught. She found her 16 years of tour organizing very "valuable, inspiring, energizing, and wonderful"[28]; and her tourists agreed.

Sister Julian Honza traced the Congregation's history of placement.

> At first we were just told where to go based on our education, if we could take the climate in that area and if we were compatible with the Sisters who were already there. Later on, I think there was a greater

---

[25] Oral interview, 16 June 2000, CDPA.

[26] Sister Jule Adele Espey, oral interview, 4 Nov. 2003, CDPA.

[27] Mary Rodulfo, "Ladies of the Lake," pp. 11-12, OLLUA.

[28] Oral interview, 8 Feb. 2000, CDPA.

emphasis on our specialty that we were teaching and what the needs were; and we were allowed to ask if we could do this.[29]

Sometimes the needs of the school took precedence over the needs of the Sister. Sister Marietta Fischer remembered that in the 1960's Mother Amata

> agonized over this way of placing the Sisters. Their personal wellbeing was very important to her. As much as possible she would talk with the Sister before placing her. As far as I know this was the first time attempts were made to discuss with a Sister how she felt about being sent to a certain place. This was different from, "Here is the need, and you have the qualifications."[30]

Superiors who followed Mother Amata discussed possibilities with each Sister throughout the year and reached mutual agreement on where her talents would be best employed. By the end of the century, docile acceptance of changes initiated exclusively by superiors was replaced by continuous dialogue and consultation between the Sisters and their leaders. The whole process of assignments became less dominating (or even traumatic), more respectful of mature adults, and more collaborative.

Negotiating with Clerics

The annual appointing or assigning, later called "missioning," was a gigantic, complicated task that resembled deploying troops to battles in a war. By 1962, for example, the Congregation staffed 105 elementary schools in the archdiocese of San Antonio alone.[31] The needs of one school had to be balanced with the needs in others. Pastors had to be chided or mollified.

Mother Angelique's correspondence with three clerics, which started just two months after her election, shows the skillful diplomacy required to keep relations smooth between rectory, school, and convent. She wrote to Bishop Joseph P. Lynch of Dallas: "For several years we have had two Sisters teaching in

---

[29] Oral interview, 28 Feb. 2000, CDPA.

[30] *CDP Times*, 16, 6 (Feb. 1996): 12, CDPA. Sister Madonna Sangalli experienced Mother Amata as "a person who was not afraid to talk to you and to hear from you even if she was going to be the one telling you what the decision was. Both she and the General Councilors began to be more accessible" (oral interview, 31 Mar. 2000, CDPA). It is to be noted that the Superior General annually assigned MCDPs as well as CDPs until 1968.

[31] Sister Marietta Fischer, group interview of CDPs who taught in Catholic grade schools, 17 June 2001. By 2002, the total number of Catholic schools in the entire archdiocese was only 47.

Pilot Point, Texas. The work is entirely too heavy for only two, and circumstances there and here make it impossible for us to send more Sisters. I am, therefore, asking your Excellency's advice in this matter."[32] The bishop replied immediately, referring to the Gospel passage where Jesus sent word to John the Baptist and said his mission was that "the poor have the Gospel preached to them."

> The people of Pilot Point are poor. They are rustics. They need to be told the simple truths of religion in a primary school conducted by the wise virgins of Christ.
>
> Please continue to give them the cooperation of your venerable and beloved organization. I have written to Father Charcut to take this matter up with you, and to arrange to relieve the Sisters of a part of their task.[33]

Poor and rustic, the people were nevertheless generous. From their pantry shower, the Sisters had surplus to share with orphans in Dallas.[34]

A few days later, Mother Angelique wrote to the pastor in High Hill, Texas, with concerns about the spiritual life of the Sisters at the school at Middle Creek, a mission of High Hill. She learned "that the people of Middle Creek cannot assure the Sisters of the opportunity of hearing Mass daily on account of present transportation difficulties. Under such circumstances we cannot ask the Sisters to return to the school. We shall await word from you in regard to this matter."[35] Transportation was arranged.

After visiting this school as part of her duties of office, the Superior General had reasons to make more demands the following year:

> The dwelling at Middle Creek has none of the conveniences that are ordinarily found in meagerly furnished houses,—no bath room and toilet facilities for the Sisters, no refrigeration for the storage of food, and a miserably cold house with very poor heating and cooking facilities.[36] Having the Sisters go through heat and cold to High Hill for Holy Mass and return for a cold breakfast at nine o'clock with a rushing to school immediately after has impaired the health of

---

[32] Mother Angelique to Bishop Lynch, 2 Aug. 1943, CDPA.

[33] Bishop Lynch to Mother Angelique, 3 Aug. 1943, CDPA.

[34] FC, April 1946: 142, CDPA.

[35] Mother Angelique to Rt. Rev. Msgr. H. Gerlach, 5 Aug. 1943, CDPA.

[36] In Westphalia, Texas, the Sisters also had no indoor plumbing. There was an outhouse and a cistern to catch rainwater. The Sisters took turns bathing in a galvanized tub in the kitchen, where they would heat bath water on the stove. Gas stoves replaced coal stoves in the classrooms, music room, and elementary central library only in 1949 (FC, Nov. 1949:14, CDPA).

both Sisters. I do not feel justified in sending the Sisters back to such privations. If the people of Middle Creek can do something to improve this situation we shall be ready to send back the two Sisters.[37]

The people responded, and in 1949 the two Sisters reported that they had four grades in each room and made a trip of eight minutes every morning for Mass, except Wednesdays "when we have Holy Mass here."[38]

The yearly correspondence between Rev. Michael S. Becker of Cloutierville, Louisiana, and Mother Angelique is also instructive. On 10 August 1943 Father Becker wrote that one of the Sister-teachers "incited some of the boys in her class to set fire to one of the outhouses, and they did so three or four times." Two years later, he still had not responded to the basic need highlighted by the fires. On 17 July 1945, Mother Angelique wrote to him that the Sisters would not return "unless the school was renovated and painted and proper desks were put in for the children and sanitary toilets built." The following year the pastor complained about another problem. He "was sorely disappointed" because one of the Sister-teachers "tried to belittle me. She had the children in her classroom compute a problem to show them how much money I threw away by smoking and attending movies."[39] If Mother Angelique re-assigned the offending Sister, she did not satisfy the pastor, because less than a year later, there was another exchange of correspondence. Mother Angelique was "very sorry to hear" that a certain Sister-teacher's imprudence had "gone so far as to be a nuisance. My writing her, I am afraid, would not make matters any better. If you think it is too great a disadvantage to have her there, please tell Sister Consortia [Klein] and let Sister Consortia bring her home. I will have no one to give in her place this year."[40]

More than three years later on 2 July 1951, Mother Angelique again threatened the pastor that "the Sisters will not return to Cloutierville until you have made provisions for a sufficient water supply to furnish them with not only kitchen and laundry facilities but bathroom use as well." Father Becker fired back: "Some of the complaint in this regard is due to the fact that Sister Consortia locked the bathrooms, from the outside, with a pad lock. I myself saw this when I went to give the good Sisters Holy Communion and to say Mass

---

[37] Mother Angelique to Rt. Rev. Msgr. H. Gerlach, 14 July 1944, CDPA. The situation in nearby Chapell Hill was similar. Sister Alice (Theresa Henry) Spies recalled sitting around a pot-bellied wood-burning stove on cold days with her fifth and sixth graders (oral interview, 13 June 2000, CDPA).

[38] FC, Nov., 1949:14, CDPA.

[39] Rev. Michael S. Becker to Mother Angelique, 26 June 1946, CDPA.

[40] Mother Angelique to Rev. Michael S. Becker, 10 March 1947, CDPA.

on Saturday morning."[41] Differences were somehow resolved, and the Sisters staffed the school until it was closed in 1967.

These examples from small schools give some idea of the challenges of making suitable assignments. Not only the educational credentials but also the health, age, personality, and ability of the Sisters to get along with each other, the pastor, and the people had to be taken into account. In larger communities, a "household Sister" did the cooking and community laundry, but the teachers did all the other housework and often were in charge of the sacristy of the parish church. In communities of four or fewer, the Sister-teachers usually took turns cooking in addition to their household tasks. This was typical of women religious. Until the late 1950s Sisters performed 95% of the teaching and administrative work in U.S. Catholic schools, yet their students from widely differing economic backgrounds performed better, as a group, than pupils in public schools.[42]

Trends in Elementary School Education

Elementary schools—parochial, private, or public—in which the Sisters taught outnumbered secondary schools, and the majority of them were owned by parishes. Often the boundary between grade school and high school was blurred due to considerable sharing of space, personnel, and other resources. For example, when Sister Marcia Havlak was teaching the primary grades in Ennis, Texas, Sister Sylvia Egan, who taught high school Latin, became ill and returned to the Motherhouse. Sister Marcia took over her Latin students, but not her space. "It was a small class. They came to my first grade room, and I taught Latin while my little ones did their work." For the next 12 years, Sister taught English, Latin, and "whatever else they didn't have a teacher for."[43]

Sister Catherine Fuhrmann analyzed some reasons why this situation did not last.

> Years ago I had over 50 children in the classroom, and I could count on the fact that when I would give them a little task, they would do it. They were not going to disturb their neighbor, so you could go ahead and teach a reading group while they were working. Today that is not the case. Children seem to be much more insecure. They

---

[41] Rev. Michael S. Becker to Mother Angelique, 16 July 1951, CDPA.

[42] James S. Coleman monograph, University of Chicago, 1982.

[43] *CDP Times*, 15, 4 (Dec., 1994):10. Sister Ferdinand Jenschke taught both first grade and high school home economics in El Reno in the 1960s (Sister Ferdinand, oral interview, 23 Nov.1999, CDPA).

cannot focus, don't like the desk and chair, and are often on Ritalin because of their hyperactivity.[44]

Rapid social changes in the last half of the twentieth century, especially population growth, had repercussions on all levels of education. The 1949 Gilmer-Aiken law reorganized Texas school administration, consolidating 4,500 school districts into "2,900 more efficient administrative units." "State funding became dependent on attendance, thus providing an incentive to increase attendance."[45] More than 1,000 schools were eliminated as small school districts were consolidated. In the tiny community of High Hill, Texas, for example, the high school consolidated with the Schulenburg public school in 1948; but elementary school pupils from other districts that were annexed were brought to High Hill Elementary School.

The Sisters who remained on the faculties of consolidated schools found ways to continue to teach religion even though the 1948 McCollum v. Board of Education decision forbade religious instruction in public schools because allegedly students were forced to participate in religious instruction or risk being ostracized by teachers and peers. In High Hill the Sisters taught catechism in the morning before school.[46] In the Olfen Elementary School in Runnels County in central Texas the Sisters could no longer catechize on "released time." Accordingly,

> each class goes to the north sacristy of the parish church for catechism. The County Superintendent advised this to avoid being charged with contempt of the Supreme Court.
>
> All the students are Catholic, so there is prayer in school as well as all the spiritual activities of parochial schools. The pupils ransom pagan babies and the children's choir sings High Mass on the third Sunday of the month as well as all Requiem High Masses.[47]

In Ennis, Texas, when the public school superintendent said the Catholic school children could no longer ride the public school buses, the pastor purchased three buses and enrollment increased. The children prayed the Rosary daily on the buses.[48]

---

[44] Oral interview, 14 June 2000, CDPA.

[45] "The Handbook of Texas on Line," *http://www.tsha.utexas.edu/handbook/online/articles/view/GG/mlg1.html*. The law also required rural public schools to increase enrollment or close their doors (FC, Dec. 1949: 43, CDPA).

[46] FC, Jan. 1947:104, CDPA.

[47] FC, Dec. 1948: 69, CDPA.

[48] FC, April 1950: 148-149, CDPA.

Most classrooms throughout the nation became even more crowded with pupils later called Baby Boomers. St. Augustine School in Laredo, Texas, had more than 600 pupils in 1946-47.[49] Three years later the State Department of Education warned that the number of students in each room could not exceed 35 if the school wished to maintain its affiliation, so lay teachers were hired for the overflow of the sixth and seventh grades.[50] St. Anthony's Elementary School in Harlingen was expanding because as many as three families were moving into the parish every week.[51] By 1960 Texas ranked third in national student enrollment.

The situation was similar in other states. St. James Grade and High School for Blacks in Alexandria, Louisiana, had 55 or more students in each classroom and a similar shortage of teachers, which forced the principal to hire two inexperienced lay teachers for the third and fourth grades.[52] By 1949 the school had 644 pupils with three grades enrolling 100 pupils; two Sisters held their classes in a rented store building nearby. The school auditorium accommodated 160 pupils and three teachers who suffered in the heat of early fall since only four windows near the ceiling could be opened.[53] In 1951 the school had 656 students, the largest enrollment to date; 205 were in high school. St. Ferdinand School in San Fernando, California, had 65 to 75 pupils in each grade in 1948, the sesquicentennial year of this historic mission. Plans were in place to add two or three new classrooms.[54] The following year the school had to turn away 174 Catholic children.[55] By 1951 the parochial grade school had 512 students and the Mission High School had 211. "The population growth out here," reported a Sister-correspondent, "is simply out of bounds."[56]

Crowded as they were and forced to interact in the classroom with neighbors who were very near, teachers and students did not forget children far away whose living conditions were deplorable. In 1945 and 1946 they collected clothes and canned goods for European sufferers. In 1947 the Curé of Cutting, France, birthplace of Jean-Martin Moye, founder of the Congregation, returned to the village from which he had been expelled five years before to find it devastated. In response to his appeal, parcels were sent from the Convent, the College, and Moye Military School in Castroville.[57] In Olfen, Texas, the pastor responded

---

[49] FC, Mar. 1947: 176, CDPA.

[50] FC, Nov. 1950: 37, CDPA.

[51] FC, Dec. 1951: 57, CDPA.

[52] FC, Jan. 1946: 70, CDPA.

[53] FC, March 1950: 107, CDPA.

[54] FC, April 1948: 17, CDPA.

[55] FC, Nov. 1948: 40, CDPA.

[56] FC, March 1951: 120, CDPA

[57] FC, Feb. 1947: 116, CDPA.

to an appeal from the pastor in Olfen, Germany, and held a collection of new and used clothing. The children from the Olfen, Texas, school also sent 20 pounds of candy to a "chaplain in the army of occupation for a Christmas party for German children in Bamberg, Germany. Some of these children had never before seen any candy."[58]

Because their founder had been a missionary to China and manifested great zeal in baptizing babies, the Sisters had a special reason to encourage their pupils to support missionaries in foreign lands. Students sold Holy Childhood Christmas seals and cards or filled mite boxes with pennies. These projects encouraged pupils to adopt a more international or global outlook and enhanced geography lessons. A popular project of Catholic elementary schools was "ransoming pagan babies." The children contributed a certain amount of money, which enabled a missionary overseas to feed, clothe, and educate a child for several years. In Ponca City, Oklahoma, Sister Mary Martin Haidusek's first and second graders ransomed six pagan babies.[59] St. Joseph Grade School in San Antonio ransomed "many" and got to select their names.[60] At San Fernando School in California, over 700 pagan babies were ransomed at five dollars apiece.[61] The students at Prompt Succor Elementary School in Alexandria, Louisiana, "sponsored the baptisms of 66 children in foreign lands through the Holy Childhood Association" in 1961.[62]

Methods of teaching are always changing, but during this half-century often they had to change because the students and their families changed. Christian Family Living was the basis of the curriculum in the Congregation's schools in the 1950s. The 1960s brought new challenges and concern about "values" on all levels of education. No longer were most of the pupils from families who lived in the same neighborhood and shared religious values. The Sisters could not take it for granted that parents shared their strong desire for the children to acquire good habits as well as to succeed in academics. Sister Josepha Regan noticed "in earlier years it seemed the parents worked wholeheartedly with the teachers, and in later years it seemed that the children were taking over because there was less training in many of the homes."[63] Sister Rosa Ruiz observed that parents "are more lenient with their children. They let their children tell them what to do."[64]

---

[58] FC, March 1947: 158, CDPA.

[59] FC, March 1946: 121, CDPA. Sister Alexia Vinklarek was director of the Holy Childhood Missions Office in the San Antonio archdiocese for four years.

[60] FC, Feb. 1947: 133, CDPA.

[61] FC, Nov. 1951: 23, CDPA.

[62] "News Flashes," First Edition, 1961: 3, CDPA.

[63] Oral interview, 21 Jan. 2000, CDPA.

[64] Oral interview, 24 Oct. 2000, CDPA.

Sister Virginia Huser observed that it was becoming more difficult "for parents really to know who their children are." She experienced parents who were "quick to criticize and blame the teacher and the school. They feel that their children really don't do anything wrong. It's hard for them to believe teachers or administrators when they say certain things have happened."[65]

As the parents at St. Anne's School in Houston, Texas, became more involved with their children's education in 1968, they demanded teachers with "more discipline" and better education. Specifically, they discovered that no Catholic school in the city had a qualified science teacher. Sister Margaret Clare Mathews, the principal, responded immediately by sending Sister Barbara (Ruth Marie) Fry, who was in her first year of teaching, to take a geology class at St. Thomas University and become qualified. Six years later, however, some vocal parents regarded the Sisters as being too cloistered and not involved enough in the parish.[66]

After the second Vatican Council, theology emphasized involvement in rather than withdrawal from the world. Welcomed by some who wanted private and parochial schools to be less insular, this accentuation led others to challenge the very reason for the existence of a separate Catholic school system. Would it not be better, they reasoned, to send all the children of the parish to public schools but provide excellent religious instruction for them at the parish facilities?[67] At the same time, some parents wanted their children's education to be permeated with values that could not be made explicit in public school classrooms. Did the parents espousing such different positions have the same definition of "values" and "religion"?

Lay teachers became the majority on faculties in the 1970s, and some of them had limited experience. The teachers had a common framework and imparted basic skills; but the pupils and their situations changed, making constant adjustments necessary. Computers speeded up delivery of information but did not secure more time for teachers because extra-curricular activities multiplied.

Children were presenting more psychological problems because of single-parent families, "latchkey" children, and lack of supervision at home when both parents were employed outside the home. All of these conditions impacted students' classroom performance, usually in a negative way. A first

---

[65] Oral interview, 2 Sept. 2000, CDPA.

[66] GC minutes, 17 April 1974, CDPA.

[67] Even before Vatican Council II, Archbishop Lucey had suggested that catechetical centers "may be a symbol of things to come when in a few years we have to discontinue elementary schools and turn them into catechetical centers." Memo of Archbishop Lucey to Rev. Virgil Elizondo, 9 Dec. 1960, quoted in Stephen A. Privett, SJ, *The Pastoral Vision of Archbishop Robert E. Lucey*, Trinity University monograph series in religion, no. 9 (San Antonio, Texas: Trinity University Press, 1988) 140.

grade teacher, Sister Ferdinand Jenschke, thought "the children were more lively because they had kindergarten now. To get them settled down was quite a job. They were so free in kindergarten, and they thought they still could be that way in the first grade."[68] Sister Esther (George Annette) Habermann, on the other hand, noted at the beginning of the twenty-first century that her pupils came to the first grade more ready to settle down and work because most of them had attended kindergarten where they received character training and experience in team work.[69]

Almost every teacher—especially in the higher grades—increasingly had to deal with problems like drugs, gangs, weapons, teen-age pregnancy, and alcohol abuse. Sister Reparata Glenn noticed a change in the students in Tulsa, Oklahoma, where she taught in the 1940s, when she returned 10 years later.

> I was still teaching some of the younger members of the same families I taught before, but those younger kids were not like their older siblings. Perhaps it was due to conditions in society in general—more radio, movies, and television. Or perhaps their parents were better educated. World War II was a big factor in the changes. The students did not seem to be as well disciplined as they had been before.[70]

Other experienced teachers made similar observations. Sister Madeleine Zimmerer noted that "as TV became more prominent, I could tell that it was harder to teach the children because I was competing with the TV screen. Videotapes were getting more popular in the classroom because we were competing with TV."[71]

The teaching of religion changed greatly. After the Second Vatican Council theology was less dogmatic and more incarnational. Love and free choice were emphasized as central to Christian living. Religion textbooks stressed Church as community and insisted less on rule-keeping and hierarchies. Discussions and multi-media presentations usually replaced the *Jesus and I* catechism with

---

[68] Oral interview, 23 Nov. 1999, CDPA.

Sister Alice Spies said "students are a lot more lively, a lot more talkative, and it takes a little more patience these days, especially when you have one that throws temper-tantrums, something you didn't have in the early days" (oral interview, 13 June 2000, CDPA).

[69] Oral interview, 28 Nov. 2003, CDPA.

[70] Oral interview, 14 Feb. 2000. Sister Martha Kuban, who taught music for over 60 years, noticed that students became "more aggressive, more assertive, more difficult to motivate. They saw too much permissiveness on television, and they tried to imitate it. It was such a delight to teach in the older days because when you said something, they did it right away" (oral interview, 20 Feb. 2000, CDPA).

[71] Oral interview, 10 Aug. 2000, CDPA.

its question and answer format.[72] Instruction focused more on inserting oneself to bring about good in this world and less on amassing merits for a future state of bliss. Catholic schools began to describe themselves as "faith communities." Their aim was to offer their pupils not only a good education but appreciation of their faith and skills to make them active members of the parish and other communities. Social justice was introduced on the grade school level.

The decline in the number of schools staffed by the Congregation was dramatic in the last decades of the twentieth century despite the excellent instruction by CDP teachers. One recognition of their competence was the "Sister Clare Maher" award given by Incarnate Word College for excellence in teaching. Sister Jane Patricia Coyne received it in 1992[73] and Sister Adrienne Marie Schmidtzinsky in 1994.[74] In 1995 Sister Adrienne Marie also received the "Secondary Teacher of the Year" award in District XX of the Texas Business Education Association.[75] When Sister Marietta Fischer was principal of St. Pius Elementary School in Tulsa in 1986, she was named as one of the top ten Catholic elementary school principals in the U.S.[76] The Constance Allen Guild for Lifetime Learning, an educational foundation of the Business and Professional Women's Club of San Antonio, annually bestows the "Yellow Rose of Texas Education Award" on outstanding contributors to education. Ten CDPs received the award between 1994 and 2002: Sisters Elizabeth Anne Sueltenfuss, Marilyn (Mary of the Assumption) Molloy, Janet (M. Gabriel) Griffin, Elaine Gentemann, Ann (Paulann) Petrus, Ramona Bezner, Margit Nagy, Adrienne Marie Schmidtzinsky, Frances Lorene Lange, and Jane Ann Slater.

The supervisory expertise of the Sisters in education was also recognized outside as well as inside the Congregation. Sister Marietta Fischer and Sister Frances Theresa Phillippus, CCVI, were the first Supervisors of Instruction in Catholic Schools of the Archdiocese of San Antonio, 1955-1961. They were succeeded by CDP Sisters Elizabeth McCullough, 1961-1964,[77] Theonilla Vrba, 1964-1970, and Eugenia Ann Stell, 1970-1971. Through them for over 15 years the Congregation provided educational leadership for hundreds of schools. Sister Eugenia Ann was Curriculum Coordinator of the diocesan office in Oklahoma City from 1966 to 1970. Sister Michael Rose Stanzel was Associate Superintendent

---

[72] The publication of *The Catechism of the Catholic Church*, however, greatly impacted religious instruction after 1994.

[73] *CDP Times*, 15, 9 (May 1995): 16, CDPA.

[74] *CDP Times*. 16, 8 (April 1996): 10, CDPA.

[75] *CDP Times*, 16, 8 (April 1996): 10, CDPA.

[76] *CDP Times*, 16, 6 (Feb. 1996): 11, CDPA

[77] Sister Elizabeth found this a difficult position because "you saw all kinds of abuses in visiting the schools, but you didn't have any authority to change things. We could only report the abuses to the superintendent. Also, we were not welcomed in some places and could not even eat with the community Sisters" (oral interview, 17 Apr. 2000, CDPA).

of Catholic Schools in the San Antonio archdiocese from 1985 to 1991. Sister Bernard Marie Horrigan served as the Alexandria, Louisiana, diocesan supervisor of schools from 1966 to 1973. She and the superintendent, Monsignor John Wakeman, were instrumental in passing House Bill No. 16 which provided aid for the 143,000 elementary and high school students attending Louisiana public schools.[78] Sister Rose Frances Rodgers founded the San Angelo Diocesan Board of Education in 1969 and served as its president.[79]

CDPs were not sheltered from the impact of world events such as World War II, the Korean War, and the Vietnam War as well as smaller conflicts like the Bay of Pigs Invasion, the Iran-Contra Affair, and Operation Desert Storm. These conflicts took human lives and caused physical and psychological damage; yet each also launched new technologies, especially in the area of communications, and exposed people to cultures they may never have explored without stimulus. Travel—actual by jet or virtual by computer—became more accessible, and economies became more globalized. Every classroom acquired a computer. Communication became increasingly instantaneous. Words like systems analysis, e-mail, microchips, genetic modification, cloning, and website entered the vocabulary.

What enabled the Sisters to adjust constantly to these changes yet maintain their dedication to those they served? Besides trust in Divine Providence, another of the "fundamental virtues" promoted by their founder was simplicity, a habit of going straight to God, "having no other aim than to please Him." They were to "act and speak with their neighbor in a direct manner, without deceit or malice."[80] To be "wise as serpents and simple as doves," the founder urged them to "simplify themselves," that is, "to get rid of all that is neither necessary nor useful."[81] The Sisters interpreted that injunction to mean they should adjust to trends and fluctuations as well as find ways to remove obstacles to good works.

Relinquishing Schools

A sampling of the history of a few schools can give some idea of the sacrifices as well as the satisfaction involved in providing good education for younger children during the rapid changes of the last half of the twentieth century. The demand for resiliency was often daunting, and the Sisters did not foresee how often they would not be able to complete a work that began well.

---

[78] "News Bulletin" sponsored by the Eastern Region, May 1969: 5. Sister Bernard Marie, "the little Sister with the big voice" was the able coordinator of the Congregation's centennial celebrations in 1966.

[79] Communication to the author, 3 Mar. 2003.

[80] *Directory* 90.

[81] *Directory* 285.

St. Rose Elementary School in Schulenburg, Texas, was the only school started by the Congregation in the nineteenth century that still had a Sister on the staff in the year 2000. It saw many changes in those 110 years and can serve as an example of ongoing adaptation while supporting cherished values.[82] Rev. John Kirch, the first pastor of St. Rose parish in Schulenburg in 1889 paid from his personal funds for the construction of a school, known at first as Santa Rosa School, which the Congregation purchased for $1,000. The Congregation prepared to withdraw from Schulenburg in 1947, but Archbishop Lucey would not approve this move.[83] In 1953 a large enrollment in the elementary school, which rose to over 275 by 1966, necessitated the employment of lay teachers for the first time. But by May 2002, the Congregation was no longer able to supply any Sisters for the school.

While St. Rose typified a school serving Anglo immigrants in a rural area, Our Lady of Guadalupe (OLG) School in Houston, Texas, was an example of an inner city school started in 1912 for Hispanic children. At first the Sisters taught gratis, and by 1929 there were eight Sisters and over 400 pupils. A new school was built in 1948, and tuition was charged for the first time. In 1950 the Scanlan Foundation began to help pay for the teachers' salaries. By 1966, 24 women from the parish had become Sisters of Divine Providence or Missionary Catechists of Divine Providence. In the 1970s the school enrolled Central American and Vietnamese refugees who made their homes in the parish.

Every avenue to obtain funds and bring education and other services to the impoverished children and parishioners was explored. The Equal Opportunity Act, Title 2, made funding for Head Start programs available in 1964. Guadalupe initiated a Head Start program in the summer of 1965. The following year Sister Madeleine Zimmerer began to teach remedial reading, funded by Title 1.[84] In 1970-71, the first year for Title VII bilingual programs, Our Lady of Guadalupe was the only Catholic school in Houston participating as a pilot group with a small class of first graders. This was also the first year it offered a Model Cities Free Kindergarten for 40 children aged 4 and 5.[85] At the same time Sister Katherine Ann Hays and Sister Emily (Maxentia) Bolcerek lived in the Guadalupe convent while working in Model Cities, which had 59 projects in the area. They were involved in Title I projects. In 1972 Sister Elizabeth McCullough wrote to Sister Colleen Hennessey, SSND, Superintendent of Catholic Schools of the Galveston-Houston diocese, that she did not "pick up from the pastor at Our Lady of Guadalupe a determined

---

[82] See *Memoirs*, II, 336-353, CDPA.

[83] GC minutes, 29 June 1946, CDPA.

[84] "CDP Newsletter," March 1970: 4, CDPA.

[85] *Nunspeak*, June 1971: 7, CDPA.

desire to keep the school open."[86] Alumni and benefactors, however, did succeed in maintaining the school.

Sister Florencia López, born in Our Lady of Guadalupe parish, taught in the school for a total of 24 years. Her devotion and initiative are typical and were appreciated, as indicated by Margarita Lemus, a sixth grader. "Sister Florencia is a great teacher. I remember one time I was in first grade, and she spent a whole hour showing me how to add."[87] Dominican Sisters began to administer the school in 1975 and Religious of the Sacred Heart of Jesus in 1983. By 1988 Sister Florencia was the only CDP of eight Sister-teachers. That year the editor of the school yearbook stated: "Sister Florencia wonders how much her first students could have learned since she was new at teaching. Well, we all know that they learned love, respect, confidence, and self-worth."[88] Even when she was no longer in the classroom, Sister Florencia supervised the "Cocinita," a small kitchen that sold food on Sundays between Masses. She was pleased that in the 1995-96 school year the Cocinita raised $10,000 while the Parent-Teacher Organization raised $7,000 for the school.[89] Sister Florencia was the last CDP to leave OLG, the oldest Catholic elementary school in the diocese, in 2000.

A small town in Louisiana benefited from the CDP services and contributed to furthering its spirit and works. St. Joseph School in Plaucheville, Louisiana, started as a Congregational elementary boarding school in 1899. At least seven families in this little community with a population of little more than 600 sent daughters to San Antonio to become Sisters of Divine Providence. In 1920 a junior high school was added, and in 1927 it became a state accredited high school.[90] In 1945 when the elementary grades moved to a new brick building constructed by the parish, the enrollment was 230. One of the priest-teachers, Rev. Joseph Lesage Tisch, paid tribute to the Sisters in a homily in 1966.

> We welcomed the Sisters of Divine Providence at the turn of the century, when they came to take over the small school that had been founded by a group of our own lay people. During these years, we know how the Sisters have been interested not merely in teaching the child seven hours five days a week, but interested in the total development of each child—mental, physical, and spiritual. When there was no other education available here, the Sisters were teaching your great-grandparents' children. During these years they have been

---

[86] Sister Elizabeth McCullough to Rev. Bernard Wagner, OMI, 8 Nov. 1972, CDPA.

[87] "Our Lady of Guadalupe School, 1988-1989," p. 2, CDPA.

[88] "Our Lady of Guadalupe School, 1988-1989," p. 2, CDPA.

[89] Communication to the author, 15 Oct. 1999.

[90] *Memoirs*, II, 254-271, CDPA.

consoling the sorrowful, rejoicing with our people in their moments of joy, and counseling both children and adults in time of doubt and crisis.[91]

When the Sisters withdrew in 1985, the parish, which had always paid the Sisters' salaries, bought the high school building from the Congregation.[92]

In Castroville in 1939, when the Congregation re-purchased the original motherhouse, the decision was made to convert it into a rather unusual school, a military school for boys, grades one to eight. Only one boy enrolled at Moye Military Academy the first semester, but by 1947 there were 107 cadets from 11 U.S. states and Mexico. Forty acres on the Medina River were purchased and became Camp Cayoca (Catholic Youth Camp), which boasted a large swimming pool, a rustic cabin, and stables with horses for the pupils to ride.[93] The Sisters taught all classes and supervised the dormitories from taps to reveille as well as took care of meals and laundry. "A commandant was in charge of the military training, and a chaplain took care of religious training."[94] The school was flourishing when it was closed in 1959 to make room for the aspirants, girls of high school age pursuing a religious vocation, who no longer fit into the overcrowded motherhouse in San Antonio. The stables were put to other uses, but the aspirants and Sisters enjoyed the camp until it was sold in 1998.[95]

Erected in 1955 to provide elementary education for fast-growing suburbs, St. Pius X Elementary School in El Paso, Texas, serves as an example of a school that always had more lay teachers than Sisters. Three Sisters and seven lay teachers instructed 410 pupils the year it opened, and the number of students had grown to 567 by 1966. Proof of its academic excellence was that 15 scholarships had been awarded by that year to students who scored highest on entrance tests

Behind the scenes, however, the demands, especially on the principal, were daunting. The experiences of Sister Mildred (Leone Therese) Leonards instantiate typical headaches of these days. Sister recalls that in 1963 she was

---

[91] *Memoirs* I, 270, CDPA.

[92] Sister Agnes Leonard Thevis, oral interview, 19 June 2000, CDPA.

[93] FC, Jan., 1947: 109, CDPA. As in many boarding schools, not all the boarders were happy to be there. Sister María Cristina Ruelas recalled that two boys left the campus and got as far as Hondo, about 20 miles west of Castroville. "It was winter, and they made the mistake of taking a blanket that said 'Moye Military,' so they were reported right away" (oral interview, 27 Mar. 2000, CDPA). Sister also recalled having to shampoo 21 heads on Saturdays when the little boys came back from Camp Cayoca with their hair full of sand.

[94] *Memoirs*, I, 52, CDPA. Sister Martha Vrba, who taught in this school for 19 years, "cherished every moment of it. The boys from Mexico didn't get to go home very often, and we got along very well since I speak a little Spanish. They have been very faithful to me all these years" (oral interview, 13 May 2000, CDPA).

[95] GC minutes, 20-21 May 1998, CDPA.

changed from a small school in Schulenburg to being principal-directress at St. Pius. In early August, she arrived in El Paso to discover she needed six more lay teachers. Only Sister Angelene (Archangela) Holzer had been at St. Pius the year before. Sisters Annalee (M. Clement) Prather and former Sister Sherry Romine were as new as herself; and a different culture, climate, and pastor who was ill also challenged them. The Sisters were excellent teachers, but many of the lay teachers were not. One of them wrote in big letters on the blackboard of her classroom, WELCOME TO THE FORTH GRADE. Since the cafeteria space was being used for other purposes, the children ate their lunches at their desks. At Christmastime, Sister Angelene, because she had experience with boarders, was moved to Palestine. The Sister who replaced her injured her back after a few weeks and had to return to San Antonio, so Sister Mildred was forced to rearrange her principal's schedule in order to teach in her place. She later asked for and received a change to Shreveport, Louisiana, the following year. A few hours after arriving she discovered she may have gone from a frying pan into a fire. She was to be "totally responsible for hiring teachers and managing the budget of the parochial school." The pastor, however, wanted no parish funds to be used; and he did not even attend monthly school board meetings.[96]

The needs of Native Americans attracted Sisters Bernadette Bezner, Anita Brenek, Regina Decker, Jane Marie (M. Alexandra) Gleitz, Cathy Parent, and former Sister Wanda Holt to teach Navajo children in Tuba City, Arizona, in the 1970s and 1980s. Sister Bernadette Bezner, besides teaching fifth and later third grade, helped Franciscan Brother Fabian Gardner teach religion to the youth on Wednesday nights and Sundays and conduct Search retreats in Gallup, a six-hour drive away. In spite of having to travel long distances and smell mutton stewing in the still air outside the hogans during Mass, she loved the sturdy people, their rich culture, and their connection with nature. It was thrilling to visit the Grand Canyon, Coal Mine Canyon, Castle Rock, and Canyon DeChelly. Sister Jane Marie found her Native American students to be

> alive, alert, interested . . . aware of the world beyond their reservation. . . . I live among an ancient people who walk the ways of their heritage, people hoping to blend the old and the new, and to fit into today's world yet hold strong to all that has been significant in their identity as Native Americans. . . . I feel very much a part of who they are, yet step back in awe and wonderment at their unique way of reaching the Divine.[97]

---

[96] Sister Mildred Leonards, oral interview, 1 Sept. 2000, CDPA.

[97] *Movements*, 3, 1 (Fall/Winter, 1999): 9, CDPA. One of the Sisters' students, Lori Ann Piestewa, 22, a Hopi convert and single mother of two, joined the military and was killed in Iraq in April, 2003.

Because the Congregation owned (or sponsored) a college and insisted on continual updating, the Sisters on whatever level they taught built on a common foundation and presented a unified approach to education stemming from a liberal arts tradition. Sister Lora Ann Quiñonez, college teacher and tenth Superior General, summarized:

> The essence of a liberal education is to free one, permit one to develop the concepts, skills, and imagination to understand life, interpret experience, and think about the meaning of things. It helps one be able to find one's way in a totally new situation because one has certain conceptual skills and capacities. Part of having a liberal education is having a framework of meaning that is philosophical and religious but also sociological and scientific. It makes one able to take real life and make sense of it.[98]

But finding meaning, she insisted, is not sufficient. A well-educated person also takes responsibility to shape meaning and influence events "according to values that are not purely private and esoteric but part of a shared sense of meaning, part of an orientation to life that takes account of the common good."

The Sisters' own faith and formation certainly influenced their teaching, whatever the subject matter; but they were not prone to pious moralizing or proselytizing; and this helps to account for why they were sometimes seen to be more human or even more "worldly" than other women religious. Part of the reason is that their formation in a Congregation rooted in Alsace-Lorraine eschewed expressions of personal emotion. A more important reason is their acceptance of the presence of a Provident God everywhere and at all times, so the secular and sacred are not completely separate. Sister Lora Ann expressed this belief clearly.

> I am reluctant to use the word "secular" as inimical to faith or religion. Some of the values of so-called secular societies are wonderful. For example, in the U.S. culture there is a tendency to think that one ought to help people when disaster strikes them. When we find people wiped out, we are rather quick to respond. I think that is a cultural value.

To avoid unthinking routine and encourage integration, Sister did not open her classes with a "Hail Mary" or an "Our Father" but with a little reflection which was sometimes connected to events of the day. "The purpose of prayer, after all, is to reflect, to become attentive and reflective in one's life."

---

[98] This quotation and the ones in the next two paragraphs are from a videotaped interview of Sister Lora Ann Quiñonez, CDPA.

Sister Lora Ann's concern was to integrate education with real life, and that requires discovering and applying values instead of merely admiring them or carrying them separately from life, like coins in a purse. In her field of English, for example, "We were always careful not to put into a literary work something the author didn't put into it to make it fit some kind of religious party line." But whatever the subject, she thought "we teachers always need to figure out better how to put into relationship with each other the content of a discipline with meanings and value. Often we either paste one on top of the other or use one to get at the other."

Following the example of its founders, Father Moye in France and Mother St. Andrew in Texas, the Congregation has looked for God's plan in the "signs of the times"—the needy calling for help, the Church pointing out new directions, or the talents and inspirations of individual women who vowed to spend their lives in this group. Some have reproached the Sisters, saying that it was a mistake to be so tuned in to the times, for they have become worldly and so God has not blessed them with new members. Would it not have been better to continue the pattern of religious life in force for several centuries, i.e.: wear an identifiable habit, lead a quasi-military lifestyle, live in large groups in semi-cloistered convents, and limit ministry to parochial and private Catholic education? Has this Congregation been deceived? The reply has to be in the negative. To have "stayed the same" would have indicated a belief that God is static and is to be found only in certain familiar people and places. This has never been the Sisters' belief. A Provident God invites rather than rejects creativity and risk-taking.

The Sisters believe in and witness to a God who is present in the great and small, in joys and sorrows, in triumphs and failures, in the settled and in the fermenting. Sister Joanne (Scholastica) Eustice, for example, went from 23 years of teaching music at St. Pius X Church in Tulsa to retirement at the motherhouse. She admitted it was hard to leave her hometown and relatives as well as her pupils, especially since no Sister would replace her. Yet she felt "God will raise up whatever He needs to take care of us and to take care of the Church."[99] For Sister Joanne and the rest of her Sisters, the measure of success was not popularity or even measurable accomplishment but unswerving fidelity to the God of surprises and constant discerning of God's next invitation to love and service. This readiness has demanded constant adjustments and trust in divine aid. In the upheavals and dramatic changes of the past 60 years, the Sisters have been committed to excellence in ministry as a grateful witness to God, who always provides what they need. The foregoing presentation of educating, together with thumbnail sketches of a few schools, illustrates this characteristic of faithful readiness, which—along with risk-taking—characterizes the Sisters of Divine Providence.

---

[99] For her part, she was ready to "relax, pray, and prepare to die"(*Eastern Oklahoma Catholic*, 22 June 2003: 19, CDPA).

CHAPTER 4

GROWING INTO A UNIVERSITY

Sisters of Divine Providence who taught between 1943 and 2000 influenced thousands of lives. Their students interviewed for this history testify to receiving a good values-based education due in large part to the Sisters' professional competence and personal interest in their students. Much credit for successful teaching belongs to the college owned and operated until 1957 by the Sisters, Our Lady of the Lake College (later Our Lady of the Lake University). At the beginning of this period it was an established small liberal arts college. A half century later it had grown in size and offerings, was separately incorporated although still sponsored by the Congregation, and had changed its character. This chapter is not a history of the college but rather a documentary of the major contribution the Sisters through the college made to the success of their graduates, particularly graduates who were members of the Congregation. Our Lady of the Lake University is an example of adaptation to changing circumstances in order to continue to attain the goal of meeting needs for quality education. It gives outstanding witness to a CDP characteristic: constant adaptation to insure excellent service, especially of the underserved.

In the 1940s OLL was a small women's college noted for its strong undergraduate liberal arts offerings, especially in music. Its home economics department was robust, and its Worden School of Social Service, the seventh Catholic graduate school of social work to be established in the U.S., was expanding. All the courses required for teacher and librarian certification were also available. The majority of the faculty consisted of CDPs, and students were typically young middle class Anglo women from San Antonio as well as from many neighboring towns and a few other states. Daughters of upper class families from Latin America were a small but steady component.

Sister Jane Coles recalled

In the seventies, our student body changed, and I think for the better. We opened our admissions more broadly and were on the leading edge of what was called an inner-city school. We began to make a direct effort to incorporate Hispanic students and to help train them to go teach their own. I believe we were doing more clearly the mission of the Sisters of Divine Providence as Father Moye would have us do. Not that our previous work was bad or wrong, but I think we were more alert to what our mission was.[1]

Thus by the turn of the century Our Lady of the Lake College had metamorphosed into co-educational, separately incorporated Our Lady of the Lake University[2] with several graduate programs and a student body comprised predominantly of middle and lower class Hispanics. In March 2001 *Hispanic Magazine* listed OLLU among the top 20 colleges and universities for Hispanics. Criteria for inclusion were "Hispanic enrollment, retention, and graduation; academic excellence; number of Hispanic student organizations and support programs; and number of Hispanic faculty."

During these fifty years, state colleges, always better endowed and offering lower tuition, had burgeoned while numerous small private colleges had failed. Why was OLL not one of their number? What caused it to become so different in such a relatively short time?

Risk Taking at OLLC, which became OLLU

To survive and thrive in a competitive and occasionally even hostile environment demanded foresight, hard work, and certainly venturesomeness. Not all the factors contributing to the development of OLL will be treated here. Emphasis will be given to projects to which the CDPs contributed significantly as administrators, teachers, and staff. Sisters who took daring steps, especially in the 1970s when they were the majority of the personnel at the college, could not have done so without backing from the Congregation's superiors and their Sister-companions.

Social work, the first graduate program at the college, and education, the second graduate program, were soon followed by a graduate program in speech and hearing begun in 1955 by the former Sister Mary Arthur (Elizabeth) Carrow

---

[1] Oral interview, 17 Jan. 2000, CDPA.

[2] Although OLLC's third President, Gerald Burns, briefly considered re-naming the college Providence University of San Antonio, the name was changed to Our Lady of the Lake University of San Antonio (GC minutes, 14 Oct. 1975, CDPA). This name reflected the fact that enrollment had grown and several graduate degrees were being offered.

in the basement of Providence Hall. This program moved to its own building, named after benefactor Harry Jersig, in 1959 and was accredited in 1969. Sister Lourdes Leal was appointed director of the Harry Jersig Speech and Hearing Center in 1970.

An MA in English was introduced in 1965, and the departments of business and psychology began to offer graduate degrees in the 1980s. The business department started as a certification program under the leadership of Sister Bernadette Marie Gremillion and Sister Rose Annelle McClung. In 1982 it added the degree of Master of Business Administration in Management. By 1996 it had 493 undergraduate business majors; 608 students were enrolled in the MBA program in 1999. In the 1980s OLL began to offer an MA in psychology, and in 1990 it initiated the first doctoral degree, a doctorate in psychology, PsyD. The honor of establishing the first doctoral program in counseling psychology to be accredited by the American Psychological Association at a "non-research I university" came to OLLU in 1995. In 2000 the majority of OLL undergraduates majored in psychology.

The program in English as a Foreign Language, started by Sister Clara Kliesen in 1966, brought international students from Africa, Asia, the Middle East, Mexico, Europe, and Latin America to OLLU every semester.[3] It evolved into the campus International Center, which initiated the Kumamoto Student Exchange program in 1990. This program enabled an OLLU student to spend an academic year in Japan.

The college strongly supported a federation of three local Catholic colleges and Oblate School of Theology in the late 1960s. It also joined the United Colleges of San Antonio (UCSA), an attempt at closer cooperation between St. Mary's University, Incarnate Word College, and Our Lady of the Lake College led by Rev. Wm. G. Kelley, SJ, a specialist in inter-institutional cooperation, from 1971 to 1974.[4] A committee chaired by former Sister Mary Arthur Carrow drew up the original proposal for UCSA.[5] OLLU officials suggested a number of possibilities for cooperation between the education departments of the three institutions, but they were not deemed acceptable; the consortium began to disintegrate when St. Mary's University withdrew after the fall semester of 1972.[6] Although UCSA was successful in the development program for fund raising and tried to initiate ethnic studies programs, it achieved little in other areas and was abandoned after five years.

---

[3] Sister Clara herself spent a semester in Japan, and Sister Margit Maria Nagy spent longer periods there while working on her doctoral dissertation.

[4] "OLL Happenings," 26 April-2 May 1970, and 15 July-27 Aug. 1971, OLLUA.

[5] Sister Mary Clare Metz, cassette tape of remembrances, ca. 1977. Hereafter, Metz oral interview, 1977, OLLUA.

[6] Metz oral interview, 1977, OLLUA.

When Sister Mary Clare Metz replaced Mother Angelique as academic dean in 1961, the availability of financial aid brought to the campus large numbers of first-generation Hispanic students. Many had not taken college-preparatory courses in high school. Sister Elizabeth Anne Sueltenfuss recalled:

> I saw a distinct difference between the students in the early 70s and those in the 50s and early 60s. Academically in terms of performance, the caliber of the students began to deteriorate. In the biology department we tried not to water down the courses, but we had to adapt in terms of preparation and motivation of the students.[7]

Sister Mary Clare, a professor of biology for many years, recognized that the increasing diverse clientele demanded different ways of teaching as well as new means of evaluating success. More students sought a college education as a means to economic advancement. "It became increasingly important" to relate universal knowledge to practice "and thereby provide the student with a profession so that he [sic] may be a productive citizen and may lead a normally comfortable life."[8]

Sister Mary Clare scheduled two important faculty conferences to stimulate thinking and surface new alternatives. The first leadership conference was held 24-25 September 1971 at Methodist Camp Flaming Arrow near Kerrville, Texas. Although limited to 55 people, the conference was open to all students, faculty, and administrators.[9] She was also idealistic, and this fueled her confidence that the motivation and dedication exhibited amply by the Sisters was attainable by everyone at the institution. In 1966-1967, the Sisters comprised 70% of the total faculty. Of the 91 Sisters assigned to various positions at the University in 1971, ten were administrators and 34 full-time teachers. But Sister Mary Clare foresaw that the mission of the college could remain even though her lay colleagues were bound to increase in number and the student body was bound to increase in diversity. "The college or university, however, that recognizes within the student a being called to share in the redemptive mission of Christ will attempt also to educate him [sic] to carry out this ultimate task of his [sic] life. This added dimension then becomes for the institution a true ministry."[10]

A second conference held in Castroville, Texas, in spring, 1972 elicited much grassroots enthusiasm and support that eventually resulted in the adoption of a competency based education program. In this "totally new venture," there

---

[7] Oral interview, 20 Oct. 2000, CDPA.

[8] *Nunspeak*, June 1971:13, CDPA.

[9] "OLL Happenings," 19-25 Sept.1971, OLLUA.

[10] *Nunspeak*, June 1971: 13, CDPA.

were no basic required courses in the general education program. Instead, each student had to furnish proof of having acquired certain basic competencies.[11] The college already accepted transfer courses from education programs at military bases. Now it started to evaluate portfolios assembled by older students to obtain credit for life-work experience. It also adopted a score slightly below the national scaled score mean as a basis for awarding credit through College Level Evaluation Programs (CLEP) examinations.

Inspired by Philip Phenix's *Realms of Meaning*, the competency based program measured students' progress not by their presence in classrooms for a certain amount of time or by their acquisition of semester hours in given subjects (although both of these continued to be required) but rather by their demonstration of skills and competencies in six areas: (1) communication (2) human and physical environment and the scientific method (3) personal and social growth and interpersonal relationships (4) religious and ethical dimensions (5) interrelations of art, aesthetic theory, culture, and creativity (6) integration and synthesis of one's own ideas with the ideas, values, and experiences of others.[12] After recording its first budget deficit of $75,000 in 1974-75, the college secured a Fund for the Improvement of Post Secondary Education (FIPSE) grant that enabled it to become among the first in the U.S. to re-organize the curriculum around the competency concept. Other colleges that adopted competency-based curricula included Alverno College in Wisconsin, Mars Hill College in North Carolina, and Evergreen State College in Washington.

The early 1970s also saw a plethora of new ventures aimed at Hispanics.[13] In the fall of 1972, 60% of OLLU students were Mexican American and 80% were dependent on financial aid.[14] With the help of federal grants, "Project Puerta Abierta" searched the region for talented prospective Mexican American students. These gifted students from low income families were then offered scholarships. OLLU cooperated with St. Mary's University in Project Unico even though the "basic philosophy of the two institutions regarding how the program was to be conducted differed considerably."[15] This project provided special counseling, tutoring, developmental courses, and other services for 125 needy minority students on each campus who had inadequate academic background for college success. At least 50% of the students were from Model

---

[11] Metz oral interview, 1977, OLLUA.

[12] "General Education Manual," 1978-1979, OLLUA.

[13] During the Christmas holidays of 1967, OLL hosted 53 Peace Corps trainees from campuses across the U.S. who came to observe local community development programs and test their dexterity in the Spanish language. "OLL Quarterly," 1, 2 (Winter 1967), OLLUA.

[14] "Title VI proposal," 1972, OLLUA.

[15] Metz, oral interview, 1977, OLLUA.

Cities neighborhoods, and OLL was recognized as a pioneer in developmental programs in Texas.

Perhaps the adaptability and creativity displayed in faculty ventures were one of the sources, or at least models, for student initiatives. The nationwide Vietnam Moratorium Day, 22 October 1969, was observed at OLL under the sponsorship of the Young Democrats Club, the Committee for the Vietnam Moratorium, and Concerned Students and Faculty after the Student Council could not muster enough support to sponsor the observance.[16] Student-sponsored Earth Day on 22 April 1970 featured lectures, panels, and participation in "the world's average lunch" in addition to a panel discussion and film symposium. César Chavez, leader of farm workers, held a press conference on campus; and his supporters staged a rally at the Worden School.[17] Amnesty International held its first regional meeting on campus in the 1980s, featuring Rose Styron, former United Nations Commissioner for Refugees. Julia Powell, an instructor in the ESL (English as a Second Language) program, was the Amnesty International adoption group leader. She attributed the high quality and success of the conference to the fact that the University encouraged leadership and gave all a chance to use their talents.[18]

On 15 June 1970, a public forum on "La Raza and the Violation of Civil Rights in Texas" took place on the OLL campus. Senator Joe Bernal and Mario Compeán, regional coordinator of the Mexican American Youth Organization (MAYO), were among the participants. On 30 March 1971, Secretary of Health, Education, and Welfare (HEW) Elliot Richardson addressed a La Raza conference held at OLLC as part of a two-day conference sponsored by the student council. Replying to a question, the secretary admitted that HEW had been focusing more attention on the Black minority. "It is only in recent months that the Chicano voice has been heard. . . . HEW will seek to identify needs and to tailor programs for the Chicano."[19]

A few months later a student-organized seminar on "the Chicano" was held during the first summer session. During the second summer session, the "Concerned Students of OLL" presented to the college administration a position paper demanding the immediate institution of a Chicano studies program. On 10 August 1971, the group staged a class boycott and rally to support their requests. Sister Mary Clare Metz remembered a demonstration staged by off-campus people and one OLL teacher who "believed they had to make OLL become a Chicano college." The group

---

[16] "OLL Happenings," 19-25 Oct. 1969, OLLUA.

[17] Position paper on ethnic studies at OLLC, 24 Aug. 1971, OLLUA.

[18] Julia Powell, oral interview, 23 Nov. 2001, CDPA.

[19] "Highlights," Office of Youth and Student Affairs, U.S. Department of Health, Education and Welfare, 1, 4 (May 1971): 20, OLLUA.

pushed into the president's office. During the confrontation, a restaurant manager waved a $1,000 check in the president's face saying that the check was being given to the student association to sue OLL because of its violation of the Civil Rights Act. . . . The college president had no difficulty defending OLL against this accusation because a representative from the Washington Civil Rights Office had very recently made his official visit to the campus before renewing five-year approval for compliance with the Civil Rights Act.[20]

Former Sister Mary Arthur Carrow recalled that as the first vice-president of OLL, she was in charge (because Dr. McMahon was ill) when about 20 people demonstrated just outside the campus on 24th Street. They protested that the College was not doing enough for minorities, but she countered that it was doing all it could within channels available. The press exaggerated the number of people involved, she stated.[21] Sister Mary Clare recalled that "bad publicity by the news media" resulted in "the loss of friends and supporters, including a large number of alumni and even many of our own CDP Sisters who ceased encouraging their high school graduates to attend OLL."[22]

Within two weeks of the demonstrations, President McMahon announced that the administration would present a position paper detailing "the commitment of the College to the best interests of the Mexican-American and other minority groups" and "concrete plans for further implementing this curriculum both in the fall Semester and in the long-range future."[23] The search committee for a Mexican-American faculty member at a budgeted salary would include student representatives.[24] A few weeks later, all incoming freshmen were bussed to the convention center downtown for a Cultural Awareness Institute sponsored by TEDTAC (Texas Educational Desegregation Technical Assistance Center) on 10 September 1971,[25] and a "Concerned Students of

---

[20] Metz oral interview, 1977, OLLUA. President McMahon was aware of campus unrest that was developing even as the University focused more attention on minorities. On 7 March 1969, he had sent a memo to Sister Mary Clare, Academic Dean, saying "I would strongly recommend that the social sciences departments in particular indicate the ways in which the Mexican contribution to our national life is being treated. . . . If there were documentation of the things that we do, we could avert possible criticism" (OLLUA).

[21] Elizabeth Carrow Woolfolk, oral interview, 17 Feb. 2003, CDPA.

[22] Metz oral interview, 1977, OLLUA. Dr. Albert Griffith also recalled the alienation of some alumni (oral interview, 3 Sept. 2002, CDPA).

[23] "OLL Happenings," Aug. 20-27, 197, OLLUA.

[24] Memo to Faculty from Sister Mary Clare Metz, Academic Dean, 16 Aug. 1971, OLLUA.

[25] Memo to Faculty from Sister Mary Clare Metz, Academic Dean, 8 Sept. 1971, OLLUA.

OLLC" group was organized the same month.[26] The following semester on 1 May 1972, four Raza Unida Party candidates spoke in Providence West Social Room on campus: Ramsey Muñíz, Alma Canales, Fred Garza, and Flores Amaya.[27] An ethnic studies program under the direction of OLL instructor Richard Santos was inaugurated in 1972.

As the students accepted and took pride in their Chicano identity, they also became aware of different means to make their desires and grievances known. They circulated a list of faculty whom they considered discriminatory and submitted their complaints to the U.S. Department of Health, Education and Welfare Office for Civil Rights, Region 5, in Dallas, Texas. They alleged disparate treatment, claiming that some faculty treated non-Hispanics more favorably. The office sent Civil Rights Investigator Aurora Rodriguez-Curry to interview students who had complained and to obtain sworn affidavits. Ms. Rodriguez-Curry, an OLL alumna, took it as a great compliment that the office valued her "objectivity and competence in collecting and safeguarding evidence." After her investigation, the office received a protest from OLL because she had been selected. An HEW official replied "that OLL should be proud that one of its own who was considered to be an excellent investigator had been sent."[28] No charges were filed. In a caucus held for the entire college community in December 1973, the item to which most time was devoted was an explanation of an affirmative action program.[29]

Monsignor Balthasar Janacek, a priest of the archdiocese of San Antonio, was the campus chaplain during this period. He maintained that a strong contribution the Congregation made to the Church and to society was

> establishing in the middle of the barrio a university which became a member of the barrio. It was established at the edge of the city, but the barrio grew up around it. Many modern institutions establish themselves in an area that is not yet developed, and they keep it from being developed except in their own way. The CDPs did not do that. They grew up with the neighborhood and served as a stepping-stone to a better life for a number of people of the area.[30]

---

[26] "OLL Happenings," 3-9 Oct. 1971, OLLUA.

[27] "OLL Happenings," "Events for 21-29 April 1972." OLLUA.

[28] Aurora Rodriguez-Curry, e-mail to the author, 7 Jan. 2003, CDPA.

[29] Twenty years later Ms. Rodriguez-Curry no longer worked for HEW, but she still tried to help people "to value their perspective and view other cultures as additional viewpoints, like different playgrounds to play in. Getting institutions to broaden their inclusion, to value differences in perspectives, cultures, lifestyles, etc. and to experience the new life this brings" was still one of her passions (e-mail to the author, 7 Jan. 2003, CDPA).

[30] Oral interview, 18 Sept. 2001, CDPA.

The cleric was also aware that it was not always easy for a predominantly Anglo Congregation to promote Hispanic culture. Some Sisters objected, for example, when he wanted to introduce hymns in Spanish at campus Masses. "The University kept trying to find ways to reach out to more students but had difficulty accepting and embracing the fact that it was becoming a Mexican-American university. It was hard to admit them and use this as a real asset."[31]

OLL belonged in the category HSI (Hispanic-serving institution), a federally recognized category of post-secondary institutions enrolling 25% or more Hispanic students, more than a decade before the category was invented in the 1980s. OLL professor Dr. Antonio Rigual was also instrumental in founding HACU (Hispanic American Colleges United) in 1986 to promote cooperation among HSI leaders. He attested that HACU "was born out of frustration institutions felt when dealing with those who controlled resources. Hispanics had no representatives in Washington and in corporations."[32] OLLU President Sister Elizabeth Anne Sueltenfuss provided released time for Dr. Rigual and space for the fledgling association from 1988 to 1991.

Meeting the needs of adult learners was another concern that received a creative response. The first Weekend College in South Texas for undergraduates was founded and directed by Dr. Antonio Rigual of the OLLU Spanish department. It began in 1978 as a new way to help adults who could not leave their full-time jobs to work for a degree. Sister Immaculate Gentemann, who was on the staff of Weekend College for its first 12 years, says she "admired the students who had the discipline to return to college and earn a degree while living the lives that they had already achieved. She was proud to be a part of this pioneering program because it helped the community."[33] Sister Immaculate was admired in turn by Dr. Rigual, who praised her love, commitment, and energy. "We worked together daily for hours. She couldn't let an opportunity to serve go by. She would even test the students over the Christmas holidays and call me at home to come advise them, saying, 'We must be there when they're ready.' There is no better person in this world than Sister Immaculate."[34] A branch of Weekend College was opened in Houston, Texas, in 1986; and by 1987 there were more than 700 adults in classes at the two locations. About 150 Weekend College students had already graduated. Another site was opened later in Dallas, Texas.

---

[31] Oral interview, 18 Sept. 2001, CDPA. "Father Balty" continued after five years as OLLU chaplain to work with the Sisters at Meadowood Acres and in the Old Spanish Missions Historical Research Library housed at OLL. He presided often at Congregational celebrations and offered the Sacraments for the retired Sisters.

[32] Dr. Antonio Rigual, oral interview, 11 Aug. 2003, CDPA.

[33] Ricardo Espinoza, "The Gift of Sister Immaculate Gentemann," in "Ladies of the Lake," Fall 1999, p. 9, OLLUA.

[34] Oral interview, 11 Aug. 2003, CDPA.

Not to detract from the originality of the Weekend College but to maintain a historical perspective, it is noteworthy that there were precedents for the flexibility and faculty mobility demanded to deliver education in this form. University faculty in the 1960s sometimes gave individual courses in off-campus locations, for example at Nazareth Convent in Victoria and Jefferson Avenue School in Seguin. In 1962 the college cooperated with Brother Fabius Dunn, CSC, of St. Edward's University in Austin to offer a joint yearlong English Language Program for Foreign students. Sister-faculty members were exchanged with the College of St. Teresa in Winona, Minnesota, and Seton Hill College in Greensburg, Pennsylvania, in the summers of 1969 and 1970.[35]

Weekend College also had a predecessor of sorts in Central America. Franciscan Sisters from the Panama Canal Zone regularly sent 20 of their members to OLLU for summer school starting in the 1950s. In order to facilitate their access to required courses as well as to save them money, the college agreed to send several Sisters to teach at Franciscan headquarters in Balboa, Panama. Sisters who taught in this extension school for the summers of 1955-1958 included: Sister Helen Mary Dolson (school music), Sister Clara Kliesen (English), Sister Reparata Glenn (chemistry), Sister St. Rita Clarkson (government and speech), Sister Angela Fitzmorris (history), and Sister Tharsilla Fuchs (school arts and art appreciation). The Sisters were able to traverse the Panama Canal on the Grace Line or United Fruit Line ships. Sister Tharsilla recalled working on an archeological site with archeologist Neville A. Hart and Alejandro Mendez, who was on the staff of a Panama art museum. She herself unearthed a baby's grave that contained a beautiful golden bell as well as a copal pellet. "I learned more than I taught down there," she insisted.[36]

The Center for Women in Church and Society was founded on the OLL campus to bridge a perceived separation between feminists and women of religion. Consonant with the Congregation's explicit goal of promoting the well being of women and girls,[37] the center was to reach beyond the campus and bring together a variety of people and disciplines. In 1977 the OLLU Planning Council approved the establishment of a center for women's studies, but attempts to include it in the Institute for Intercultural Studies and Research were not successful. In the spring semester of 1981 Sister Margit Maria Nagy and Sister María Carolina Flores developed a formal proposal which was supported by OLL President Sister Elizabeth Anne Sueltenfuss. The Center was imagined as a safe

---

[35] Sister Frances Jerome Woods taught at the Catholic University of America in Washington, D.C. in 1956 (GC minutes, 1 Dec. 1956, CDPA). Another example of flexibility was that in the summer of 1975 students enrolled at OLLU could receive credit for a class taught at the Mexican Cultural Institute in downtown San Antonio (OLLUA).

[36] Videotaped interview for the OLLU Center for Women in Church and Society. Hereafter Videotaped interview.

[37] This was always an implicit goal, but it was explicitly stated in Goal 5 of the General Chapter of 1973.

and neutral ground where current social and ecclesial problems affecting women could be discussed in an environment that would be supportive for visioning solutions and improvements.[38] On campus it served to meet student needs for building contacts, friendships and networks to further spiritual development and a sense of identity.[39] In 1987 the Congregation agreed to provide a director while the university provided a secretary, space, and operational expenses.[40] Former Sister Jane Shafer became the first director in fall, 1987 and was succeeded by Susan Klein in 1992.[41]

As the Center was forming, the General Council of the Congregation perceived a "serious morale problem" among the Sisters working at the university. The Council met with the University Sisters' Organization (USO) on 22 January 1982. Agenda items included campus housing and remuneration for the Sisters' services. Personnel from the USO met with the OLLU President's Council and indicated a desire to identify "creative ways" in which the Sisters' services would be "permeated with values that truly make a difference." That these values were not impacting older students was a concern, and they thought that the whole faculty needed to show more leadership in communicating values.[42]

Teacher Training

One factor that contributed greatly to the Sisters' reputation for excellence as educators was the fact that the Congregation staffed its own college, and its significance cannot be underestimated. In its whole history in Texas, fewer than a dozen Sisters came from families where the father was a physician, attorney, college professor, or owner of a large business. Most of the Sisters' fathers were farmers, merchants, or employees of small businesses. Members of the family who became CDPs were usually the first in their families to obtain a college degree. That 42 CDPs and one Missionary Catechist of Divine Providence (Sister Anita DeLuna) earned doctorates is a significant accomplishment.[43]

The first Sisters who came from France had normal-school training to be teachers; and from the first days in Texas the Superiors had provided this

---

[38] Dr. Albert Griffith, oral interview, 3 Sept. 2002, CDPA. See also Sister Margit Maria Nagy to Superior General, Sister Mary Margaret Hughes, 27 Dec. 1981, CDPA.

[39] Dr. Robert Gibbons, oral interview, 29 Jan. 2003, CDPA.

[40] GC minutes, 24 Mar. 1987, CDPA.

[41] GC minutes, 11, 13-15, 18-21 May 1992, CDPA.

[42] GC minutes, 4 Oct. 1983, CDPA.

[43] See Appendix IV for a list of Sisters with doctorates, all of whom taught at Our Lady of the Lake University. This list does not include a number of Sisters who had earned several Master's degrees.

training, at first by CDPs educated in France, then by faculty coming from the Catholic University of America in Washington, D.C. (CU). As state certification requirements became increasingly stringent and OLLU began to offer liberal arts courses and degrees, teachers with higher degrees were needed, so CDPs were sent to earn doctorates from various universities. These Sisters were role models of competent professionals for generations of students. Almost half of the Sisters elected to the Congregation's own general administration between 1943 and 2000 had been teachers and/or administrators at its college. Training teachers was training leaders and also, in many cases, future administrators of schools and other institutions.

When all the Sisters came to the motherhouse each summer for studies and spiritual exercises, they also listened to visiting lecturers and compared notes with each other on their pedagogical, and other, successes and failures of the past year. Each year the April issue of the "Family Circular" included the summer school schedule and listed the textbooks for each course. In 1948, for example, the Sisters knew before they left their missions that 66 courses were to be offered. Among them was English 203, the Novel, which was scheduled to meet all morning, offered six semester hours of credit, and required each student to read 22 novels.

Sisters stationed in San Antonio often took courses after school or on Saturdays at the college, in addition to their full teaching loads. In the 1959-60 school year, a creative arrangement enabled two annual professed Sisters to complete their degrees while each taught half-time at Providence High School in San Antonio. Sister Patrice Sullivan had a homeroom and three classes every morning while Sister Imelda (Mary Cyril) Maurer took courses at OLLU. In the afternoon Sister Patrice took college courses while Sister Imelda taught biology, Algebra II, and Chemistry at PHS. The arrangement involved coordinating with Peter Lagutchik, the convent chauffeur, and using the PHS station wagon since there was no direct bus line from the high school to the college.[44]

Mid-century was a time of ferment and change in Texas education. Teachers in the education department at OLL had been aware of the deadlock in the 50th Texas state legislature over the passage of a minimum-salary law for Texas public school teachers in 1947.[45] Soon an elected State Board of Education reorganized Texas schools and appointed the Commissioner of Education of the newly created Texas Education Agency. Among their mandates was a nine-month

---

[44] Sister Patrice Sullivan, oral interview, 27 June 2000, CDPA.

[45] The Gilmer-Aiken Committee formed as a result of this law proposed three bills in 1949, one controversial measure being the prohibition of the use of school buses by parochial schools (Handbook of Texas Online *http://www.tsha.utexas.edu/handbook/online/articles/view/GG/mlg1.html*).

school year.[46] Family economics, however, sometimes took precedence over laws and led to changes in school schedules. "The new law which forbids farmers to employ Mexican children under 16 years of age made it necessary for the children of each family to help pick the cotton" for one week beginning 9 October in Rowena, Texas.[47] The new law also set minimum standards for teacher training and teaching facilities.

The CDPs welcomed rather than resisted these changes. Increasing state regulation coincided with readiness at OLL to offer more graduate work. The chief source for graduate degrees for numerous CDPs as well as Sisters from other Congregations was the Catholic University of America in Washington, D.C. The Congregation even built a house of studies for such students near that campus in 1914. Twelve CDPs received doctorates, and a larger number received Master's degrees from this university between 1920 and 1949.[48] Then the Congregation was ready to decrease its dependence on CU by initiating the second graduate school at OLL. The OLL Graduate School of Education opened in the summer of 1950, the same year that TEA first recognized graduate professional degrees.

The MEd degree immediately attracted local educators with values similar to those of the Sisters. One of the first to enroll was African American Dolores Burton Linton (1910-1980) who at age 21 had opened a school for Black children of West San Antonio Heights in a former dance hall and taught all six grades using second-hand textbooks. She earned her master's degree from OLLC in 1952, the same year that, at her instigation, a modern four-classroom school replaced a one-room school that had no water, indoor plumbing, or electricity.[49]

In 1953, 62 CDPs received MEd degrees, a record number to that date. The following year the school received accreditation from the American Association of Colleges for Teacher Education (AACTE) and continued to receive it from

---

[46] Before this time, rural schools in cotton-raising districts often began classes in August and closed some weeks later so the children could help in the cotton harvest. See Rev. W. F. Bosen, Rowena, Texas, to Mother Angelique, 18 July 1944; and FC, Dec. 1947: 65, report from St. Peter's School, Lindsay, Texas, CDPA.

[47] FC, Nov. 1950: 16, CDPA. Sister Ann Theodore Wiesmann, who grew up in Muenster, Texas, remembered "Our farm required lots of work. Picking cotton and other fall harvesting kept us out of school until Christmas. By then my class was always a semester ahead of me, and my teachers told me they couldn't teach the first semester over. I had to do the best I could. I was accepted 'on trial' in the fifth, sixth, and seventh grades. I did not complete the eighth grade" (*Signs of Providence*, 2, 8 [December, 1998]: 8, CDPA).

[48] In 1956 the Congregation sold its house of studies to the Grey Nuns of the Sacred Heart of Philadelphia. By this time the Congregation was sending Sisters for graduate studies to a variety of universities. In 1956, for example, six Sisters received MA degrees from the University of Michigan, Peabody College in Nashville, Columbia University, and Texas Women's University in Denton while one obtained a doctorate from Yale University.

[49] *San Antonio Express-News*, 11 Oct. 1980; and *San Antonio Light*, 24 Aug. 1975 and 5 Oct. 1980.

its successor, the National Council for Accreditation of Teacher Education (NCATE). In 1955, the same year the Texas State Board of Education approved new standards for the evaluation of undergraduate and graduate programs of teacher education, it began to offer graduate certification programs in Supervision and Administration, Psychology and Guidance, and Curriculum and Instruction.

Although OLLC did not officially become co-educational until 1969, men were accepted in its graduate program in Social Work a year before the passage of the 1944 so-called GI Bill, the Servicemen's Readjustment Act. By 1947, 49% of college students in the U.S. were veterans, and the first male undergraduate to attend OLL was a veteran accepted into the bachelor of music program in 1949. In 1966, when there were 324 students in the Graduate School of Education, there were 30 men in the whole college.

During the first decades of the MEd program at OLL, most of the degree candidates were women religious. The majority of CDPs who entered the convent after 1950 earned bachelor's degrees in elementary education and then MEd degrees at OLL. The college gave tuition discounts to many Dominican, Mercy, Benedictine, and Marianite of the Holy Cross Sisters as well as Daughters of Charity, Canonesses of St. Augustine, and Sisters of the Holy Ghost and Mary Immaculate, who enrolled in large numbers. In the early 1960s, for example, members of more than 32 different religious congregations studied at OLL every summer. Between 1956 and 1966 the total number of religious enrolled at OLL more than doubled, but their proportion to the total enrollment decreased since more lay students entered into all of its programs.[50]

By 1955 there were two and a half million students in U.S. colleges, and by 1960 Texas ranked third in national student enrollment. The decade 1957-1967 saw renewed intellectual emphasis engendered by Sputnik, more demand for specialists because of advances in technology, and greater interest in minorities because of the U.S. Supreme Court ruling on desegregation in 1954, the Civil Rights Act in 1964, and President Lyndon Johnson's "War on Poverty" in 1965.[51] In spite of the fact that small schools were being eliminated and small school districts consolidated, the National Defense Education Act of 1958 followed by federal grants and student loans promoted college enrollment growth everywhere.

---

[50] Duncan, "An Analysis" 69. Although the Congregation did not have the custom of leaving a Sister in a position of authority for a lifetime, a number of Sisters were very successful principals of grade schools or high schools for 20 or more years in the last half of the twentieth century.

[51] Duncan, "An Analysis" 307. James Gaines, President of the San Antonio Chamber of Commerce, noted in 1964, "We are the third largest city in Texas, but our residents have the lowest per capita income of any major city in the U.S." *San Antonio Express-News*, 4 April 2003.

By 1972, 80% of the undergraduates at OLLU were receiving financial aid. Others were grateful for scholarships, as Jessica A. Morin explained in a note to the Congregation:

> I am the first child in my family to attend college. I am living proof that dreams can become a reality. I am very committed to community service, and I have wanted to attend OLL for as long as I can remember because the Education program is so well known in San Antonio. Thanks to the Congregation of Divine Providence, I am able to accomplish my life long goal of becoming a Special Education teacher.[52]

Close cooperation between the College and the Congregation to provide qualified teachers on all levels continued. Sister Adelaide Marie Heyman, mistress of studies of the Congregation, and Sister M. Lucina Schuler in 1953 developed with the cooperation of student teachers a detailed *Handbook for Student Teachers*. Dr. Harold Wren, head of the School of Education, reported in 1961 that although the college had been separately incorporated in 1957, it was still "a branch house and an educational unit of the Congregation of Sisters of Divine Providence" whose primary obligation to the Congregation was the education of its members.[53] In 1974 there were enough CDPs enrolled at OLL to warrant a separate summer school schedule for them.[54]

Although tuition in the OLL graduate school in 1964 was a low $25 per credit hour, the amount of money the Congregation saved by not having to pay tuition for Sisters enrolled in OLLC was substantial. Even though it was always possible that highly educated Sisters might decide to leave the Congregation, the Congregation never begrudged the money spent on educating its members. As Sister Madonna Sangalli, former General Treasurer of the Congregation, explained: "As women religious we began to understand that an investment in an individual is an investment. Whether we saw the return on that or not, we knew we had done a good thing to help a lot of people. Those Sisters in whom we invested by helping them get an education did use those talents within the Congregation, at least for a while."[55]

---

[52] Jessica A. Morin to Sister Antoinette Billeaud, 31 October 2001. Another recipient said her scholarship "certainly relieves some of the stress my family and I have had to deal with. I participate in many volunteer activities because I want to gain experience working with others, especially children, before I graduate to become an elementary teacher" (Yvette Salinas to Sister Antoinette Billeaud, 30 Oct. 2001).

[53] Education Department papers, OLLUA.

[54] But the courses scheduled were open to all students.

[55] Oral interview, 31 March 2000, CDPA.

To further the preparation of good teachers, the OLLC Education Department continued to initiate new degrees and programs as needs for counselors and early childhood educators became apparent; it also adapted to its clientele by beginning evening and weekend courses in 1961.

The most foresighted and innovative program was the 1965 Project Teacher Excellence (PTE). Dr. Harold Wren submitted a proposal to the federal government to subsidize the education of low income students so they might return to their own neighborhoods to teach. Newly-hired Dr. Guy Pryor was put in charge of PTE and began to identify Mexican American high school students on the west side of San Antonio whose values and determination, more than grade point average or scholastic achievement, indicated high potential. With much personal counseling and help in overcoming deficiencies, they became remarkably successful students. Almost all of these women and men not only graduated from college but went on to make outstanding contributions in different professions.[56] This program was expanded in 1972 into the Department of Bilingual/Bicultural Teacher Education. In 1974 the college was one of only four chosen to pilot a bi-lingual/bi-cultural child development associates training project.

OLL also cooperated with nearby Edgewood School District to help district teachers finish their degrees. By the end of the century it was the U.S. university with the highest percentage of undergraduate Hispanic women who completed doctoral programs.[57]

Besides preparing hosts of teachers for their profession, OLLC was also a training ground for many librarians. It was the first college in the area to offer library science courses in 1925 and soon inaugurated BA and later MA degrees in Library Science. This MA degree was dropped in 1955 but reinstated ten years later. In 1978 the library science department was incorporated into the school of education.

Attending OLL classes and reading books were the Sisters' chief means of learning since their lives were still somewhat cloistered.[58] In the 1960s and 1970s, however, many Sisters received National Science Foundation grants for post-graduate summer studies. Their horizons were widened as they took advantage of cultural as well as educational opportunities at colleges and universities in other areas of the country. In 1957, for example, 29 Sisters studied off-campus; and in 1966, 31 did so. Of the 20 Sisters doing post-graduate studies

---

[56] The great success of PTE contributed to OLLU's winning in 2000 a similar grant, PSE (Project Student Excellence) which was not limited to teacher-education students.

[57] "Moving Forward Together," Fall 2002: 28, OLLUA.

[58] As late as 1966, for example, Archbishop Lucey sent out letters concerning the attendance of the Sisters at night programs and night meetings (GC minutes, 8 Jan. 1966, CDPA).

off-campus in 1969, 14 had NSF grants. In 1971, nine of 31 had NSF grants. Sister María Guerra remembered

> I got three of these grants, so I took advantage of them. I studied at Portland University in Portland, Oregon, one summer how to integrate chemistry into physics. I studied radiation mycology and physics at the University of Wyoming in Laramie, Wyoming, the following summer. Then I studied biochemistry and new ways of teaching science at Ball State University at Muncie, Indiana. I loved those studies at each one of those places because it gave me a broader view of what I was doing so that I could apply it in my teaching of high school classes.[59]

In 1965 only three Sisters earned MEd Degrees from OLLC; but four earned MA degrees from Immaculate Heart College in Los Angeles, Catholic University of America in Washington, D.C., and the University of Texas in Austin; and one earned a PhD from St. Louis University. Thirty Sisters held PhDs in 1966. In 1971 when the Congregation numbered a few more than 600 Sisters, 25 (about 4%) held PhDs; 76 (about 14%) had MAs; and 21 (about 3.5%) had obtained master's degrees in Science, Music, Social Work, or Journalism. The largest number, 128 (about 21%), held MEd degrees. Almost all of the remaining Sisters, except for those involved in housekeeping, possessed BA or BS degrees.

Higher studies were becoming more individualized in the 1980s. Instead of being told by superiors that they would study in a certain field in order to serve on the college faculty, Sisters themselves were asking—and being asked. Sister Margit Maria Nagy, for example, "discovered Asia" and was told she could begin Asian studies if she obtained a grant. For two summers she studied intensive Japanese and then earned an MA in East Asian Studies. In 1973 she was given a choice of continuing her graduate studies or teaching, and she chose to go on for a PhD.[60]

The General Council developed guidelines that showed more cognizance of the Sisters' maturity as well as their talents. One of the Councilors was to meet with the Sister asking to study to (1) determine what and when she wanted to study, (2) discover the plan she had for ministry upon completion of her study,

---

[59] Oral interview, 3 June 2000, CDPA. The following year (1972) only 23 Sisters were studying off campus and not all were pursuing degrees. After that date the numbers continued to decline.

[60] Sister Margit Nagy, oral interview, 17 Nov. 2000, CDPA. In the spring of 1992 on a post-doctoral Fullbright grant she taught American civilization to Hungarian university students in Budapest. Although a number of CDPs were born in foreign countries, Sister Margit is the only refugee who became a member of the Congregation.

(3) examine how this plan related to the Congregation's goals and projections, (4) help the Sister complete the required request forms, and (5) urge the Sister to investigate the possibility of applying for a scholarship.[61] At the same time, the University instead of the Congregation began subsidizing the doctoral studies of Sisters studying in other universities who would be able to teach at OLLU. If they left the Congregation, they were to repay the loan to the university.[62]

Not all Sisters who acquired higher degrees spent the rest of their lives teaching at OLL. Some entered areas new to the Congregation. For example, Sister Patrice Sullivan became an attorney, and Sister Deborah Ann Fuchs became a midwife.[63] Some joined the faculties of other colleges. They included Sister Angelina Breaux at Gallaudet College for the Deaf, Washington, D.C.; Sister Suzanne Dancer at the University of Texas, Austin, Indiana University in Bloomington, and University of Wisconsin in Milwaukee; Sister Virginia Clare Duncan at the University of Texas, El Paso and Northwestern State University in Natchitoches, Louisiana; Sister Janet Griffin (M. Gabriel) at Tulsa Junior College; Sister Ann Petrus at Benedictine College, Atchison, Kansas; Sister Mary Christine Morkovsky at Sacred Heart School of Theology, Milwaukee, Wisconsin; and Sister Madlyn Pape at St. Philip's College, San Antonio. Sister Mary Christine and Sister Madlyn also taught at Wadhams Hall Seminary-College in Ogdensburg, New York.

The education department of OLLU kept its students abreast of trends that succeeded each other at this time—team teaching, modules, phonics, and multi-age classes.[64] In the 1970s individually guided education was emphasized as well as classes for the gifted. Testing for learning difficulties became imperative. Again the college was ready, for in 1969 it was the first college in Texas, and one of only 18 out of 190 in the U.S., to be certified by the American Speech and Hearing Association to award the MA degree in speech pathology. It was the second college in the south to have met the standards.[65] In 1971 the education department introduced two new certification programs in Language and/or Learning Disabilities and in Educational Diagnostics.

OLLU's graduate education department continually kept up with ever changing trends and developments as well as regulations regarding teacher certification. In the 1970s, for example, TEA made major changes, eliminating

---

[61] GC minutes, 17 Sept.1988, CDPA.

[62] In 1993 the Congregation forgave a $25,000 loan for one former Sister and paid $40,000 owed to the university by another (GC minutes, 12-15 Jan. 1993, CDPA).

[63] *CDP Times*, 1, 1 (Oct. 1980): 5, CDPA. Sister Patrice, who provided legal ministry to the poor in Catholic Charities of Fort Worth, Texas, earned her Doctor of Jurisprudence when she was 46 years old and practiced law for the next 17 years.

[64] Sister Eugenia Ann Stell, oral interview, 29 Aug. 2002, CDPA.

[65] "Happenings," 16-22 Nov. 1969, OLLUA.

bachelor's degrees in education and requiring that each teacher major in a content field in addition to taking education courses and fulfilling supervised practice teaching requirements. In 1976 OLL was the first university to establish a competency-based teacher education program. In the summer of 1992 the Texas Commission on Standards for the Teaching Profession asked for a new set of outcome-based standards for Texas' beginning teachers. Once again OLLU's Education Department implemented 14 outcomes defined through knowledge, disposition, and performance statements.

The Sister Faculty of OLL

OLLU was the center of the intellectual life of the Congregation until the 1980s because of a faculty (largely Sisters) both well prepared and easily available for consultation. The Sisters also profited from the strong Education Department as well as numerous lectures and workshops by contemporary experts in many fields which the college offered to all of its students. Ida O'Keeffe, sister of Georgia O'Keeffe, for example, was an instructor in painting in the OLL art department for one year.[66] Outstanding speakers included author John Howard Griffin (1965), ecumenist Gregory Baum (1969), theologian John L. McKenzie, author Joseph Heller (1970), psychologist Rollo May (1971), U.S. Secretary of the Treasury Romana Acosta Bañuelos (1972), newsman Daniel Schorr (1973), African American poet Nikki Giovanni (1976), and former Secretary of Defense Elliot L. Richardson (1978). Le Treteau de Paris performed plays in French regularly in the 1960s and 1970s.

To honor Dr. John McMahon on his 25th jubilee as president of OLLC, Sister James Aloysius Landry of the French department organized a lecture series on the thought of Teilhard de Chardin, paleontologist and spiritual writer. National figures in the fields of theology, biology, philosophy, and sociology illuminated the contributions of the controversial Jesuit. The series took place during the 1966-67 school year and culminated in a faculty-student forum and interdisciplinary student panel.

Through the initiative of former Sister Dorcas Mladenka, a Cinema Arts Program sponsored by OLL and St. Mary's University offered films from England, France, India, Spain, Germany, Japan, and Sweden. Thanks to a HUD grant obtained through the Model Cities Department of San Antonio, eight Creative Arts of San Antonio (CASA) programs were launched under the auspices of OLLU.[67] Sister Ethel Marie (Charles Marie) Corne, OLL art professor, actively

---

[66] Interview of Mother Angelique by Irma de B. Sompayrae, associate editor of *Art and Artists Today*, n.d., OLLUA.

[67] "OLL Happenings," 12-19 Dec. 1971, OLLUA.

participated in this program. The Audubon Society began showing Audubon Screen Tours on campus in 1955 and continued for several decades.

The college consistently promoted interest in many cultures. For the "Salute to Mexico Series" held during four consecutive spring semesters, 1968-1971, former Sister Mary Arthur Carrow was instrumental in bringing outstanding artists, musicians, dancers, and lecturers on various topics from Mexico and obtaining some financial support from San Antonio community groups. Another initiative stretched to Middle Eastern culture. Very Rev. Msgr. John Trad, a native of Lebanon and pastor of the local St. George Maronite Church, offered a course on campus in beginning Arabic in the spring and fall of 1966. A decade later the university opened its men's dormitory to Berlitz students from Iran and Saudi Arabia who needed to learn English for jobs, such as those for aircraft mechanics, in the technological sector. They were able to offer first-hand descriptions of their countries.

Keeping the college up to date required new faculty to replace retiring veterans. At the annual National Catholic Education Association (NCEA) meeting in Chicago in April 1960, a "Personnel Policy for Sister College Teachers" with nine points was proposed. OLLU responded with alacrity and a strategic plan. By 1961 it had listed all the Sisters teaching at the college, their expected date of retirement, and the names of young Sisters who showed promise for replacing them. In 1969 Sister Mary Clare Metz, academic dean of OLLU, wrote to Sister Elizabeth McCullough, the Superior General: "It appears imperative that a plan be made for the education of members of the Congregation who might fill some of the vacancies if the Congregation plans to retain the control of this institution." She attached a plan containing a list of the present staff nearing retirement, a departmental breakdown on the present faculty and a proposed plan to fill various needs as they arose.[68] Four Sisters were due to retire that year and about a dozen more within the next two to five years, and Sister Mary Clare named eight Sisters who could begin graduate studies between 1969 and 1972. All of them did so.

Sister Lora Ann Quiñonez remembered:

> The Sisters at the College took a personal interest in preparing their successors, so to speak. Sisters who were good at a particular subject, who showed real talent for that particular content, were often chosen and tutored by the Sisters at the College, who then began to advocate on their behalf to the religious superiors of the Congregation. Sisters Marilyn Molloy, Lourdes Leal, Mary Arthur Carrow, Kathryn [Mary Michael] Keefe, and I were identified early on as having real

---

[68] Sister Mary Care Metz to Sister Elizabeth McCullough, 3 Jan. 1969, OLLUA.

potential for college teaching. That was a very important grooming and mentoring effort by the Sisters in cooperation with the superiors of the Congregation.[69]

This practice also led to some disappointment for Sisters in the Congregation who were not "groomed" and concluded they were not considered college instructor caliber.[70] The practice of coaching successors waned as the proportion of Sisters on the college faculty diminished and some younger Sisters on the faculty who had been mentored left the Congregation. Sisters Charlotte Kitowski, Phyllis Ann (Marie Bernard) Bunnell, and Maria Carolina Flores earned doctorates after 1983 and taught full-time at the college even though they had not been "mentored" by Sisters who were college teachers.

The Superior General and Mistress of Studies were constantly looking for Sisters who showed promise of becoming college teachers. When Mother Angelique, dean of the college, and the Sister who served as the Congregation's Mistress of Studies both lived in the college community, a unanimous decision on who should undertake graduate studies was easy. During the time Sister Mary Clare Metz was the academic dean, 1960-1972, she did not live in the same community with the Mistress of Studies and had less direct access to the Superior General. Some Sisters turned to her rather than to the Congregation's director of studies to advance prospective candidates or nominate themselves for higher studies. In March, 1969, for example, former Sister Barbara Joan (Sidonia) LeBlanc asked to join the college faculty. Sister Mary Clare informed her that although she had ability, she did not have enough advanced courses. She was also reminded that the Superior General made the final decision in such matters.[71]

Sister Mary Clare was also open to suggestions from CDPs who were not on the college faculty. In April 1967 Sister Miriam Fidelis Mellein, who was stationed at St. Mary's High School in Lawton, Oklahoma, recommended Sister María de la Cruz Aymes, SH, author of the *On Our Way* series in religious instruction, for a summer weekend workshop. Sister Mary Clare checked with the Mistress of Studies and the Sister who taught theology at the college. She

---

[69] Videotaped interview, CDPA. Sisters Bernadette Marie Gremillion and Marion Walter Coyle recommended that Sister Madonna Sangalli major in business administration so she could succeed them (Sister Madonna Sangalli, oral interview, 31 Mar. 2000, CDPA). Sister Suzanne Dancer said, "The part of my education which I most enjoyed was pursuit of my graduate degrees. After seven years on the mission, I was permitted to pursue a PhD. Those teaching assignments were OK, but I knew I was just biding my time until I could go to graduate school. My real desire was to teach at the university level" (oral interview, 15 Nov. 2003, CDPA).

[70] Dr. Robert Gibbons, oral interview, 28 Jan. 2003, CDPA.

[71] Sister Mary Clare Metz file, OLLUA.

then wrote to Sister Miriam Fidelis that the way was cleared and asked her to carry on the negotiations and complete the arrangements with Sister María de la Cruz.[72]

Former Sister Regina (Eutropia) Richter, who was teaching biology at Bishop Kelley High School in Tulsa, Oklahoma, informed Sister Mary Clare.

> I have been watching the growth of this new [biology] curriculum for a full two years now; and, believe me, this is no new fad. It is here to stay! And we don't want to be trailing behind. . . . It is far different from anything the traditional method is offering at the present. You are going to love the "labs." I can hardly wait to try them out, and the same is true of students I'm teaching.
>
> I feel that, with the training I can get this summer in the basic philosophy of the new curriculum, I can offer a good course in 1963 for our biology teachers.[73]

This type of feedback and suggestions from high school teachers helped to keep the college courses relevant and useful and to maintain the students' enthusiasm, thus contributing to OLL's steady growth.

The college in turn helped the Sisters teaching in grade school and high school stay up to date. Science and math teachers, for example, held an annual meeting in early June to exchange ideas.[74] Sister Reparata Glenn founded a newsletter in 1966 for CDP science and math teachers. It was published seven times a year with information on conventions and meetings, teaching methods, and equipment. Sister Cecile Clare Vanderlick succeeded her as editor.

Two teachers in the math department were noteworthy for their availability to students. The Sisters could consult Sister Laetitia Hill, who was noted not only for mathematical skill but also for her eccentric habit of using a spyglass to peer at the ducks on the lake as well as the homework papers she asked her students to raise up during class. Almost always covered with chalk dust, she delighted in asking after she had presented an intricate problem and solution, "Now isn't that cute?" Sister Ann Petrus also remembered her subtle spiritual motivations. One day Sister Laetitia wrote on the board, "Any moment not spent for God is frittered away for all eternity." She stated simply to the class, "I read that in

---

[72] Sister Mary Clare Metz file, OLLUA.

[73] Former Sister Regina Richter to Sister Mary Clare, Bishop Kelley High School, Tulsa, Oklahoma, 28 Jan. 1962, OLLUA.

[74] "CDP Newsletter," Central Region, 1 Jan. 1970; 11, CDPA.

my meditation this morning" and began the day's lesson.[75] Few realized that this math genius had sight in only one eye. Another teacher in the math department, Sister Marilyn Molloy, communicated her love for math and physics as well as for research to her students. She graded every student's problems herself and wrote them notes. Known as a strict teacher with great common sense, she also liked to play baseball and mow the lawn. She never concealed her devotion to the Dallas Cowboy football team or affection for pet cats and dogs.

High school English teachers met and heard from Sister Generosa Callahan about better ways to teach grammar or composition. Years later, Sister Generosa defended her high standards and her reputation as a demanding professor. "I know I was a hard teacher, but I wanted my students to know how to write. If their sentences and paragraphs were not well constructed, I had to point this out to them. Otherwise, they would never learn; it was my responsibility to see that they did."[76]

Sister Lora Ann Quiñonez of the English department also shared the insights that won praise from students such as Anne Keehan: "Although I did not like the classes, Sister Lora Ann truly made, maybe not a silk purse, but an acceptable one out of this sow's ear when it came to writing. Somehow she succeeded where my high school teachers did not."[77] Sister Lora Ann encouraged the Sisters to teach contemporary works such as Bernard Malamud's *The Fixer* or J. D. Salinger's *Catcher in the Rye* while instructors in other schools were still debating with their principals and PTAs the suitability of these books for teenagers.

Experts in classical languages were also available and happy to be consulted. Sister Agnes Clare Way translated several of St. Basil's letters from the Greek. Sister Inviolata Barry in cooperation with Dr. Roy J. Deferrari of Catholic University not only compiled an Index to the works of St. Thomas Aquinas but also a concordance to Ovid that totaled 2,219 pages.

Some Sisters also became authors and editors even though it was not the custom to receive "released time" for such efforts. Sister Frances Jerome Woods, sociologist, wrote eight books including three textbooks.[78] Dr. Lucy

---

[75] Sister Ann Petrus, oral interview, 30 June 2000, CDPA.

[76] *CDP Times*, 13, 3 (Nov. 1992): 12, CDPA.

[77] Letter of Anne Keehan to Sister Antoinette Billeaud, Christmas, 2002, CDPA.

[78] *Mexican Ethnic Leadership in San Antonio Texas* (Catholic University of America Press, 1949), *Cultural Values of American Ethnic Groups* (New York: Harper and Row, 1956, 402 pp.), *The American Family System* (New York: Harper and Row, 1959, 585 pp.), *Introductory Sociology* (New York: Harper and Row, 1966, 439 pp.), and *Marginality and Identity: A Colored Creole Family through Ten Generations* (Louisiana State University, 1972), a major contribution to understanding Colored Creoles in the U.S. One of her books, *Value Retention Among Young Creoles: Attitudes and Commitment of Contemporary Youth*, 1989, vol. 5 in the Mellen Studies in Sociology series, was considered a model study of intergenerational continuity and the impact of social change on cultural retention within a cultural system.

M. Cohen, Professor of Anthropology at Catholic University in Washington, D.C., testified:

> Sister Frances Jerome was well ahead of her time in the problems and questions she addressed. Her keen appreciation of cultural values and socialization in communities enabled her to conduct exemplary investigations among marginal groups in American urban and rural societies. Her studies provide contemporary generations of researchers with inspirational models to emulate.[79]

Dr. Cohen also experienced Sister Frances Jerome's "outstanding intellectual generosity with colleagues. She was an innovator, disciplined and always ready to travel."[80]

Sister Frances Jerome single-handedly instilled a love for the new field of sociology at OLL and tirelessly promoted the importance of research in all areas. She was Sister Marian Angela (Rose Duchesne) Aguilar's "big mentor. She was gruff, but she was a wonderful mentor for me. I would bring drafts of my articles or proposals to her; and she would review them, saying 'Oh, dearie, don't do this,' or 'Well, honey, this is the way you should do it.'"[81] After writing her dissertation on Mexican ethnic leadership in San Antonio, which continues to be cited by sociologists as well as historians, Sister Frances Jerome spent many years researching a community of Louisiana Creoles, publishing books and articles about their unique culture. Her commitment to her religious vocation was central in her life, and she guided the Congregation to full participation in national surveys of religious, especially after the second Vatican Council. In 1989 she received from the Catholic University of America an achievement award for outstanding research and scholarship.

Sister James Aloysius Landry and Sister James Elizabeth González of the Modern Languages department guided students and teachers of French and of Spanish. They also conducted a pilot program in modern languages at Lackland Air Force Base Training School on the west side of San Antonio. In the fall of 1965 they held classes in French and Spanish six hours a week for 27 weeks for military personnel.[82]

Sister Jane Marie Barbour, director of the graduate department of Library Science, was always alert to extending influence beyond OLL. She founded the

---

[79] Communication to the author, 2003, CDPA.

[80] Communication to the author, 2003, CDPA.

[81] Sister Marian Angela, oral interview, 21 June 2000, CDPA.

[82] "Alumni News," XXIV, 1 (Jan. 1966): 7, OLLUA. The college received grants from the NDEA for Spanish Institutes during the summers of 1963, 1964, and 1967 as well.

Teen Age Library Association (TALA) and was very active in library associations on local, state, and national levels. In 1966 President Lyndon B. Johnson appointed her to a two-year term on the eight-member Advisory Council on College Library Resources. That same summer the department of librarianship sponsored two summer institutes financed by NDEA grants, school library services for bilingual youth and teaching reading to bilingual children, ages 4-9.[83]

Former Sister Mary Arthur Carrow initiated the speech and hearing clinic on campus and was the first woman religious to be named a Fellow of the American Speech and Hearing Association at its annual convention in Chicago in 1965. Similarly, Sister M. Immaculate Gentemann was the first woman religious to serve as a director of one of the 60 graduate schools of social work in the U.S. She held that post from 1959 to 1969.

Music was a strong department at OLL until the 1960s. Sister Amabilis Hanley and her successor, Sister Lucy Marie Green, chaired summer meetings of all the music teachers in the Congregation. Topics included improving classroom teaching as well as private music. For example, St. Joseph's, a Congregational school in Abilene, Texas, boasted eight pianos, many violins, several accordions, and a number of wind instruments attesting to the importance of music in the curriculum.[84]

All the Sisters who taught music accepted the hardships of long hours and sometimes inferior instruments along with assurances from their leaders that their financial contribution to the Congregation was needed and appreciated. Often music recitals, band or choral festivals, pageants, and operettas were also a school's main public relations projects.

Difficulties and annoyances experienced by music teachers did, however, have compensations. It was rewarding to awaken children to the beauty of music.[85] As Sister Anna Marie (Janice) Kaeberle expressed it, "I strongly believe it's important to give students in this culture of instant gratification and high technology the experience through music of a deep emotional outlet. The place of quality music is extremely important to our civilization, our culture, and our human spiritual and emotional interaction." For her, music also led to ecumenical experiences:

> First I was in Catholic schools and parishes, then Protestant churches, and next I taught private students, who are not even Christians any more. I have a number of Buddhists, eighteen Chinese students, and

---

[83] *Phoenix* xxxi (28 Oct. 1966), OLLUA.

[84] FC, Dec. 1949: 38, CDPA.

[85] Music teachers group interview, 13 June 2001, CDPA.

a number of Muslim children whose parents are from Iran, India, and Pakistan. It has been a very broadening experience to learn about their holidays, which are so different from ours, as well as their music which is also different from Western European traditions.[86]

Sister Helen Mary Dolson was the OLL expert on school music. At the 37th Modern Music Masters awards ceremony in 1972 she was honored for her contribution to the yearly music festivals held at OLL, which brought in student performers from a wide geographic area.[87] In 1972, for example, 13 high school choral groups competed. CDP musicians were active in the National Guild of Piano Teachers that scheduled auditions every spring for private piano students, and they served as officers of various professional organizations. The CDP music teachers in 1950 launched Tri-M (Modern Music Masters) in San Antonio.

The Sisters also used their musical talents off campus. Sister Lucy Marie Green, who taught piano at the college for over 60 years, was a member and officer of the Music Teachers National Association for over 50 years; and she performed publicly in the Tuesday Musical Club's piano ensemble from 1976 to 2000. Sister Emelene Matocha played the violin in local ensembles and orchestras and the organ for Protestant and Catholic Sunday services at a military base. Sisters Madlyn Pape and Anna Rose Bezner sang in San Antonio choral groups.

Sister Elaine Gentemann, gifted organist who served under five OLL Presidents, prolific composer, and lively teacher was a continual inspiration. The secret of her serenity and optimism? "I feel like I've been swimming in grace. It's so evident God is watching over me."[88] Sister's output of over 500 compositions included music for piano and organ, chorus, string quartet, and string orchestra as well as 23 Masses, music used for speech therapy and for teaching foreign languages, and a three-act operetta. One Mass was based on African American spirituals, and her Mass in honor of Kateri Tekakwitha incorporated Native American melodies. She produced a hymnal and also authored three inspirational booklets containing reflections and jokes titled "Respond, Reflect, Rejoice," "Read, Relax, Enjoy" and "Lines for Living." Born with perfect pitch and ability to play by ear, she was noted for her compositions for special occasions—patriotic, religious, or ethnic. Sister Elaine confessed that

---

[86] Sister Anna Marie Kaeberle, oral interview, 20 June 2000, CDPA. Sister Anna Marie taught music in California for 25 years. When she came home for the summer, she and Sister Emelene Matocha, a violinist, frequently staged concerts. When she retired, Sister Anna Marie offered piano lessons to lay employees as well as Sisters at the motherhouse.

[87] As soon as a music festival was over, Sister Helen Mary and her helpers would conduct a "post mortem" and begin planning for next year's festival (Sister Jule Adele Espey, oral interview, 4 Nov. 2003, CDPA).

[88] Oral interview, 31 Jan. 2000, CDPA.

her own favorite occupation and special gift was to make arrangements, for example of "Phantom of the Opera" tunes for piano solo. She was named Texas Composer of the Year in 1960. In 1970, for example, she published nine new compositions: Masses, music for the revised New Marriage Rite, and piano solos and duets.[89] Her steady creative output continued into her late 80s.

Famous musicians such as Daniel Pollock, Hazel Griggs, and Lilly Kraus not only performed and/or lectured at the college but also became personal friends of the Sisters. Justin Harrison, noted African musician, and Harold Robinson were among many who gave summer workshops. Local musicians were generous to the Sisters. Sister Mary Clare Metz expressed "sincere appreciation" to Dr. Victor Alessandro, conductor of the San Antonio Symphony Orchestra, "for the privilege granted to the Sisters to attend the Symphony rehearsals. It has meant much more to them than you can possibly know."[90]

The first Sisters who came across the Atlantic Ocean brought a love of and skill in music that remains strong to this day in the motherhouse in France, and excellence in this field was always encouraged. At OLL a Sisters' choir and, in the 1930's and 1940's, a Sisters' orchestra showcased the talents of many Sisters.[91] Sister Hortensia Gaertner, born near St. Jean de Bassel in France, was not yet a teenager when she came to Texas determined to be a missionary. Most of her life was spent at the college, and she was responsible for training generations of Sisters in sight-reading and artistic singing, which was preserved on a 33RPM record cut in 1968.[92]

For the centennial of the Congregation in Texas in 1966, Sister Elaine composed the music for an elaborate pageant, "The Light Shines in Darkness," staged by the Sisters in San Antonio's Municipal Auditorium.[93] That year there were 45 Sisters teaching music (5 in college, 9 in high schools, two in aspirancies,

---

[89] *Nunspeak*, June 1970: 10, CDPA. *Movements* Fall/Winter 2007/08, pp. 16-19.

[90] Sister Mary Clare to Dr. Victor Alessandro, 21 April 1962, OLLUA.

[91] Sisters Blanda Basner, Teresita Schulz, Agnes Rose Halbardier, Hortensia Gaertner, and Madlyn Pape were outstanding choral directors. Instrumentalists included Sisters Joan of Arc Heinrich, flute; Emelene Matocha, violin; Gloriosa Burkholder, trumpet; and Joanne McCreedy, marimba. Sister Leola Ann Doerfler played daily "reveille" and "taps" on the trumpet for the students of St. Thomas Aquinas School in Dallas (Sister Frances Klinger, oral interview, 6 June 2000, CDPA). Sisters Elsa Mary Bennett and Corona Hill played the French horn and clarinet in a German orchestra in San Antonio.

[92] Sister Hortensia did, however, leave campus to teach singing to the Holy Ghost Sisters on Yucca Street in San Antonio in the early 1950s. In 1988, former Sister Amabilis (LaClaire) Hermann also taped the Sisters' choir.

[93] Sister Kathryn Keefe, who had just earned her PhD in speech and drama from Northwestern University, received the script only six weeks before the scheduled performance. Nevertheless she enjoyed the "wonderful experience" of working as artistic director of the pageant with professional and non-professional volunteers (oral interview, 25 Aug. 2000, CDPA). Sister Louise Miksch also remembered teaching eurhythmic dances to some teenagers for a pageant celebrating the CDP centennial that took place in New Braunfels (oral interview, 19 May 2000, CDPA).

one at the motherhouse, and the rest in grade schools). Their numbers were decreasing, however, so in 1966 the music teachers generated and circulated among themselves a questionnaire for prioritizing factors that might account for the decrease. These ranged from long teaching hours, isolation from community life, and conflicts with other teachers to lack of motivation and more choices on the part of students and lack of understanding as to how music contributes to a child's development.

Besides its prominence in performances and formal celebrations, music was always a part of informal fun times for the Sisters. Talent shows contributed to hilarity in the summertime with numbers like "Grandma's Lye Soap" or "The Kazoo Choir." When hootenannies became popular during the Civil Rights Era, a number of young Sisters learned to play the guitar so they could accompany summer songfests.[94]

By the turn of the 21st century, OLL University was much larger and more Hispanic than it had been in 1950, and lay faculty greatly outnumbered Sisters.[95] The institution decreased its emphasis on morality, religion, and Catholic identity, and increased emphasis on intellectual development and professional training.[96] Probably no one person in 1950 anticipated this evolution. It came about step by step by responding to invitations, launching new projects, and continuing the tradition of providing for the underserved. No one can foresee 2050, but the Sisters and the laity who "caught" the Sisters' charism of trust in Divine Providence were sure a Provident God would continue to send invitations for improving and extending beneficial education.

---

[94] The Sisters were sometimes entertained by Sister Euphrosine Honc on the harmonica, Sister Dorcas Mladenka on the guitar, or Sister Madeleine Zimmerer on the accordion.

[95] On 23-25 March 1973, the Sister-faculty of OLLU gathered to discuss for the first time various aspects of their apostolate.

[96] Sister Virginia Clare Duncan, "An Analysis" 296-297.

Sister Ramona Bezner teaches math,
St. Martin Hall, San Antonio, 1960s.
(Joe Bacon)

Sister Teresa Pauline Hereford coaches baseball players,
St. Anthony's School, San Antonio, 1960s.
(Joe Bacon)

Sisters of 32 religious communities attend
summer classes at Our Lady of the Lake College.
(Alamo Messenger, 15 July 1966). (Used with permission of *Today's Catholic*)

Under the auspices of
U.S. Congressman Henry B. Gonzalez
Sister Frances Jerome Woods (OLLU)
conducted a study of the San Antonio
Model Cities Program.
(K. Jewell, 1990/CDP Archives)

In 1995, Sisters Angelina Murphy, Immaculate Gentemann (in habits worn in 1895), Sisters Elizabeth Anne Sueltenfuss and Lora Ann Quiñonez commemorate the move from Castroville, Texas to San Antonio. *(CDP Archives)*

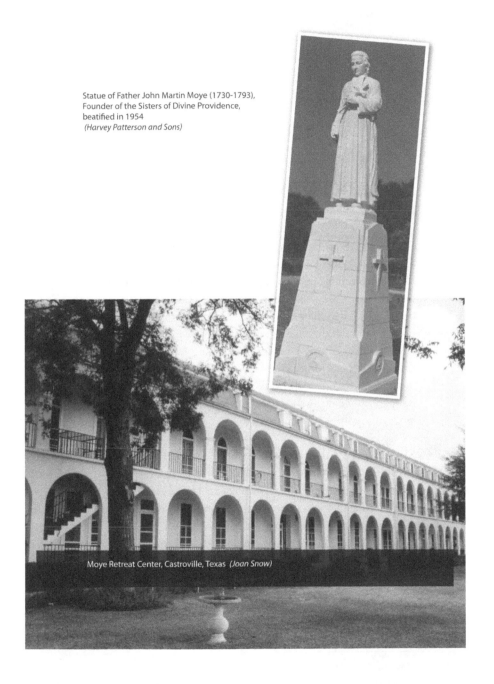

Statue of Father John Martin Moye (1730-1793),
Founder of the Sisters of Divine Providence,
beatified in 1954
(Harvey Patterson and Sons)

Moye Retreat Center, Castroville, Texas (Joan Snow)

CHAPTER 5

EMPOWERING HISPANICS

> We teach over 100 students under the trees in a vacant lot between
> two railroad tracks on Chihuahua Street on San Antonio's west side.
> We are surrounded by piles of junk—bottles, old cars and car parts,
> pieces of machinery, huge tanks, and battery cases which the children
> use as seats when the rough wooden benches are filled. Dogs bark,
> play, and distract the children; occasionally we hear roosters crowing.
> The children walk six blocks from Johnson Elementary School, so
> they are tired when they arrive and often either perspiring from the
> heat or shivering from the cold. After the religious instruction, there
> is supervised craft time—sewing, embroidering, or making different
> kinds of toys.[1]

In 1946 Sister Mary Paul Valdez and Sister Carmen Rocamontez, Missionary
Catechists of Divine Providence (MCDPs), were engaged in one of the
most traditional and time-honored tasks in the church: teaching children
the rudiments of the faith. In the next few decades, MCDPs would be
sharing their faith not only with children but with adults and not only
on the west side of San Antonio. By 1989 they had grown from a small
society of laywomen to an autonomous pontifical Congregation of 45
professed Sisters. Motivated by their own experiences, they were poised
"to empower others to become clearer in their identity and stronger in
their leadership."[2]

---

[1] Adapted from FC, March 1946: 119-120, CDPA.

[2] Sister Anita DeLuna, MCDP, "The Rise of the Missionary Catechists of Divine Providence from barrio anonymity to autonomy and national recognition," MCDP website, http://www.mcdp.org/history.asp

Thus the Congregation of Divine Providence through one of its Sisters was instrumental in initiating a new religious Congregation in the church. For several decades CDPs mentored MCDPs as they responded to the needs of Latinos and worked with Archbishop Lucey to obtain their autonomy. They also facilitated the beginning of a new branch of the CDP in Mexico.

Missionary Catechists of Divine Providence

Sister Benitia Vermeersch, CDP, foundress of the MCDPs, was born in Belgium and raised at St. Peter and St. Joseph's orphanage in San Antonio. When she was 15, she volunteered for missionary work in Saltillo, Mexico, with the Sisters of Charity of the Incarnate Word. Fluent in Spanish when she returned to San Antonio, at age 18 she joined the CDP. In 1915 she was assigned to Our Lady of Guadalupe School in Houston where the number of Mexican immigrants coming to Texas after the Mexican Revolution was rapidly increasing and the Great Depression was soon to multiply economic problems. When she and the other Sisters at the school in Houston could not satisfy the great need for religious instruction on the part of children in the barrio, she started enlisting the help of young Hispanic women whom she herself trained. The future Sister Margarita (Frances Louise) Sánchez, CDP, recalled:

> When I was about 14 or 15, Sister Benitia let me teach, which in those days was just to help the children learn the prayers by memory. We were young, and we had a good time! We went to school dressed in a black skirt and a white blouse. About 2:30 p.m. we left the class, put on this long black dress and veil, and went out to teach at different places. We would go on the bus free.[3]

In 1928 Sister Benitia organized a group of these young women into the Society of St. Teresa, which prefigured the Missionary Catechists of Divine Providence, the first and only religious order of predominantly Mexican American women founded in the United States.

Sister Benitia's strong character and legendary skill at eliciting donations contributed to her success. Sisters remember the tiny pecan seedlings she brought from New Mexico that grew into the CDP Motherhouse pecan grove. A trunk full of corsets was another unusual gift she accepted. She was persistent, intrepid, and challenging. Sister Inéz Terán, who accompanied her on some of her begging missions, recalled: "She got any and everything from everybody.

---

[3] Oral interview, 13 Jan. 2001, CDPA.

But I used to cry at night because it hurt me to see the way she would do it. I used to say to Sister Florencia Lopez, 'I didn't join the Congregation to go begging!' And she would say, 'Well, Sister, just do what she tells you, and you'll be on her right side.'"[4]

Sister Helen Louise Rivas grew up in San Antonio, and her first assignment as an MCDP was to make home visits in a neighborhood near the tannery, which her family considered to be dangerous and off limits. "It was very difficult. My first reaction was to say to myself, 'Did I go through all that preparation just to come back to the street my mother wouldn't let me come to?' Then I said, 'Well, if that is what you want, Lord, I'll do that.'"[5]

In 1938 Sister Benitia continued her ministerial approach in San Antonio at Providence House near the Chancery building downtown. Besides coordinating catechetical centers, her Missionary Catechists also offered retreats for various groups of adults as well as social services and leadership training. By 1946 they were instructing more than 1,100 pupils in over 14 centers. Each of these centers in turn spawned "Miniature Catechetical Centers" in which self-appointed lay teachers found their own pupils in the neighborhood. They looked for five or six year-olds, never more than six to a group, who wanted to make their First Communion. After the Sisters had explained the prayers, the laywomen made sure the pupils understood and knew them by heart.[6] The following year the MCDPs had fifteen catechetical centers in San Antonio as well as four near Houston.[7] Some of their students were African Americans.[8] By 1965, the MCDPs staffed catechetical centers at seven San Antonio parishes as well as in nearby towns. That year they reached more than 30,000 students in Texas alone.[9]

Sister Benitia was basically a social worker, and her catechists did not hesitate to meet any legitimate needs as they arose. They distributed government surplus food, visited families, found lawyers for immigrants in trouble, or instructed prisoners. Later they readily responded to calls for training adult teachers and parents, forming seminarians, and serving as chaplains in hospitals, prisons, and funeral parlors. They ministered in parishes all over the U.S., on Native American reservations, with immigrants in Alaska, and on military bases in Europe.

Archbishop Lucey recognized and appreciated the potential of this cadre of catechists and contacted Sister Benitia within four days of his installation as archbishop of San Antonio. He had started the Confraternity of Christian

---

[4] Sister Inéz Terán, oral interview, 8 Apr. 2000, CDPA.

[5] Oral interview, 17 Oct. 2000, CDPA.

[6] FC, April 1949: 144, and March 1950: 123, CDPA.

[7] FC, Dec. 1946: 85, CDPA.

[8] Sister Gabriel Ann Tamayo, MCDP, oral interview, 5 Dec. 2000, CDPA.

[9] "The View," 1, 3 (10 Dec. 1965): 1, CDPA.

Doctrine (CCD) in north Texas while he was the bishop of Amarillo, 1934-1941, and formally launched the CCD in San Antonio on 1 January 1942.[10] The cleric and the foundress shared a "desire to eradicate the ignorance of the poor and the exploited with regard to their fundamental human dignity and basic rights. Religious education was, for Lucey, a dangerous enterprise that threatened established ways."[11] He saw in the CCD the potential "for raising the consciousness of both the victims and perpetrators of injustice and for effecting those structural changes within society that were part and parcel of the Church's evangelizing mission."[12] These views anticipated by 30 years Pope Paul VI's insistence that evangelization involves "ensuring fundamental human rights" and securing "structures safeguarding human freedoms."[13] The Archbishop, like the foundress, wanted the catechists to concern themselves with "the actual living conditions of those with whom they worked" and offer "athletics, handcrafts, singing, Scouting, and direct social work." Moreover, he considered "most important activities" of the CCD to be "adult discussion clubs and the parent-educator movement."[14] His vision for the CCD even extended "beyond religious education for Catholic students in public schools" to include "non-Catholic youngsters who should be considered as 'our wards in Christ.'"[15]

Over 6,000 people attended the first regional Inter-American Catechetical Congress held in San Antonio 23-25 October 1947. Taking advantage of enthusiasm generated by the Congress, Archbishop Lucey had the courage to address the reality of financial compensation for religious instruction. The CCD relied on many part-time lay volunteer teachers, helpers, fishers (home visitors), leaders of discussion clubs, and parent-educators. But the women religious who worked full-time in this area were not volunteers; they relied on their earnings to meet their living expenses. Financial decisions in this matter, however, could not be made by the Archbishop alone. He requested his priests to pay a salary to the MCDPs who had been providing instruction and home visiting services gratis. The priests decided "to pay $40 a month for those living in their own convents and $30 per month for those living in parish convents."[16] Subsequently "at regular two-year intervals (1947, 1949, 1952) the archbishop instructed every pastor to raise the wages of women religious teaching in the parish school and of those doing catechetical work; he

---

[10] "Yearbook of the Archdiocese of San Antonio, 1874-1974" 31.

[11] Privett, *The Pastoral Vision* 38.

[12] Privett, *The Pastoral Vision* 157.

[13] *Evangelii Nuntiandi* # 39.

[14] Privett, *The Pastoral Vision* 29, 30.

[15] Privett, *The Pastoral Vision* 17.

[16] Sister Mary Paul Valdez, MCDP, *The History of the Missionary Catechists of Divine Providence*, (privately printed, 1978) 53.

insisted that catechists receive the same pay as school teachers."[17] The importance of Archbishop Lucey's vision and support become even more evident when one discovers that twenty years later Sister Gabriel Ann Tamayo, superior of the MCDPs from 1968-1972, was still trying to secure salary commitments of $15 or $20 per month for the MCDPs serving in other dioceses.[18]

Catechetical programs and parochial schools were not meant to be rivals. The object of the CCD "in addition to strengthening evermore the parochial schools, is to provide for the Christian way of living, by various methods of teaching, for the benefit of localities and persons outside these schools."[19] In the 1940s, the Congregation would sometimes staff a parish school with CDPs and the parish catechetical centers with MCDPs. In Alice, Texas, for example, in 1943 four CDPs taught 170 pupils while two MCDPs, 12 lay catechists, and 10 helpers took care of 350 children who were almost all Mexican American. The pastor received permission from Mother Angelique to start a club for the Catholic girls going to public schools because he and the Sisters viewed it as a way to promote vocations to the religious life.[20]

While Archbishop Lucey opposed inequalities in the pre-Civil Rights climate, he could not shield the MCDPs from the effects of cultural domination by Anglos which they experienced in the Congregation as well as in their ministry. At first their relationship with the CDP was one of mother to daughter, "like children dependent utterly on the parent Congregation to take care of everything." Until 1967, the MCDPs usually resided in CDP convents, but the arrangement was never ideal. The catechists' main work was after regular school hours, in the evenings, and on weekends. Their rule specified different communal prayers from those of the CDPs. "Infrequent opportunities to interact with one another resulted in less than accurate assessments of the other from both sides."[21] MCDPs were mostly Mexican Americans, so their upbringing and traditions differed from those of CDPs, who were mostly Anglos. The CDP General Council recognized this in 1945; it was reluctant "to incorporate a large number of Latin Americans who would be able to work devotedly amongst their own, but who would have difficulty in adjusting to the Anglo-American culture or way of thinking that is now characteristic of our group."[22]

---

[17] Privett, *The Pastoral Vision* 150-151.

[18] Sister Gabriel Ann Tamayo, MCDP, oral interview, 5 Dec. 2002, CDPA.

[19] Address delivered to the Third National Catechetical Congress, St. Louis, Missouri, 9-12 October 1937, in *Addresses and Letters by Most Reverend Amleto Giovanni Cicognani* (St. Anthony Guild Press, Paterson, New Jersey, 1947) 31.

[20] File for Alice, Texas, CDPA.

[21] De Luna, "The Rise," MCDP website.

[22] Privett, *The Pastoral Vision* 129.

Mother Angelique recommended separate organization and the "prerogative to select those Sisters who would collaborate closely with the MCDPs." CDPs were responsible for "MCDP assignments to mission, dismissals, and acceptance of members, etc. MCDPs had no voice anywhere unless it was in their out-of-town missions where they usually managed everything once they were there."[23] Until 1964, a CDP was in charge of MCDP formation. A group of five MCDPs told an interviewer in 1984 that in their experience this formation was "aimed at replacing Hispanic practices of piety with a more mainline style of Anglo Catholicism." They were not allowed to speak Spanish. "The tag, 'little catechists,' was popularly attached to the Missionary Catechists, and this diminutive designation was the self-image that was reinforced throughout the Catechists' training period for some years."[24]

Being members of a religious congregation, even in predominantly Catholic areas, did not protect the Mexican American Catechists from discrimination by Anglos. When two MCDPs opened a catechetical center in Moulton, Texas, in 1965, for example, the local restaurant refused to serve them. Sister Ann Regina Ross, MCDP (who was not Hispanic) catechized in Castroville and recalled that in the village as well as in the church and in the convent:

> there was a lot of prejudice. The fact that we worked with the Mexican community somehow meant we weren't the same as the other Sisters. We seldom interacted, and we usually ended up eating after the other Sisters were finished. Also, Father would not allow us to use the parish car to visit the Latin Americans, so we had to walk to everything that we did.[25]

Mother Angelique wanted the MCDPs "to have a [college] degree because the time was coming when catechetics was going to be a professional career, and she wanted them to be in the forefront."[26] Most of them earned a BA at OLLU with a major in theology and a minor in philosophy. Archbishop Lucey was confident that the MCDPs had a future because their association with the Sisters of Divine Providence guaranteed them access to the congregation's educational resources.[27] He designated Rev. John Ilg to study the organization

---

[23] DeLuna, "The Rise," MCDP website.

[24] Privett, *The Pastoral Vision* 132.

[25] Oral interview, 8 June 2000, CDPA. Sister Mary Elizabeth Shafer had the opposite experience. When she was a librarian in a public school in Laredo, Texas, from 1978 to 1990, she was the only non-Hispanic in the school and reported that she experienced no prejudices as an Anglo (oral interview, 21 Jan. 2000, CDPA).

[26] Sister Marian Frances Margo, oral interview, 3 May 2000, CDPA.

[27] Privett, *The Pastoral Vision* 127-130.

of Sister Benitia's catechists and had Monsignor Leroy Manning draw up a constitution for them. In 1945 he asked the Apostolic Delegate, Amleto Giovanni Cicognani, to obtain Vatican recognition. This was granted the following year, and the archbishop then received the vows of the first five Sisters. During a trip to Rome in 1949 the Archbishop praised the MCDPs fine work during a personal audience with Pope Pius XII as well as during a visit to the Vatican Congregation for Religious. In 1953 he "asked for final approval of the order" and reported to the Pope that "the Catechists were 'indispensable' in working effectively within the 'peculiar circumstances surrounding the lives of our Spanish speaking Catholics' and in providing the 'special care' to which these people were entitled."[28]

Considered a "filial adjunct" of the Congregation of Divine Providence, MCDPs practiced the four fundamental virtues recommended by Father John Martin Moye: poverty, simplicity, abandonment to Divine Providence, and charity. Sister Benitia, who never joined the MCDP group but remained a CDP, exhorted them also to appreciate humility, love, loyalty to the society, and a spirit of obedience. Their spirituality became characterized by strong relationships with friends and family, joy, and love for the poor.

Several successive general administrations worked for 17 years to prepare for the independence of the Missionary Catechists of Divine Providence. Sister Madonna Sangalli, who was a General Councilor from 1981 to 1987, said, "We did not feel that their desire for independence was any reflection on the Congregation. We were proud that they felt they could stand on their own and continue their dedication to ministry."[29]

> The Missionary Catechists of Divine Providence requested autonomy, believing that what they did for themselves they did for the entire Mexican American community. In order to empower others to become clearer in their identity and stronger in their leadership, they themselves would need to model such behavior. . . . The MCDP story parallels the Mexican American collective experience moving from being guests in their own territory, to their quest for recognition and identity, and finally to the self-determination and affirmation of their dignity.[30]

---

[28] Privett, *The Pastoral Vision* 131.

[29] Oral interview, 31 Mar. 2000, CDPA. Sister Anita DeLuna, MCDP, corroborates this observation. "Perhaps it was their [MCDPs] own apostolic approach to leading that led them to respond to the invitation to become independent and therefore more equal partners with the parent congregation." *"Evangelizadoras del Barrio*: The Rise of the Missionary Catechists of Divine Providence," *U.S. Catholic Historian*, 21, 1 (Winter, 2003): 62.

[30] Anita DeLuna, MCDP, *"Evangelizadoras"*: 70 and 71.

The 1960s in the southwest U.S. were a time for claiming Mexican American identity. The Chicano movement as well as liberation theology were prevalent. These trends encouraged not only more personal autonomy but also shared leadership and greater cooperation with the laity. The CDP General Chapter of 1967 decided to allow the MCDPs to experiment with their own leadership team. Mother Amata Regan appointed a superior, councilors, a secretary, and a treasurer even though they were still financially dependent on the CDP. Twenty-seven out of 45 MCDPs voted in favor of independence on 26 May 1983. In 1985 they incorporated so as to receive property deeds and finance the education of the Sisters. They also began to write their own Constitutions. The formal ritual of autonomy was held in May 1990. Affiliation with the CDP remained relational rather than governmental and was based on personal bonds, shared resources and expertise, and mutual consultation.

Sister Anita De Luna, a member of the appointed team, was elected the first MCDP Superior General in 1989 and served in that position until 1995. She was also the first Latina elected as president of the national U.S. Leadership Conference of Women Religious (LCWR) in 1991. Sister Anita received an honorary doctorate from Notre Dame University in 2004 for "the work of the order for the evangelization of the faithful of the southwest."

Additional service opportunities presented themselves as MCDPs continued to follow migrating Mexican Americans. They took on a variety of new ministries such as counseling, nursing, diocesan administration, and social work. They launched a "Masters Catechist" program in English and Spanish and set up the Benitia Family Center on the west side of San Antonio for community outreach and advocacy. When they submitted a Constitution to the Vatican in 1984, officials in Rome asked whether they wanted affiliation or independence. By this time the "MCDPs recognized themselves as the trained Hispanic leaders called for in the U.S. Bishops' 1983 pastoral letter, 'The Hispanic Presence: Challenge and Commitment.'" Forty-four Sisters voted in favor of autonomy; three Sisters abstained and transferred to the CDP. When their autonomy was officially granted in 1989, the MCDPs considered it an endorsement of their aim "to empower others to become clearer in their identity and stronger in their leadership."[31]

The importance of education, initial and ongoing, for ministry—which is a legacy and tradition of Father Moye's followers—continues to be appreciated by the Missionary Catechists of Divine Providence. It was also a factor in the origin and development of a branch of the CDP in Mexico.

---

[31] De Luna, "The Rise," MCDP website.

Congregation of Divine Providence, Mexico Region

While the well-educated MCDPs were contributing to the success of Archbishop Lucey's strong catechetical program, a bishop from Mexico aimed to strengthen his catechetical program with the help of Sister Rachel Moreno, CDP. Rev. Pedro Moctezuma, Vicar General of the diocese of San Luís Potosí headed by Bishop Gerardo Anaya, revealed his plans to Sister Rachel, who was working closely with the MCDPs at Providence House and the Girls' Club in downtown San Antonio. This enterprise, however, did not turn out as the clerics expected.

Sister Rachel, a native of Mexico, had been one of the presidents of Sister Benitia's first catechetical society in Houston. After entering the CDP, she earned a Master's degree in Social Work from the Catholic University of America. In 1950 she served as translator and guide for Sister Mary Immaculate Gentemann, who went to Mexico to offer scholarships for the Worden School of Social Service at OLLU.[32] While they were in San Luís Potosí, Sister Rachel's hometown, Father Moctezuma asked her to obtain permission from Mother Angelique to come to his parish to train some girls as lay catechists. "I want you to give them a pedagogical foundation, to teach them to teach, to found and govern catechetical centers, to train secular catechists, to keep records, statistics, etc."[33] Although Mother Angelique was interested and even explored some property available in Mexico, nothing concrete developed. In the fall of 1953 the priest brought five young women who wanted to be lay catechists to Providence House in San Antonio. Sister Rachel took charge of them, teaching them the same material weekday afternoons in Spanish that she presented to the MCDPs weekday mornings in English. During the formation program which was supposed to last three years, slowly it dawned on the young women that they were actually being treated like candidates for religious life.

A year after their arrival, Bishop Anaya wrote to Archbishop Lucey concerning these young women. "I am pleading with you to give them guidance so that with the help of God we can develop a [religious] congregation [of missionary catechists] to transmit religious instruction to this diocese."[34] Instead of offering help, however, Archbishop Lucey decided that the "grey girls," as they were called because of the color of their uniforms, must return to Mexico.

---

[32] Most of the material in this section comes from Rose Marie Gallatin, CDP, "An Hour of Providence, Resource Book for a History of the Sisters of Divine Providence in Mexico, 1953-1983," n.p., n.d., p. 29.

In 1986 Sister Rachel translated a manual by Alfonso Navarro Castellanos, MSpS, *Fundamental Evangelization, God's Love for Man* (San Antonio Press, 1986).

[33] Father Moctezuma to Sister Rachel, 7 May 1953, CDPA.

[34] Most Rev. Gerardo Anaya to Archbishop Lucey, 15 Dec. 1954, CDPA.

They did not leave right away. In November 1955, Father Moctezuma was still trying to calm the fears the young women had of becoming religious rather than lay catechists.

Bishop Anaya bought a house that could serve as a convent in San Luís Potosí. He envisioned a diocesan congregation whose members would immediately begin to teach, but CDP superiors in San Antonio insisted that future women religious would need more education before undertaking ministry. The bishop did not accept the suggestion that the house could serve as a second novitiate of the MCDPs in Mexico. The young women, now insisting that they did indeed want to become religious, were also asking for more training as well as papal affiliation for the proposed congregation. Complicating matters were months of negotiations between the CDPs and a would-be donor of a hacienda in Galindo, Mexico, that came to naught. After much consultation and dialogue, the laywomen were released from any obligations to the San Luís diocese. In the fall of 1957, the CDP sent them to complete their training as catechists and religious with Sister Rachel in Querétaro, Mexico.

Their living quarters were crowded and poor. At first they used wooden produce crates for chairs and tables. Since the government at that time did not allow religious orders to own property, a so-called "anonymous society" was formed and later purchased for the Sisters a small estate that had served as a monastery and later a botanical garden in the colonial center of Querétaro.[35] There five young women—Sisters Adela Teresa Barcenas, Susana María Cárdenas, Lourdes García, Rosa Margarita Martínez, and Maria Rodriguez—were invested as MCDP novices in 1961 and professed on March 25, 1962. In 1965 the central administration in San Antonio asked the Sisters to decide whether they wanted to become an independent group, remain Missionary Catechists, or join the Sisters of Divine Providence. They chose to be CDPs, and Sister Dorothy Louise (Alberta Marie) Hoog was appointed to be their superior. A dozen years after leaving San Luís Potosí they were confident enough in themselves and in God's Providence to take this definitive step.

On 22 April 1965, the bishop of Querétaro dedicated on the outskirts of the city the Father Moye Religion School, which already had a weekly attendance of 600 youths and adults. The center also provided social and counseling services as well as training for lay catechists. The Sisters instructed a total of 1,600 persons during this year, and they continued to expand their catechetical field.[36] Although the means they used to share their faith was basically the same

---

[35] GC minutes, 17 Apr. 1958, CDPA. The government later confiscated some of the property. GC minutes, 28 June 1971, CDPA.

[36] "The View," Special Centennial Opening Edition, 1, 4 (3 Jan. 1966), CDPA; and Sister Susana Cárdenas, oral interview, 11 Aug. 2000, CDPA.

as that of their Sisters north of the border, the Sisters' circumstances were often unique and noteworthy. From their home base in Querétaro in north central Mexico, Sisters went to remote missions where travel was arduous and often hazardous and the people seldom met "outsiders." Southeast of Mexico City in San Matéo del Mar, Tehuantepec, Oaxaca, on the Pacific coast they worked among natives who had syncretized their gods with the Christian God presented by the Dominican missionaries in the 1500s. In the mountains of Ahuacatlán northeast of Querétaro, they traveled by horseback and donkey to remote villages to catechize. These missions lasted three years. Later the Sisters also ministered in Chiapas to the south, in the northern state of Coahuila, and in the jungle region of Jalpan, where they journeyed to isolated communities to teach and pray with the people in their own little huts.

> To reach these remote areas, the Sisters ride in the back of a pickup truck for about an hour. After arriving, everything else is on foot, a walk of about an hour to the next community on sometimes slippery, muddy roads and roads that go "straight up." Often it is already dark, very dark, and the Sisters must carefully follow the guide in front of them.[37]

A photograph of Sister Lourdes Leal when she was a member of the Jalpan missionary team captured the flavor of the arduous climb. It showed Sister wearing a straw hat and backpack clenching her long skirt in her teeth so as to keep from tripping on it and leaving her hands free to clutch trees and vines, the only method of hoisting oneself up the steep hill.

People from distant areas regularly gathered at the catechetical center in Jalpan, an unfinished chapel that was also the Sisters' home. The Sisters provided not only training but also meals and sleeping space there at weekend meetings for as many as 100 potential leaders:

> Besides weekly meetings with leaders of small communities on how to prepare and share the liturgy of the word, the Sisters held evening workshops for catechists on content and methodology. The workshops have proved successful with as many as 80 persons attending the sessions. The CDP trio also helped to organize a prayer and discussion guide to be used with the rosary and litany for the 46 evenings prior to the feast of Our Lady of Guadalupe.

---

[37] *Movements*, 3, 1 (Fall/Winter, 1999): 16, CDPA. Sister Assunta Labrado also evangelized in the mountains and remembered that "sometimes we would really suffer because we didn't have any supper to eat or we had to sleep on a mat instead of a mattress" (oral interview, 29 May 2000, CDPA).

Initiating youth ministry in the area was especially challenging—and rewarding! Weekly three-hour sessions, with approximately 40-50 youth and adolescents from the extended communities, have focused on leadership skills and a variety of group dynamics. After several sessions, some of the young adults have moved on to begin work with youth groups in their own communities.[38]

Identifying adults and youths with leadership potential and teaching them methods and skills, the Sisters multiplied their influence as their students went back to their remote hamlets to share their faith. A revival of interest in prayer and religious practices among the people was one concrete effect of strengthened lay leadership.

The CDPs of Mexico also worked in Mexico City parishes, at first with the Oblates of Mary Immaculate, assisting newly arrived immigrants from rural parts of the country. Their convent in the Casas Alemán suburb also served briefly as a residence for women university students.

Sister Benedict Zimmerer also became interested in ministry in Mexico when she volunteered for the Los Niños program based in San Isidro, California, in 1984. Subsidized by parishes or communities where CDPs were stationed, for two years she visited the sick and helped very poor people in Baja California. She felt that the poor taught her much more than she gave them. For example, an old man she was visiting once told her, "When I die I'm going straight up to heaven." She asked, "Goito, what makes you say that?" He replied, "God loves the poor, and I've been poor all my life."[39] His faith in the Gospel promises bolstered her own "preferential option for the poor." In 1986 Sister Benedict began to work in Nueva Rosita in northern Mexico, becoming the first U.S.-born CDP to minister with native Mexican CDPs in a non-administrative position.

In 1999 Sister Lourdes Leal, who had served as a college teacher and administrator after earning her doctorate, readily accepted an invitation to join a CDP catechetical team in Mexico. She stated that "at various points in my life I have been called to re-choose religious life and figure out what is really central. To me, we live religious life to be doing more faith sharing, talking about the faith, talking about God. That has become more important to me."[40] Sharing faith in another culture led to learning experiences.

I realize that I am still a foreigner down there. At first I thought the distrust was because of my personality, but I discovered that some

---

[38] *Movements*, 3, 1 (Fall/Winter, 1999): 16, CDPA; and Sister Estela Solís, oral interview, 8 Aug. 2000, CDPA.

[39] Sister Benedict Zimmerer, oral interview, 4 Aug. 2000, CDPA. Sister also served as a house mother in a day care center in Morelos, Coahuila, from 1996 to 2000, CDPA.

[40] Sister Lourdes Leal, oral interview, 8 Aug. 2000, CDPA.

of it is just because I am coming from another country. They don't really want to hear too many solutions that aren't part of their own culture. So I am probably more reserved there than I would be in the U.S. But I enjoy the people, mixing with the people and working on the projects we do together.[41]

Although the number of professed Sisters in Mexico has never exceeded 20, they have zealously responded to the needs of the poor who hunger for the Word of God but also lack basic material necessities. The Sisters have lived in huts with no electricity or running water, slept on the ground and in hammocks, learned to speak native dialects, and sometimes had reasons to fear for their lives. During a time of disputes between native peasants and wealthy landowners in Oaxaca, for example, the Sisters were once accosted on an isolated road by armed bandits. In this tropical region they also had to deal with poisonous snakes that appeared in their shower stall.[42] Despite hardships, the Sisters have learned to employ both traditional and new ways to evangelize their own people. In Mexico they have the reputation of being well-educated, cooperative, and willing to undertake new tasks

The novitiate of this group has always been in Mexico, and they depend on the CDPs of San Antonio for financial support. Until 1980 most of the Sisters appointed by the Superior General in San Antonio to direct and form these Sisters were from the U.S. As the general administration became more aware of a kind of colonial mentality that occasionally surfaced in relationships and wanted to prevent undesirable dependency, they implemented plans for greater autonomy of the Sisters of Mexico. In 1999 the group numbered 17 native Mexican professed Sisters and formed the first Mexican region of the Congregation, electing their own regional superior and two regional councilors.

When asked, "What are the advantages of belonging to a Congregation with headquarters in the U.S.?" the Sisters from Mexico immediately reply, "It gives us a broader vision of religious life." Latin American groups such as Confederación Latinoamericana de Religiosos/as (CLAR) keep them connected to their own history and challenges, but interacting with Sisters from the U.S. gives them a different and wider perspective. They cherish the richness of belonging to a Congregation with roots in France as well as in the United States.

Being financially dependent on the Generalate gives the Mexico region a measure of freedom from fiscal concerns, but it also presents the challenge of having to explain regional needs and plans to people who live in another

---

[41] Sister Lourdes Leal, oral interview, 8 Aug. 2000, CDPA.

[42] Sister María Luísa Sierra, oral interview, 9 Aug. 2000, CDPA.

country and a different culture.[43] Since the Sisters from the North seldom have first-hand experience of the communities in Mexico, it is harder for them to get a real picture of what is happening there. The Sisters from the Mexico region, therefore, have to take more initiative; and they appreciate the encouragement to do so.[44] They have also negotiated within the Congregation the difficult situation which is often found in former colonial countries: dependence on people from a different culture to supply basic needs.

Language can be an obstacle to union; however, most of the Sisters from Mexico have learned English, and some of the English-speaking Sisters have learned Spanish. In spite of obstacles, the Sisters from Mexico have overcome language barriers. When they came to the Motherhouse in San Antonio, they experienced their U.S. Sisters as hospitable, open, and ready to share. Improved telephone, FAX, and e-mail service enhanced exchange not only between the leaders but among all the Sisters on both sides of the border.

The chief disadvantage of having one's motherhouse in another country, the members from Mexico averred in individual interviews in 2000, is distance. Communications take time to arrive, and direct contact is infrequent; so it is hard to build interpersonal relations. Occasionally an older Sister may still refer to them as "little Sisters." While not intended to be disparaging, this language shows, at the very least, that some of the Anglo Sisters have not learned the names of their own Hispanic Sisters. Mother Angelique herself after praising the first Sisters received in Mexico wrote "The five are lovely children."[45]

The CDPs who came from France in 1866 worked with European immigrants, but as they became rooted in the border state of Texas, they took note of the needs of immigrants from Mexico. Some women who entered the Congregation were from Mexico and others were children of Mexican immigrants. Being bilingual, they were key persons in offering services to Mexican Americans. These Sisters were equal members, but Jim Crow laws in Texas often excluded all people of color, and local customs promoted prejudiced attitudes which were not entirely absent from the Congregation. The dedication and perseverance of Sister Benitia Vermeersch and Sister Rachel Moreno led to the creation of new groups on both sides of the border. The Missionary Catechists of Divine Providence became an autonomous Congregation while the Sisters who catechized in Mexico became a region of the CDP. Both groups perpetuate Father Moye's vision of trusting God's Providence to enable them to serve the needy.

---

[43] Sister Miriam Fidelis Mellein was one of the most zealous fundraisers for the Congregation's mission in Mexico. Stationed in Laredo, Texas, for over 20 years, she sponsored numerous raffles and collected clothing. Her projects also supported construction and repair of chapels in northern Mexico.

[44] Sister Estela Guadalupe Tovar, oral interview, 13 May 2000, CDPA.

[45] Mother Angelique to Hannah Deutchmann Gaines, n.d. [1960], OLLUA.

CHAPTER 6

SHARING FAITH AND GUIDING

Teaching Church doctrine was the main way to share one's faith in the mid-twentieth century, and the main persons to do it were classroom teachers. In addition to his concern for religious instruction, Archbishop Lucey was motivated by the increasing presence of Protestant proselytizers to promote religious education throughout his archdiocese. During his first summer in San Antonio, there was a 300% increase in religious education programs.[1] In a 1944 letter to Mother Angelique he lamented, "A substantial group of English speaking people [in Poteet, Texas] have practically ceased attending Mass. These and a large number of Spanish-speaking children will soon be lost to us if something is not done about it." Unfortunately, the Archbishop could not always count on his own clergy. "The pastor lives on his own farm about seven miles from the church and devotes a great deal of zeal and energy to his farm while the faithful under his jurisdiction have received almost no religious care whatever."[2] The archbishop asked that the Sisters extend religious vacation school in this parish to four weeks instead of two. He was sure he would find in the Sisters what he found lacking in one of his clerics—zeal and dedication as well as sound teaching.

Almost forty years later the Congregation's general leadership, responding to a 1983 survey by the International Union of Superiors General (IUSG), identified a trend to move away from Congregation-owned ministries such as schools and hospitals to more diversified ministries within the Congregation and to ministries in parishes and dioceses as well as in public institutions.[3] Instead

---

[1] Privett, *The Pastoral Vision* 16.

[2] Archbishop Lucey to Mother Angelique, 16 May 1944, CDPA.

[3] GC minutes, 5 April 1983, CDPA.

of being predominantly teachers of children, CDPs became facilitators and co-learners on teams with lay people. They accepted invitations to new fields such as adult education, leadership on the diocesan level, and domestic as well as foreign missions. Instead of "catechizing" and "apostolates," they began to speak of "faith sharing," "evangelization," and "ministry."[4]

Some religion teachers easily segued from classrooms into positions such as administrators and supervisors of diocesan programs and directors of religious education (DREs) in parishes. Becoming more directly involved in the parish led to the recognition of other needs they could fill such as adult education or visits to the elderly and shut-ins. Sisters also became leaders of Scripture study and reflection, youth counselors and grief counselors, chaplains, caregivers in nursing homes and hospices, leaders in charismatic renewal, and pastoral associates. Success in these areas, as well as increasing shortage of priests, led to invitations to join parish ministry teams where they also served as trainers of leaders and administrators. As pastoral associates, they performed all the functions traditionally reserved to priests except the actual administering of the Sacraments.

CDP Catechists

While the MCDPs were full-time catechists, CDP teachers often catechized after school hours or on weekends, especially in rural areas.[5] Between 1945 and 1951 in the archdiocese of San Antonio alone, from 50 to 100 CDPs each year instructed from 3,000 to 3,700 pupils. They also taught "religious vacation schools," classes that lasted several weeks and were usually held in June after the end of the spring semester or in August before the regular school term began. The Sisters had only a few weeks to instruct children of all ages, with special attention to those preparing to make their First Communion and to altar servers. Often classes were conducted under difficult conditions—outdoors, in a tiny sacristy, or in hot public school classrooms. The Sisters surmounted hardships rather than fled from difficulties. In the summer of 1949, for example, Sister Praxedes Martínez and the former Sister M. Solano Griego from San Fernando School in San Antonio, who were teaching a two-week religious vacation school in Tilden, Texas, discovered that the only water available to them was undrinkable. Instead of leaving their post, they sent an S.O.S. to the convent for four gallons of water.[6]

---

[4] See Pope Paul VI, "On Evangelization in the Modern World" (1975). He proclaimed that the whole Church receives from Christ the mission to evangelize and lists some "apparently new ministries." See # 15 and # 73.

[5] Sister Marcia Havlak, for example, taught CCD classes in towns near Olfen, Texas for almost 30 summers, *CDP Times* 15, 4 (Dec. 1994): 11.

[6] FC, Nov. 1949: 10, CDPA.

When it was difficult for students to travel to one location, the Sisters themselves took to the road. For example, before there was a Catholic school in Pasadena, Texas, two Sisters from Immaculate Conception School in Houston traveled to Pasadena to teach religion. Nine Sisters from St. Joseph's School in Yoakum, Texas, went out to four little settlements as far as 17 miles away to teach 187 pupils in both English and Spanish. Rev. W. Pechal, pastor of the Church of the Immaculate Heart of Mary in Abbott, Texas, expressed his gratitude to these traveling teachers: "Last year the good Sisters from West were permitted to teach Catechism to our 120 children of Abbott on Saturday mornings. May I here state that they did a swell job and that this is so appreciated by every parent at Abbott. I do not know what we would do without them. The bottom would simply drop out."[7]

Some Sisters traveled even greater distances. Rev. Mycus, pastor of St. Thomas Church in Corcoran, Minnesota, asked for Sisters for summer as well as fall classes in 1966.[8] In the summer of 1972, six CDPs taught CCD in the Milwaukee area; and 24 Sisters responded to a call from Auxiliary Bishop Patrick Flores to be present to migrants from Texas who were working in Freemont, Ohio. Sister Anna Rose Bezner recalled they went in pairs, one Anglo and one Mexican-American Sister. She told Sister Elizabeth McCullough, "I know no Spanish, and I don't know anything about migrants." The answer she got was, "Just take your guitar and your personality and go on." The Sisters went by bus and stayed eight weeks. As it turned out, the migrants spoke English, and "it worked out fine."[9]

While pastors appreciated the Sisters' services, Archbishop Lucey relied on them to help promote the CCD not only locally but nationally and internationally. He called on the expertise of members of the Congregation and their associates, as shown at the session on religious instruction at the archdiocesan teachers' meeting in 1947. Sisters Berenice Trachta, Suzanne Marie Cleaver, M. Dolores Cárdenas, and M. Rachel Moreno made presentations as did Dr. John McMahon, OLLC president, and Mary Jane Coles, the future Sister Jane Coles.[10] At the Archbishop's recommendation, Sister M. Antonina Quinn of the OLL college faculty was appointed to a special national committee on teaching Catholic doctrine.[11]

At OLL College Sister Mary Clare Metz, biology teacher, had already responded to the need for catechetical instruction around 1935. "The most notable catechetical center we started was the one begun in the garage of Jimmy González located next to San Fernando Cemetery," she recalled. Along with

---

[7] Rev. W. Pechal to Mother Amata, 14 June 1958, CDPA.

[8] GC minutes, 13 Sept. 1966, CDPA.

[9] Sister Anna Rose Bezner, oral interview, 1 May 2000, CDPA.

[10] FC, March 1947: 139, CDPA.

[11] GC minutes, 25 Sept. 1943: 49, CDPA.

some college students she began to teach catechism at the Extension Society's mission, which later became St. Jude's Church. She continued this instruction every Sunday morning as well as during the week for the next 20 years. By 1949, sixty students from OLLU were instructing about 1,200 children in 12 active centers.[12] Sister Jane Coles was a college student at this time, and every Saturday morning she taught catechism "to the children in the neighborhood. We taught either in the yards of the children's poor little homes or in the beer hall, the tavern. The children would sit on the beer kegs while we taught them."[13] Former Sister Mary Catherine Griffin remembered that as an OLL freshman in 1960 she was sent by Sister Agnes Clare Way to teach in a three-sided shed with a dirt floor, a few chairs, and a portable blackboard. "There was very little, but the children were happy and responsive."[14] In 1965 Sister Jane Ann Slater, faculty advisor to the CCD at OLLU, supervised 40 students teaching catechism in four different parishes and at Lackland Air Force Base.

In 1940 Sister Mary Clare asked that Sister M. Berenice Trachta, who also taught biology, become the moderator for the Confraternity of Christian Doctrine on the OLL campus.[15] Aware of the dearth of materials for forming CCD teachers, in 1948 Sister Berenice published *A Course in Methods for Confraternity Teachers*, which was "used extensively in the formation of CCD lay catechists" in "dioceses all over the United States." Fifteen years later she wrote *Catechetics Today*, a manual that gave "religion teachers an even better foundation in the principles of catechetics."[16] The book included discussion questions and selected references after each chapter as well as insights from contemporary experts in catechetics. Written before the documents of Vatican II were easily available, the book included both principles and very practical examples. After Sister Berenice retired from the religious education department of OLLU, she continued to teach Scripture classes in local parishes until she was 90 years old.

Sister Euphrosine Honc, CDP, published a 32-page booklet, "Mass Prayers for Children" in 1944.[17] Archbishop Lucey wrote to Mother Angelique that he had received a copy and sent it to the Censor Librorum.

---

[12] FC, April 1949: 144, CDPA.

[13] Oral interview, 17 Jan. 2000, CDPA.

[14] Oral interview, 30 July 2000, CDPA.

[15] Metz oral interview, 1977, OLLUA. The future Sister Helen Louise Rivas was one of the children taught by OLLC students at St. Alphonsus parish (oral interview, 17 Oct. 2000, CDPA).

[16] Rev. Joseph R. Till, "Foreword" to *Catechetics Today: A Manual for Training CCD and Parochial Teachers of Religion* (San Antonio, Texas: Confraternity of Christian Doctrine, 1963) vii and viii. The book went through two editions and emphasized a kerygmatic catechetics with a biblical-liturgical orientation (Author's Preface, p. ix).

[17] She also published a 90-page prayer book, *Talking with Jesus: Meditations for Children* (Milwaukee, Bruce Publishing Co.) in 1958.

> I am particularly happy that the little booklet has been written in English as I fear that we have made some mistakes in the past in allowing our children to use more largely a foreign tongue even though most of them were born right here in this Archdiocese and will be seriously handicapped in their future lives if they do not have a good command of English.[18]

The Archbishop insisted that diocesan priests learn Spanish and he himself became proficient in this language.[19]

Hispanic CDPs had an advantage in catechetics "because we knew Spanish and could make a child or an elderly person understand what we were saying."[20] The first vacation school for Spanish-speaking children in La Coste, Texas, took place in August, 1949.[21] But there were also disadvantages for Spanish-speaking CDPs. Because she was bilingual, Sister Inéz Terán "did a double job" for 24 years. After rushing to close the spring semester as a classroom teacher, she would teach CCD in a small town and arrive at the Motherhouse a week or more after the start of college classes. To catch up, she stayed up late at night copying notes from classmates.[22]

As the number of children needing religious instruction increased in the 1960s and the place, personnel, and finances needed for this service were inadequate, some pastors began to consider closing parish schools and bolstering catechetical programs. When Sister Frances (Mary Leonard) Trochta experienced for the first time the closing of a school in 1968, she reasoned, "the fact that I'm leaving this school does not mean that there are not people here in the parish who need me, who need religious leadership with Sisters. That was when I really started looking at changing my ministry to parish ministry."[23] Instead of lamenting the past and resisting change, many CDPs saw school closings as opportunities "to go to them when they could not come to us."[24]

Sister Teresa Pauline (Francis Pauline) Hereford, for example, felt that she was responding to unmet needs for religious formation of adults and children in public schools. "The opportunity to know the parishioners and people outside the school environment is much greater if I'm working in a parish faith formation program. I increased the number of those with whom I worked and to whom I

---

[18] Archbishop Lucey to Mother Angelique, 22 March 1944, CDPA.

[19] See Privett, *The Pastoral Vision* 135-136.

[20] Sister Jerome Carrión, oral interview, 3 Dec. 1999, CDPA.

[21] See FC, April 1949: 155-156; Nov. 1949: 14 and 18, CDPA.

[22] Sister Inéz Terán, oral interview, 8 April 2000, CDPA.

[23] Oral interview, 20 June 2000, CDPA.

[24] Sister Leola Ann Doerfler, oral interview, 21 Jan. 2000, CDPA.

ministered."[25] Sister Helen Marie (M. Lawrence) Miksch also appreciated the wider scope and variety of parish work. "I get to work with so many different age levels. I get to know the whole family as I work with students in the context of the rest of their life."[26]

Directors of Religious Education (DREs)

A study conducted by the U.S. Bishops showed that the number of children receiving no formal religious instruction more than doubled between 1965 and 1974.[27] Sister Marian Frances Margo and Sister Redempta (Leonita) Bradley were the first two CDPs who, after years of classroom teaching, definitively left the classroom to become full-time religious educators in 1963. Sister Redempta's experience can serve as a case study of similar trajectories by a number of CDPs.

Sister Redempta taught at St. Joseph School in Shreveport, Louisiana, in the 1950s and returned to serve as assistant DRE in 1964. She was convinced that catechetics involves a holistic approach.

> Religious education is not a head-trip. It is more faith sharing. If we are catechists, we are not simply teachers but are persons who are sharing the faith. The books today are beautifully written, and catechists teach the doctrine; but teachers always end up applying it to our life and getting the children involved. We have to help them not only to know their religion but to love it and go out and do something about it.[28]

Four years later Sister Redempta helped to organize and supervise St. Cletus School of Religion in Gretna, Louisiana. The greater part of her time was not spent with the children but instructing parents and training volunteers to teach the children. This was an effective way "to provide the finest, educationally and spiritually, for all members of our Church." Sister Redempta stated, "I find real joy in enabling lay persons to become effective not only in their work as catechists and youth ministers but also as more committed members of their parish communities."[29]

---

[25] Oral interview, 9 Sept. 2000, CDPA.

[26] Oral interview, 2 April 2000, CDPA.

[27] By 1974 "6.6 million Catholic children received no formal religious education. That is 43.5 per cent of the young people in elementary and secondary schools" (reported in "CDP Newsletter," 3, 8, 1 April 1976: 153, CDPA).

[28] Oral interview, 16 Sept. 2000, CDPA.

[29] "CDP News Bulletin," Northern Region, Jan, 1969: 6, CDPA, and written communication, Sister Redempta Bradley, ca. 1985, CDPA.

Next, Sister Redempta inaugurated an elective program for high school students at St. Genevieve Religious Education Center in Lafayette, Louisiana, which served 1,058 children from five parishes.[30] The pastor called her "a Master Con-artist." "Wherever I've been," she said, "I've had to recruit volunteers."[31] It was often difficult to get volunteers to make long-term commitments, and at the turn of the 21st century the recruiter had to exercise extra caution as scandals in the Church impacted religious education. New policies required everyone who worked with children to be screened and fingerprinted. While a catechist teaches, an aide must always be present in the room.

In some respects, however, conditions did not change. After more than 30 years in religious education Sister Redempta observed that although lay catechists became better prepared and more competent, their gifts and services were still not sufficiently remunerated nor appreciated.

> Sometimes religious education was treated like a second-class citizen. The school was taken care of and took a large part of the budget. In Ennis, Texas, for example, there were over 200 children in the parish school. They had a principal, assistant principal, faculty, and two secretaries—all paid a salary. We got "the scraps." We had over 450 children of the parish in religious education; and I, the DRE, was the only paid person. Yet the 25 catechists and their 25 aides were some of the cream of the crop of the parish. And my volunteer secretary had a PhD in geology and worked at the nuclear testing ground in Los Alamos before she retired here. So the parish was really getting a good deal. [32]

Sister Redempta also served as Assistant Director of Religious Education for the Diocese of Oklahoma City and as consultant for Silver Burdett Publishing Company. When she heard in the 1980s that some day religious education would be in cyberspace, she thought, "I'll never live to see it." But she did live to see it. "*Faith First* has a website; and if you buy their books, you have free access to it. They have a family front porch, games, stories of saints, and prayers for the family to say—all arranged by grade levels."[33] This corroborated her own experience that "catechetics was always at the cutting edge of change. I never did get into a catechetical rut."[34] In 2005 Sister Redempta received

---

[30] "CDP Newsletter," Central Region, 1 June 1970: 10, CDPA.

[31] Sister Redempta Bradley, oral interview, 16 Sept. 2000, CDPA.

[32] Oral interview, 16 Sept. 2000, CDPA.

[33] Oral interview, 16 Sept. 2000, CDPA.

[34] Oral interview, 16 Sept. 2000, CDPA.

an Excellence Award for her region from the National Association of Parish Catechetical Directors.

Sister Marian Frances Margo was finishing an 11-year term as Director of MCDP Postulants and Aspirants in 1963 when Father Marvin Bordelon recruited her for his religious education program in Shreveport, Louisiana. He paid all her tuition expenses at the Catholic University of America in Washington, D.C. and furnished airfare, room, board, and spending money for five summers. Sister Marian Frances was especially grateful to Father Gerard S. Sloyan, head of the Religious Education Department, who "took a special interest in me and encouraged me to write my thesis on the work that I was doing. It was printed in the *Living Light* magazine."[35]

She recalled her pioneer experiences:

> The position of coordinator of religious education for both the Catholic school and the parish CCD was unheard of in those days, and I had to pay a price at the beginning. At first I had a very difficult time being accepted by the parents because they felt I had taken away one of their Sister-teachers from the parish school. My salvation was the altar boys. I was also assigned to take care of them, and they loved me. So they spread their good feeling to the parents, and gradually I was accepted.[36]

Difficulty with parents of children in Catholic schools was not the only tension experienced by Sisters who became full-time DREs. They also found themselves competing with classroom teachers for space and funding, endlessly searching for volunteers who would be both qualified and reliable, and requesting considerations equal to those given to priests whom they replaced.

When Sister Carolyn (Monica Rose) Pelzel was DRE at Anunziata parish in Houma, Louisiana, "It was really uphill as the pastor was not always behind me. I had 100 teachers and 1,000 students. He provided us with paper and pencils, but he would not buy books for us. Not even teachers' manuals." But Sister Carolyn was resourceful. "I got one set of samples from Sadlier and mimeographed as much as I could. I re-wrote the teacher materials and met monthly with the teachers."[37] Sister Mildred Leonards also recalled a challenge when she was DRE in a conservative Louisiana parish.

---

[35] Oral interview, 3 May 2000, CDPA. See "Developing a Parish Religion Program," *The Living Light*, 4, 4 (Winter 1967-68): 35-41.

[36] Oral interview, 3 May 2000, CDPA.

[37] Oral interview, 26 Nov. 1999, CDPA.

> The CCD instructors had no supervision; they were just a group of women who were willing to teach. When I first got there, they were fighting with the children the whole hour. Once I decided to teach a third grade class to show the teacher how it could be done. The students were just terrible. So I said, "You, you, and you, I'm going to take you home." So I took them home and talked to the parents. I told them, "Look, we are providing these services, and your child is more than welcome. But if they are disrupting, I will give you the book, and you can take care of it." Then their children calmed down.[38]

Teaching religion demanded stamina as well as adaptability. Sister Miriam Fidelis Mellein related that at St. Benedict's parish in Houston in 1968, "We had 1,900 in the elementary school, 200 in high school, and 200 in pre-school. We had CCD every day after school, and I also taught two speech classes. It was hard, but I enjoyed it."[39] Former Sister Rose Marie Salinas taught the sixth grade at St. Genevieve Elementary School in Lafayette, Louisiana, until 1 p.m. and after that coordinated a released time religion program for three public schools, which enrolled about 700 students from five parishes. Sister Rose Marie also helped prepare 56 teachers for grades 7-12 in 10-week preparation sessions in the fall and the spring. And she did have spare time! On her "spare evenings" she met with parents and children preparing for First Communion and Confirmation. All these activities prepared her for full-time religious education work in Texas the following year.[40]

Sister Ann Regina Ross was involved in parish ministry for the whole of her active life as a religious. In the 1980s at Holy Rosary parish in St. Amant, Louisiana, she supervised 77 lay teachers for almost 900 students. Most of the teachers had college degrees and were teaching in the public schools, so her main concern was to work with them for certification for religious education. It was one of her "most powerful and positive experiences in parish work."[41] She noticed great changes in religious education over the years. "Earlier, large classes were common; and it was easy to hold the pupils' attention." Gradually she limited class sizes to twelve students, adjusted to parents who spent less time in the home, and employed more visual aids because "today due to television, computers, and our instant society, children want everything yesterday. People say they want you to discipline the children, but they really don't mean it. You

---

[38] Oral interview, 1 Sept. 2000, CDPA.

[39] Oral interview, 13 June 2000, CDPA.

[40] "News Bulletin" sponsored by the Eastern Region, May, 1969: 4 and 5, CDPA.

[41] Oral interview, 18 June 2000, CDPA.

have to be careful because of lawsuits. And I wouldn't think of going to a class today without an overhead or a video."[42]

Two CDPs directed catechetics for the U.S. military overseas in the 1980's. A contact with an Episcopalian woman led to Sister Emily Rabalais' becoming the supervisor of religious instruction for U.S. military families at 60 army bases in Europe from 1980 to 1992. She was a civil service employee with a G 12 rating and traveled to all U.S. army and air force bases in England, Holland, Belgium, Greece, and Italy. She introduced the Rite of Christian Initiation of Adults (RCIA) to Germany, where no parish offered this program. One of her greatest satisfactions during her years abroad was serving as spiritual moderator of the Military Council of Catholic Women, trying to help them see that being a Catholic woman meant much more than reciting the rosary. She got people to do what they did not know they could do instead of waiting for the priest to initiate everything.[43]

For five years Sister Zélie (Rita Margaret) Dolan worked for the 21st TAA (Theater Army Area) Command in West Germany, supervising liturgical training in a territory of 144,000 square miles in Belgium, Holland, and part of Germany. Sister Zélie also developed lay leaders and trained youth ministers. She organized and computerized a catalog for the largest video library in the army. Another part of her work was to defuse tensions between staff, religious education teachers, youth ministers, and chaplains. One high point was a task that took three years to complete: planning and staging a religious education conference for English-speaking religious educators from all of Europe. She said, "I love creating programs. I love going into a place, seeing needs, finding the resources, and helping. It is not like it's mine, but I get people to help support the project."[44]

As the number of young Catholics in high schools and colleges increased, especially after World War II, it became evident that parish religious instruction alone would not meet the distinctive need of teenagers and young adults for more comprehensive religious education. "Newman clubs" for Catholic students on secular campuses multiplied. Campus ministers on secular campuses were a Catholic presence, planned all kinds of liturgical celebrations, and promoted ecumenism. Leadership training and informal counseling were other aspects of their work.

Sister Angelina Breaux became the director of the Catholic Campus Student Center in Huntsville, Texas, in 1984. She served there for twelve and a half

---

[42] Oral interview, 18 June 2000, CDPA. Sister entered the MCDPs in the 1940s and transferred to the CDPs in the 1960s.

[43] Sister Emily Rabalais, oral interview, 14 Feb. 2000, CDPA. A noteworthy event in her life during these years was shaking hands with Pope John Paul II minutes before he was shot on 12 May 1981. Her traveling companion, Rose Hall, was one of two women wounded in that incident.

[44] Oral interview, 18 June 2000, CDPA.

years and especially loved "working with people in a non-educational setting, answering their questions, and teaching informally."[45]

Sister Gloria Ann Fiedler worked with young adults in the diocese of Brownsville, Texas, before she became campus minister at the University of Texas there in 1990; nine years later she transferred to the diocese of Fort Wayne, Indiana, where her task was to be present on three college campuses and create a ministry for young adults in all parishes of the diocese. She met with pastors, created ministry core teams of young adults, and gave them leadership training. She particularly liked "to see the spiritual, psychological, and emotional growth of the students."[46]

In the 1980s Catholic high schools were also awakening to the fact that offering religion classes and providing for reception of the Sacraments of Reconciliation and Holy Eucharist were insufficient to satisfy the spiritual hungers and needs of their students. They began to provide a more comprehensive campus ministry at Catholic high schools. Sister Louise (Henry Louise) Miksch, in addition to teaching religion at Providence High School in San Antonio from 1983 to 1985, was its campus minister. She planned liturgies, gave off-campus weekend retreats for the students, and was available for consultation on religious topics. Later she worked at a diocesan high school in Beaumont, Texas, which enrolled numerous non-Catholic and non-Christian students. In this setting she along with her students grew in appreciation of other religions. "We had Muslims and Hindus. One boy let us see a video on the Hindu custom of cremation. He told us that as the oldest son he would have to light the fire for his father's burial." She also seized opportunities to participate in different worship styles. "I also enjoyed the Gospel choir in the Black parish. When I really needed a lift, I would go to Sunday morning Mass there."[47]

Adult Education

Announcing the Good News was never limited to formal instruction. For example, Sisters stationed in the 1940s and 1950s at Providence House, headquarters for the MCDP catechetical centers in San Antonio, also offered retreats for adult groups as well as social services and leadership training. In the 1960s CDPs who were used to leading students progressively through textbooks and daily personal contact began to exchange the regularity and predictability of schools to undertake parish ministry with and for adults. Rev. Mario Arroyo

---

[45] Group interview of campus ministers, 20 June 2001, CDPA.

[46] Group interview of campus ministers, 20 June 2001, CDPA.

[47] Sister Louise Miksch, oral interview, 19 May 2000, CDPA.

of the Galveston-Houston diocese, who worked with CDPs for more than 25 years, identified qualities that facilitated this transition:

> I find it characteristic of your Sisters that they do not have an a priori agenda; they don't need to have everything tied down. They are balanced and do not give excessive attention to superficial matters or abandon a project when they get bored or are not appreciated. They are not fair-weather volunteers but hard, steady workers focused on the mission.[48]

Sister Leola Ann Doerfler worked with teenage youth in parishes in the El Paso area of Texas from 1974 to 1979. She also used her home economics background in this mountain area to show mothers how to read recipes, use government commodities, and sew for their children.[49] Sister Marie (de Chantal) Doebel left teaching high school in 1968 because she did not relish having to be a disciplinarian. After chaplaincy training, she spent twelve years working at Fort Sill military base in Oklahoma. "I could not be called the chaplain, but I was to act like one, visiting the homes and counseling. Later my work became more specialized in the Catholic field. We introduced RCIA, which proved very effective, and visited all the patients in the hospital and the community. I was accepted beautifully."[50]

In a few instances, lack of support from parents was one factor in a Sister's decision to leave the classroom. If what the student sees and hears at home contradicts what the teacher is advocating, frustration and failure result. Sister Frances Trochta was the principal in a school where the parents of the children did not hold the same values as the ones the Sisters were trying to inculcate. "I didn't want to spend the rest of my life trying to teach children something that was not supported at home by their parents. So I decided I wanted to work with adults."[51]

Work with adults had a transforming effect that Sister Fran did not expect, and she articulated another reason why some older Sisters began to feel somewhat confined in an elementary classroom. Like some mothers who spend almost all their time with very young children, some Sisters felt keenly the lack of adult company and conversation. Sister Fran said, "When I started working with adults and at an adult level, I experienced a lot of community because I was talking about faith and about things that concerned them in their families and

---

[48] Oral interview, 17 Feb. 2003, CDPA.

[49] Oral interviews, 21 Jan. 2000, CDPA.

[50] Oral interview, 11 Dec. 1999, CDPA. Services to low income families and families on welfare were completely free of charge.

[51] Oral interview, 20 June 2000, CDPA.

their own crises." Her lay colleagues became peers and friends and helped her to keep "growing in faith and in skill in my work. There is something bonding about that. It is a mutual kind of relationship of learning in support of one another."[52] Sister Fran noted that this tremendous amount of affirmation as well as stimulation from the laity could be especially gratifying if the Sisters' community was not very affirming.

Educating adults, the Sisters also discovered, brought its own problems and challenges, both for the individual Sister and for the community. They had to be more knowledgeable of the latest Church pronouncements and current events and more adaptable to changing circumstances. Adults were more apt than children to articulate problems and challenge opinions. Sister Olga Zotz noted that "people have changed because they too have become educated. They don't believe everything they hear like they used to. Today you'd better know what you are telling them!"[53] Sister Agnes Marie Marusak, who pioneered in teaching adult education classes in Ponca City, Oklahoma, gave an example: "Helping people understand that birth control and abortion were two totally different things made me realize how women and families had to suffer through this. It was very difficult to plan and at the same time remain faithful and obedient to the Church."[54]

Ministry to adults sometimes required detachment from one's own ideas and preferences. Sister Louise Miksch articulated an experience common to a number of Sisters. "I have changed. In the beginning I wanted everything to be more ordered, to be in place. I think I have learned to listen better to all kinds of people. Now I say, 'Let's plan, and then let's go the best way that it works out.' It's not all-important that it happens exactly the way I wanted it."[55]

Changing ministries also entailed changes on the community level. Sister Teresa Pauline Hereford recalled that she found the transition from classroom teaching to directing the parish religious education program for high school students in Ennis, Texas, "really challenging and stimulating. The only trouble was that now I was on a totally different schedule from the teachers in the school, so it made community life somewhat more difficult."[56] Life together in community became less predictable as ministry needs took precedence over the schedule; consequently schedules varied, often from day to day.

The Sisters not only traveled beyond their former beaten path from convent to school to church but also interacted with a greater variety of people. Some learned to form community with Sisters from other Congregations. Sister Inéz Terán, for

---

[52] Sister Frances Trochta, oral interview, 20 June 2000, CDPA.

[53] Oral interview, 23 Feb. 2000, CDPA.

[54] Oral interview, 11 Aug. 2000, CDPA.

[55] Oral interview, 19 May 2000, CDPA.

[56] Oral interview, 9 Sept. 2000, CDPA.

example, lived with three Holy Cross Sisters and served 750 families in Dolores parish in the Montopolis area of Austin, Texas. In addition to coordinating the adult education program at the parish and religion classes, she also trained military personnel at Bergstrom Air Force Base who were teaching catechism.[57]

Ministers to the Elderly and Shut-ins

The number of retired Sisters in the Congregation increased along with the burgeoning elderly population in the U.S. at the end of the twentieth century. The idea of spending their last years traveling or being entertained was not attractive to women who found fulfillment in service. Many found they could continue to express their personal concern by assisting the elderly. Their concern was actually more focused and intense because they were less preoccupied with duties that could distract from basic human needs for affection and meaning.

When Sister Olga Zotz was 72 years old in 1986, she took a sabbatical after more than a dozen years as an elementary school principal and then looked for needs she could fill. "I felt like I did not want to be a teacher any more; I wanted just to visit the elderly in their homes. But that was very hard because at that time people were not thinking that much of the needs of the elderly." Eventually she was able to fulfill her desire. "I really enjoyed visiting people in their homes because I could really take my time. I would sit down and talk to them because usually they are by themselves. I would listen to them and then have a little Communion service. They would always ask about others who were alone in their homes." Later in Lindsay, Texas, she was like a hospital chaplain in that she spent one morning a month with the sick in the hospital and spent every Friday bringing Communion to people in five nursing homes.[58]

Sister Ermelinda Cannady recalled the effect her calls had in St. Francis Xavier parish in Enid, Oklahoma. "Whenever I visited these older people, their eyes lighted up and smiles came to their faces. They just couldn't wait for me to come. I was so welcomed, and they had so many stories to tell me; and some of those were very sad stories. They always felt that it was special when Sister came to visit."[59]

When Sisters Mary Grace and Pauline Mary Doebel, blood sisters, were in their 70s, they undertook a ministry of visiting patients in nursing homes and

---

[57] *Nunspeak*, Summer 1972: 13, CDPA.

[58] Sister Olga Zotz, oral interview, 23 Feb. 2000, CDPA. Sister Margaret Clare Mathews also ministered to the sick and shut-ins at St. Brigid parish in Hanford, California, from 1986 to 1999 (oral interview, 26 May 2000, CDPA).

[59] Sister Ermelinda Cannady, oral interview, 9 Dec. 1999, CDPA.

hospitals as well as those confined to their homes in Abilene, Texas. A few years later they transferred to St. Patrick's parish in Brady, Texas, primarily to be a religious presence. The parish was too poor to provide a salary, but it furnished the Sisters with a house and a car. They visited the sick and took Communion to them and also worked with the RCIA. "We had time to garden, to read, to pray, and to be available to the people, to 'just be' for others."[60] As the number of Sisters in the OLL retirement center grew, their spiritual needs could not be met by the one priest-chaplain. In 1986 Sister Marie Habetz became the first director of pastoral care for the residents of the center; Sister Thérèse Pousson was her assistant. Besides coordinating the prayer schedule, they arranged for spiritual direction and visits to the sick Sisters in the retirement center or in the hospital.

Ministry to the elderly contributed to the Sisters' deeper awareness of their role in collaborating with the Church and with others. Sister Theodore Mary Von Elm, for example, developed a program for the elderly homebound in St. Patrick's parish in Oklahoma City which quickly spread to other parishes.[61] In all these outreaches, the Sisters' priority remained "being ecclesial women in mission for the Kingdom."[62] Ageing did not mean for them less contact with people or more self-absorption. Perhaps they could not work as long and as hard as before, but their gifts were still available for the Church.

Parish ministry teams

Sister Regina Decker was the first pastoral associate in the San Angelo, Texas, diocese.

> Bishop Pfeiffer requested that I come in 1985. When I went to meetings in several places in the diocese that spring, I was always surprised to hear people say, "Well, most bishops will put a Sister in a small parish and send the priest who was there to a large parish as a second priest or a parochial vicar." But Bishop Pfeiffer did not do that. He said, "If St. Ann's, a large parish comprised mostly of well-educated people, can't make it with lay ministry, then nobody can."[63]

---

[60] *CDP Times*, 13, 7 (Mar. 1993): 10, CDPA.

[61] *CDP Times*, 13, 9 (May 1993): 14.

[62] Response to a survey from the International Union of Superiors General (IUSG), GC minutes, 5 April 1983, CDPA.

[63] Oral interview, 8 Nov. 2000, CDPA.

He told Sister Regina "not to do anything that she could not teach someone else to do." Her assignment was "to train the laity to take leadership and ownership of different things in the parish."[64]

Also in the San Angelo diocese, Sister Estela Guadalupe Tovar after 25 years in a variety of ministries in Mexico served as coordinator of a parish with no resident priest in Sanderson, Texas, from 1990 to 1995.[65] Sister Frances Klinger served as a pastoral associate at Assumption, St. Jerome, and St. Michael parishes in Houston, Texas. At Assumption she was the public relations coordinator as well as coordinator of Communion calls to the sick and shut-ins. She also arranged for home liturgies.[66]

Sister Carolyn Pelzel and a young priest from Ireland ministered to four rural parishes in the vicinity of Stephenville, Texas. "Every Sunday Father would say Mass in two parishes, and I would hold Eucharistic Services in the other two. That is when the 'Sunday Celebration in the Absence of a Priest' became a necessity. I enjoyed preaching every Sunday, and I made some significant changes there." She also helped organize the parish councils, worked with the volunteers in the religious education programs, and updated the textbooks. Holy Week was especially challenging because services were conducted "in all four parishes, each of which celebrated in its own unique way. Since most people had to travel 30 miles to church, they had never celebrated Holy Week before. It was hard work for us two ministers, but it was worth it."[67] In the 1990s Sister Carolyn was pastoral associate of a large urban parish in Midland, Texas, where she supervised the principal of the Catholic school, the director of religious education, the music director, and the youth director. She also directed the RCIA program, which had 50 to 100 catechumens each year, and prepared couples for marriage.[68]

As the shortage of priests intensified, more Sisters discovered they were qualified to administer parishes where the priest's role was to provide the Sacraments. Sister Olga Zotz, for example, taught CCD, helped with the RCIA, and presided at Communion services and prayer services because in Cyclone, Texas, where she lived, there was no priest. She remembered, "I did everything except say Mass and hear Confessions in that place. It was okay by me."[69] From campus ministry in a large city Sister Louise Miksch went to the small town of Moulton, Texas, as its first pastoral associate. "I thought how much my experience

[64] Sister Regina Decker, oral interview, 8 Nov. 2000, CDPA.

[65] Oral inverview, 13 May 2000, CDPA.

[66] *Nunspeak*, Summer 1972: 16, CDPA.

[67] Oral interview, 26 Nov. 1999, CDPA.

[68] Sister Carolyn Pelzel, oral interview, 26 Nov. 1999, CDPA.

[69] Oral interview, 23 Feb. 2000, CDPA.

was like that of Father Moye and the first Sisters whom he sent to a tiny village in a rural area of France. I even had to live by myself and be a pioneer in this parish like Marguerite Lecomte, the first CDP." Monsignor Stanley Petru, pastor of the hamlets of Hostyn, Cistern, and Plum, Texas, boasted later that Sister Louise was "the best deacon he has ever had."[70]

Sister Lourdes Leal considered herself a "missionary in the Valley," the southern tip of Texas which has a very large Hispanic Catholic population but few priests. She began to serve as a pastoral associate in St. Mary's parish in Brownsville and St. Anthony's parish in Harlingen, where she was in charge of a little chapel near a housing project that had about 250 dwellings. "I visited the housing project to help in the food dispensary and get rides for people or help them with their immigration papers. I was probably doing more social work than anything else. But I was also in charge of the chapel. When the priest was busy, I got to conduct the Sunday service." In Brownsville she basically organized the parish and put structures into place at the invitation of the pastor, who had never been in charge of a parish. There she prepared adults for the sacraments, headed the RCIA, and offered spiritual direction to priests, Sisters, and laypeople. Everything had to be conducted in both Spanish and English. Sister Lourdes was instrumental in bringing to the parish some consultants from a program run by evangelicals in Mexico. She found it fascinating to watch how from charismatic prayer meetings the program evolved into small Christian communities/*comunidades de base*.[71]

Another Sister on the U.S. side of the border who strengthened ties between immigrants and a local parish was Sister Lora Ann Quiñonez. After she completed her term as superior general in 1999, she moved to the Outer Banks of North Carolina for a sabbatical during which she intended to do some writing. Before she died of cancer in 2002, she told Sister Suzanne Dancer that

> she felt God had a purpose in making her bilingual. This purpose revealed itself in new ways in fall 2000 when, between chemotherapy treatments, Lora Ann began to work with a group that affectionately came to be known as "her Latinos" of various Central American origins, persons who graced North Carolina with a rich faith life but were unable to participate fully in Church and civic life because of language barriers.[72]

---

[70] Sister Louise Miksch, oral interview, 19 May 2000, CDPA.

[71] Sister Lourdes Leal, oral interview, 10 Aug. 2000, CDPA.

[72] *Movements*, 5, 2 (Spring/Summer, 2002): 15, CDPA. Between the time she was executive secretary of LCWR and Superior General, Sister Lora Ann worked for the federal government in the Office of Bilingual Education, where her duties included speech writing.

Her language skills helped her to connect them to Holy Redeemer Catholic Church.

Sister Lora Ann accompanied women to clinics and served as an interpreter. She invited several CDPs from Mexico to give a leadership-training workshop to the Latino parishioners, who named themselves "Lora's Angels."

> Her work called her to draw upon her Honduran roots in ways she never could have imagined. And indeed, anyone who saw her in action with her Latinos can testify to the fact that in this work she had come home. Despite being tired to the bone after three years of chemotherapy, in the presence of her Latinos she had an energy and radiance that can come only from returning to one's source and "being home."[73]

Diocesan Administrators

Some Sisters who started as DREs soon accepted invitations to expand their vision and share their wisdom beyond a parish to a whole diocese. The Sisters' gifts as administrators, facilitators, and trainers of leaders were needed; and once again they responded willingly. Frequently they were the first women to hold a particular Church position.

Sister Marian Frances Margo was head of the Religious Education Office of the Alexandria, Louisiana, diocese from 1968-1975. Bishop Charles P. Greco, who was also chair of the Episcopal Committee of the CCD, asked her to take this post because Father Aloysius Olinger did not want it. She traveled all over the diocese, often at night, teaching teachers in the deaneries of Shreveport, Alexandria, Monroe, and Avoyelles and helping with the CCD programs. "This diocese is missionary country, needing an army of workers to help it open up to what has to be done in meeting its most pressing needs."[74] Sister Marian Frances did not find an army, but she did recruit at least eight CDPs who were regular volunteers. Sisters from Prompt Succor parish also went to the Louisiana State School for Girls for Sunday Mass, where they led and accompanied the singing.[75]

As the need for religious education increased, the self-image of the catechists also changed. Exposed to the ideas of Ivan Illich and Paolo Freire,

---

[73] *Movements*, 5, 2 (Spring/Summer 2002): 15, CDPA.

[74] "News Bulletin" sponsored by the Eastern Region, May, 1969: 1, CDPA. Sister Marian Frances also experienced criticism from the group called CUF, Catholics United for the Faith, who objected to the new textbooks (oral interview, 3 May 2000, CDPA).

[75] "CDP Newsletter," March 1970: 1, CDPA.

they became more aware that pedagogy and reflecting together on Scripture can be tools for liberation. Sister Marian Frances Margo, a diocesan director of religious education, noted, "The role of the religious educator is of necessity shifting away from that of a mere content specialist and record keeper to that of facilitator and co-learner, especially in the process of an education which liberates."[76] Religious education programs had the serious responsibility of producing "leaders and collaborators of Christ in His great work of Redemption." In addition to actual instruction, religious educators needed to (1) work and pray for their own willingness to confront their needs and deficiencies as well as strengths and resources; (2) form communities to provide honest, trusting, and supportive dialogue; and (3) propose structures to provide continuity without oppression.[77] Sister Marian Frances also experienced the growing trend of "making full use of the ample room for a lay and feminine presence recognized by the Church's law."[78] But the full use still did not come with full benefits.

In 1974-1975 Sister Marian Frances trained her successor, Father Buddy Ceasar. "So I gave up my office and took over the little storeroom while he had my former office."

> When I left the diocesan office after seven years, I was being paid much, much less than what Father Buddy Ceasar got. I learned that when I was involved in preparing the finances. Before I left, I went to the accountant and said, "I have to say this before I leave: I have been running the office, and I have to teach Father to run this office, and he gets paid so much more. I don't think that is just. I have done the work. Why was my pay so much less? Is it because I am a Sister? Or is it because I am a woman? That should be corrected." I am happy to say that when Sister Ann Regina Ross took that post, they upped her salary, so it paid to go and say my piece.[79]

Some Sister-administrators spent most of their time on the road rather than behind a desk. Sister Inéz Terán, a CCD director for the San Antonio Archdiocese, had as her territory three deaneries: Victoria, Del Rio, and Floresville. Floresville alone contained 15 parishes and 15 missions. Each

---

[76] *Nunspeak*, Summer 1972: 15, CDPA. Sister Mary Ann Phillipp said liberation theologians, the Gospel from Solentiname in Nicaragua, and the biography of the Guatemalan native, Rigoberta Menchú, gave her a new view and respect for people struggling for their rights (oral interview, 15 Oct. 2000, CDPA).

[77] *Nunspeak*, Summer 1972: 20, CDPA.

[78] Pope John Paul II," Angelus Reflection," 3 Sept. 1995.

[79] Oral interview, 3 May 2000, CDPA.

weekday night found Sister in a different small town.[80] Sister María Guerra was Assistant Director of Religious Education in the San Antonio archdiocese from 1981 to 1987. Her territory included the west side of San Antonio and reached to the Mexican border about 150 miles away. Sister Louise Miksch developed programs of ongoing education for religious education teachers in the religion department of St. Mary's University in San Antonio. Her work involved constant traveling in the San Angelo, Corpus Christi, and San Antonio dioceses. In 2000 she continued to travel 70 miles, one way, once a week to teach in the Victoria diocese pastoral institute for adult education.[81]

After decades of kindergarten teaching, Sister Suzanne Marie Cleaver joined the staff of the Archdiocesan Religious Education Office in New Orleans as director of pre-school and adult education. Among her qualifications were that she had been a national supervisor for Head Start programs after setting up an outstanding Head Start program in San Antonio and had given the keynote address at an annual meeting of the National Catholic Educators' Association in Chicago.[82] Sister Suzanne Marie also assisted the former Sister Teresa Mary Kempf in Gretna to supervise 45 lay teachers and some regular teacher substitutes. Only a year after its opening, this school served the religious education needs of 580 children and a number of adults and also provided junior and senior Catholic Youth Organization (CYO) and adult education classes.[83] In the 1980s Sister Elsa García trained 2,000 people in the diocese of Brownsville, Texas, in listening skills so they could exercise a ministry of presence in parishes. The manual on visiting ministry that she co-authored is still being used in this diocese.[84]

At the invitation of Bishop Thomas Tschoepe of Dallas, Sister Helen Louise Rivas established the Office for Ministry to Hispanics and headed it from 1978 to 1990. Her task was empowerment of Hispanics living in a predominantly Anglo culture who often were inhibited and afraid to try things because they thought they didn't know how. Sister Helen Louise employed a "hands on" approach.

> I thought they could learn better by doing than by taking leadership courses. So I asked them to share responsibilities in planning and executing the diocesan celebration of the Feast of Our Lady of

---

[80] "CDP News Bulletin," Northern Region, Jan. 1969: 8, CDPA. Sister Inéz "taught teachers how to teach religion" from San Antonio parishes as well as St. John's Seminary, Oblate College, and Lackland Air Force Base. At one time she would also take a group of CDP novices to teach catechism in Elmendorf, Texas, on Sunday mornings (Sister Inéz Terán, oral interview, 3 April 2000, CDPA).

[81] Sister Louise Miksch, oral interview, 19 May 2000, CDPA.

[82] Oral interview of Sister Suzanne Marie Cleaver by Sister Angelina Murphy, 1983, CDPA.

[83] "CDP Newsletter," Central Region, 1 Jan. 1970: 9, CDPA.

[84] Sister Elsa García, oral interview, 21 Aug. 2000, CDPA.

Guadalupe. I didn't tell them how to do it but encouraged them to decide. This was a very good way for them to learn. After this success, they initiated a convention with an invited speaker and went on to organize a program for youth.[85]

Sister Helen Louise was able to reach an even larger audience when she became Diocesan Director of Lay Ministry in San Angelo, Texas, in 1991.[86]

An area that required tact and listening skills was serving on diocesan marriage tribunals. As a Procurator Advocate in the Marriage Tribunal of the Archdiocese of San Antonio, Sister Elizabeth McCullough obtained testimony and presented it in court. Sister Agnes Leonard Thevis performed the same ministry in the diocese of Lafayette, Louisiana. Sister Lucille Ann (Cordelia) Fritsch worked with the liturgy commission of the diocese of San Angelo, Texas; and Sister Madlyn Pape did the same in the diocese of Ogdensburg, New York. Sister Denise (Rita Louise) Billeaud was the executive secretary to the bishop in Lafayette, Louisiana, and Sister Susana Cárdenas held the same position in Mexico City, Mexico.

Sisters who began to pray with charismatic groups after Vatican Council II experienced a mutual strengthening of faith. Some discovered that this prayer style was particularly appropriate and satisfying for their spiritual growth.[87] Contacts with charismatic prayer groups eventually led to diocesan directorships of charismatic renewal in the diocese of El Paso for Sister Kathryn Keefe and Sister Assunta Labrado.[88] Sister Kathryn coordinated two national charismatic symposia. Sister Assunta also coordinated conferences for 3,000 to 4,000 people that featured national and international speakers. Sister Margarita Sánchez started the Hispanic Charismatic Renewal at Our Lady of Guadalupe parish Houston.[89] Sister Jule Adele Espey was very active for 15 years in providing music for charismatic prayer groups in San Antonio.[90]

Faith sharing also includes sharing with others the inspiration and motivation that leads a person to enter religious life. In mid-century men and

---

[85] Oral interview, 17 Oct. 2000, CDPA.

[86] Sister Helen Louise Rivas, oral interview, 17 Oct. 2000, CDPA, and GC minutes, 20-24 May 1999, CDPA.

[87] Similarly, Sister Mary Florence Volz was attracted to the Focolare movement and spent a nine-month sabbatical in Rome "studying the spirituality of unity and the charisms of our different founders and foundresses" (oral interview, 8 April 2000, CDPA).

[88] Sister Assunta was Director of Evangelization for the diocese of El Paso from 1988 to 2000.

[89] Sister Margarita Sánchez, oral interview, 13 Jan. 2001, CDPA.

[90] Oral interview, 4 Sept. 2003, CDPA. Sister Bernadette Phillipp was encouraged by Sister Huberta Gallatin to become involved with Camp Further Out (CFO), a non-denominational group of charismatic prayer healers (Sister Bernadette Phillipp, oral interview, 30 Oct. 2000, CDPA).

women attracted to religious life or the priesthood generally knew what to expect if they entered, and they consulted priests or Sisters whom they knew to find out about details. Archbishop Patrick Flores of San Antonio, for example, credited Sister Benitia Vermeersch with recognizing and supporting his vocation to the priesthood. She also encouraged Sisters Aquilina Martínez and Florencia Lopez to enter the CDP and other young women to enter the MCDP and other Congregations. As fewer people experienced Catholic school education or had personal acquaintance with priests and religious, dioceses and religious orders began to designate personnel for vocation promotion.

Cooperation with other Congregations in vocation work and searching for potential candidates who had completed college or had experience in a profession began to characterize recruitment efforts in the 1970s. Some difficulties in this orientation were experienced by Sister Lourdes Leal, who supervised a diocesan house of discernment for five or six girls in Edinburg, Texas, from 1984 to 1987. "The emphasis of the diocese was to find priests. They did not really care about what happened to the women. They were giving all the money to the men, and they paid for their college education." As a vocation director, if Sister Lourdes found interested women, she "had to connect them to the Congregations, which expected them to find their own funding."[91]

Sister Barbara Fry was a pioneer in vocation work in Texas as the Associate Director from 1976 to 1980 of the first vocation office in the diocese of Austin. She helped to plan the first national training for vocation directors held at Niles High School in Chicago for women and men religious and priests and was also on the National Sisters Vocation Conference Board. From this conference the National Catholic Vocation Council evolved.[92] Sister Rosalie (Edwardine) Karstedt was in vocation work for the diocese of Galveston-Houston for 22 years. She noted that lack of support and money were factors that helped to account for the paucity of entrants despite the efforts of Sister vocation recruiters.

In the 1980s some Sisters began to work in seminaries. Sister Madlyn Pape was the music director at Wadhams Hall Seminary-College in Ogdensburg, New York, from 1984 to 1987; and Sister Mary Christine Morkovsky was head of the philosophy department there from 1983 to 1991 and a member of the spiritual formation team at Sacred Heart School of Theology in Hales Corners, Wisconsin, from 1991 to 1999. These Sisters found that facilitating discernment or working with seminarians deepens one's appreciation of the Church and of the necessity of solid formation for priests and religious.

---

[91] Oral interview, 8 Aug. 2000, CDPA. In 1965 the Congregation for the first time asked candidates to sign an agreement promising to pay for their education, room, and board if they decided to leave during the formation process (GC minutes, 8 March 1965).

[92] Sister Barbara Fry, oral interview, 27 Oct. 2000, CDPA.

Animating and supporting professed religious in their vocation is another form of sharing faith. Sister Mildred Leonards was Vicar for Religious as well as Director for the Propagation of the Faith in the diocese of Lafayette, Louisiana, for more than 20 years. As Vicar she was the liaison between the bishop and the religious Brothers and Sisters. Visiting and counseling them as well as arranging meetings and prayer services were her main tasks. Sister Rose Ann (M. Francetta) Blair performed the same services in the diocese of Lake Charles, Louisiana, and Sister Regina Decker did the same in the diocese of San Angelo, Texas. Sister Dianne Jean (Roberta Rose) Heinrich was the first Sister to be the Vicar for Religious in the diocese of Baton Rouge. She accompanied the bishop on parish visitations and helped him formulate recommendations for improvement.[93]

Like the other Vicars, Sister Charlene Wedelich, co-Vicar for Religious in the San Antonio Archdiocese for more than 20 years, learned that her position gave her easier access to the Ordinary of the diocese, who came to rely on her advice and insights, especially with regard to religious life. Accompanying Sisters of many Congregations in their joys and sorrows, large and small, replaced the older notion that the Vicar's main duty was to help Sisters who were leaving their Congregations. National meetings and regular gatherings in Rome expanded the vicars' vision and strengthened their skills.

Closely related to vicars is the organization that represents the women religious of a diocese. Sister Bernadette Bezner was president of the Sisters' Senate in the Brownsville diocese. Sister Martina Zea headed the conference of women religious in Saltillo, Mexico, when she was stationed in Villa Unión, Mexico, and continued this service in the newly created diocese of Piedras Negras, Mexico.

Missionaries in Foreign Countries

Before World War II, Sister Reparata Glenn "really wanted to be in a foreign mission. But it was the middle of the depression. I had no way of getting to New York to go to the Maryknoll Missionary order, and Dad didn't want me to go anyhow. It was one of those things that were impossible, so I had to work on what was possible." She joined the San Antonio CDPs, but after two or three teaching assignments, in the early 1940s she talked to Mother Angelique about her desire.

> Mother was very interested. She said, "Where would you want to go?"
> I said I wanted to go to the Orient. "You know, we have CDPs in Manchuria," she said. She pulled out a book and showed me pictures

---

[93] Sister Dianne Heinrich, oral interview, 20 June 2000, CDPA.

of an orphanage there run by daughters of Father Moye from the motherhouse in Portieux, France. The Japanese were having some conflict with China at the time, however; so it was not safe to go to that territory. But then Sister Frances Jerome Woods applied for a scholarship to study in the Philippines. Mother Angelique said, "If she gets that scholarship, I'll let you go with her to see what you think of the area and see what you can find there that you would like to do."[94]

Sister Reparata's hopes were high, but she never got to Asia. "Of all the many grants that Sister Frances Jerome applied for and got, this was probably the only one she did not get. It did not work out, and I think God was trying to tell me that I was supposed to stay here."[95]

More than three decades later, the Congregation investigated international ministry in an organized way due to a corporate groundswell of interest. Ideas of establishing a foreign mission surfaced in the 1980s, and the General Assembly of 1991 acknowledged that some Sisters felt a call "to go where Providence would send them." The General Chapter of 1987 decided to focus on a country, and the General Assembly of 1994 promulgated "Our Vision of International Ministry."[96]

Sister Lourdes Leal's experience with former foreign missionaries in the Rio Grande Valley was useful when, as a General Councilor, she was put in charge of the international ministry project. If CDPs became missionaries in other countries, they would need strong group support. The call to be a missionary is personal, but it is also an invitation to the whole Congregation to be present, attentive, and generous—through the missionary—in another country. Sister Lourdes felt that

> the Congregation made great progress as the General Council defined international ministry and articulated its goals. We were task-oriented and did not get bogged down in personalities. We gathered support by working in this way closely with the CDP Representative Assembly (RA) and at cluster meetings, step by step. In this way an unstoppable momentum for international ministry developed.[97]

---

[94] Oral interview, 14 Feb. 2000, CDPA.

[95] Oral interview, 14 Feb. 2000, CDPA. Sister Reparata did request a foreign mission ministry again in 1981, but her request was not granted (GC minutes, 23 Nov. 1981, CDPA).

[96] Material for this section was taken from letters and other materials in the CDPA as well as from interviews of Sisters, CDPA.

[97] Sister Lourdes Leal, oral interview, 10 Aug. 2000, CDPA.

The General Council sent Sisters to explore possibilities in Guatemala and consulted with CDPs in Melbourne, Kentucky, a province of the French motherhouse of St. Jean-de-Bassel, who staffed a mission in Africa. Conditions in Guatemala were deemed unfavorable, but the Sisters in Kentucky welcomed cooperation with their Sisters who had been in Ghana since 1983. Twenty-five Texas CDPs volunteered, and four were sent to a missionary training workshop offered by the School Sisters of Notre Dame. Finally, Sisters Frances Lorene Lange and former Sister Mary Catherine Griffin were selected for missionary training followed by a three-year assignment to Ghana. Bishop James Kwadwo Owusu, DD, gladly welcomed them to the Kwasibuokrom-Japekrom, New Drobo area.

Started as a private Catholic mission school in Kwasibuokrom (KBK) in 1989, Our Lady of Providence School (OLPS) in 1994 had been absorbed into the Ghana Education Service, which paid teachers' salaries and gave small grants for operations. Students in the three-year senior secondary school were girls and young women ages 14-34. English was the language of instruction. The pupils espoused a number of Christian denominations as well as Muslim and indigenous African religions. Sister Frances Lorene reflected after three years in Ghana.

> I have a sense that for this particular moment in history, somehow for some reason Providence really does work through us Sisters of Divine Providence to be manifested in Ghana in a new way. God's Providence, through our Congregation's charism of trust in God's Providence, connects with the same spirit already present in the people. I think the Ghanaians through and with us are having an experience of Providence that matches their spirituality quite well.[98]

The national motto of Ghana, *"Onyame Bekyere,"* which means "God provides" is displayed prominently on public buildings and private dwellings and even taxicabs and T-shirts. Although the Sisters did not proselytize, and fewer than one-third of their students were Roman Catholic, every year a few students would ask to be instructed in preparation for Baptism.

The problems faced by the school in Ghana were rather typical of those generally associated with agricultural, politically dominated, poor, and low income areas anywhere on the globe. Although they did not prevent faith sharing, they raised the age-old challenge of bringing the Good News to people who are unemployed, under-employed, hungry, and oppressed in countless ways. The Sisters had experienced similar conditions in parts of Texas for many years. The need of secondary education for Ghanaian women was not widely recognized,

---

[98] Oral interview, 1 July 1999, CDPA.

and poverty contributed to a lack of funds for the education of girls. In their homes the students lacked an environment conducive to study as well as parental supervision, understanding, and support of the value of punctuality, discipline, and consistent study habits. Teenage pregnancy outside of wedlock was common. All of these factors contributed to a high dropout rate. In addition, qualified teachers did not want to come to an area that lacked basic amenities such as electricity, good roads, and medical services. Even non-teaching staff was hard to recruit, and worker morale was low. Few citizens saw the need for secondary schools, so both diocesan and government funding for such schools was scarce.[99]

Although the problems were familiar to the CDP missionaries, the daily school schedule and its physical conditions were not. Divided into three semesters, classes were held for 40 weeks of the year, beginning at 7:15 a.m. Some of the students came with poor English language skills. Sister Janet Griffin spent two months as a visiting teacher in KBK in the summer of 1997 and noted that the students "work very hard with limited resources. We had only a blackboard; chalk and paper were scarce. The poverty is unbelievable; I was inspired by the people's quest to survive in spite of all their difficulties."[100] Nevertheless, OLP School ranked fourth among 56 Ghanaian Schools in the Brong Ahafo region whose students took the national certification exam in 1999.

Besides learning the native language, Twi, a dialect of Akan, the Sisters from Texas had to adjust to different weather, food, and neighbors (both human and animal, including troublesome insects) as well as to the British system of education. Everyone carried a tea towel or large handkerchief to wipe away perspiration during the hot season. The school had no electricity when the Sisters arrived. They had to carry water from a well, a borehole topped by a pump, some distance away in their compound. They also collected water in cisterns during the annual rainy season to tide them over the hot, dry season. The Sisters did more than endure these conditions or take them in stride. They considered it "a privilege to work with the people and be invited into their lives,"[101] and the benefits far outweighed the hardships. Sister Frances Lorene concluded:

> Getting to know another people, relating to them, and enjoying them brings many blessings and learnings. I have found that to live among the people in Ghana is to experience in actuality our charism. It seems that they innately trust in Providence; for them, God is always present. They learn this from childhood on. After experiencing their deep faith, I feel called to live even

---

[99] From answers by CDPs in Kwasibuokrom to a questionnaire from the Sunyani diocese, 27 June 1997, CDPA.

[100] "Lake Currents," XIX, 1 (8 Sept. 1997), OLLUA.

[101] Sister Frances Lorene Lange, videotaped interview, CDPA.

more radically this trust in a provident God. . . . Their simple lifestyle speaks loudly to our fundamental virtue of simplicity. Their simple life holds a freedom and a joy that we in the U.S. can't even understand.[102]

Sister Frances Lorene felt great love and respect from the Ghanaians who sometimes called her their "grandmother," a title of great honor in a country where only 8% of the population is over 65. Ghanaian friendliness and hospitality are legendary.

Sister Frances Lorene was not only a teacher but also the overseer of the seamstresses who sewed the pupils' uniforms. She was "the compound's first aid station" as well as an architect. Somewhat to her own surprise, Sister succeeded in drawing up plans for a new home economics building and had the satisfaction of having them accepted and developed by government officials. Whoever responds to a call from God attests to an experience of divine power working in human weakness. Sister Frances Lorene said,

> I don't feel worthy to carry such a gift of God. I pray that I can carry it to others. That particular splendor of God's self-manifestation to humanity must continue. God works through all of us wounded healers. No matter how scarred the situation, God works with it. I'm handicapped, disabled, physically limited. This is my "thorn in the flesh." Others have drawbacks such as divorced parents or physical abuse as a child. But God is the primary healer, and we are instruments of healing for one another.[103]

The Sisters in Ghana were fascinated by the lively African Eucharistic celebrations, which lasted three or four hours and took on "a rich cultural, colorful character with drumming, singing, dancing, and traditional dress." Both former Sister Mary Catherine and Sister Frances Lorene found that their own faith was greatly strengthened by participating in such ceremonies as well as through communicating their religious beliefs, even in taxing conditions, to people from another culture.

Sister Frances Lorene mused

> What difference has it made to the Congregation that some of us were in Ghana? For myself, I see that we the community have expanded our vision of the world. We have embraced another part of the world. When the word "Ghana" appears on a newscast or in a newspaper,

---

[102] *Movements*, 4, 2 (Spring/Summer 2001): 20, CDPA.

[103] Videotaped interview, CDPA.

we say "Ah!" Sisters living in the U.S. tell me that they will never again take a shower without thanking God for running water. Or when the electricity unexpectedly goes off, they say to each other, "Just remember Ghana." Something is happening among us, little though it might be. Somehow we are all in Ghana. If one of us is somewhere, we are all there.[104]

Sister Lourdes Leal thought that "the experience of these Sisters in Africa challenges us to live simply and to share what we have. Their presence in another country inspires us to live like missioners here and to be conscious that there is more in life than the daily problems we encounter."[105]

Former Sister Mary Catherine Griffin returned to the U.S. in 1999. Sister Frances Lorene continued at OLPS until the Sisters from Kentucky relinquished it to the Congregation of Jesus, Mary, and Joseph from the Netherlands in November 2000. She then spent seven months sharing her experience by giving spiritual direction and helping in the formation of native leaders at St. Joseph Retreat Center in the city of Sunyani.[106]

Even though CDPs no longer live in Ghana, the Congregation's support for the Church in this African country continued in the form of supplying room and board for Sister Martha Mabel Anobaa, SMMC, a native of Ghana who was recommended by the Conference of Major Superiors of Ghana. Sister Martha received a full-tuition scholarship for an MA in Counseling from OLLU and planned to serve at a counseling center in Ghana after graduation.[107]

Missionaries at Home

Sister Ida Marie Deville also felt a strong call to missionary service, but she chose a mission on U.S. soil, St. Vincent Mission in the town of David, Martin County, in the Appalachian region of Kentucky.[108] At an age when many people retire, she began visiting the remote "hollers," organizing craft outlets and thrift

---

[104] Oral interview, 1 July 1999, CDPA.

[105] "Hermanas de la Divina Providencia en ultramar," *Revista Maryknoll*, marzo 1997: 25, translated by Sister Sharon García, CDP, of San Antonio.

[106] Sister María Cristina Quiñonez, who taught Spanish at OLLU, went to Brazil and taught English in the state of Minhas Gerais before she left the Congregation in 1999. She considered her classes to be means by which many Brazilians could rise out of poverty.

[107] *Signs of Providence*, 6, 5 (May 2002): 6, CDPA.

[108] St. Pius X Parish in Tulsa, Oklahoma, generously subsidized Sister Ida Marie as well as Sister Marcella Marie Frazier (GC minutes, 6-10 April 1992, CDPA).

shops as well as helping the people fill out necessary forms for medical and social services. When she "retired" to Louisiana two decades later, she continued her missionary services.

> I have started a new program called Providence Mission, which includes a food pantry in St. Augustine Catholic Church in Isle Brevelle, Louisiana, and one at the First Baptist Mission in Natchez. I generated funds to buy the food from people in the local area and donors outside the state. At Thanksgiving we had 30 boxes to distribute. It was only after that first Thanksgiving that I really got accepted by the African American people of the area. They trusted me because I fed them. By Christmas they accepted me enough to invite me to be one of the speakers in their church. I also generated enough money to support 15 senior families with 50 pounds of food a month. This can be done for $100 a year for each family.[109]

She and her helper of many years, Sister Marcella Marie Frazier, knew they did not have to preach much with words as long as people saw their deeds. They "worked very closely with their CDP Associates to get them involved in prayer life, in discussions, and in work for other people in the community. We repair houses, especially by building handicap ramps, new porches, and new roofs. While the men repair, the women prepare their noonday meal." Sister Ida Marie also planned "in the future to bring in some volunteers from other states, perhaps some of my friends from Wisconsin."[110]

Sisters Ayleson and Bertina Maxwell also served in the home mission field where clergy were unable to be present and Roman Catholics were few. Sister Ayleson came to Noel, Missouri, in 1990 and with characteristic style, grace, and energy plunged into meeting the needs of her new community. She was the only active Church representative in McDonald County, Missouri. Despite her parish commitments, she still found time to offer her personal talents to serve others. The poultry processing plants operating around the city created a demand for labor that was filled by migrants, mostly from Texas and Mexico. Sister served as translator for them as well as for social agencies, law enforcement authorities, and the medical community. Two or three people came to her door every day for counseling or help with rent or utility bills or food needs. She depended upon the generosity of Catholic Extension's Mission Partners to continue her work.[111]

---

[109] Oral interview, 20 June 2000, CDPA.

[110] Sister Ida Marie Deville, oral interview, 20 June 2000, CDPA.

[111] "Mission Partner Update" *Catholic Extension Society*, reproduced in *Signs of Providence*, 6, 2, (Nov. 2001): 4.

Similarly, Sister Rose Ann Blair found she did not have to leave the U.S. to preach the Gospel to marginalized people. During her parish ministry in Missouri in the 1980s, she discovered multiple needs of the rural poor. Many of the people did not know how to read or write. Undocumented Hispanics from Central and South America were coming to work in the maize and corn fields. In addition to helping them find food and housing, she assisted them with their immigration papers. She stated, "I love working with the poor. They have a special place in my heart. I was able to stand with them and help them come to the realization that they are beautiful and have many gifts to offer. I tried to empower them, to instill in them the belief that they could do anything they wanted to do. They became more involved in the parish."[112]

While the Sisters who volunteered for Africa followed a planned discernment process, sometimes Sisters found themselves to be missionaries even though they did not intentionally seek this role. Sister Deborah Ann Fuchs, a nurse-midwife at Trinity Mother Frances Hospital in Tyler, Texas, in 1995 said, "What we didn't know when we went to Tyler, Texas, is that it is missionary country, I think, as much as Mexico, Ghana, and the rest of the distant places we've gone. The theology of this place is pre-Vatican II, and it's a very inbred community where strangers are not well accepted." The Sisters concluded that "we were led into missionary country by the Spirit without even realizing that is what we were doing at the time."[113]

Taking the Good News of the Gospel to people different from themselves has been an enriching experience for all the Sisters, even those who "stayed at home." Sister Frances Lorene thought that "as a Congregation we have gained a sense of completeness and humility through our multi-cultural ministries. No matter the skin-hue, language, or cultural pattern, each human being is a beautiful creation, each an expression of love to be reverenced, each an enhancement of and gift to others."[114]

Guidance, Formal and Informal

Counseling offered by a religious can also be considered a form of faith sharing since often its purpose is to build up another's faith and hope. Every teacher does

---

[112] Oral interview, 19 June 2000, CDPA. In the late 1980s Sister Rose Ann had the unfortunate, traumatic experience of realizing that a pastor was abusing children. When she told the bishop, the pastor threatened her life. The parishioners publicly told the pastor of their concern for their children and for his health. Instead of receiving help, he was sent to another parish (oral interview, 19 June 2000, CDPA).

[113] Oral interview, 23 June 2000, CDPA.

[114] *Movements*, 4, 2 (Spring/Summer 2001): 17, CDPA.

some form of academic counseling; and if she shows interest in the lives of her students, she might be called on to do some psychological counseling as well. Some, like Sister Adrienne Marie Schmidtzinsky, had the title of guidance counselor. Sister Catherine Walker was lauded by many former students as the founder and sustainer of the counseling department at OLLU. She herself derived particular satisfaction from aiding priests of the archdiocese of San Antonio to obtain counseling degrees at the time they were in difficulties with the archbishop.[115] Sister Blandina Paul set up the counseling office at Teurlings High School in Lafayette, Louisiana, and drew up policies for it. She was also a counselor at Xavier Preparatory High School, an all-Black girls' school in New Orleans.[116]

Sister Mary Martin Haidusek, who had an MA in psychology and counseling, enrolled in CPE night classes after she became semi-retired in 1988. For 14 years she spent every Thursday as a chaplain and counselor in the University Hospital System in San Antonio. She

> used to help Dr. John Sharp, the psychiatrist at the jail. He would consult with me before he sent me a prisoner for counseling. It was almost like confession. All they really wanted was to tell their stories, and the most important thing was to listen to them. We would pray together to ask God's forgiveness. I would give them a word of encouragement and ask them to be sensitive to the crime they had committed.[117]

She also counseled pre-operational patients, AIDS patients, and those who were terminally ill. She worked with drug addicts and suicidal teenagers and also baptized babies.[118]

Sister Karen Kudlac undertook doctoral studies after working as a family counselor. "One of the reasons I went to get the degree in counseling," she said, "was that I was noticing more and more teenagers becoming pregnant, and that concerned me. I felt we were raising this entire society of children who had basically only one parent." In Port Neches, Texas, she also dealt with family crises due to marriage problems or divorces as well as with many custody-type battles.[119]

---

[115] In September 1968, 51 priests of the San Antonio archdiocese sent a letter to Pope Paul VI asking for the removal of Archbishop Lucey. The Archbishop removed some of them from their positions before he retired in 1969 (Privett, *The Pastoral Vision* 22).

[116] Sister Blandina Paul, oral interview, 26 June 2000, CDPA.

[117] Oral interview, 22 Feb. 2000, CDPA.

[118] Kenneth Redmond, "Ladies of the Lake," p. 18, OLLUA.

[119] Sister Karen Kudlac, oral interview, 14 June 2000, CDPA. Sister went on to say that divorce was almost the norm. Her eight-year-old nephew told his mother he wished his parents were divorced so he could go away to visit his daddy on

Sisters who were social workers did counseling; and Sisters María Guerra, Margaret Clare Mathews, and Sharon Rohde served as bereavement counselors. All of these Sisters found the trust of their clients to be both rewarding and humbling; they considered the time spent listening to their stories to be sacred time.[120]

The ministry of spiritual counseling or spiritual direction became more formalized in the past 30 years, partly as a result of the popularity of directed retreats. Sister Charlene Wedelich articulated the satisfaction of "working with people to cultivate a relationship with God as friend or God as lover. It is so life-giving and energizing to listen to God in other people. It is a real grace to see how God leads."[121]

Some Sisters counseled others without having the title of counselor. Two can serve as examples that neither age nor physical infirmity is an obstacle for someone who wants to share with others her belief in a loving God whose Provident care is always available. One used her pen and another used her confinement to access others' deeper spiritual needs and desires. Sister Dolores Cárdenas, the first CDP whose native language was Spanish, began to write a weekly meditation column for *El Sol*, a Houston newspaper, and continued to utilize this way of inspiring people during her retirement until her death at age 100 in 1991. At age 25 Sister Victor Valek was preparing to leave her work in the OLL laundry to begin studies to become a teacher when she was diagnosed with an inoperable tumor on her neck. For 21 years she was unable to leave her bed, but this did not block her access to people in need. A steady stream of visitors came to ask for her prayers and often her advice. No one left this invalid's room without feeling spiritually nourished.

Teaching, administering programs, visiting the sick, sharing Scripture reflections, counseling, and training leaders are some important ways to evangelize or impart the Good News; but there are countless other ways as well. Listening to the Spirit, which blows where it will, and discerning the Spirit's movement in everyday situations is indispensable for faith sharing. In their professional as well as in their personal lives, Sisters of Divine Providence have grown more adept, especially over the past 30 years, at detecting and articulating God's invitations and helping others detect the divine presence in their lives.

---

weekends like his friends did.

[120] Group interview of counselors, 18 June 2001, CDPA.

[121] Sister Charlene Wedelich, oral interview, 9 May 2000, CDPA.

CHAPTER 7

SHOWING COMPASSION IN HEALTH CARE

Although their founder had urged the first Sisters to care for the sick, they concentrated on teaching both in Europe and in the New World. Health care became an acknowledged and publicized apostolate of the Texas CDP in 1940 due to several factors. The Congregation received a woman in her 30's, the future Sister Annella Foelker, who was a registered nurse; and some Sisters showed talent for nursing. A greater variety in apostolates seemed desirable as the Congregation grew in numbers.

Taking over a small financially strapped clinic that grew into a hospital was the first of many financial outlays for buildings in several Texas communities. Besides providing training for Sisters to become nurses, technicians, dieticians, and housekeepers, the Congregation during the next few decades sent Sisters Thérèse Pousson, Amata Regan, Huberta Gallatin, Lydia Leehan, and Laverne Mettlach for studies in hospital administration. The boom was short-lived, however. After flourishing in the 1950s and 1960s, both of the Congregation's hospitals closed by 1974; and its clinics closed within the next two decades.[1] In this field, as well as in education and social service, the legacy of the spirit of Providential care lives on in the Sisters' co-workers, patients, clients, and students.

Why did a teaching Congregation go into health care? The answer in essence is because of a need no one else was filling and Sisters willing to fill it. According to the ethos of the Congregation, opportunities to serve and personnel able

---

[1] Reasons for the closures will be discussed later. McCullough Hall was the Congregation's only sponsored health care facility in 2000.

to respond were signs of a call, and such calls had to be pursued to test their genuineness.[2]

Sisters willing and able to "learn on the job" were necessary as the Congregation entered a new apostolate. Sisters had to manifest some aptitude before they were released for training that would be expensive and lengthy. Usually the testing ground was the convent infirmary. Sister Genevieve recalled how she began her ministry of compassionate care that lasted over 40 years. "I loved health care, and when I was a candidate and postulant they sent me to St. Joseph's Hall. I helped give baths in the infirmary to the retired Sisters. I helped Sister Electa Schlueter downstairs in the pharmacy. We also helped give out the trays in the halls."[3] To go from this step to hospital duty without going through formal training demanded not only natural talent but intelligence, energy, and a good amount of courage and daring. That the Sisters learned fast and performed well is proved by the fact that the hospitals quickly and easily passed inspections by the American Medical Association and other certification groups.

When Sister Genevieve received her first assignment to a hospital, she learned all about the laboratory and x-ray department by watching the lay technicians, reading manuals, and practicing when she was not on duty. Later she passed the examination for registry and went on to train at least four other persons who became registered x-ray technicians.[4]

Sister Geraldine Theresa (Aloysius Gonzaga) Bourg also "learned everything first hand." After serving five years in the convent infirmary, she went to St. Ann Hospital in Abilene, Texas. "Late at night when we weren't busy, Sister Joachim would go into surgery, open up the big set used for laparotomy, and have me name all the instruments. She also taught me how to run the big steam autoclave." While this preparation for nursing in the operating room was going on, Sister Geraldine was also learning about other departments. "Sister Yvonne bought me a book on obstetrics that I learned by heart. I would go with her when a patient came in during labor and stay through all the stages to delivery and post-delivery. So I had wonderful opportunities few nurses have."[5]

---

[2] Father Moye advised the first Sisters to be concerned about their neighbors who were ill. "Let your immediate concern be for the sick. Go and console them, encourage and relieve them. Render them all kinds of services. Try to be present at deathbeds," *Directory*, 98-99.

[3] Sister Genevieve Prochaska, oral interview, 15 Sept. 2000, CDPA.

[4] Oral interview, 15 Sept. 2000, CDPA. Sister Alice Spies is an example of Sisters who discovered that care for the sick did not suit their natural disposition. "I was going to go into nursing, and the first year out of the novitiate I worked in St. Joseph's Hall. Then during the summer I went to relieve Sisters in Abilene and was put on night duty with the infants. I missed all the community life, so I asked to come back. I did, and the next year I went into teaching" (oral interview, 13 June 2000, CDPA).

[5] Sister Geraldine Theresa Bourg, oral interview, 15 May 2000, CDPA.

Later the Sisters who served in hospitals received their training before their assignments. Two Sisters explained how in those days it involved bridging two worlds. Sister Lydia Leehan, who had worked in a hospital x-ray department before she entered the convent, and Sister Bernadette (Mary Cabrini) Phillipp had to blend their training as laboratory technicians at a secular institution, Nix Hospital in downtown San Antonio, with a lifestyle replete with Catholic convent traditions and practices. In the early 1950s they had to wear a floor-length black wool cloak over their white uniform when traveling to and from the hospital because this would be sure to identify them as religious. They mixed freely with the lay personnel while working, but taking food with them would have violated the Constitutions; so they had to eat their lunch "in the cloakroom in the hospital basement. There were cages of rabbits for pregnancy tests, people's old shoes, and all kinds of things in that cloakroom." Their daily lunch consisted of "a sandwich made by the convent dietary department, a piece of fruit, and a canister of coffee in a thermos." Mother Eugenia Kaiser, superior of the Motherhouse, was sensitive to the incongruity of the arrangement and tried to make it more bearable. She gave them "a roll of nickels so we could have a coke every day."[6]

Hospitals

The Congregation seized the opportunity in 1940 to buy the 18-bed DeBerry Clinic in Abilene, Texas, and re-name it St. Ann's Hospital. Work began to renovate and enlarge the buildings while Sisters were selected to study. Sister M. DeLellis Kasberg and Sister Mary Joachim Geagan went to Providence Hospital in Waco, Texas, for a three-year nursing course. Sister Jane Frances Meis was sent for an eight-month course of studies in anesthesia at St. John's Hospital in Springfield, Illinois. When Sister Sarah Kainer took charge of the hospital kitchen, she was sent to St. Louis, Missouri, for dieticians' workshops which also included units on psychology.[7]

When St. Ann's Hospital first opened, "there were at times so many infants that dresser drawers served as bassinets. Patient beds were in halls. However, the Gray Ladies and the Auxiliary helped by making bands, binders, and bandages, and by providing nursery accessories and bed linens."[8] Each employee had to be focused as well as versatile. Busy employees and crowded conditions did

---

[6] Sister Lydia Leehan, oral interview, 8 July 2000, CDPA.

[7] Oral interview, 19 May 2000, CDPA.

[8] *Memoirs*, I, 1, CDPA. St. Ann's was "known for the special care that premature babies got and how many survived. We had quite a record on that" (Sister Geraldine Bourg, oral interview, 15 May 2000, CDPA).

not, however, indicate sub-standard care. The hospital was approved by the American Medical Association and the American College of Surgeons in its first year of operation. By 1950 it had admitted 12,971 patients of whom 97% were Protestant and 3% were Catholic. During the next ten years it admitted 24,065 patients of whom 87% were Protestant and 13% were Catholic.[9] Although St. Ann's was still a small hospital of about 40 beds, by 1959 "the Sisters had such a good reputation for giving wonderful care that the people loved St. Ann Hospital. The doctors were really very happy to practice there. The hospital was booming, and the occupancy rate was high."[10]

Besides much personal attention, patients as well as doctors appreciated the power of the Sisters' prayers. Sister Genevieve Prochaska recalled a very good doctor, who also had a temper.

> Once he was in surgery trying to remove a stone from a patient. He was having a hard time and getting edgy, and the nurses were too. I was there to take an x-ray, and he turned to me and said, "Sister, are you praying?" I replied, "Yes." "Well, what are you praying for?" Spontaneously, I said "First that you calm down, and then that you get the stone out." In a few minutes he got the stone out. Speaking to the patient's family later, he even gave me credit; and later when he left Abilene he called to thank me for "keeping him on the straight and narrow path."[11]

Although doctors or patients might not have been able to articulate it, the ministry dimension of their care was never far from the Sisters' minds. As Sister Barbara Lynn Hyzak expressed it, "In the midst of all the technological and medical advances, perhaps the most effective 'medicine' health care professionals can offer to their patients is compassion and understanding."[12]

Appreciation of the Sisters' dedicated, compassionate care in Abilene motivated the Congregation to consider an offer to take over the city hospital in Denison, Texas, established in 1913.[13] The initial appeal came in 1943 from Rev. T. S. Zachary, a pastor in the city and OLLU alumnus, who had once been a faculty member at St. Joseph's, the Congregation's high school in Abilene, Texas. A bond issue proposal failed, and an appeal to the Federal Works Agency was refused. The city council then offered the hospital, along with $10,000 to assist

[9] "News Flashes," First Edition, 1961: 1, CDPA.

[10] Sister Madonna Sangalli, oral interview, 9 Sept. 2000, CDPA.

[11] Oral interview, 9 Sept. 2000, CDPA.

[12] *Movements* Fall/Winter 2000:23.

[13] Material for this section is from *Memoirs*, I, 63-82, CDPA.

in its renovation, to the Sisters of Divine Providence. The Congregation actually spent more than $175,000 before it opened as 45-bed Madonna Hospital in 1945.[14] During its first year of operation, 3,054 patients received care, and 489 babies were born. Thirty infants and 23 adults were baptized.[15]

In 1951 the first of several new buildings was added to Madonna Hospital. Five years later the local paper paid tribute to the hospital during National Hospital Week.

> Another milestone has been reached by the Sisters of Divine Providence, a community young in the hospital sphere but remarkably efficient in the performance of the spiritual and corporal works of mercy as taught and commanded by the Divine Founder of Christianity, Jesus Christ.
>
> At Madonna alongside the best in physical care is found an absolutely essential adjunct, the pervading influence and fragrance of Christian charity under whose inspiration the Catholic Hospital originated and without which it must necessarily disintegrate.[16]

Madonna Hospital opened a school for Licensed Vocational Nurse Training in 1958. Sister Lydia Leehan, who was also vice-president of the Texas Catholic Hospital Association, started the school; and Sister Sylvan Durbin was the main instructor from 1960 to 1964. Sister Sylvan recalled, "We had good students. We never had any failures when they took their state boards, and every year one in my class was one of the top ten in Texas."[17] In 1965 the school was incorporated into Grayson County Junior College. Among the Sisters who worked in the supplies and dietetic departments was Sister Rita (Daniel) Fritz, who said she enjoyed her ministry of cooking for the Sisters. "I have to say, though, that it was a little more fun when `diet concerns' were not so common and `cholesterol' was unknown. Seriously, though, I liked helping the Sisters this way. They should concentrate on their own work and not have to be worrying about preparing their meals."[18] Sister Josephine Marie Pape did all the printing for Madonna Hospital.

---

[14] The Congregation asked for an indult to borrow $60,000, anticipating the hospital would cost $92,000 (GC minutes, 12 Oct.1944, CDPA). The annex built in 1951 cost $90,000, and a new rectory built in 1959 cost $14,000.

[15] FC, March, 1947:156, CDPA.

[16] *Denison-Herald,* 11 May 1956, CDPA.

[17] Oral interview, 6 June 2000, CDPA. Always on the night shift, Sister Sylvan also nursed later at the Railroad Hospital and the King's Daughter's Hospital in Temple, Texas; Presbyterian Hospital and Walnut Place in Dallas, Texas; and Ferris Nursing Care Center in Ferris, Texas.

[18] *CDP Times,* 16, 3 (Nov. 1995): 10, CDPA.

Nine CDPs were assigned to this hospital in 1961, and by 1969 five young Sisters were student nurses. But the doctors' desire for greater independence as well as increased specialization in medical institutions everywhere threatened the continuation of Madonna Hospital. Also, the Sister-nurses preferred to work in a larger hospital which could offer them opportunities for broader nursing practice.[19] In 1973 the General Council became aware that to remain effective Madonna Hospital would either have to construct a new building and remain a general hospital or become a specialized hospital. Neither alternative was feasible, so a year later they sold it for $400,000.

Despite their busy schedules, the Sisters found time for works of charity outside the hospital. Sister Bernadette Phillipp recalled that one administrator,

> Sister Huberta Gallatin, was very innovative and was really a model for me. When she visited the patients, she became aware of a young family with many children, including twins. She got to know them; and in the evenings she would go out to their home, bathe the twins, and be with them just so the parents could have some time off. Even today her example influences my life. I feel very comfortable now just seeing the needs of other people and giving them a break.[20]

Thanks to Sister Huberta's example, some of the Sisters began to conduct Bible classes for adults. Sisters Geraldine Bourg, Mary Lin Koesler, and Marie de Chantal Doebel visited needy families and did some home nursing. Sisters Bernadette Phillipp and Aline Hrncir worked with the CYO and CCD in the parish as well as at nearby Perrin Air Force Base.[21]

The third hospital staffed by the Sisters was leased rather than owned by the Congregation. After several years of negotiations, the Congregation agreed to staff the new 29-bed Floresville Memorial Hospital, the only hospital in Wilson County just south of San Antonio. Groups from all religious denominations in the town raised funds and donated furnishings. Bishop Stephen A. Leven dedicated the facility on 10 April 1960, and an emergency surgery was performed that very evening.[22]

Although the hospital was small, the number of Sisters staffing it was relatively large, often 12 to 17. Sister Barbara Lynn Hyzak recalled:

[19] GC minutes, 27 Feb.1973 and 3 Apr. 1973, CDPA.

[20] Sister Bernadette Phillipp, oral interview, 30 Oct. 2000, CDPA.

[21] "CDP News Bulletin," Northern Region, Jan, 1969: 7, CDPA.

[22] Memoirs, I, 113-116, CDPA.

> It was a good experience, and community life was very enjoyable. The standards were high; and we had very good relationships with the physicians, nursing staff, and administration as well as the surrounding community. They really appreciated having this hospital. The difficult thing for us young ones was having to take call and take whatever came along. We learned to cover all areas and in a few years were supposed to be able to be in charge.[23]

Sister Daria Rush found in this atmosphere an outlet for her zeal even after she retired. "I feel that my mission in Floresville was to the employees and patients. I served as a sort of spiritual guide, and I stay in touch with many former employees."[24]

Lay employees at this hospital appreciated their training and mentoring by the Sisters, who also instilled values and "respect for each other." They worked together united as a team and "never felt threatened." Shirley Brenek, an employee for over 30 years, remembered consistent encouragement from the Sisters who would say, "Keep it up! You can do it." She was confident "I would always have a job if I did my job well." The Sisters "would never ask us to do anything they themselves wouldn't do." As a result, the employees felt a personal interest in the hospital. When the census was down, they would voluntarily "wash walls or scrape wax buildup so it would look nice."[25] Armando Castellanos in his 29th year of service in this hospital said, "I stayed here because of the Sisters whom I admired. They were so giving; they worked for next to nothing and always gave extra care. They prayed with us before every function and taught mostly by their deeds, not words." He especially liked the fact that the Floresville hospital was "a family even more than a team. Everyone was on a first-name basis, and we knew one another's families. We had pot-luck dinners and played volleyball with the Sisters."[26]

Sister Laverne Mettlach, the first woman to graduate from the hospital administration program at Trinity University in San Antonio, was the administrator of the Floresville Hospital from 1969 to 1983. She appreciated the Sisters' reliability and commitment to excellence. "There was a Sister in charge of every department except maintenance. They knew what they were doing, and they did it well." Because they were able to respond quickly and

---

[23] Oral interview, 18 Jan. 2001, CDPA. After 20 years as a nurse, Sister Barbara Lynn studied to become a nurse practitioner and valued being able "to retain my autonomy as a registered nurse but also have the luxury of being one-to-one with patients."

[24] Oral interview, 14 Nov. 2000, CDPA.

[25] Shirley Brenek, oral interview, 4 Aug. 2004, CDPA.

[26] Oral interview, 4 Aug. 2004, CDPA.

efficiently at any time, she was free to pursue some of her interests, including starting ambulance service.

> I love anything mechanical, and I was free to supervise some construction. I also worked in the health care section of AACOG (Alamo Area Council of Governments), which had jurisdiction over our county and 11 neighboring counties. I lacked just a few hours from being a paramedic in the EMS system. Frequently I rode out on ambulances as a volunteer. I usually took weekend shifts. Unlike the nurses in San Antonio, we were also allowed to ride with firemen on fire trucks.[27]

Sister Laverne found that women were the majority on her volunteer squad. While the men volunteers were at their regular work during the day, the women staffed the ambulances. "Whoever was the most trained would take care of the patient, and the lesser trained would do the driving. When we were on call, we would carry a big monitor with a loud beep. I used to pray that it would not go off during Mass when I took it to church."[28]

Sister Laverne also became an associate professor at the University of Texas Health Science Center because she taught students from that center who were rotating in the Floresville Hospital to earn credit in rural health nursing. Residents from this center also received credit for rural health as family physicians by rotating through the hospital. Their presence raised the level of health care for the entire community.[29] The hospital also cooperated in training programs at nearby airbases by using MATS (Military Assistance to Traffic and Safety) helicopters and crews to transport its patients to San Antonio hospitals before those hospitals started to offer their own service called Air-life.[30]

The Congregation considered staffing a fourth hospital in Edinburg, Texas. Sisters Thérèse Pousson, Aline Hrncir, Marie Antoine (Jo Marie) Toudouze, and former Sister Sylvia (Ann William) Cárdenas worked in this 50-bed hospital from 1965 to 1966. They discovered a great need to renovate and update, for example, the surgical suite; but elected officials told them no funds were available. The Sisters realized it would be necessary to work with local politicians. Having neither preparation nor taste for this type of "political organizing," they left without signing a contract with the county. They informed Rev. John J. Lazarsky, OMI, of additional reasons for declining

---

[27] Oral interview, 13 June 2000, CDPA.

[28] Oral interview, 13 June 2000, CDPA.

[29] Sister Laverne Mettlach, oral interview, 13 June 2000, CDPA.

[30] Armando Castellanos, oral interview, 4 Aug. 2005, CDPA.

to locate in Edinburg: "our lack of Sister personnel and our inability to secure lay personnel in small towns."[31]

Sister Bernadette Phillipp spent years in the Congregation's hospitals as a medical technologist. She loved the Sisters' communities and the ministry but voiced a regret shared by other Sisters in health care ministry:

> In the summer we would come home for a retreat, but it was usually a silent retreat, so we weren't able to talk much. We liked coming home, but we always felt left out. We didn't know what was going on. The teachers got to spend about two months at home, and we got only a week. That didn't allow us to take part in activities at the convent. We didn't get to know the Sisters very well.[32]

Sister Lydia Leehan added that Sisters who worked in hospitals "also got assigned to give a certain number of bed baths in St. Joseph Hall when they were in San Antonio, so retreat was certainly not a relief or a vacation."[33]

During the school year, Sister Bernadette said, "the hospital Sisters were always on call, and they were working on the holidays so that the lay people could be off. I never knew what Saturday and Sunday could mean until years later because those were always workdays during my life in the hospital." Sister Bernadette appreciated the fact that the Congregation allowed for diversity in ministry, but she sometimes felt that she was known and appreciated more for her work than for who she was as a person. In hindsight, Sisters in other ministries besides health care would agree with her assessment.

> I was always "a Sister at Madonna Hospital." After we sold it, I had to find out that I was Sister Bernadette. That was happening to many of us when we no longer had our institutions. I had lived in an institution all of my religious life, and suddenly it was no longer there. But releasing our institutions was the greatest thing that ever happened personally for my own growth.[34]

---

[31] GC minutes, 29 Oct. 1963, CDPA. The Congregation also turned down offers to take over Houston East Community Hospital (GC minutes, 18 July 1964, CDPA), a hospital in Longview, Texas (GC minutes, 24 Nov. 1965, CDPA), and the proposed Hondo Memorial Hospital (GC minutes, 4 Nov. 1961, CDPA). Sisters continued to work in hospitals not owned by the Congregation. Sisters Leola Ann Doerfler and Mary Elizabeth Jupe after teaching home economics in high schools became registered dieticians and worked with dietary staffs in various hospitals.

[32] Oral interview, 30 Oct. 2000, CDPA.

[33] Oral interview, 8 July 2000, CDPA.

[34] Oral interview, 30 Oct. 2000, CDPA.

She described her "spiritual awakening," which was experienced by a number of other Sisters in the 1960s and 1970s, as "messy and terrible, but I knew I didn't want to leave the Congregation."[35] She went on to work in the area of holistic health and alternative health care. In 2002-2003 under the auspices of the International Association of Human Values Foundation, an NGO (non-governmental organization) member of the United Nations, Sister Bernadette served the poor in Bangalore, India.[36] The group engaged in service and education projects related to home health, hygiene, human values, and harmony in diversity. Sister Bernadette learned that

> religion and spirituality in some cases are not as foreign to these people as they are to many Westerners. Almost everyone knows the wisdom books of all religions and can tell you the meaning of names, events, and more. They know many languages. I feel very poor in this respect in comparison with them.[37]

After the CDP hospitals were closed, some Sisters found sharing faith with the sick, both children and adults, a rewarding ministry. After developing a package on spiritual care for patients of different denominations discharged from a hospital, Sister Rose Ann Blair became a hospital chaplain at Christus St. Patrick's Hospital in Lake Charles, Louisiana. A number of Sisters successfully completed units of Clinical Pastoral Education (CPE). Sister Bernadette Bezner served as a CPE instructor as well as a prison and hospital chaplain.[38] She recalled her year of residency at Children's Medical Center in Dallas in 1985. "It was very, very strenuous and tough because we would do calls at Parkland, a thousand-bed trauma unit, as well. We would see six patients a night and take bodies to the morgue, tag the toes, and take care of the entire chart. I attended 52 deaths of little children that year."[39]

When the Congregation no longer had its own institutions to staff, Sisters felt even more free to develop their talents and inclinations without having to ask how they would fit into existing structures. Concomitantly they acquired the task of representing the Congregation and its mission as individuals without the visible support of a community of co-laborers. They illustrated the trend in all ministries of the Congregation to move into public ministries where they

---

[35] Oral interview, 30 Oct. 2000, CDPA.

[36] *Signs of Providence*, 7, 1: 13, CDPA.

[37] Sister Bernadette Phillipp, e-mail to Sister Margit Maria Nagy, Jan. 2003.

[38] Sister Sharon Rohde founded a group for separated, divorced, and widowed persons in Tulsa, Oklahoma, before she entered the Congregation. Sister Martha Anne Hunter was one of her helpers.

[39] Sister Bernadette Bezner, oral interview, 17 Sept. 2000, CDPA.

collaborated with other religious or lay groups.[40] In the process they became more aware of their own gifts as well as their deficiencies or deprivations.

Stella Maris Clinic, San Antonio, Texas

At the same time the Sisters staffed hospitals, the Congregation had personnel in two clinics serving predominantly low income Mexican Americans as well as Mexican immigrants: Stella Maris Clinic in San Antonio, Texas, and Guadalupe Clinic in Rosenberg, Texas. When the MCDPs began to catechize in the Las Colonias neighborhood on the west side of San Antonio, they discovered that the families, largely migrants who worked on the fertile farms owned by Belgians, had multiple medical needs. These people were isolated because there were no stores or public transportation in the vicinity. The low salaries earned by the men did not reach far enough to provide for their children. There was no pavement on the streets and no running water inside the crowded shacks. Infant mortality among Hispanics on the west side was 500% higher than among non-Hispanics.[41] Babies died of diarrhea because of improper food; mothers had no way to get pre-natal care. Colds and influenza spread easily because of unsanitary conditions and because the people had never been told to cover their mouths when they sneezed. There were cases of smallpox as well as tuberculosis, influenza, and hepatitis. Mother Angelique responded to their request for help by selecting Sister Nelda González, a teacher at San Fernando School in San Antonio, to study nursing at the Catholic University of America in Washington, D.C. In addition to earning an RN degree *cum laude*, Sister did specialized studies in psychiatry and field work at Seton Institute in Washington, D.C.[42]

When Sister Nelda returned from her studies in 1951, she used to walk more than two miles from the Motherhouse to the clinic on Castroville Road, which originally consisted of one big room and one chair. She admitted that kind people frequently offered her a ride. "I had to go out and find the people. I could not expect them to come. They couldn't walk with those babies, especially when it rained and got muddy. Even when I got a car, every time it rained I had to get somebody to pull me out because it would get stuck."[43] Miss Marguerite Higgins, a retired anesthesiologist living at OLLU, gave her car to Sister Nelda, who could then transport supplies as well as people. Pinning her starched coronet as far back on her head as she could in order to have unobstructed peripheral

---

[40] GC minutes, 5 April 1983, CDPA.

[41] Privett, *The Pastoral Vision* 79.

[42] *San Antonio Light*, 26 July 1989.

[43] Oral interview by Irma González, 1989, CDPA. Much of the material in this section is taken from this interview.

vision, Sister left the Motherhouse early each morning and usually returned late at night.

> They always needed everything, and I even brought them food. I got milk for the babies and showed the mothers how to feed and bathe them. It was troublesome because I had to heat water on their little stoves before I could bathe the babies.
>
> Two [MCDP] Catechists helped me teach basic hygiene, and later Mrs. Rodriguez from the funeral home gave me enough little beds to fill a room at the clinic. So we used to put all the babies in those little beds while I taught the mothers how to fill and sterilize bottles and bathe their babies.[44]

Having been a teacher for 16 years, Sister Nelda was convinced that education was essential for advancement of any kind. Her home visits corroborated the fact that in 1945 the average daily truancy record for Hispanic children in San Antonio was 12,000.[45] She knew that schools were located at a distance and transportation to them was not available. Her determined protesting and persuading were instrumental in getting schools for the area around the clinic, later named the Edgewood Independent School District.

Sister Nelda was described as a "feisty, witty, intelligent woman who has worked both hard and smart to see 'her' clinic succeed."[46] Almost immediately she secured the volunteer services of Doctors Pedro Miniel, Cornelius Nau, and Felipe Estrada. They saw about 300 patients a week, and later a dozen more doctors offered their free services. Sister Nelda credited Mother Angelique with persuading Miss Adelia (Dela) Chacon, Director of Nursing in the San Antonio Health Department, to send visiting nurses to the clinic two days a week. They were especially helpful with immunizations, and some of them continued to volunteer after they retired from the health department. The owner of a maternity hospital on the east side of the city offered its furnishings to the clinic as a gift. Regretfully, Sister Nelda refused the offer because the General Council decided "we do not have the personnel to carry on the work of a Maternity Hospital for Latin Americans."[47]

Sister Nelda also quickly became a skilled mendicant and a fundraiser for the clinic, which provided medical services gratis. She explained, "When the patients asked us how much we would charge, I always told them, 'Whatever

---

[44] Oral interview, 1989, CDPA.

[45] Privett, *The Pastoral Vision* 79.

[46] *San Antonio Light*, 26 July 1989.

[47] GC minutes, 27 Jan. 1953, CDPA.

you can give us. If you can, give us something; but we don't ask for anything.' We were the ones that were supposed to give to them instead of their giving to us because they didn't have anything."[48] She persuaded dairies to donate milk. She and her two MCDP helpers made and sold tamales, enchiladas, and tacos to buy equipment; but this income was far less than the growing expenses.

U.S. Representative Henry B. González suggested that Sister Nelda form a club to help finance the clinic. She got her friend, optometrist Dr. José San Martín, to organize the Stella Maris Support Club for professional people and wealthy patrons, most of them Hispanic. The Belgian farm owners, grateful for Sister's care of their migrant workers, also organized the Martin de Porres Club, which held festivals, dances, and beauty contests and banked the profits for the clinic. By 1951 the two clubs, which merged in 1963, had saved enough money to construct a three-room building named Stella Maris Clinic. The clinic was also able to finance Sister Mary Raymond Meng's pharmacy studies at the University of Texas in Austin. A new clinic was constructed in 1966. In 1974 Dr. San Martín stated that "without this little 'dynamo' (Sister Nelda) the clinic's operation wouldn't have progressed at the rapid rate since its origin. Sister's dream is that someday a charity hospital can be built in that community."[49] Dr. San Martin wanted to build a maternity hospital near the clinic, but the CDP General Council advised instead that the clinic be incorporated and operating policies and procedures be written.[50]

When the city and county began to offer services in the area in 1975, Stella Maris Clinic was seeing as many as 800 patients per week. Sister Nelda took up residence next door to the clinic and used an annex to Stella Maris convent to shelter indigent expectant mothers and aged women. Sometimes she helped people adopt children.[51]

Stella Maris was the first clinic on the west side, 12 miles from any city or county health care services. The perseverance and dedication of Sister Nelda and those who supported her cause brought to the neediest people medical services which no one else was able or willing to offer. More than 25 years after she started, the Old Highway 90 Public Health Clinic was completed. While Stella Maris Clinic was "a self-maintained health institution funded solely by fundraisers and the generosity of the community," the new clinic "was financed with a combination of the 1970 Bond Issue Share, $190,737, and the Hill Burton Grant of $134,974."[52]

---

[48] Oral interview, 1989, CDPA.

[49] *San Antonio Light*, 28 July 1974.

[50] GC minutes, 30 Sept. 1960 and 29 Mar. 1963, CDPA

[51] Oral interview, 1989, CDPA.

[52] Irma González, oral history project, 5 Dec. 1989, CDPA.

Barbara Mann Wall, assistant professor at Purdue University School of Nursing, became interested in the history of Stella Maris Clinic through a colleague, Nelda Martínez, Sister Nelda's namesake. A native of San Antonio, Nelda Martínez remembered Sister Nelda's frequent visits to her family home to check on one of her sisters who was ill. Dr. Wall found it especially interesting that Stella Maris Clinic never received government money for its prodigious services.

In the 1960s the Congregation's general administration had ongoing concerns about bookkeeping, accountability, and the expense of maintaining the clinic even though it was pleased that the clinic was meeting great needs. Sister Nelda took a three-month leave while some organizational changes were implemented, and another Sister managed the clinic until she returned. Sister Nelda's input helped shape objectives, job descriptions, and lines of communication that were then implemented. Sister Nelda, who began to limit her services to house visits in 1987, was succeeded by Sister Barbara Lynn Hyzak, who faced problems dissimilar to those her pioneer predecessor had solved. After almost 40 years, the neighborhood population still included recently arrived immigrants, but it had newer challenges such as constantly rising medical costs, constantly increasing medical liability, and a diminishing number of physicians providing services on a volunteer basis. Doctors increasingly preferred to see patients in their own offices where they had their own equipment and would be reimbursed by Medicaid. In view of decreasing personnel and clients and in order to avoid duplication of services, in 1992 the Stella Maris Board decided to lease the clinic building to the Bexar County Health District, which was interested in bringing health services to the west side neighborhood.

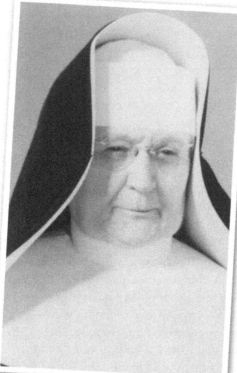

Sister Benitia Vermeersch (1882-1975),
Foundress of the Missionary Catechists
of Divine Providence

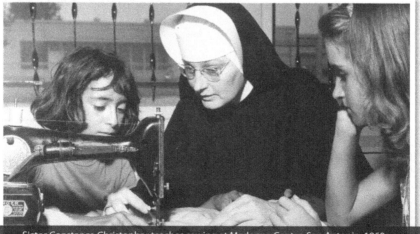

Sister Constance Christopher teaches sewing at Madonna Center, San Antonio, 1960s.
(Joe Bacon)

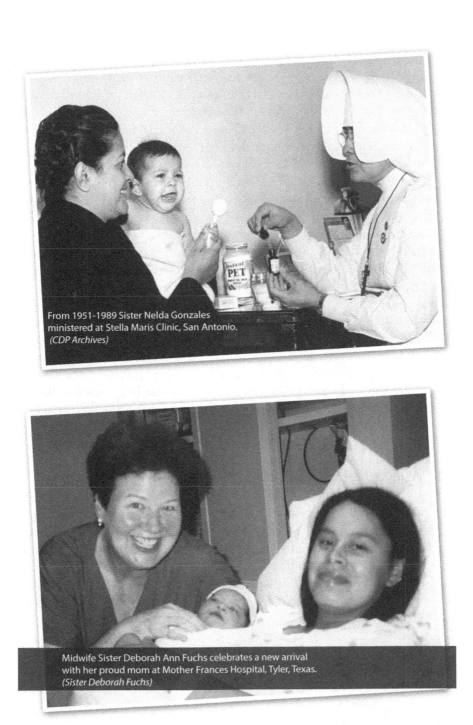

From 1951-1989 Sister Nelda Gonzales ministered at Stella Maris Clinic, San Antonio. *(CDP Archives)*

Midwife Sister Deborah Ann Fuchs celebrates a new arrival with her proud mom at Mother Frances Hospital, Tyler, Texas. *(Sister Deborah Fuchs)*

Our Lady of Guadalupe Clinic, Rosenberg

Bishop Wendelin Nold had a dream of a clinic for the predominantly Mexican families from the town and farms around Rosenberg southwest of Houston. He envisioned it would be staffed by a CDP and an MCDP with a registered nurse in charge.[53] The Basilian priests in charge of Our Lady of Guadalupe parish, where the Congregation staffed a school from 1942 until 1963, would manage the finances. The clinic became a reality even though its staff was not as the Bishop imagined. Its mainstay was nurse Sister Mary Walter Gutowski, CDP.

Sister Walter helped Rev. John F. Collins, CSB, and Rev. Joseph Dillon, CSB, in 1951 convert an old ten-room frame house in Rosenberg into a clinic. After three months, Sister Walter was assigned to St. Ann's Hospital in Abilene but returned to Rosenberg in 1955 after she completed nurse's training at Providence Hospital in Waco, Texas. She administered the clinic until her sudden death in 1993. A Polish farm-girl from Chapell Hill who never lost her appreciation for *czarnina* (goose blood soup), over the years Sister Walter became fluent in Spanish and adept at meeting every kind of need through her contacts with professionals, merchants, and other donors.[54]

Sister Martha Vrba as Regional Superior visited the clinic on 11 October 1965, and her report is a good description of the community. She commended them for "unusual evidence of the spirit of generosity and charity," good relationships in and outside the community, outstanding manifestation of interest in apostolic work, and good support between the Superior and the Sisters. She also recommended that they be more faithful to time for meditation and spiritual reading, observe small silence, and accept small privations in a spirit of dependence upon God.[55]

Conditions and corresponding health problems of the lowest economic level of the population in this small town were similar to those on San Antonio's west side. They did indeed call for generosity and love of the suffering people. While patients from small towns around San Antonio came to Stella Maris Clinic, Sister Walter sometimes traveled out to the sick in small communities near Rosenberg, and local traffic officers tended to turn a blind eye to her "heavy foot" on the accelerator. "There was an absolute void of services for the poor in the early 1950s, and it's not much better county-wide now,"[56] Sister Walter

---

[53] GC minutes, 13 Feb. 1951, CDPA.

[54] Details of Sister Walter's life were given during an oral interview in Rosenberg on 14 Feb. 2003. Interviewees were the pastor, Rev. James Blocher, CSB, who first met Sister Walter in 1977 and gave the eulogy at her funeral; Mrs. María Rosales Martínez, who worked closely with Sister Walter since she was a child; Mr. Alex Aguilar; and Mrs. Nora Dominguez.

[55] Reports of Regionals, CDPA.

[56] *The Herald Coaster*, 23 June 1986.

observed around 1977. Not only were there no government agencies to help them, but regulations made by the medical associations and government agencies were drawbacks rather than incentives. Schools required immunizations, but their parents could not bring their children to county clinics because of their "inflexible hours." Some families could not get food stamps, much less milk for their babies.[57] Once again CDPs stepped in to fill a gap.

Sister Walter found that the poor Mexican and African American people in Rosenberg and surrounding communities were fearful and distrustful of doctors and hospitals. The doctors, on the other hand, were afraid to donate their time lest they lose paying patients. She began to build bridges of relationship. Her relentless advocacy for the sick poor led doctors to volunteer their services, and soon from three to seven of them came several times a week to Guadalupe Clinic.[58] Patients were treated mostly for diarrhea and pneumonia as well as pink eye, skin infections, and malnutrition. The clinic provided immunizations, injections, and tuberculosis tests; and it also filled prescriptions. Pharmacists and dentists as well as friends of the clinic collected medicines and samples. Father John S. Broussard, CSB, who was pastor for 18 years of Our Lady of Guadalupe Church located across the street, acquired a two-ton truck that was used to collect medications.[59]

Like Sister Nelda González in San Antonio, Sister Walter Gutowski made education a priority. The clinic provided instruction on how to care for a baby as well as classes in home nursing and Red Cross nursing for mothers and young women. Some local professionals used the classes to renew their Red Cross certifications. But Sister Walter had other lessons in mind as well. "Money is not the main object of my work. I want to help people and teach them love and kindness toward each other."[60]

When the clinic was 40 years old Sister Walter, one of 13 children whose own mother was a midwife, could boast, "I never lost a baby or a mother. I saw them for prenatal care, and if I foresaw any difficulties I would send them to an obstetrician. On occasion they had to go to the hospital for Caesarean sections. We delivered 1,890 babies all together."[61] Two years later, she was credited with having delivered more than 3,000 infants.[62]

---

[57] George Scott, *The Herald Coaster*, n.d. (ca. 1977), CDPA.

[58] These included physicians Franz Amman, Samuel Boswell, Sylvester Vaughan, and ENT specialist Dr. Phillips, who also donated milk from his cows to the clinic.

[59] Rosenberg group interview, 14 Feb. 2003, CDPA. People also remember that an 18-wheel truck from out of state occasionally delivered rolls of cloth, handkerchiefs, and sundries.

[60] Sister Walter to Sister Angelina Murphy, ca. 1971, CDPA.

[61] *Texas Catholic Herald*, 6 Dec. 1991, 16.

[62] *Herald Coaster*, 17 May 1993: 5.

When babies were in danger of death, Sister Walter baptized them. In one case, a Mrs. Rivera gave birth to triplets. The family was not practicing any faith, so Sister Walter instructed them in the Catholic religion and was their *madrina* (godmother) when they were all baptized. She also helped them move into a low-cost house in nearby Richmond, which they bought with small monthly payments. She often served as a kind of employment agency because her many contacts enabled her to match people who needed jobs with people who were looking for workers.

Sister Walter was an unabashed workaholic, and she did not slow down much after she suffered a heart attack in 1990. "If I retired, I would die within a week," she insisted.[63] To make sure the community knew about the clinic, she mimeographed its weekly schedule in two languages and handed them out after each of the three Sunday Masses.[64] In the evenings she crocheted afghans for Christmas gifts which, along with pecans or persimmons from a neighbor, she gave to the doctors who volunteered at the clinic. She was voluntarily on call 24 hours a day, seven days a week. A small card on the front door of the clinic said "Smile, God loves you and I love you too." Her patients had overwhelming proof of Sister Walter's love for them.

But Sister Walter also knew how to play. She amused herself with the two convent dogs. She played the organ and the accordion, but she was not a singer and did not enjoy cooking. She did take time off to go fishing or crabbing in Matagorda Bay or to pick blackberries in the spring, peaches in the summer, and pecans in the fall. She also went water-skiing even though she wondered if this was "permissible." In a letter describing her grueling daily routine interspersed with a little time at the coast she insisted, "Do not worry—I know how to take care of the old donkey."[65]

Sister Walter solicited support of all kinds and acknowledged that the clinic's success was dependent on many people. One of her helpers, Anna Kasberg, a former CDP, began to assist at the clinic in 1985. At Sister Walter's urging, Anna, who had left the Congregation in 1952, re-entered and was professed in 1990. She came back to Rosenberg as Sister DeLellis in 1991 and died in 1993, seven months after Sister Walter. Another faithful helper was Sister Rosina Lewandowski, who "would even be called outside to help a mother who was about to deliver her baby in a truck or car, and she would try to get her into the clinic before it was too late. Sometimes it was too late."[66] Sister Rosina also oversaw an extensive program of food and clothing distribution, cooked meals,

[63] Article by Bob Giles in *Texas Catholic Herald*, 13 June 1986.

[64] FC, Mar.1952:120.

[65] Sister Walter to Sister Angelina Murphy, n.d., ca. 1971, CDPA.

[66] *CDP Times*, 13, 2 (Oct. 1992):15. CDPA.

kept records, and submitted public health reports. Donated clothing was either given to the needy or sold and the proceeds used to buy medicine.

The convent was next to the clinic, and plainly people's needs always took precedence over Church customs or Congregational rules about religious decorum, cloister, or silence. For example, when families had no way to pay for a burial, Sister Walter sometimes obtained cemetery space and a coffin through Mr. José Hernandez, a local funeral director. More than once, she performed the burial rites herself, surrounded by relatives and neighbors of the deceased.[67]

The clinic contributed to the local economy. Most of the patients at first were from sharecropper families, and farming was risky. Later many immigrants, documented and undocumented, asked for help. Using Guadalupe clinic enabled them to spend less on health care since it did not charge for medicines and services and hence to have more money to buy other necessities. Sister Walter did ask for $200 for prenatal care and delivery; but she knew her patients usually could not pay, so—like Sister Nelda González—she accepted whatever they gave. She amassed their small cash payments in envelopes filed in numerous shoeboxes.

The Rosenberg clinic relied on support from members of the Basilian Congregation who conducted fund drives in the Northern U.S. and Canada and brought seminarians from Toronto, Canada, in the summer to help with building in the parish complex. Parishioners also held bake sales, raffles of cotton bales, and a monthly meal to raise money for the church, school, and clinic. Grants from the Catholic Extension Society and foundations insured survival.[68] Father John Collins, CSB, was officially the Clinic Director; he reported directly to Bishop W. J. Nold and personally handled all of the clinic's finances with copies to no one.[69] After Father Collins' untimely death in the fall of 1969, Sister Elizabeth McCullough, the Superior General, asked that Sister Walter's salary be raised to $200 per month "so that she would be able to set something aside for her retirement." She asked that Sister Sophie Kubicek, who was also constantly on call, receive $50 a month.[70]

The Scanlan Foundation assumed financial support of the clinic in 1972 and replaced the frame house with a brick building containing rooms for deliveries, consultation, supplies, and medications. The clinic had three incubators. When the new clinic was functioning, Sister Elizabeth asked Mr. Frank A. Rudman of the Scanlan Foundation to pay Sister Walter $500 a month and her helpers, Sister Sophie Kubicek and Sister Casimir Vermaelen, $250 apiece per month. After Sister Walter's death in 1993, the Congregation could not provide a replacement.

---

[67] "CDP Newsletter," 1, 8 (20 Feb. 1974), CDPA.

[68] The Sisters also collected cans and glass to help themselves.

[69] John Collins, CSB, to Rev. Mother Amata, 1 July 1963, CDPA.

[70] Sister Elizabeth McCullough to Father Jackson, 20 Oct. 1969, CDPA.

The following year the foundation conveyed ownership of the clinic property to the Galveston-Houston diocese, which turned over the responsibility of the clinic to Our Lady of Grace parish.[71]

Sister Walter was legendary for her healing touch and the high standards she set for her co-workers, who easily observed that she walked extra miles with her patients. She personally escorted the brother of a friend to the Hazelden Foundation in Minnesota for alcoholism treatment, found him a mobile home when he returned, and saw to his burial when he died in a nursing home. She arranged for adoptions that led to valuable opportunities for the children of unwed mothers. The Alex Aguilar family, for example, adopted a daughter, Annette, who became an ophthalmologist. The José Hernández family adopted María Teresa, who became a social worker specializing in counseling people contemplating suicide. After 15 years in this profession, she decided to earn a PhD in anthropology from Rice University.[72]

Sister Walter also became the guardian for some patients from the State School for the mentally retarded who lived near her clinic. She explained:

> The Mental Institute from Austin chose us to check on the mental patients that they sent home. We keep tap [sic] on them and check on them to see that they take their medicine. It will be a year since this was set up. We had great success as none of the patients returned to the Institute. I should pet [sic] myself on the shoulder. I counsel them and give them nice motherly talk. How about that?[73]

Although she did not seek the limelight, honors came to Sister Walter that acknowledged how a woman religious who was "spirited, candid, and possesses a dry sense of humor"[74] worked marvels. In 1976 the Roman Catholic Church bestowed on her the *Pro Ecclesia et Pontifice* award "given to persons distinguished for personal charity and reputation and for zeal evidenced by their outstanding work beyond the parochial level."[75] She received the prestigious Jefferson Award initiated by the American Institute for Public Service and presented for distinguished public service at the local level in 1985. In 1991 she was honored as "the Irish Houstonian of the Year for her service to the poor in the Rosenberg-Richmond area." This award was sponsored by the Shalom Center, "an organization founded to provide spiritual and

---

[71] Rosenberg newspaper, May 1994, CDPA.

[72] Rosenberg group interview, 14 Feb. 2003, CDPA.

[73] Sister Walter to Sister Angelina Murphy, n.d., CDPA.

[74] Bob Giles article, *The Texas Catholic Herald*, 13 June 1986.

[75] "CDP Newsletter," 3, 5 (5 Jan. 1976): 134.

psychological services to clergy and religious leaders" and was presented at a dinner-dance at the Wyndham Hotel Greenpoint in Houston.[76] Sister Walter used such occasions to acknowledge her gratitude for others' support and also to solicit donations for her projects.

In 1986 Sister Walter celebrated her 25th anniversary as administrator of Our Lady of Guadalupe Clinic and also her golden jubilee of religious profession. One sign of her popularity was the fact that parishioners traveled 200 miles to the ceremony in San Antonio in a chartered bus donated by Rosenberg-Richmond merchants.[77] Our Lady of Guadalupe Clinic closed after Sister Walter's death, and the building was converted into Our Lady of Guadalupe Pastoral Center where counseling takes place for teens and families. The collection and distribution of food and clothing continued under the direction of Mrs. María Rosales Martínez, who helped Sister Walter for many years, in the former convent and office building built next door to the clinic in 1973.[78]

The affection and admiration Sister Walter received from her patients continued after her death. A bronze bust of Sister Walter, modeled on her golden jubilee photograph, was sculpted and donated by Bernadette Carman, a parishioner of St. Vincent de Paul Church in Houston. The bust was installed in the patio of the clinic in Rosenberg in 2000.[79] Mr. George Zepeda, who began in 1993 to collect toys for the children at Christmastime, and Dr. Eric García, a local dentist, solicited donations and sponsored a dance to raise funds for the bust. The people of Rosenberg still revere Sister Walter as a "quirky" but saintly person who gave of herself completely to show them God's care. Like the founder of the Congregation and many of its members down the years, Sister Walter declared, "I have dedicated my life to the poor, and I love to work for them because they need it the most."[80]

Contemporaneous Stella Maris Clinic and Our Lady of Guadalupe Clinic were directed for four decades by strong, focused Sisters who set no limits to service to disadvantaged people. Both clinics had Boards that gave the Sisters virtually free reign in their work. Although one clinic was urban and the other more rural, their clients were largely Mexican American and African American families struggling to make ends meet. The clinics' services were free, thanks to volunteers who were qualified professionals, successful business men and women, or laypeople and Sisters who were usually of retirement age.

---

[76] Rosenberg newspaper, 9 March 1991, CDPA.

[77] *Herald Coaster*, 23 June 1986, CDPA.

[78] Mrs. Martínez recalled examples of Sister Walter's dedication and self-sacrifice when she had emergency surgery for a burst gallbladder and later when she refused to accept a pacemaker.

[79] *Texas Catholic Herald*, 8 Dec. 2000.

[80] Article by Stephen Johnson, *Houston Chronicle*, 24 Mar. 1980: 3, 3.

In their holistic outlook on health, Sister Nelda and Sister Walter emphasized education and dealt with adoption, mental health, and other agencies. For financial support, they relied on donations and small money-raising events rather than on community or public sources of support. Some of their accounting practices were haphazard if not slipshod because these women although perfectionists in their work had little patience with bureaucratic details. Neither one trained a successor. In San Antonio the times called for acceding to another health provider; in Rosenberg, no one could be found to fill Sister Walter's shoes.

Health-related Ministries

The Harry Jersig Speech and Hearing Clinic at Our Lady of the Lake University began in response to a plea from the Sunshine Cottage School for Deaf Children in San Antonio. Afraid that the school would have to close for lack of qualified personnel, the school's administrators appealed to Dr. William Wolff, the Congregation's physician. He in turn presented the need to Sister Adelaide Marie Heyman, and she obtained Mother Angelique's approval to send the former Sister Mary Arthur Carrow to be trained in 1950. Sister received an MA from Texas University in Austin, which qualified her to work with the deaf, but meanwhile Sunshine Cottage had met its needs. Sister went on to earn a PhD at Northwestern University in speech and hearing and started an undergraduate program and clinic in speech pathology and audiology on the OLLU campus for children and adults. Thanks to referrals from pediatricians and others, the program grew rapidly and soon outgrew its quarters. Even though she was warned that non-hospitals were unlikely to be financed by Hill-Burton funds, Sister Mary Arthur obtained a Hill-Burton grant of $40,000, which was matched by Mr. Harry Jersig of the Lone Star Brewing Company to construct a clinic.[81]

In the 1960s and early 1970s the closing of two of the Congregation's hospitals made it possible to undertake new ministries to the sick and, increasingly, to the retired. Four Sisters served at the Regis Retirement Residence, the former Roosevelt Hotel built by Hilton in 1926, in Waco, Texas. Owned and operated by the Allen McDonald Foundation, the Residence was sponsored by the diocese of Austin, Texas. The building of 12 stories had 300 rooms. It housed 132 residents who received nursing

---

[81] Elizabeth Carrow Woolfok, oral interview, 17 Feb. 2003, CDPA. After she left the Congregation in 1969, Elizabeth wrote two books and numerous articles on language theory and disorders, started speech and language clinics in four hospitals in the Houston area, and developed five instruments to test language comprehension of children and teenagers.

care around the clock. Medicare funded Home Health Services for 150 active residents. Sisters Annella Foelker, Mary Joachim Geagan, Henry Ann Fuhrmann, and Benigna Rossy worked on four floors where the residents required custodial care or were on Medicare. Residents from the other seven floors, however, often came to the Sisters to discuss their personal, social, financial, and spiritual problems.[82]

Although the Congregation never staffed orphanages, many Sisters had years of preparation for this type of ministry in the Congregation's various boarding schools. In St. Joseph's Children's Home in Oklahoma City, CDPs served as "mothers, nurses, sister-confessors, entertainers, teachers, and fairy god-mothers" from 1965 to 1978.[83] "Care of the children at St. Joseph's Home is one of our very special apostolates," Sister Elizabeth McCullough assured Msgr. A. A. Isenbart, head of Catholic Charities in Oklahoma City.[84] It also presented unique challenges because it was "a 24-hour-a-day job, seven days a week, with the expected and unexpected always taking place, such as grass fires in the wee hours of the morning, children going AWOL, burglarizing in the dorm, and children's activities."[85] Superiors were aware of how busy the Sisters were, still they counseled deeper reflection and mutual support rather than less activity. Sister Henrietta Schroeder, regional superior, after a visitation of the community wrote: "I realize how busy your days are, giving much of your time and energy to this worthy apostolate. However, I encourage you to take some time from your daily activities to examine the deeper meaning in your lives."[86] Sister Henrietta's successor, former Sister LoRayne (Charles Ann) Hoge, also counseled: "Because your coming together is, of necessity very seldom, I would encourage you to make these moments golden opportunities whereby you encourage one another, listen to, build up, and edify one another."[87]

St. Joseph's had begun as the diocesan orphanage in Bethany, Oklahoma, in 1912 and was staffed by a number of different religious Congregations as well as lay people until 1965. When the orphanage building became the CDP Headquarters, the children and their CDP caretakers moved to a new building in Oklahoma City. The character of St. Joseph's home changed in 1976, two years before the Sisters left. It began to accept temporary custody of "abandoned, neglected, unwanted, and juvenile delinquent children," usually

---

[82] *Nunspeak*, June 1970:11, CDPA.

[83] *Nunspeak*, June 1970: 9, CDPA.

[84] Sister Elizabeth McCullough to Rt. Rev. Msgr. A. A. Isenbart, 5 Oct. 1970, CDPA.

[85] "CDP Newsletter," 3, 8 (1 April 1976): 153.

[86] Canonical Visitation Report, 5 Nov. 1968, CDPA.

[87] Canonical Visitation Report, 20-24 Oct. 1971.

awarded through juvenile courts. At that time the 36 children were enrolled in ten different schools.[88]

A different segment of the population of needy children came to the Sisters' attention in Texas: children infected with auto-immune deficiency syndrome, AIDS. At the urging of Dr. John A. Mangos, head of pediatrics at the University of Texas Health Science Center in San Antonio, Providence Home and Family Services was established in 1990. Dr. Mangos saw a growing need for services to babies born with AIDS whose mothers could not care for them. Dr. Mangos asked CDPs to provide this service. In 1990 the annex to Stella Maris Convent was transformed into Providence Home and Family Services, a licensed residential facility for children with AIDS. This was made possible because of great financial and in kind support from local businesses, individuals, and numerous volunteers.

Sister Barbara Lynn Hyzak was the first Director of the home, which served as a 24-hour residential care facility for six children while the University of Texas Health Science Center provided the necessary medical care. A few years later the home expanded to include the former Stella Maris Clinic, which was converted into a learning center for children from 18 months to 6 years of age and later added services for infants from birth to 18 months. These infants and children were either themselves infected or came from families affected by HIV-AIDS. By 1997 a second cottage residence was added. Advances in research were improving the treatment for AIDS-infected persons. Perceptions towards AIDS-infected people were changing. Also the number of AIDS-infected children who had no care-givers was decreasing. New legislation required other facilities to admit AIDS-infected children, and financial help was available for their families. The Board began to consider its future in light of all these realities. It conducted a thorough investigation and consulted many in the San Antonio community. When it was clear that the need for which the home was founded had been met and other facilities could easily meet the needs of the people who used its services, Providence Home was closed in 2000 upon the recommendation of a committee chaired by Dr. Mangos. More than 200 clients had been served, and more than 400,000 services had been provided by staff and volunteers.[89] The Home celebrated its closing in a spirit of completing a job well done.

The buildings were leased by AVANCE, an early head start program that provided comprehensive and continued service to young children and their families. AVANCE was founded by Mrs. Gloria Rodriguez, an alumna of OLLU who was a member of the first Project Teacher Excellence program.[90]

---

[88] "CDP Newsletter, 3, 8 (1 April 1976): 153.

[89] *Signs of Providence*, 5, 1: 1, CDPA.

[90] *Signs of Providence*, 5, 1: 7, CDPA.

Sisters in Health Services

Some Sisters had extensive teaching experience before they went into nursing. Their age did not prevent them from starting a career that attracted them and suited their tendencies and gifts. Sister Felicia Beck, who lived to be 102, taught school for 25 years before in her "high 50s" she started what she *really* wanted to do, nursing. And she did that for 35 years. A former student at Moye Military School in Castroville, Texas, admits that he would go to Sister Felicia, the school nurse, with every little cut or bruise because she bandaged so sympathetically and always gave him a cookie. One of the assignments she cherished was taking care of Mother Angelique during the last years of Mother's life when she was confined to St. Joseph Hall. Even after Sister Felicia herself retired, she continued to take care of the other retired Sisters' toes and feet until her eyesight failed.[91]

Sister Evangelista Karlik began a two-year nursing program when she was 57 years old. She used her skills at Mercy Hospital in Laredo, Texas, in El Campo Czech Catholic Home, and at Yoakum Hospital before spending several years doing private nursing in New Braunfels, Texas.

Sister Cecile Clare Vanderlick managed to satisfy her love for teaching and for nursing at the same time.

> I've spent most of my 49 years in ministry as a high school chemistry teacher, but I am also a registered nurse. For seventeen years in two ministries at the same time—education and health care—I taught five or six classes in science scheduled consecutively early in the day and went to nurse at St. Frances Cabrini Hospital in Alexandria, Louisiana, on the late afternoon and evening shift or on the weekends.[92] I not only cared for the sick, I was also there to call the priests in for the Sacraments. I have baptized many people on their deathbed.[93]

Sister Cecile Clare was well positioned to encourage her students and her sister, Sister Virginia Lee, to volunteer at the local hospital and accompany the Sisters when they visited the sick and the grieving.

Sister Marlene Quesenberry, on the other hand, was never attracted to teaching, but she was attracted to the charism of Providence and trusted that her attraction for nursing would be recognized and encouraged.

---

[91] See *Movements*, 3, (Fall/Winter 1999): 12-15.

[92] *Movements*, Spring/Summer, 2001: 12, CDPA. Sister Cecile Clare obtained her degree in a pilot program at Louisiana State University in Alexandria (oral interview, 21 July 2000, CDPA).

[93] CDPs stationed in Alexandria also profited from her medical advice (Sister Esther Habermann, oral interview, 28 Nov. 2003, CDPA).

> Nursing had been my number one interest since I was four years old. When I entered the Congregation, there was absolutely no guarantee that I would go into nursing; they told me I might be teaching. I did look into several nursing orders, but they just weren't a good fit. The CDP charism came through even when I was very young, so I entered the CDPs. I took the chance. Then Providence put Sister Elizabeth McCullough, my eighth grade teacher, into office. She understood where I was coming from, so I had no trouble getting permission to go into nursing.[94]

After nursing at Madonna Hospital in Denison, Sister Marlene worked in San Antonio at McCullough Hall. Next she moved into ministry sites outside the Congregation: the Southwest Migrant Association, the Barrio Comprehensive Family Health Care Clinic, and Southwest Methodist Hospital. Then she became a school nurse for 20 years in the Edgewood Independent School District where she did state-mandated testing and health teaching as well as gave general first aid. "We have severely and profoundly handicapped children to care for with tube feedings. Right now I am taking care of a little boy dying of progeria. His body is like a 90-year old. He has had strokes and heart problems and is in hospice no-resuscitation."[95]

Caring for the whole person continued to be Sister Marlene's concern, and she found opportunities to show compassion in more ways than giving vaccinations, treating playground injuries, or dispensing pills. "So many of our parents are single mothers, and I have two or three conferences a day with parents concerning their children's health and well being. Sometimes these moms just need to air things out to someone with a listening ear."[96]

Sister Barbara Lynn Hyzak, who was the chief administrator at Stella Maris Clinic and later at Providence Home and Family Services, found that "Over the years, my desire to heal and comfort the whole person has been a constant in a life of continuous change and transition, professionally and personally."[97] In her itinerary through small and large, urban and rural hospitals as an Adult Nurse Practitioner she noticed a trend: the increasing frequency and importance of ethical questions in the medical field.

> A continuous challenge to all professionals today is the advancement of technology. Changes in health care procedures and treatments have led to ethical questions and led people to believe that there are

---

[94] Oral interview, 21 June 2000, CDPA.

[95] Oral interview, 21 June 2000, CDPA.

[96] Oral interview, 21 June 2000, CDPA.

[97] *Movements*, Fall/Winter 2000: 23, CDPA.

"instant cures" for almost everything that can be wrong with them. However, they fail to realize that there are times to sit back and make a judgment call on the "quality of life" of the patient as the key indicator of what measures to take.[98]

Sister Barbara Lynn has had numerous opportunities to make those judgments in her profession of caring for the sick.

Sister Marie (Marie Anna) Gubbels had unique, but increasingly common, experiences as a patient that resulted in special empathy for people with the sickness of addiction. After overcoming her own addiction to prescription drugs, she wanted to help addicts. She knew from experience what others learned only from textbooks.

> People take drugs because they want to be free from some problem tension, or unpleasant situation or relationship. But soon they take them because they like the feeling and continue even when the pain is no longer there. The hardest part for me was knowing it was wrong and knowing that as a Sister I should not do it, but I was a junkie.[99]

She learned to accept the fact that addiction is a disease rather than a moral failure and that she could relapse. She was convinced that the 12 Steps Program, especially its emphasis on the necessity of having a spiritual life to stay sober and recognizing dependency on a Higher Power, is the most effective help for all types of addiction. "One of the biggest factors in a person's turning to drugs is feeling unloved, not accepted, or not good enough. If these needs are not met, a person may look for comfort in a bottle or a pill." The availability of drugs is another factor. "Today it is easier than ever to get drugs without a prescription; and I think that doctors prescribe drugs more readily because they are overwhelmed, rushed, and do not want to deal with deeper problems the patient may have."[100]

After overcoming her own addiction, Sister Marie earned an MA in mental health and substance abuse. She was a counselor on the staff of the Hazelden Community Prevention and Professional Education Division of Minneapolis, Minnesota, from 1983 to 1992. Among her assignments were giving workshops and talks on Alcohol/Chemical Dependency.[101] Later she gave lectures on

---

[98] *Movements*, Fall/Winter 2000: 23, CDPA.

[99] Oral interview, 20 May 2004, CDPA.

[100] Oral interview, 20 May 2004, CDPA.

[101] Sister Rose Ann Blair participated in a family program at Hazelden before beginning parish ministry in Lake Arthur, Louisiana. The pastor, Msgr. Charles Dubois, had identified a large number of parishioners with drug and alcoholic addictions whom Sister Rose Ann counseled (oral interview, 19 June 2000, CDPA).

chemical dependency to students at OLLU and was instrumental in getting several of them to accept help for their addictions.

Sister Marie added that her experience gave her a new appreciation for two virtues CDPs try to manifest: trust in God and simplicity. More than ever she experienced a need for God, "lots of God" in her life. Being kind and truthful also had added meaning as day by day she aimed to be genuine, honest, and straight.

Sister Marian Angela Aguilar was employed as a social worker in 1978 at John Sealy Hospital in Galveston, Texas, to work with women who had cancer and with their families. She recalled

> I saw the suffering and dying, the negative aspects. Sometimes it was depression and lack of family support rather than the cancer which killed them. Of the 200 patients, we used to lose about seven a month. But then we had the survivors, those who would live with their cancer. These survivors grew as persons and were really a source of edification for me and for their whole community.[102]

Some Sisters who were not social workers found their sympathy awakened for people desperate enough to contemplate ending their own lives. Sister Ann Carmel Maggio while she was a laboratory technician at St. Ann's Hospital in Abilene received a commendation from the Abilene Association for Mental Health for her volunteer work with the Suicide Prevention Service.[103] While stationed in Ennis, Texas, Sisters Rose Corrine Medica and Elizabeth Dale (Marie Therese) Van Gossen started a crisis line and spent hours on the phone every weekend in Waxahachie, Texas.[104] Sister Carolyn Pelzel worked at Seton Healthcare System in Austin, Texas, with patients who had tried to commit suicide.[105]

Among the changes after Vatican Council II was the possibility of Sisters' living with sick or aging relatives to care for them when no one else in the family could do so and institutional care was not an option. To appreciate the impact of this change, it is important to recall that the Sisters' contacts with their relatives had been very limited. If they visited on campus, which was permitted one Sunday afternoon a month, the Sister was not supposed to take food with them. Visits home were short and infrequent.[106] Caring for sick relatives was labeled "leave of absence" in the community assignment list and was limited to a two-year stay

---

[102] Oral interview, 21 June 2000, CDPA.

[103] "CDP News Bulletin," Northern Region, Jan. 1969: 8, CDPA.

[104] Sister Rose Corrine Medica, oral interview, 16 June 2000, CDPA.

[105] Sister Carolyn Pelzel, oral interview, 21 June 2000, CDPA.

[106] Sister Josepha Regan explained, "Sisters whose close relatives lived in San Antonio could go visit them one Sunday each summer for half a day. Those whose families lived out of town could visit home only every five years for a week with a

until Canon Law changed. Then the assignment was called "family ministry" and had no time limit. Sister Elsa Mary Bennett said this change "was like a ton of rocks off my shoulders"[107] when she had to leave to care for her mother.

In 1982 Sister Herman Mary Zimmerer went home to care for her 94-year-old mother. She recalled the experience as "one of the happiest years of my life, though very trying and difficult at times. It was very rewarding because many things Mother did made me feel important. She related stories that I needed to hear to bring back memories of my childhood.[108] Sister Josepha Regan found a common thread between teaching and family ministry. "In the classroom I was always thinking about improving my teaching methods and seeing how much the children could accomplish." Caring for family members she realized she was still thinking of others rather than of herself. "I began to see values that I hadn't seen before. What is most important in life? It's not what we do; it's what we are, our very presence—just being there, thinking of others, not of ourselves."[109]

At first Sisters cared only for their parents. In 1973 Sisters Natalie Jean and Agnes Rita Rodriguez asked to live with and look after their brother who was ill. They were told that "by policy the Congregation has not allowed in any instance a Sister to continue teaching and to reside at home to care for a brother or sister."[110] Less than two years later, however, Sister Miriam Parker was allowed to stay with her ill brother and sister-in-law until they found a live-in caregiver.[111] Soon afterward Sister Jane Patricia Coyne received permission to live with her sick sister in San Antonio and continue teaching at St. Anthony's School.[112] After the Congregation opened McCullough Hall to relatives of CDPs, the parents and siblings of a number of Sisters spent their last days in the Congregation's nursing center.

Sister Deborah Ann Fuchs, a certified nurse-midwife, illustrated a well-known CDP trait: if others cannot or will not do it, I will educate myself to do it. Her involvement in midwifery came "by chance—or by Providence."[113]

In the 1970s I taught Lamaze classes in Floresville, Texas, educating couples about childbirth and alternatives in childbirth. I was

---

companion. Later on we could visit home without a companion as often as possible if it did not interfere with our ministry" (oral interview, 21 Jan. 2000, CDPA).

[107] Oral interview, 28 July 2000, CDPA.

[108] Oral interview, 29 Feb. 2000, CDPA.

[109] Oral interview, 21 Jan. 2000, CDPA. More than 35 Sisters performed family ministry.

[110] GC minutes, 27 Feb. 1973, CDPA.

[111] GC minutes, 22 Jan. 1975, CDPA.

[112] GC minutes, 30 April 1975, CDPA.

[113] Quotations in the next two paragraphs are from Sister Deborah Fuchs, CDP, "The Joy and Privilege of Being a Nurse-Midwife," *Movements*, Spring/Summer 2001: 3-5.

encouraging men to be involved in the birth of their babies, but the doctors refused to allow the couples to participate and do the things they were taught in my classes. That frustrated me and the couples. When I realized I couldn't change the doctors, I decided I would have to get educated and become qualified to do the births myself. So began my journey into midwifery.

She observed that "midwives tend to be spiritual people who believe in the awesomeness of God." She also saw this profession as an opportunity to live out the CDP mission more fully because she could work "with indigent women, with the needy in society. They struggle with basic life issues on a daily basis. Oh, how I admire them! I try to help them recognize the power that they hold. In return I find it a joy, a privilege, and an inspiration to work with women during this special, vulnerable time in their lives."

Sister Deborah Ann was employed at Su Clínica Familiar in Raymondville, Texas, where she also had the experience of being a minority.

The people put us up on a pedestal, but that meant we were not part of the community. All the services in church were in Spanish. At first I didn't know a single word of Spanish. When the translator was not present during deliveries, I used sign language. I felt like an outcast and thought, 'This is what we have done to minorities. We have excluded them because we can't speak their language.' It feels like nobody supports them; nobody cares. I appreciated that experience.

Later Sister Deborah Ann taught at Parkland School of Midwifery in Dallas, Texas, and worked at the Family CARE Clinic in Tyler, Texas. She also spent one day a week at the Birth Center in Trinity Mother Frances Hospital in that city.

Sister Deborah Ann first started taking massage therapy evening classes in order to relax and reduce stress in her personal life. That small step led in an unexpected direction. She invited some massage therapists who did prenatal and labor massage to make a presentation at a national meeting of midwives. Attending a workshop at that meeting on Reike, an ancient art of healing, Sister was profoundly moved. "I had a really healing experience of letting go of anger with some people who had really hurt me in the very recent past. When I was able to let go of that, I thought, 'This is something I now want to incorporate into my life.'"[114] Soon afterwards as a certified massage therapist she was able to incorporate Reike and massage therapy into her clinical practice.

---

[114] Oral interview, 23 June 2000, CDPA.

Pregnant women always have what we call common discomforts, and most health care providers just say they can't do anything about it. But I have learned to apply massage therapy to help relieve the painful symptoms. To my utter amazement, when I started doing this, the patient would get up off the table and say, "Ah, the backache in my lower back is completely gone. Thank you!" When she came back some weeks later, I would say, "How is your back?" and she would reply, "I haven't had any problems with it since the massage." I was awed that Reike and other alternative-type treatments really worked. So I use them to help women understand what is happening to their bodies, and I try to find natural relief measures for symptoms rather than just prescribing medicine and more medicine.[115]

Alternative medicine, natural remedies, and healing through touch became better known in the last quarter of the twentieth century; and some Sisters saw them as means to further healing ministry. Sister Barbara Lynn Hyzak said she realized the tendency in her early training was to use medication to avoid discomfort or have an easy fix. Later she tried to help people employ more noninvasive ways to care for themselves. She came to realize that "caring for someone doesn't necessarily mean that we are going to cure them. Rather, we will be and walk with them so that healing can take place. To me nursing is being a support and not necessarily just having the answer or thinking that something has to change." She also discovered Tai Chi and Reike, "alternative ways to allow myself to grow and also invite others to be in touch with who they are."[116]

Sister Jacqualine Kingsbury came to the ministry of massage therapy by a different route, influenced at least in part by tragedies. Within a short period, her mother died of cancer; a brother died in a boating accident; and the president of her parish youth group was abducted and killed in the neighborhood while she was working at Our Lady of Sorrows parish in Houston, Texas, in the 1980s. After sixteen years in youth ministry, she sensed a need for change. She took a sabbatical for a year at a center staffed by Franciscan Sisters in Little Falls, Minnesota, to deal with her grief as well as mid-life issues. She then remained for over six years at Wholistic Growth Resources as a massage therapist, finding great satisfaction in working with the staff and 30 to 35 religious every year.

In contrast to the parish, I was able to focus on one person at a time in massage therapy. I developed my intuitive side and some very good listening skills. At times, these women had been abused in childhood

---

[115] Oral interview, 23 June 2000, CDPA.

[116] Oral interview, 18 Jan. 2001, CDPA.

but did not remember the incidents. One woman I remember had been brutally abused, and she would go back into those spaces and relive them. I just had to let God be the healer and be present and be empathetic.[117]

Next Sister Jackie moved from Minnesota to Florida. While obtaining a massage therapy license, she worked with an outreach program for mothers in danger of losing custody of their children because of abuse and neglect. She taught Tai Chi Chih as well. Sister Bernice Eidt, who at one time was a counselor at OLLU, later learned Tai Chi Chih and gave Tai Chi Chih lessons in the Dallas, Texas, area. Sister Eugenia Ann Stell became a qualified Tai Chi Chih instructor in order to use these movement patterns with the retired Sisters.

Sister Elsa Mary Bennett majored in physical education at OLLU and taught PE there from 1979 to 1984. In 1988 while working with the City Parks and Recreation Department in the Handicapped Access Office, she made a film slide show of all the places in San Antonio accessible to the disabled. In 1989 she received a certificate from the San Antonio Institute for Natural Therapeutic Services which qualified her to give massages anywhere in Texas, and she became a physical therapist for the Warm Springs Rehabilitation Hospital. After teaching physical education in San Antonio public elementary schools for the following 14 years, Sister Elsa Mary dedicated herself to exercise and massage therapy for the retired Sisters of the Congregation.[118]

Sister Rose Marie (Marie Camille) Uhlig was a Certified Registered Nurse Anesthetist and became a Nurse Practitioner in Anesthesia in 1970. Sister Roberta Haby became a certified occupational therapy assistant in 1996.[119] Both Sisters made good use of their professional as well as their personal experiences when they were assigned to minister to the retired Sisters.

The Sisters' devoted care of individuals has also impelled them to do what they can to relieve sufferings and problems on a societal level through lobbying and legislation. Sister Sylvan Durbin exercised this influence through the Texas Nurses' Association of which she was an officer for 10 years. She organized its members to defeat a pro-abortion position.[120] Sister Annella Foelker was President of the influential Texas Catholic Hospital Association. Sisters Barbara Lynn Hyzak and Deborah Ann Fuchs were instrumental in bringing health-related bills to successful passage in Texas as well as in national legislative bodies. Both are concerned about ethical issues in health care due to

---

[117] Oral interview, 20 June 2000, CDPA.

[118] Oral interview, 28 July 2000, CDPA.

[119] Sister Roberta Haby, oral interview, 26 July 2000, CDPA.

[120] Oral interview, 16 June 2000, CDPA.

rapid advances in technology. Sister Barbara Lynn said "it behooves us to stay involved and try to see how we can impact decisions."[121]

Health Care for CDPs

Caring for the sick members of the Congregation was not only a tradition but also an obligation. The *Constitutions* of 1927 # 49 stated that "the sick shall be the object of the most vigilant charity, and the most generous devotedness." Because a number of Sisters succumbed to tuberculosis at the beginning of the twentieth century, the Motherhouse built a "glass house" near the infirmary where patients could be isolated and treated. Four-story St. Joseph Hall, built in 1933, included an operating room, dentist's chair, water therapy facilities, and a "pharmacy" for dispensing medications. It was completely renovated in 2000 to provide independent living options for retired Sisters. To make it possible for sick and retired Sisters to benefit from the latest medical care without leaving the Convent premises, Ancilla Domini (later called Regan) Hall was built in 1960 and Regan Hall Annex, (later called McCullough Hall) was constructed in 1970.[122] The retirement center also included Ancilla Domini Chapel, later named Annunciation Chapel, with exterior and interior statues by Charles Umlauf and stained glass windows by Emil Frei Studios.[123] After former Sister Joan Okonski earned a degree in occupational therapy, she and Sister Constance Christopher, MSW, planned and implemented a full program of crafts and recreational activities in 1972 for the retired Sisters in Feltin Center located in the basement of St. Joseph's Hall.

McCullough Hall was licensed on 26 August 1992 to take full advantage of available government funds as well as to prepare for the time when having fewer Sister-patients would make it possible to accommodate laypeople in the facility. This decision also meant that McCullough Hall was subject to periodical inspections, audits, and required detailed record keeping. Among the problems faced and resolved were difficulties in obtaining qualified employees, maintaining professional supervision of accountants, and formulating policies for

---

[121] Oral interview, 18 Jan. 2001, CDPA.

[122] Sister Geraldine Bourg remembered that she and Sister Mary Magdalene Bartinski, with the help of convent maintenance men, moved all the Sisters from St. Joseph Hall to their new quarters in one day. "It went like clockwork" until evening when "all the commodes began to overflow." An unskilled workman had poured liquid cement into a pipe, so other workmen had to tear up the new floor and replace some of the pipes (Sister Geraldine Bourg, oral interview, 15 May 2000, CDPA).

[123] GC minutes, 14 Feb.1959, CDPA. Emil Frei studios in Germany also made the stained glass windows in the main chapel. A large outdoor crucifix by Charles Umlauf was installed at the Generalate in Helotes, Texas, and moved to the grounds of the motherhouse in 2001.

ethical decisions. In 1999 Sister Constance Christopher was trained by a Bexar County agency as a qualified ombudsperson to work with residents and staff to maintain quality care in the facility. In 2002 McCullough Hall was separately incorporated from the Congregation of Divine Providence.

Healing the sick by means of medication alone has never been the ideal or the practice of a Sister of Divine Providence. The most essential remedy does not come out of a pill bottle. Moved by compassion to relieve suffering, they have drawn on the example of Christ the Healer and the strength of a caring God in all their attempts to relieve and comfort those who are ill in mind or body.

CHAPTER 8

PROMOTING EQUALITY
FOR AFRICAN AMERICANS

In 1953, eleven years before the passage of the Civil Rights Act, San Antonio Archbishop Robert E. Lucey asked the Catholic schools the archdiocese of San Antonio to accept any Black students who applied. Mother M. Rose Kallus, IWBS, Superior General of the Sisters of the Incarnate Word and Blessed Sacrament who staffed Nazareth Academy in Victoria, Texas, asked Mother Angelique's advice about complying. Mother Rose was concerned about losing accreditation since state schools were still segregated and Jim Crow laws were in effect. Mother Angelique replied:

> We received a letter such as you did, from His Excellency, and of course we shall comply with the directive, hoping that all other schools in the City will do likewise. We are to accept one or two if they apply. We do not need to go out soliciting. The less we say about it the better it will be.
>
> We have had Negroes in our graduate department for the past four years, and there has been no difficulty. . . . It will be better for us to comply than to wait until the other schools have begun to accept them, and it is surely going to be general pretty soon. I hope we may always do what is right in this matter. It will help to get the State laws set straight.[1]

---

[1] Mother Angelique Ayres to Mother M. Rose Kallus, 1 July 1953, CDPA. Actually, Negro students enrolled at OLLC as early as 1939, "Alumnae News," XXIV, 1 (Jan., 1966): 5, OLLUA. "African American" is today the preferred term. Other terms used were: colored, Negro, or Black as well as Creole and mulatto.

Two years later, some Sisters from the college were involved in public protests against segregation. Sister Marilyn Molloy recalled that

> many of the Sisters at the College organized with students and picketed the downtown theatres that refused to allow Blacks to have seats except in the balcony. We would also get in the ticket line, but instead of buying a ticket we'd carry on a conversation with the ticket seller. This slowed the process so terribly that they changed their policy. We did win that one. In 1956 we again took a strong stand with local restaurants which did not let Blacks enter by the front door.[2]

In 1973, a group of CDPs at Holy Savior Menard Central High School in Alexandria, Louisiana, recommended that the Congregation withdraw its personnel because instead of promoting integration the school was supporting "white flight."[3]

How did the Congregation move from rather passive acceptance of the status quo to more active opposition to inequality? The exclusion of African Americans and other groups, especially women, from benefits raised consciousness in the 1950s and 1960s and sparked concerted efforts to promote greater respect for human dignity. In 1950 "separate but equal" higher education was challenged in *Sweatt v. Painter*, but unequal educational opportunities in elementary and high schools took longer to address. Strong catalysts for social change in the 60s, 70s, and 80s were the Civil Rights movement, the Chicano movement, Vatican Council II, liberation theology, and feminism.

This chapter will show how CDPs supported justice causes and how defending rights of African Americans significantly impacted the Congregation and its works. Located in Texas and Louisiana, a notoriously prejudiced section of the U.S., many individual Sisters became more aware of the evils of injustice and prejudice and tried to promote understanding and respect in their sphere of influence. By the mid 1970s all institutions staffed by the Sisters were integrated. Although several mulatto women entered the convent, none of them stayed.[4]

---

[2] Oral interview, 26 Dec. 2000.

[3] Sisters Theresa Anne Billeaud, María Carolina Flores, Charlotte Kitowski, and Imelda Maurer to Sister Elizabeth and members of the General Council, 18 January, 1973, CDPA. In this case, "white flight" referred to the departure of whites from public schools which were increasingly enrolling Blacks.

[4] No Sister of the San Antonio Congregation of Divine Providence is African American. In 1963 "a Negro aspirant of a good Catholic family had applied for admission to the aspirancy. The Council approved considering her for entrance" (GC minutes, 9 July 1963, CDPA). Sharon Metoyer, the last African American to enter, left in 1970 because she "never

Some Sisters actively promoted the welfare of Mexican Americans and members of different immigrant groups. Others were actively engaged in promoting justice through responsible corporate investments and systemic change. Sometimes conscientization led to confrontation and called forth new forms of perseverance and courage.

African Americans

Mother Angelique knew from her youth in Mississippi and East Texas how divisive and even deadly racial clashes could become. If principles were at stake, she was ready to transgress accepted protocol that could lead to censure.[5] In 1936 she facilitated a gathering of whites and non-whites for an evening of musical entertainment, which "was considered flaunting the white community's values and the long-standing taboo of strict separation of the races."[6] Members of the Alpha Tau Omega chapter of Alpha Kappa Alpha Sorority, which since 1913 had been a channel for college-trained African American women to improve socioeconomic conditions, were "deeply appreciative" of her support. They wrote, "In this era of conflict and misunderstanding, it is fine to discover that here in San Antonio are people of wisdom, sincerity, and a 'will for understanding,' such as you." The women also praised the spirit, which prompted your cooperation and the sacrifice you made in doing so.

> To be able to recognize and understand the needs and aspirations of other peoples establishes one's kinship with God. The transmission of that spirit to large groups of young people, as you are doing, can not other than go far toward smoothing out discords, and establishing a harmony that will tell for the good of our common life.[7]

Mother Angelique preferred to ignore rules and regulations rather than to confront directly. In 1941 there was no college for Negroes in San Antonio, and Fannie Mae Edmerson because of her teaching schedule could not go out

---

'felt at home'—the food was different, the music was different, the culture was different, etc." (Sister L. Suzanne Dancer communication to the author, 15 Nov. 2003).

[5] Such behavior is "political," an act for a *polis*, for a whole people. See Robert R. Treviño, "Facing Jim Crow: Catholic Sisters and the 'Mexican Problem' in Texas," *Western Historical Quarterly* 14 (Summer 2003):156.

[6] Treviño, "Facing Jim Crow": 156.

[7] Mrs. Mattie T. Lewis, Mrs. Edna Morris, and Mrs. Euretta K. Fairchild to Mother Angelique, 5 March 1936, Dean's Correspondence file, OLLUA.

of town for two courses required to renew her teaching certificate. Mother Angelique asked two OLL teachers to give her private courses on Saturdays. Probably no CDP would object to Ms. Edmerson's presence on campus, but the attitude of the Anglo students and their parents was not predictable, so she entered through the back door of Providence Hall. Sister Tharsilla Fuchs, who taught her school arts and design, met and accompanied her wherever she went on campus.[8] Ms. Edmerson's credits were transferred to Prairie View College, and her teaching certificate was renewed. Sister Tharsilla did not see her again until they happened to sit together at the dedication of the Carver Cultural Arts Center in San Antonio in 1977. Undoubtedly this experience contributed to the fact that Sister Tharsilla "donated most of her best [art] works for the benefit of the United Negro College Fund."[9]

In 1943 Archbishop Lucey asked superiors of congregations of women religious to establish inter-racial clubs on all levels of education. He recommended that the groups meet "among themselves" to grasp the problems and then "with Chinese, Latin-American and Colored students" to establish better relations.[10] Mother Angelique was pleased to report some progress in a letter that also reveals her strategy for reducing racial tension and her penchant for situating events in a wider context.

> I think these casual meetings, such as in the Confraternity [CCD] group, give the opportunities for forgetting race and accepting individuals. Your Excellency will be interested in knowing that among our students are not only Anglo—and Latin Americans, but two Chinese girls, and even one Japanese girl, and they are living in normal school-girl peace.[11]

African Americans not only had separate schools but also separate churches or, if their number was small, they were assigned to pews in the back or on the side in white churches. Few clerics were ready to defy this custom, but in 1961 Sister Praxedes Martínez braved the wrath of the white community in Cloutierville, Louisiana, where the Congregation staffed St. Mary's School for whites and St. Joseph's School for blacks. She was principal of the black school and decided "since the church was segregated, white in the middle and blacks

---

[8] Videotaped interview. Sister Tharsilla did not recall that the college ever made a formal decision to accept African Americans, but it did receive threatening phone calls later when it did so.

[9] *CDP Times*, 12, 4 (Dec. 1991):11, CDPA.

[10] Archbishop Lucey to Mother Superiors, 25 Jan. 1943, CDPA. See GC minutes, 8 June 1953, CDPA.

[11] Mother Angelique to Archbishop Lucey, 19 Oct. 1943, CDPA.

on the side, she was going to sit with 'her' Black people."[12] Besides teaching blacks, some CDPs later worked in black parishes. Sister Redempta Bradley was Director of Religious education at St. Anthony/Uganda Martyrs parish in Okmulgee, Oklahoma. Sister Mary Bordelon administered St. Catherine parish in Arnaudville, Louisiana.

One of Archbishop Lucey's first acts upon arriving in San Antonio had been to call together a group of priests, brothers, and laymen to consider what to do about desegregating the schools. OLL President John McMahon was active in this group, which eventually developed into the Catholic Interracial Council.[13] After twelve years of urging institutions to "stop the sin of racial segregation and to treat all human beings as children of God," Archbishop Lucey formally ordered all schools in his jurisdiction to be integrated in 1953, six weeks before the 1954 decision of the Supreme Court. More than 10 years later the city of San Antonio, anticipating the 1968 Hemisfair held to celebrate the 250th anniversary of the city's founding, "promoted the 'voluntary' integration at public eating places, to avoid the embarrassment of hosting a world's fair in a segregated city."[14] The prelate's initiative in the schools contributed to smoother integration in other places.

The state changed slowly, however, and the College remained cautious about promoting integration in residence halls. The head of the graduate education department took note when the college was preparing for re-accreditation that presently "the school is integrated in all its departments. Until now there have been no Negro resident students (one during a summer session), but this is true only because none have completed admission requirements." Socials were also not fully integrated. "In the undergraduate school there is one requirement enforced by the school: Negro students who attend the college dances must bring their own escorts, and dance only with their own, or other Negro students' escorts."[15]

Some Sisters promoted appreciation of black culture through their scholarship and publications rather than through protests and marches. Sister Elaine Gentemann composed a Mass embodying Negro spirituals. Former Sister Helen Rose (Betty Joyce) Fuchs' Master's thesis at the University of Texas in Austin was on "Contact and Prejudice-reduction Among Colored Creoles."

---

[12] Sister Lucille Ann Fritsch, oral interview, 9 Sept. 2000.

Sister Clarice Trumps, who taught at St. Joseph's School from 1958 to 1964, interviewed when she was 82 noted that the black people lived in a neighborhood surrounded by whites, "who weren't as nice to them as they should be" (oral interview, 12 Jan. 2000, CDPA).

[13] Privett, *The Pastoral Vision* 152.

[14] John McCormack, "The Fair that Changed Us," *San Antonio Express-News*, Sun., April 4, 2003: K4.

[15] Education Department files. Appendix No. 6, (hectographed) n.d., Dr. Harold Wren to members of the Committee on Purpose. OLLUA.

Based on surveys of students in grades 5 to 12, she researched "how attitudes toward other ethnic groups change when individuals are first in contact with groups different from themselves."[16]

As the Civil Rights movement gained momentum, sometimes the parents' professional standing in the community facilitated their children's acceptance in the all-white school. In Fredericksburg, the father of the first African American students in St. Mary's School was a veterinarian and their mother was a librarian. At St. Martin Hall in San Antonio the first African American students were from families stationed at Lackland Air Force Base. In other schools, the Sisters refused to withdraw their support of integration even under pressure. Ku Klux Klansmen burned a cross in front of Our Lady of Prompt Succor School in Alexandria, Louisiana, after an African American student was accepted into the seventh grade.[17] When an African American student enrolled in the third grade in Texarkana, he was not dismissed even when some white parents withdrew their children in protest. Tensions heightened sensitivity to whatever might become a racial issue. Sister Miriam Fidelis Mellein found she had to be extremely careful casting students for a play in Tulsa, Oklahoma, in 1966. "In those days you didn't cast a black and white as husband and wife."[18]

In the 1960s the Congregation still had four schools for African Americans, all in Louisiana. In 1964 Sister Jane Marie Gleitz became principal of "the mulatto school" in Cloutierville. Three Sisters in the community taught in the white school and three in the mulatto school, where physical conditions were not easy. Sister Jane Marie recalled, "Our school was in the cotton field, and we got our water out of the well outside of the door. We pulled the bucket up in the morning and filled the metal container in the classroom."[19] Sisters in the black schools made light of the hardships and stood up for their pupils despite growing criticism of "separate but equal" education and dwindling numbers of Sisters who volunteered to teach in these schools. Sister Jane Marie "cried buckets" when the school was closed in 1967; she could not understand the closure. "One of the black people came and said, 'Sister, why are you leaving us? Who needs you more than we do?' Which was true. I never understood how the Congregation, if we were for the poor, pulled out of such a place or why we kept sending our oldest Sisters to those places."[20]

---

[16] "CDP News Bulletin," Northern Region, January 1969: 3, CDPA.

[17] Sister Euphrosine Honc oral interview, 18 May 2000, CDPA.

[18] Oral interview, 13 June 2000, CDPA.

[19] Sister Jane Marie Gleitz, oral interview, 28 April 2000, CDPA. Sister Lucille Ann Fritsch, who taught in the white school, remarked, "We could wave to one another across the cotton field, but we could not teach in the same building" (oral interview, 9 Sept. 2000, CDPA).

[20] Oral interview, 28 April 2000, CDPA.

Rev. Marvin Bordelon, pastor of St. Joseph's, a white school staffed by CDPs in Shreveport, Louisiana, "planted a black girl from a wealthy family from another part of Shreveport in the school. The children accepted her, but she was the only black student and was not very outgoing." Sister Mildred Leonards concluded, "it wasn't good for her or the rest. The people called Father a 'Nigger Lover.'"[21] St. Joseph's joined the Great Books program but withdrew as soon as it became known that the black school in Shreveport staffed by the Holy Ghost Sisters was not allowed to participate. The boycott caused the sponsors to relent, and soon both schools joined the program.[22]

Sister Reparata Glenn, among other Sisters, did what she could in the classroom to question segregation.

> In my religion classes at St. Mary's in Natchitoches, I would ask why the Blacks from St. Anthony's couldn't come to our school since there was room. The students would get furious with me because of what I said about "their Christian duty." Then I would remind them how talented some of these blacks were. They were just as smart; they just had a different color of skin. Any time they would say something against the blacks, they'd hear from me.
>
> One student said, "I don't care what you say. I hate them anyhow." That was their attitude. But, you know, sometimes if you keep drumming it in, it begins to sink in. A girl, daughter of a doctor, who was a leader in the class, at first was avidly against my lectures. After a while, she didn't say too much; but she was really a thinker. One day there was a discussion about Jackie Robinson, who had been admitted to a baseball team and was a terrific player. This girl was a baseball fanatic, so she began to think that Jackie Robinson was all right. When one of the boys spoke against him, she jumped all over her fellow-student. After that, some more of the students began to speak up for Robinson.[23]

Sister Lydia Leehan, administrator of Madonna Hospital in Denison, Texas, 1957-1963 was distressed that black mothers and their babies were segregated from the general population in the hospital. After delivering on the third floor, the mothers were sent to the ground floor, and their babies had to be transported back and forth for nursing. Sister Lydia knew in her heart that this was not right. She was very uncomfortable with the arrangement; however, the hospital

---

[21] Oral interview, 1 Sept. 2000, CDPA.

[22] Sister Sylvia Schmidt, SSS (former CDP), oral interview, 3 Feb. 2003, CDPA.

[23] Oral interview, 14 Feb. 2000, CDPA.

staff was not ready to accept a change. Eventually she got up enough courage and determination to face objections. She announced that the obstetrics area would be integrated. "One doctor said, 'Sister, are there any alternatives?' I said, 'No, not really.' Then he said, 'Gentlemen, this is academic; and we might as well accept it.' So they did accept the fact that we were going to be integrated." Sister added that Madonna Hospital "was probably one of the first hospitals in North Texas to be integrated. In fact, I don't know any other at that time that was integrated."

Sister Lydia put all newborns in the same nursery and all new mothers on the same floor. She also discovered that many black employees "were getting a free meal in lieu of a boost in their salaries, and they just had to take whatever dietary served them." She thought this was unjust, so she called the prime orderly, who was black, and asked him:

> "What would you think if I gave you a raise and then you could buy anything you want in the dietary? You wouldn't have to take whatever they serve you." Oh, you would have thought I had given him a piece of heaven. The nurses said, "What did you tell Mitch? He is just floating on a cloud?" I said, "Well, I just gave him status as a person."[24]

Sister Angelina Murphy recalled that students were often more tolerant than their parents. At Bishop Kelley High School in Tulsa, Oklahoma, students "refused many times to patronize skating rinks, prom centers, cafeterias, and swimming pools unless the Negro students could also be accommodated. . . . Their student council president for 1965-66 was a Negro Baptist boy. . . . 'Miss Courtesy' at OLL High School in 1964 was a Negro girl."[25]

Sister Mary Bordelon was pastoral associate in African American parishes for nine years. She discovered how Black parishes in Lafayette, Louisiana, "fought (and continue to fight) to stay open so they can worship as they please and have their own parish council and not be 'tokens' on the parish councils in white churches."[26] She became aware that "we Anglo-Saxons are not used to being the minority; and situations when we are can be very jolting for us. Everybody else is thinking the very opposite of the way we might be thinking." In subtle ways book knowledge is presumed to be superior. "True, we may have education in religion that some parishioners don't have. They might not know what Canon Law or current theology says on a particular topic," but they

---

[24] Oral interview, 8 July 2000, CDPA.

[25] "Alumnae News," XXIV, 1 (Jan. 1966): 5, OLLUA.

[26] Sister Mary Bordelon, e-mail to the author, 28 July 2004.

might have very valuable insights. "So it's important to reach a balance between dictating and being sensitive to the culture while also sharing knowledge we have. Sometimes it was awkward or difficult, but I found it very stimulating and growthful." Sometimes Sister found it hard to come back into an all-white situation. "It was like a culture shock because I got used to thinking more like African Americans think."[27]

"By and large Catholics, either black or white, were not in the forefront of the Civil Rights movement or among the leadership of the protest organizations."[28] Anti-segregationist sentiment in Louisiana, however, aided by the support of school superintendents and the attitudes of Sisters—most of them young—assigned to teach there, precipitated the abrupt closing of the Congregation's black schools in that state. Unlike Archbishop Lucey, Bishop Charles P. Greco of Alexandria, Louisiana, tended to support the segregated status quo. In a letter to the clergy and laity of his diocese on 6 August 1963, he quoted Pope John XXIII to bolster his argument that the Church's support for segregation had been a legitimate "adaptation" to a local practice and had wisely prevented the "imitation of social reform" from taking precedence over the "all-important work of sanctifying souls." Ten years after the 1954 Supreme Court decision ended legal segregation in U.S. schools, this same bishop asked the people of his diocese "to accept the inevitable" and to recognize that desegregation "will gradually be enforced in every part of our country." At the same time, he urged the black Catholics of the diocese to "elevate" themselves so that they could "merit acceptance as did other peoples . . . in the course of the development of this country."[29]

Most of the Sisters who took a stand against segregation in the Alexandria diocese were born after World War II, were aware of the decision in *Brown vs. Board of Education* that abolished segregation in public schools, were sympathetic to the Civil Rights movement, and were beginning to experience the impact of the second Vatican Council. The Congregation's interim "Constitutions, Norms and Commentary, 1968," defined two concepts used in the Vatican Council documents and endorsed by the Sisters, collegiality and subsidiarity. All of the Sisters had experienced collegiality by being involved in generating grass-roots proposals with rationales for the General Chapters held at this time. They were involved in experiments with government structures, community forms, and garb as the Congregation implemented the decrees of the Council. They had also experienced subsidiarity because they were expected to deal with situations on the local level according to their best judgment and not wait for minute

---

[27] Sister Mary Bordelon, oral interview, 20 July 2000, CDPA.

[28] Cyprian Davis, *The History of Black Catholics*, (New York: Crossroad, 1990) 256.

[29] Privett, *The Pastoral Vision* 19. Bishop Greco was consecrated Bishop of Alexandria on 24 February 1946.

instructions from higher authority before acting. These experiences contributed to their readiness to initiate action to change practices they considered unjust.

Sister Pearl (Paul Elizabeth) Ceasar was one of three Sisters in annual vows nominated by Sister Frances Jerome Woods to prepare for teaching at OLLU. She was to earn a PhD in sociology and continue Sister Frances Jerome's research on the mulattos in Isle Brevelle, Louisiana, where she was assigned to teach in 1968. Sister Pearl had recently accepted some of the new ideas of Vatican II when she taught in Tulsa, Oklahoma, and attended lectures by forward-looking priests. Her experience in Isle Brevelle was eye-opening and life changing. She learned why Sister Agnes Louise Zotz said she had "a special place in her heart for the people in Isle Brevelle, whom she taught for fourteen years. . . . The people in this Cane River area are very special and unique. They are Creoles, a beautiful people who have suffered a great deal of rejection in the past. They have a deep spirit of faith and unity, and they were an inspiration to me."[30]

St. Joseph's School in Isle Brevelle had closed in 1967, so in 1968 Sister Pearl and Sister Tiolinda Marotta were the first Sisters teaching at the public school there which was called St. Matthew's. Half the students were black Baptists and the other half were mulatto Catholics. Sister Tiolinda reported some hardships in the convent and in the school. The school was two miles from the house. She and Sister Pearl, went "into Natchitoches to buy groceries, to wash our blouses at St. Mary's, and to get drinking water once a week. . . . We bathe and wash in river water so we smell like the river."[31] They received their teachers' manuals the day before school started and only because they requested them. Sister Tiolinda reported that some "teachers go around with whips so the children respond only to the whip. Slowly but surely we're taming them down without the whip. . . . Our students miss school frequently. Most of them have repeated at least two or three times, so I have a 16-year-old young man in my sixth grade."[32]

Sister Pearl recalled that to finance new cafeteria equipment, staff and students for one full year ate rice and beans—"red beans, pinto beans, lima beans, navy beans, every kind of bean you could imagine." And what happened? "The new cafeteria equipment went to an affluent school with an all-white student body, and Sister Ceasar's school was given the all-white school's castoffs. It was a lesson the teacher never forgot."[33]

Sister Pearl found herself making comparisons between her students in Louisiana and the students she had the previous year in Oklahoma. How were such inequities possible? In Isle Brevelle she taught 22 black children of plantation

---

[30] *CDP Times*, 15, 3 (Nov. 1994):16, CDPA.

[31] "CDP News Bulletin," Northern Region, Jan. 1969: 1, CDPA.

[32] "CDP News Bulletin," Northern Region, Jan. 1969: 1, CDPA.

[33] Sister Pearl Ceasar interview, "Profiles of Faith," *Texas Catholic* (Dallas), 15 Aug. 2003.

workers in the first and second grade, including two boys aged 11 and 12 who did not know how to read. The sharp contrast between the "incredibly bright students" she had taught in Tulsa and her present African American students "shook" her. The ones in Tulsa "had everything going for them and could have made it on their own. Of those 22 in Isle Brevelle, only five kids—and that is a high estimate—stood a shot at life."[34] Sister Miriam Fidelis Mellein who followed Sister Pearl in Isle Brevelle found little had changed. She discovered the students really could not read. "The mulattoes did well; they knew what they were doing because they and their families had gone to school to our Sisters. But the black children had a hard time; I got some special workbooks for them, but the principal wouldn't let me use them, saying 'They have to pass those standard tests.'"[35]

Looking back 35 years later, Sister Pearl identified her experience as radicalizing, "an amazing turning point in beginning to understand what God wanted me to do with my life." She elaborated:

> What I came to understand was that I could have stayed out there the rest of my life, but I would have very little impact outside of that classroom.
>
> Those people were powerless and I realized that I can't bring about change without power. I wanted to be a part of a larger strategy to bring about change.
>
> She vowed to use her talents and energies to empower ordinary people to negotiate effectively with the government and private institutions that affect their lives.[36]

Coming back to San Antonio in 1969, Sister Pearl and Sister Christine Stephens "talked about what would happen if the Congregation sent its younger Sisters to the Black schools." They decided they would ask to be assigned to St. Anthony's School, a Black school not far from Isle Brevelle in Natchitoches, a town of over 18,000 inhabitants. "We wanted to make the school into a top notch model school for Blacks and show that the Congregation had a continued role there. The three Sisters who were there were close to retirement and were well respected. We wanted to continue the congregational commitment."[37] The two Sisters secured

---

[34] Oral interview, 18 Aug. 2000, CDPA.

[35] Sister Miriam Fidelis Mellein, oral interview, 13 June 2000, CDPA.

[36] Sister Pearl Ceasar interview, "Profiles of Faith," *Texas Catholic* (Dallas), 15 Aug. 2003. Sister Pearl became a community organizer and helped citizens obtain better conditions for their communities in the San Antonio, El Paso, Brownsville, and Dallas areas.

[37] Sister Pearl Ceasar, oral interview, 18 Aug. 2000, CDPA. At this time she also told Sister Frances Jerome that college teaching was not for her. She wanted to work more directly with people.

the permission of Sister Elizabeth McCullough, the Superior General; but they were never assigned because "the administration made the decision to withdraw from all of our black schools and integrate our white schools."[38] After 1969, the Congregation did not staff any schools for Blacks in Louisiana.

The U.S. Supreme Court ordered immediate school desegregation in 1969,[39] and the Congregation's schools in other states experienced no particular problems with the ruling. At St. Joseph's School in Killeen, Texas, for example, there was an enrollment of approximately 200 students which fluctuated "frequently and sharply" since "Killeen itself existed primarily because of Fort Hood," and military personnel changed often. But the school population was a "thoroughly integrated group, with many different ethnic backgrounds."[40]

Closing Schools in Louisiana

The dramatic events that occurred during the Civil Rights movement, especially in the South, clearly manifested the fear and hatred directed at Blacks for many years. They had "their place" separate from whites, and segregationists wanted them to stay in it. The 26 congregations of women religious in the Archdiocese of New Orleans stated in 1970 that "we can no longer contribute to or permit ourselves to be instruments in the perpetuation of racial segregation, which is unjust and immoral." The Sisters promised to "welcome cordially members of minority groups," to be "ready to accept teachers and students of all races and cultural backgrounds" and to "regretfully withdraw from a parish which does not accept and abide by this Policy on Christian Education and Racial Integration."[41]

Natchitoches

Founded in 1714, Natchitoches was the oldest permanent settlement in the Louisiana purchase. Famous for its "City of Lights" Christmas festival and unique almond tea, many of its older houses exhibit French Creole style architecture with cast-iron grillwork galleries. Its first bishop, Auguste Marie Martin (1803-1875), a native of France, "openly embraced the institution of slavery and sought to

---

[38] Sister Pearl Ceasar, oral interview, 18 Aug. 2000, CDPA.

[39] The Court had already said in 1955 that desegregation in public school systems should proceed with "all deliberate speed" (http://www.tennessean.com/special/desegregation/archives/03/07/35869764.shtml).

[40] "CDP News Bulletin," Northern Region, Jan. 1969: 6, CDPA.

[41] Statement of 15 January 1970, reported in "CDP Newsletter," 12 June 1970: 5-6, CDPA.

show how it could be a force for good."[42] In this city pioneer CDPs began their first school outside of Texas in 1888.

Sister Mary Margaret Hughes, who grew up in Natchitoches, remembered once asking her mother why some people were better than others, why some people did not associate socially with others. Her mother replied, "Well, honey, that is just the way it is." Interviewed in 2000 at age 79, Sister recalled "when I was Mardi Gras Queen in Natchitoches, there were certain friends I invited to be my maids and others that I didn't. I was feeling bad about these friends that I excluded." Has inequity and intolerance been eliminated? She observed, "I still see discrimination everywhere today; we haven't made much progress. We have not yet come to grips with accepting everybody as Jesus does."[43]

"During the school year," 1969-70, Sister Elizabeth McCullough, the CDP Superior General, promised, "we will consider the dual school system in Natchitoches and will take definite action there."[44] The General Council decided on 13 March 1970, to withdraw the Sisters from St. Anthony's School for Blacks in Natchitoches, which had an enrollment of 190 students, claiming there was an insufficient number of Sisters to staff it.[45] Sister Pearl Ceasar and Sister Christine Stephens were assigned to St. Mary's School in Natchitoches in the fall of 1970. They would soon be involved in a series of events resulting in the closing of all CDP schools for African Americans in Louisiana.

St. Mary's was a private school owned by the Congregation for 73 years before it was sold to the parish in 1961. Sister Huberta Gallatin remembered that Natchitoches had a large African American population. "The Civil War had been fought there. A relative of U.S. Grant and a relative of Robert E. Lee, two lovely girls, were in my first class. We had a special school [a short distance away] for the colored taught by two of our Sisters. There were no blacks in St. Mary's School."[46] A new St. Mary's School was built and opened in September, 1965; in 1971 it had 466 students, all white. Sister Pearl summarized the situation.

> As the public schools of Louisiana integrated, whites flocked to the Catholic schools; and we accepted them. The enrollment doubled in 1970. Sisters of our Congregation had been there for 83 years, and the curriculum had not changed. The only thing that had changed was that the public schools were being integrated.

---

[42] Cyprian Davis, *The History*, 50. The bishop's pastoral letter of 1861 caused him trouble with the Roman Curia.

[43] Sister Mary Margaret Hughes, oral interview, 18 June 2000, CDPA.

[44] Sister Elizabeth McCullough to Bishop Charles P. Greco, 10 July 1969, CDPA.

[45] GC minutes, 13 March 1970, CDPA.

[46] Oral interview, 1 Apr. 2000, CDPA.

Our hearts were in the right place, but we did not know how to deal with that situation. We did not have the skills to bring about integration.[47]

Sister Christine Stephens remembered their getting into trouble with the pastor of Immaculate Conception Church, Father Henry F. Beckers, who was also the administrator of St. Mary's School in Natchitoches.

Several young African American laywomen from Philadelphia were working at St. Anthony's. Pearl and I reached out to them, got very close to them, and spent time with them. Father Beckers, the pastor at St. Mary's in Natchitoches, thought we were organizing the African Americans and planning to picket St. Mary's, so he fired us in January 1971 along with Sister Ida Marie Deville, the principal. Basically he was using the integration of the public schools to build up his Catholic school, mostly with non-Catholic students whose parents did not want them in integrated schools. This was contrary to everything we stood for.[48]

The central administrators of the Congregation spent the month of February 1971 in intense, often unpleasant negotiations triggered by a letter written to them by the eight Sisters assigned to St. Mary's School.[49] The Sisters identified a crisis in the school due to the "large number of non-Catholic students in flight from integration." One-third of the high school population was non-Catholic. The policy on admissions enforced by the pastor was not in accord with (1) the statement of the National Association of the Council of Major Superiors of Women, September 1970; (2) the declaration of the bishops of Louisiana, January 1970; and (3) the order by Monsignor John Wakeman, diocesan superintendent of schools, to "avoid at all cost even the appearance of the use of our schools to circumvent the law." The Sisters concluded that "since Father Beckers continues to take in these students whom we feel are fleeing integration in the public schools, then we, as a community of St. Mary's School, Natchitoches, Louisiana, do not feel that we could continue to work here under these conditions."[50]

---

[47] Oral interview, 18 Aug. 2000, CDPA.

[48] Sister Christine Stephens, oral interview, 18 June 2000, CDPA. In her oral interview (18 Aug. 2000, CDPA) Sister Pearl added that Father Beckers "wanted us out of the school and out of town the same day."

[49] Sisters Ida Marie Deville, Elise Bengfort, Blandina Paul, Macaria Kelly, Patricia Kimball, Bernice Simar, Pearl Ceasar, and Christine Stephens.

[50] Sisters of St. Mary's School, Natchitoches, Louisiana, to CDP General Council, 24 Jan. 1971, CDPA. In 1973 when Sister Christine Stephens was doing social work at St. Theresa's parish in Houston, Texas, she was subpoenaed to testify in a

Sister Elizabeth McCullough and Sister Mary Margaret Hughes, a General Councilor, visited Father Beckers shortly after receiving the letter; but he refused to change his position.[51] Next they met with members of the lay board and finally with Bishop Greco and his Vicar General, Monsignor Frederick Lyons, who on the Sisters' suggestion agreed to modify the diocesan school policies to (1) limit the construction of new classrooms, including the ninth grade, (2) prohibit the transfer of non-Catholic students from public schools into Catholic schools, and (3) inform non-Catholics already registered for 1971-1972 that they were ineligible. Father Beckers reluctantly agreed to the conditions but demanded a new Sister-principal. The Congregational administrators informed the Sisters of the agreement, but two days later he met with the lay faculty of St. Mary's School, complained that the prospects for a football team[52] were doomed, and declared he would allow only three Sisters to return.

The school's coach, an ally of Father Beckers, told students all about the meeting; and on 23 February, Teachers' Appreciation Day, some of them appeared with signs saying "We Support Father Beckers and Coach French." The school secretary added to the tension by phoning the rectory to tell the pastor "he had better get over to the school if he was the administrator." A local news commentator interviewed Father Beckers and began to broadcast that "St. Mary's would be open next year, would have a football team, would have Sisters, and would have a lay principal." The same afternoon Father Beckers met with the high school teachers and with the Sisters, with whom he was "quite upset over the image the Sisters are projecting in the community." He said he "would abide by the Diocesan policies but hoped to get some of them changed."

On 24 February at a school assembly Father Beckers explained the situation and allowed four of the Sisters to make some clarifications. Sister Cecile Clare Vanderlick, superior of the Eastern region of the Congregation, was present and noticed that most of the students either did not see accepting non-Catholics fleeing from integration as a moral issue or did not see why the school should take a stand. She also remarked that Father John Cunningham, who had some influence on the lay teachers, "feels that the Sisters are imposing their consciences on everybody else." Ten days before, Dr. Joe Thomas, a past president of the St. Mary's School Board, had told Sister Mary Margaret Hughes that he believed "since Father pays the bills, he should be free to make the decisions regarding admissions."

---

suit some parents from Natchitoches brought against Father Beckers. On the stand she was asked only to verify that a letter shown her was the letter the Sisters in Natchitoches sent to Father Beckers (Sister Charlotte Kitowski, oral interview, 13 Mar. 2000 CDPA; and Sister Christine Stephens, oral interview, 18 June 2000, CDPA).

[51] The account of events given here is from a detailed report in the CDPA.

[52] The first-ever football program was started at St. Mary's in September, 1970.

The General Council decided to withdraw from St. Mary's School on 30 March 1971, and announced their decision on 20 April in three separate letters. To Bishop Greco Sister Elizabeth wrote that Father Beckers had hired a lay principal after telling her that he wanted a Sister-principal. Reluctantly the Sisters terminated their services because "continuing confusion and contradiction" in discussions with Father Beckers as well as "tensions and pressures" due to accusations produced by some people in the town made it impossible for them to work effectively in Natchitoches." To Father Beckers she also wrote that the Sisters' work "would be ineffective in the prevailing atmosphere of suspicion and confusion" exacerbated by his conflicting statements, actions that contradicted agreements, and the lack of unity caused by non-acceptance of "the principle that all men are created equal."

In a letter to the parishioners of Immaculate Conception Church and the students and parents of St. Mary's School Sister Elizabeth expressed how painful it was to have to leave a parish "where so many of us have experienced the warmth, affection, and kindness of its people." She explained that the Congregation was attempting to implement the Supreme Court's decision to integrate public schools as well as the policies of the Louisiana Bishops and the Major Superiors of Women of Louisiana. However, St. Mary's School in the past two years "accepted a significantly large number of Catholic and non-Catholic students who acknowledge they are transferring from the public schools in order to escape integration." The Sisters must leave this school because "we are convinced that we are being true to the Christian Principle that all men are created equal and have equal rights. At this moment in history, it is important that we state publicly this conviction."[53]

This letter was summarized and quoted in the *Natchitoches Times*, the *Shreveport Times*, and the *Alexandria Town Talk*. Reactions were mixed. Some people considered the Sisters disobedient and attempted to make them feel guilty. Lawyer Arthur C. Watson wrote to Sister Elizabeth to say that he "disagreed entirely with your attitude. You seem to be saying that unless the game is played your way, you refuse to play. I do not think that this is a very Christian way to behave or a Christian attitude to take." He also disagreed with the Sisters' departure the year before from St. Anthony's because the school was not integrated. "What did you hope to prove by pulling out and leaving these colored children without any religious education at all? This might have made you feel noble but did it do the children any good?" He detailed his own financial support of St. Mary's School

---

[53] CDPA, letter from Sister Elizabeth McCullough to parishioners of Immaculate Conception and Students and their Parents of St. Mary's School, Natchitoches, Louisiana, 20 April 1971. "Natchitoches is a small city, and everybody knew that students were in flight. We said we could not have that image" (Sister Elizabeth McCullough, oral interview, 17 April 2000, CDPA).

which educated so many of his relatives and his disagreement with the Bishop, who decided to take for Alexandria schools half of a legacy which had been designated for the Natchitoches school. Mr. Watson had disagreed, "but respected the Bishop's opinion. I would not dream of telling him where to get off as you Sisters seem to be doing now." Finally, he pointed out that 10 per cent of St. Mary's students were colored, which was the same as the average in the town.[54]

Mrs. John C. (Anne K.) Hoffman, on the other hand, considered the Sisters' letter "the most magnificent example of Christian witness I have ever seen." She explained:

> Three years ago we withdrew our four children from the parochial school. One young nun in particular pandered so blatantly to the homogeneous-affluent-conservative ethic that I was sure I could never again respect the sisterhood.
>
> If such courageous stances as yours were more common, perhaps the large number of Catholics here would awaken.[55]

Sister Christine Stephens told Sister Elizabeth, "If you had not stuck by us, I'd have never stayed in the convent. I would have thought we were morally bankrupt. But you and your council as well as Sister Ida Marie stuck by us."[56] Meanwhile, Archbishop Philip Hannan of New Orleans asked for Sisters to administer a community center in Houma in southern Louisiana that served African Americans. Sister Pearl and Sister Christine were assigned to Houma.

After the Sisters left Natchitoches, Monsignor Beckers reported to the police in May 1972 that he had received threatening phone calls before two shots were fired through his bedroom window in what he called "attempted murder." But then he admitted at Sunday Mass that he himself had fired the shots. Later Monsignor announced his resignation and his plans to return to his native Belgium. No charges were filed.[57]

Soon after the confrontations in Louisiana in 1973 the Congregation elected a new general administration headed by the seventh superior general,

---

[54] Arthur C. Watson to Sister Elizabeth McCullough, Natchitoches, Louisiana, 27 April 1971, CDPA. Charts and statistics provided by Sister Bernard Marie Horrigan, CDP, from the Alexandria diocesan school office showed that in the Natchitoches public schools 64% of junior high students and 55% of senior high students were African American at this time.

[55] Anne K. Hoffman to Sister Elizabeth McCullough, Alexandria, Louisiana, 25 May 1971, CDPA.

[56] Oral interview, 18 June 2000, CDPA.

[57] Monsignor Beckers became pastor of Sacred Heart Church in Pineville, Louisiana, and died of leukemia in 2001 (Sister Ida Marie Deville, communication to the author, 3 May 2003). Sister Elizabeth McCullough stated "we were probably dealing with a sick man all along. We couldn't talk to him about the school, and we couldn't talk to him about integration, so it became an impossible situation" (oral interview, 17 April 2000, CDPA).

Sister Charlene Wedelich. Sister Lora Ann Quiñonez, as Councilor in charge of ministry in the new central administration, visited Natchitoches on 27 April 1976, and prepared a report to give to the Sisters who had been there when the CDPs withdrew. She noted that the "black enrollment now was 5% as compared with 10% at the time we withdrew" and non-Catholics students were 28% of those enrolled. She observed that parents seemed unable to guide children in a strong formation program and that people still "did not understand the reason for our withdrawal." She "suggested that a ministry team be formed to work in various areas, setting up policies, training adults, and empowering the laity to carry on the work which sisters will no longer be able to go in and do on a long term basis."[58] In response to a request, on 1 July 1976, the General Council decided no Sisters would return to Natchitoches. In 1978 Father Harry Barker asked Sister Charlene Wedelich if Sister Huberta Gallatin could be sent to assist him in Natchitoches for one year with adult religious education and teacher training. Sister Charlene consulted with Sisters Elizabeth McCullough, Pearl Ceasar, and Christine Stephens and then granted permission.[59] Sister Huberta came from St. Catherine's parish in Shreveport, Louisiana, where she had been Director of Religious Education for six years. She stayed in Natchitoches from 1978 to 1986.[60]

In retrospect, Sister Pearl thought that

> the decision to close all of the black schools in one sense was a very courageous decision because the administration was saying "We will not support a segregated school system." But in another sense, there were ramifications and consequences that we had not anticipated. The integration of Catholic schools did not happen as we had anticipated, and the public schools were not offering a good education for blacks. Consequently, the blacks did not have another type of school to attend. The blacks could not afford the higher tuition at the white school. Also, these were parish or diocesan schools, and we did not plan with the diocese for a more aggressive recruitment of blacks into those schools. The few blacks that did go there were a minority and did not have a place.[61]

---

[58] GC minutes, 3 June 1976, CDPA.

[59] GC minutes, 21 June 1978; and Sister Charlene Wedelich to Father Harry Barker, 6 Aug. 1978, CDPA. In 1987 the General Council refused permission for Sister Virginia Clare Duncan to teach two English classes at St. Mary's School because of the 1971 decision (GC minutes, 15 Jan. 1987, CDPA).

[60] Sister Huberta then returned to minister in Shreveport until her retirement in 1996.

[61] Oral interview, 18 Aug. 2000, CDPA. She added "To protest as we did was admirable, but in the long run nothing really changed."

Although Sisters were withdrawn from segregated schools, they were assigned elsewhere in Louisiana because the Congregation wanted to continue its advocacy for minorities.

Alexandria

CDPs began teaching black children in Alexandria in 1894 and continued to do so when St. James School for African Americans opened in 1916. In 1951 St. James had its largest enrollment to date, 656 students, 205 of them in the high school.[62] When the Sisters withdrew in 1969, more than 500 students were enrolled.

Persistent demand for excellence over the years paid off, for the school became known for excellent college preparation. For example, from the graduating class of 1945 two students were accepted at California universities, two at Xavier University in New Orleans, and one at Dillard University.[63] Alumna Willie Dell Metoyer was the organist at the cathedral in Alexandria, Louisiana, for many years.[64] Alumnus Anthony Hollins spent 38 years in federal service and wrote, "You made a difference, and I am sure that many of us who benefited from those years applaud you and your accomplishments.'"[65]

Offering quality education was not always easy. Sister Elise (Josephine Elise) Bengfort, who was the principal from 1963 to 1969, recalled:

> In Louisiana the state supplied the textbooks, and the black schools always got the leftovers. Those books were so outdated it was pitiful. I made many trips to the school board office and demanded that they give us decent textbooks. They finally did, but it took a lot of time, effort, and just standing your ground, saying "We've got to have these books!"[66]

Sister also noted that widespread prejudice contributed to the pupils' lack of self-esteem. However, the students also had "a different, much more cooperative spirit. They knew education was their way out of poverty, so they studied very seriously. The students were most appreciative of what we did. They gave us great joy by their custom of coming back to share their successes with us."[67]

---

[62] FC, Nov. 1951:13, CDPA.

[63] FC, Jan. 1946: 71, CDPA.

[64] Sister Julian Honza, communication to the author, 18 Mar. 2003.

[65] Anthony Hollis to Sister Rose Frances Rodgers, 26 Dec. 2002.

[66] Oral interview, 27 Sept. 2000, CDPA.

[67] Sister Elise Bengfort, oral interview, 27 Sept. 2000, CDPA.

The athletic program was strong at St. James, and the music department was famous. For example, noted soprano Eileen Farrell was a classmate of Father David C. Marshall, CSSp, the school's music director. While in town for a concert at Bolton Public High Auditorium, she graciously sang at St. James Church.[68] For school operettas such as "The Belle of Barcelona," Mr. James Freidman taught the singers and Sister Julian Honza taught the dancers. When the St. James choral group and student pianist Malcolm Breeda performed at a musical festival in San Antonio, "several of the CDP postulants who observed the group during their visit here made inquiries as to how one gets to teach in a colored school. They are ready to answer the first call for volunteers."[69]

When Sister Lucille Ann Fritsch was asked to teach at St. James, she remembered: "I came face to face with an awareness in myself. Although I always said I wanted to work with black people, I discovered that I did have prejudices and a bit of fear. I didn't quite see them as equal to myself." Her attitude soon changed, however. "I became aware of their suffering, their hardships; I saw so many grandmothers, for example, rearing grandchildren without complaining. I really fell in love with those people, and I got along with them."[70]

Sister Elsa Mary Bennett was attracted to the Congregation because Sister Francisca Lott told her it had several black schools. When she was assigned to St. James, both in the school and in the neighborhood she

> had no problems adjusting to blacks or mulattoes. Two women who lived right across the street from us, Mabel and Gertie, had been children of slaves. You had to be very careful with the words you'd use, like "boy" and "girl." I had to be very sensitive to their culture. Even the blacks and the mulattoes had to be very careful of what language or wording they used with each other.[71]

Sisters teaching at St. James were involved not only in their immediate neighborhood but in the larger Alexandria community. For example, through the efforts of Sister M. Gerard Lysaght the gravel road in front of St. James High School and convent was paved in 1960. The Sisters also shared some of the

---

[68] FC, Feb. 1951: 93, CDPA.

[69] FC, Jan. 1950: 51, CDPA. Only Sisters who volunteered were missioned to colored schools of the Congregation. Some, such as Sister Celeste Lehmann, taught 30 or more years in black schools in Louisiana. "CDP Newsletter," 3, 8 (1 April, 1976): 158.

[70] Oral interview, 9 Sept. 2000, CDPA. Sister Karen Kudlac was also inspired by the thankfulness, strong extended families, and strong manifestations of faith she saw in African American students in Houston (oral interview, 14 June 2000, CDPA).

[71] Oral interview, 28 July 2000, CDPA.

hardships and humiliations of the segregation against which they fought. The St. James team performed well in the black basketball league. When their games were scheduled in New Orleans over 200 miles away, there was only one place on the road where they could buy food or use the restrooms. Sister Anna Rose Bezner, music teacher at St. Francis School in Alexandria, invited the St. James choral group to a music festival. Three days before it was scheduled to begin, she received threatening telephone calls warning, "Your life is in jeopardy for inviting those from the black school" and daring her to have a "mixed festival." The festival was held, but security was heightened and plainclothes men were around to protect her.[72] The St. James singers won second place.

While Sister Elise Bengfort was the principal at St. James, she received a phone call from the mayor of Alexandria after one of the teachers, Sister Jane Marie Gleitz, took her class on an outing to a nearby park. The mayor said: "I should put you in jail. You let one of your classes go to the city park, and that's against city law." "If that's what you have to do, then that's what you have to do," she replied. Knowing that the African Americans would protest, the mayor backed down. Sister Elise also remembered shopping in a department store in Alexandria where a clerk asked, "Are you at Prompt Succor or St. Francis [the "schools for whites"]?" "No, I'm at St. James," Sister replied. The clerk walked away and would not ring up the purchase.[73]

The year the Supreme Court ruled for integration, Sister Elizabeth McCullough, the CDP Superior General, advised Bishop Charles P. Greco of Alexandria, Louisiana, that the Sisters would withdraw from St. James School for blacks in that city with the encouragement of Monsignor John Wakeman because it was time to take a critical "look at a separate school system for the Negro." Civil authorities were pressuring for one unified system. It is a "mistake for the Church to continue to maintain a dual system; it is a stand we can no longer justify." The Sisters, therefore, would leave St. James "with the expectation that students will be admitted to Menard High School," a Catholic school they staffed which was located in the same town.[74] Former Sister Sherry Pittman, "the very best teacher from St. James," was assigned to Menard. After Bishop Greco closed St. James School, Sister Elise Bengfort and Sister Jane Shafer worked in St. James parish from 1974-1977, departing only because of disagreement with the pastor over appropriate religion textbooks.

Sister Carolyn Pelzel recalled that after St. James School closed, many of its students came to Prompt Succor, the grammar school, where she was teaching

---

[72] Oral interview and CDPA, *Movements*, 3, 1 (Fall/Winter, 1999): 8.

[73] Sister Elise Bengfort, communication to the author, 21 Jan. 2003.

[74] The African American students who transferred were not charged tuition, a fact that the parents of some of the white students resented.

first grade. Students whose parents objected to desegregated public schools came as well. "We were a small school, then suddenly we were being stormed by many white parents who had never wanted Catholic education before. Now they did not want their child to sit next to a black child in the public school, so they came to us." Sister Carolyn testified that Sister Frances Trochta, the principal, took a stand when she became aware of the situation. "Sister Frances led the community in saying that unless attendance at Catholic school had been the family's priority in the past, we would not accept the new student."[75] Sister Frances herself recalled that CDPs at Prompt Succor School experienced a "conflict of values not only with the hierarchy there but with the families and the culture." She felt that she received "tremendous support" from Sister Elizabeth McCullough, who "recognized that this was a social justice issue and told the pastor: 'If you let Sister Frances go, we will not send a replacement for her.' I had not had the experience in my own life of a Superior General taking a stand against a pastor and contradicting his wish."[76] The following year, Sister Carolyn remembered, "our contracts were not renewed, and we were asked not to return. The pastor wanted the school as full as possible, so he hired other Sisters."[77]

"White flight" was a concern that motivated an unsuccessful lawsuit filed by a group of black parents in Marisville, Louisiana, against the diocese of Alexandria in April, 1972.[78] Some of the Sisters stationed nearby shared that concern. In the 1972 spring semester, a year after the CDPs left Natchitoches and three years after they withdrew from St. James School, Sister Imelda Maurer, assistant principal in Menard High School in Alexandria, informed the General Council that Father Warren T. Larroque, the principal, no longer needed two Sisters in the theology department. The General Council felt that "if Menard continues to accept students in disregard of the ruling on integration, the administration need not support the school by replacing personnel on a one-to-one basis." A suit pending against the bishop could lead to a change in its admission policy.[79]

The following semester, four younger Sisters teaching at Menard High School in Alexandria[80] sent a letter to the General Council. Sister Theresa Anne Billeaud and Sister María Carolina Flores had been at the school for three years. Sister Imelda Maurer had been there for two years, and Sister Charlotte Kitowski was in her first year. Sister Theresa Anne had already requested and received

---

[75] Sister Carolyn Pelzel, oral interview 21 June 2000, CDPA.

[76] Sister Frances Trochta, oral interview, 19 June 2000, CDPA.

[77] Sister Carolyn Pelzel, oral interview, 21 June 2000, CDPA. Congregational records show that CDPs were at this school until 2000, CDPA.

[78] See *San Antonio Express-News*, 4 April 1972; and *National Catholic Reporter*, 5 Jan.1973, CDPA.

[79] GC minutes, 14 April 1972, CDPA.

[80] Two other Sisters in the community did not sign the letter.

permission from the General Council to transfer from a parochial to a public school system "so that she could give special attention to the needs of the blacks in the integrated public school."[81] She, along with Sister María Carolina Flores and former Sister Sherry Pittman who was stationed at St. James School, had supported some African Americans who were boycotting the largest department store in downtown Alexandria. Sister Theresa Anne remembered that the U.S. Bishops had gathered Catholics together to discuss how to implement Pope Paul VI's Apostolic Letter, *Octogesima Adveniens, A Call to Action,* and the Rome Synod of Catholic Bishops' document, *Justice in the World,* both published in 1971. Bill Callaghan, SJ, from Washington D.C.'s Center of Concern was giving a workshop on the work of the U.S. Bishops' and others on these documents. Sister Imelda Maurer, Coordinator of the community at Menard, encouraged Sister Theresa Anne to go to this workshop. "It was just a really big turning point in my awareness of the social documents and what was going on in the world."[82]

The four Sisters had noticed that "a large number of students throughout grades 9-12 were transferring to Menard from the public schools and about nine from the private academies here."[83] When they asked the principal, Father Larroque, whether he was implementing the diocesan admission policies, he claimed not to be aware of the policies.

Sister Imelda scheduled several meetings with Monsignor John Wakeman, diocesan School Superintendent, and others; but she was not satisfied with the outcomes. The "major concern" of these Sisters was "the social injustice, the scandal of the situation and the contradiction between the actuality at Menard and what the Major Superiors and the document, 'Quest for Justice,' have called for. We feel that the Congregation needs to take a public stand on this issue."

> If there is no way in which diocesan officials and Father Larroque could be made to see and resolve the conflict between their flaunting of the Bishop's admission policies and our Congregation's convictions on this matter, then we would recommend that our Congregation withdraw its personnel from Menard High School.[84]

---

[81] GC minutes, 11 Oct. 1972, CDPA.

[82] Sister Theresa Anne Billeaud, oral interview, 20 June 2000, CDPA.

[83] Information for this section is from the 8-page letter the four Sisters sent to the Central Administration on 18 January 1973. The letter includes quotations from the Sisters' Constitution; the 1971 letter of Sister Elizabeth McCullough to the people of Natchitoches; the policy statement of the Louisiana Conference of Major Superiors of Women, 15 January 1970; and "Quest for Justice," a document of the 1971 Synod of Bishops.

[84] Letter of the four Sisters of Holy Savior Menard Central High school to Sister Elizabeth and Members of the Council, 18 Jan. 1973, CDPA.

Three of the four signers, however, were willing to remain at Menard if replacements could not be found.

The General Council discussed the letter and "the need to personally interview students to determine their purpose in coming to Menard. Clouding the issue were high emotions and personality conflicts between a number of the parties involved," so the topic was tabled, and no decision was reached. Sister Mary Margaret Hughes visited the Menard Sisters and reported to the Council that they "showed varying attitudes and values." The issue was white flight, but it was noteworthy that "since Menard offered free tuition this year for blacks and blacks did not apply, perhaps this shows blacks are not interested in Menard." The Council was also aware that the financial situation at Menard was not secure. They had a lengthy discussion of the "type of Sister who could likely do the most good in the situation which involved the students, the faculty, the administration, the parents, the Sisters themselves, the total Congregation, and the civic community of Alexandria."[85] Of the six Sisters assigned to Menard in 1972-1973, only one returned the following year along with four new Sisters. Starting in 1994, only one CDP was assigned to Menard.

Broussard

The Sisters had withdrawn from their Louisiana schools for African Americans, and the students who had attended these schools were enrolling in public rather than Catholic high schools. Meanwhile in the Evangeline country farther south, Sister Bernie (Robertine) Galvin was sent to be Principal of St. Cecilia's Elementary School[86] and Coordinator of the community in Broussard, a small town ten miles south of Lafayette, Louisiana, in 1970.[87] Broussard, like most of southern Louisiana, was predominantly Roman Catholic. Rev. John P. Kemps, a native of Holland, had been the pastor there for more than 40 years; and more than a dozen of his parishioners had become Sisters of Divine Providence.[88]

Sister Bernie remembered "the second year that I was there, I took steps to integrate the school. I almost brought the white community down on my head, but I survived it." She began by asking the School Board members "why there weren't blacks in our community and why after all these years were there no

---

[85] GC minutes, 27 Feb. 1973, CDPA.

[86] St. Cecilia's High School had closed in 1964.

[87] Sister Bernie taught in Louisiana for the first time at St. Mary's in Natchitoches during the 1969-1970 school term.

[88] Similarly, in Plaucheville, Louisiana, a community with fewer than 700 residents where the Congregation started an elementary boarding school in 1899, seven families had daughters who became CDPs (Sister Agnes Leonard Thevis, oral interview, 19 June, 2000).

black kids in the school. They said it was because they couldn't pay the tuition. So what I did was to seek wealthy individuals who would just privately, quietly pay the whole year's tuition for black kids."[89] The state superintendent of schools, Louis Micheaux, was one of the persons who responded to her appeal. Five or six black students enrolled, and the new situation was addressed at the next school board meeting.

> One woman said, "Why do we have those black children in our school? Why didn't you tell us that there were going to be black students or that there were new students this year?" I said, "I didn't know we had a new policy that I had to tell you new students were coming to school. We didn't have a policy that said that the Principal had to check with the Board when new students come to the school." There were just these icy stares as I continued, "Unless you are implying that in some way the new black students are somehow different from the new white families that come in." That was the end of that.[90]

This meeting, however, was the beginning rather than the end of tensions within the community and in the diocese as well as in the Congregation. The integration of the Broussard school illustrates the difficulty of answering the call to both justice and unity in difficult times of social transition and of balancing individual convictions with Congregational membership. "Maybe our ordinary bent has been to work toward justice without alienating our benefactors, our community members, and the general public; but 'being a sword of division' has also been a recurring theme in our history."[91]

Sister Bernie next started to tutor black children in the community after school. In the sugar cane plantations, especially in St. Martinville and St. John's plantations, Sister Bernie found "absolutely appalling" situations and "began to feel drawn more and more to minister there. The more I became involved with sugar cane workers simply by visiting them in their houses, the more the wrath of the local sugar cane plantation owners, farmers, and politicians came down on me."[92]

---

[89] Oral interview, 12 Sept. 2000, CDPA.

[90] Oral interview, 12 Sept. 2000, CDPA.

[91] Sister Margit Maria Nagy, communication to the author, 29 July 2004. Some factors that increase the difficulty of interpreting reported events in Broussard include the confidentiality required of Congregational leaders, the importance of training for effective social advocacy, and attitudes to racial and ethnic groups molded by one's family, economic status, and personal experience. Other factors include how others view the personalities and methods of those who advocate change.

[92] Oral interview, 12 Sept. 2000, CDPA.

In October 1972 the Executive Director of the Southern Mutual Help Association (SMHA), Sister Anne Catherine Bizalion, a Dominican from France, had informed sugar cane growers in the Lafayette area that, thanks in part to efforts by Ralph Nader, a federal court decided they were to grant back pay to the sugar cane workers for the 1971-72 harvest season. Sister Bernie and Mrs. Curley Bernard, a leader in the Broussard black community, asked Sister Anne Catherine to meet with local small farmers. By January white farmers on small farms informed Monsignor Kemps that they were angry about the meeting, blamed him for supporting Sister Bernie, and threatened to withdraw support from the school. A very emotional meeting was held on January 18, 1973. Besides the farmers, local police officers and politicians were present. After the meeting, tensions escalated. Sister Bernie was called a Communist and attempts were made to defame her character. Although the Congregation had decided to assign Sisters to Broussard for 1973-1974, the decision began to be reconsidered. In February Monsignor Kemps read at all Masses a statement issued by the Congregation and asked not only his parishioners but all citizens of Broussard to complete a survey concerning support for the school and the Sisters.

Letters of support for Sister Bernie and Monsignor Kemps included letters from Sister Theresa Drago, President of the Council of Religious Women; Bishop Gerard L. Frey; and Rev. William Crumley, CSC, co-chair of the "Poverty and Related Concerns Committee' of the New Orleans Provincial Conference of Bishops and Priests' Councils. Father Crumley said he and the bishop both thought "it would be a mistake to close the school in Broussard as well as a mistake to replace Sister Bernie."[93]

In April 1973, Sister Bernie petitioned the Congregation's Personnel Board to replace two of the Sister-faculty at the Broussard school. In previous years, six Sisters had been assigned to Broussard. Only Sister Bernie and Sister Mildred Leonards were missioned there in the fall of 1973. Sister Mildred, who grew up in the area on a rice farm rather than a cane plantation, remembered Sister Bernie as an excellent principal. She would spend the weekends going to the plantations while Sister Mildred went home to visit her mother, who was ill. Looking back, Sister Mildred said that although she was aware of injustices, she did not have a militant attitude. "In those days there were many things we did not question. That's just the way it was, so I don't think I even understood the situation enough. I think my feeling was, 'That's wrong, but what do you do?'"[94]

Both Sister Mildred and Sister Bernie resigned in April 1974. The General Council decided that the Sisters who resigned would not be replaced "not just because of the principles as stated by Sister Robertine. . . but because of other

[93] Statement by Rev. William Crumley, CSC, 3 March 1973, CDPA.

[94] Oral interview, 1 Sept. 2000, CDPA.

irreconcilable differences which have been building up for many months and which make the bearing of Christ's message impossible for the Sisters in Broussard at this time."[95] Out of concern for Sister Bernie's safety, the Superior General asked her not to return to Broussard." She replied, "My obedience is to the Spirit, and I feel called by my conscience to return to Broussard."[96]

The new pastor, Father Harry Benefiel, asked Sister Bernie and Sister Imelda Maurer (who had come to Broussard the year before to do social ministry in Abbeville, Louisiana) to move out of the convent. They moved into a nearby house owned by Father Kemps while they worked full time with sugar cane workers.[97] Upon the recommendation of Father Crumley, Sister Imelda petitioned for this assignment because she was attracted by the purpose of SMHA, "to remedy the *causes* of poverty and injustice through trying to change legislation, by working with legislators, through a program of public relations" that aimed "to involve more of the public at large" and inform them "of situations which exist but are ignored."[98] In 1975 the two Sisters moved into a house inside the black community in Broussard. They refused financial support from the Congregation and took part-time jobs as court reporters in Crowley, Louisiana.[99]

Although Sister Bernie and Sister Imelda obtained support from individuals inside and outside of the Congregation when they stood up for the rights of black workers in the community where their school was located, they also experienced lack of support there as well as within the CDP. Their stance did not stimulate a corporate commitment or a united effort on the part of the Congregation to combat racism or poverty at this time.

The three situations in Louisiana reviewed here differed from each other, but the scenarios had common elements: a few Sisters took a stand against segregation; they met opposition; the Congregation closed the institution or withdrew the Sisters; these Sisters found other outlets to work for social justice.

Other minorities

From their first days in Texas the Sisters taught pupils from different ethnic backgrounds belonging to groups that were self-contained in a small rural area. Pupils were often immigrants or children of immigrants of German, Polish, and

---

[95] GC minutes, 16 May 1974, CDPA. St. Cecilia School in Broussard, staffed by lay teachers, continues to this day.

[96] Oral interview, 10 Sept. 2000, CDPA.

[97] GC minutes, 13 July 1974, CDPA.

[98] From a 4-page statement on Holy Savior Menard Central High School letterhead by Sister Imelda Maurer, 14 March 1973, CDPA.

[99] Sister Bernie Galvin, oral interview, 10 Sept. 2000, CDPA.

Czech descent. Often the Sisters helped preserve their culture by teaching their language. For example, Father Charles Weisnerowski wrote to Mother Philothea Thiry that he was disappointed she did not send a second Polish-speaking Sister to his Catholic school in Brenham, Texas. Sister Laura Bielski taught Polish to 160 out of the 180 students in the lower grades each day for half an hour. The priest's motive was to maintain enrollment. He feared to "lose parents" who send their children six to eight miles for Polish instead of to nearby public schools.[100] That he also had other motives later came to light. Two years later Mother Angelique wrote

> I regret that I am unable to comply with your request for Sister Laura to return. It had become uncomfortable for her to be used as an intermediary in financial matters, and she herself asked for the change on this account. . . . [S]he also felt that her people would be ready to contribute as far as was within their means, and that it would be painful to them to have to refuse you through her.[101]

Later some Sisters were able to cooperate in international outreach projects. Sister Margit Maria Nagy, born in Hungary, for decades built bridges of understanding and appreciation for Asians, especially between Asians and Hispanics on the west side of San Antonio. She received two Fullbright grants to Japan and served as consultant for the International affairs Department of the City of San Antonio during a trip to its sister city, Kumamoto. In 1989 she founded the Japan Information Center, a free telephone information service to the general public on Japan; and in 1990 she was the keynote speaker for the opening of the City of Kumamoto's Women's Center.

When the number of immigrants from Asia increased after the Vietnam War, some Sisters were also ready to help. Sister Angelina Murphy and Sister Ermelinda Cannady, for example, taught English to Vietnamese immigrants in Oklahoma in the 1980s and Sister Nicole Bunnell tutored Hmong immigrants in Milwaukee in the 1990s.

The greatest number of minorities with whom the Sisters were in contact were immigrants from Mexico and their descendants who settled in urban as well as rural areas. As indicated in previous chapters, these Mexican Americans were often treated like Blacks, segregated and the object of deliberate neglect and prejudice. The Congregation started a school in Comal Town near New Braunfels, Texas, to accommodate Mexican American students not welcomed in the parochial school where CDPs were teaching. In 1953 Mother Angelique

---

[100] Rev. Charles Weisnerowski to Mother Philothea, 21 Aug. 1941, CDPA.

[101] Mother Angelique to Rev. Charles Weisnerowski, 12 Aug. 1943, CDPA.

wrote, "The School in New Braunfels is ours, but there is no Catholic School for the Colored there, and the [Colored] children were accepted without question."[102] In 2001, however, Sisters recalled that white parents in New Braunfels did threaten the pastor when Blacks enrolled in the parochial school, and Archbishop Lucey had to settle the dispute.[103] Mexican children remained segregated in the Comal Town school until it closed in 1960.

During group interviews conducted in 2001, Sisters mentioned instances of prejudice against Mexican Americans. For example, a pastor in San Antonio would not admit a Hispanic child into an Irish school in 1947. Sister Jane Ann Slater a dozen years later discovered that the local barber in Castroville, Texas, would not cut Mexican people's hair. The hair of Joe Fuentes, a valuable football player at St. Louis High School, exceeded the required length. "Coach Keller said he himself would cut Joe's hair if Joe would get to his house before dark because he cut hair in the garage, which had no lighting. Joe worked and couldn't be there that early, and coach wouldn't let him play without the haircut. It was a no-win situation."[104] Eventually the coach and Joe worked it out, and Joe continued to play on the football team.

OLL College and OLL High School always enrolled Mexican students from both sides of the border, mostly from families that could afford private education. Sister Elizabeth Anne Sueltenfuss thought that "when we were an all-girls' school, there was a real sense of collegiality." But when she was teaching biology in the 1950s and 1960s, Mexican American students came to be about 25% of the student population. Some of them, unlike the resident students from Latin America, were economically poor. She remembered that a Mexican American "student biology major went with a group to Corpus Christi for a conference. Returning, she came into my office sobbing because she had felt all kinds of prejudice. The Anglos did not include her in any social aspects of the trip."[105]

Although individual Sisters fought for individuals who were the objects of prejudice, the Congregation did not take a public stand against discrimination against Blacks or Mexicans. In general the Sisters accepted the local social status quo. By the early 1970s, however, CDPs began to approve the Civil Rights movement and attempt to put Gospel and Vatican Council II principles, as well as new civil policies on integration, into practice. They were well informed and more articulate than many Sisters had been in pre-Council times and were being encouraged to make more decisions for themselves. They had also been

---

[102] Mother Angelique Ayres to Mother M. Rose Kallus, 1 July 1953, CDPA.

[103] Group interview of Sisters who ministered to African Americans, 14 June 2001, CDPA.

[104] Oral interview, 25 May 2000, CDPA.

[105] Oral interview, 20 Oct. 2000, CDPA.

"conscienticized" during their formation as religious or later by closer contact with laypeople and their problems, especially those due to discrimination and poverty. For them the call of the second Vatican Council to apostolic religious was to leave the cloister and find God in the world. As Sister Patrice Sullivan stated, "we cannot live our charism of trust in and abandonment to Divine Providence without inserting ourselves into the whole of creation and the earth and being part of trying to right some wrongs."[106]

Sister Jane Coles concluded that the seeds for greater involvement in social issues were planted by Sister Elizabeth McCullough. "She brought broader views of social justice to the Chapter of 1973. That was the first Chapter in which we set goal statements instead of just formulating rules and regulations. We made direct goal statements which related to social justice."[107] One of the five goals of this Chapter was to support justice by uniting with others in order to liberate individuals and groups.

Sisters eager to implement Church teachings, however, often met resistance from influential clergy as well as lay people. When individual Sisters wanted to reform institutions served by the Congregation, their efforts seemed to be stymied at every turn. The institutions were closed or the Sisters were withdrawn by order of superiors.

Sister Bernie, along with a number of other Sisters, thought:

> When I look at the closing of the schools, it is sad because I think that was one of the greatest impacts that Sisters made. . . . Most of those [schools] were in little rural areas, and that's what we were founded for: to teach the poor kids in rural areas. But closings may also have been a factor in Sisters' moving into other areas of ministry. More of us are in social justice areas now, so that may have been a positive move.[108]

Instead of dampening their zeal or causing them to lower their ideals, obstacles led some Sisters to search for other outlets and partners. As a result, the influence of the Congregation was increased and widened through them.

---

[106] Oral interview, 27 June 2000, CDPA.

[107] Oral interview, 17 Jan, 2000, CDPA.

[108] Oral interview, 12 Sept. 2000, CDPA.

MCDP Sister Carmen Zita Villasana and CDP Sister Berta Anguiano, Mother Amata Regan and Sister Rosa Margarita Martinez admire a gift from Mexico, 1960s.
(Joe Bacon)

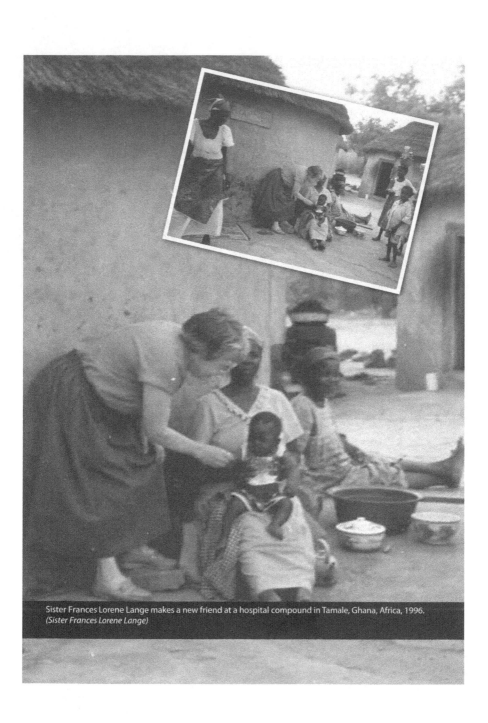

Sister Frances Lorene Lange makes a new friend at a hospital compound in Tamale, Ghana, Africa, 1996.
(Sister Frances Lorene Lange)

Sister Rachel Moreno visits a family in Querétaro, Mexico, 1979.
(CDP Archives)

Sisters Jean Marie Halleux, Charlene Wedelich, Marie Emmanuelle Bernt, and Luz Maria Escudera at the Eighth International Meeting of the Sisters of Divine Providence in San Antonio, 1981 (CDP Archives)

CHAPTER 9

SERVING THE MARGINALIZED AND DISENFRANCHISED

"Social justice" is a relatively new word in the long history of the Roman Catholic Church. In the last 50 years it has been a prominent and often contentious topic as minorities spoke up for their rightful piece of prosperity and liberation thinkers supplied theoretical frameworks and reasons for challenging those who benefit most from the current status quo. This chapter will detail how some individual Sisters addressed unjust situations, how feminism impacted the CDP, and how the Congregation, along with other U.S. women religious, moved from "cultural conventions of interaction . . . to patterns and processes expressive of American egalitarianism, openness of purpose, and fascination with the experimental." The Congregation was not prominent among groups whose "active presence in social transformation is constitutive of their identity,"[1] but its efforts were steady and persevering.

Individual Efforts to Promote Justice and Peace

The Sisters involved in opposing segregation in Louisiana in the1970s, as detailed in the previous chapter, were considered "troublemakers" or "radicals," even by some of their own Sisters. A survey of the subsequent ministries of each of them shows their continued interest in the plight of the disadvantaged and their efforts to alleviate, if not eliminate, their suffering.

---

[1] Lora Ann Quiñonez, CDP, and Mary Daniel Turner, SNDdeN, *The Transformation of American Catholic Sisters* (Philadelphia: Temple University Press, 1992) 72.

226

Sister Ida Marie Deville went on to assignments in traditional CDP ministries in Texas and Oklahoma until she was finally able to realize a lifetime dream to be a missionary. She did not go overseas but to St. Vincent's Mission in David, Kentucky, in 1981. There she was instrumental in raising the educational and economic level, especially of women, in the Appalachian region.

After leaving Alexandria, Sister María Carolina Flores moved into the Mirasol Housing project bordering the Motherhouse in San Antonio and was subsidized by the Congregation to do social work at Meadowood Acres, a development carved out of a pasture full of mesquite trees west of the city. Its inhabitants were displaced from their homes in central San Antonio by the 1968 Hemisfair. The developer who sold them land did not provide basic services. In the little time remaining after their long commutes to work in San Antonio, the residents with her help united to meet their basic needs and improve their dwellings.

In 1983 and 1984 Sister María Carolina went to Nicaragua with the Witness for Peace project, which advocated "non-violent resistance to the U.S. overt or covert intervention" and changes in U.S. foreign policy.[2] She served as a translator and saw for herself the suffering as well as the courage of the people.[3] Sister María Carolina also persistently supported the Chicano and feminist movements in her classes at OLLU. She was instrumental in the initiation and continuation of the campus Center for Women in Church and Society. In her opinion, the social justice involvement of the Congregation at the turn of the century is still "not cutting edge." She suggested some reasons why: (1) The Congregation in its early days defied a bishop and suffered for it, so it is in the habit of avoiding any trouble with Church leadership. (2) Many Sisters are from rural areas, which tend to be conservative and "red-neck" in this part of the country. (3) San Antonio is a conservative town, and we do not want to offend supporters and donors. (4) We are more institutionalized and have more to risk if we challenge the status quo.[4]

Sister Charlotte Kitowski's concern for minorities found an outlet in teaching remedial English courses so they would have a better chance of succeeding at OLLU. In the summer of 1975 she was employed off-campus and donated her salary to relieve world hunger.[5] From 1977 through 1987 she promoted methods to achieve more equity in the election of Chapter delegates to the Congregation's

---

[2] GC minutes, 29 Feb. 1984, CDPA.

[3] Oral interview, 25 May 2000, CDPA. Six years later the Sandinista government was replaced. The new president, Violeta Barrios de Chamorro, widow of martyred newspaper editor Joaquín Chamorro and the first woman to govern a Central American country, had attended Our Lady of the Lake High School some 45 years earlier.

[4] Sister María Carolina Flores, oral interview, 25 May 2000, CDPA.

[5] GC minutes, 1-3 Apr. 1975, CDPA.

General Chapters. Later she returned to the public school system, educating predominantly black and Hispanic students.

Sister Theresa Anne Billeaud taught math to Black students at Landry High School in New Orleans for four years and was involved in the Gallo wine boycott. After earning a Master of Theology and Ministry degree with a focus on social ethics from the Jesuit School of Theology in Chicago in 1981, she directed the Congregation's first, and only, Office of Social Justice for three years. She was told to give special emphasis to "the Congregation's public commitment to stand with the materially poor."[6] The Congregation, she felt, "was ripe for the emphasis on social justice and looking at the structural causes of problems in our world."[7] While she was director, she conducted a social analysis of Providence High School. During this time, the Congregation on the local level lent money to the Westside Parish Coalition project to build affordable houses[8] and cooperated with Communities Organized for Public Service (COPS) and the Industrial Areas Foundation (IAF).[9]

During her time as director of the Congregation's Social Justice Office, Sister Theresa Anne realized that other religious in San Antonio were also looking for ways to address social concerns. Together they founded and for five years she directed Camino a la Paz, an inter-congregational office for peace and justice efforts in San Antonio. Among her projects was helping to found the Refugee Aid Project, on whose board she served. She continued to be involved in social justice ministry, especially through her membership in Pax Christi New Orleans.[10] She and several other members joined tens of thousands who gathered outside the School of the Americas in Georgia to protest the training of military officers, predominantly from Latin America.

After leaving Menard High School, Sister Imelda Maurer offered basic education for plantation workers under the auspices of the Southern Mutual Help Association. She wrote a peri-natal care manual for women in the sugar cane plantation and used it as the final requirement for her Master's Degree in Science Education from the University of Texas in Austin. She organized workers

---

[6] GC minutes, 8-10 Sept.1981, CDPA.

[7] Oral interview, 20 June 2000, CDPA.

[8] GC minutes, 11 Oct. 1984, CDPA.

[9] IAF's mission is to train people to organize themselves and their institutions to take responsibility for solving problems in their communities and to renew the interest of citizens in public life. Its goal is to make democracy work through a restructuring of power and authority relationships so that the powerless can come to understand for themselves that they not only can but also should actively participate in economic and political structures that affect their lives. (Description supplied by Sister Christine Stephens)

[10] Pax Christi USA, a section of Pax Christi International, the Catholic peace movement, promotes peace by exploring, articulating, and witnessing to the call of Christian denominations to create a peaceful world.

to address plantation problems, which included bad housing, meager education, poor nutrition, and low wages. After 10 years she noted some improvement:

In 1980 Sister Imelda and Sister Bernie left Louisiana for Greenville, South Carolina, where they worked in a J.P. Stevens mill to "become immersed" in the culture of the textile worker.[11] After a year they moved to Bennettsville and became involved in the Hanes plants, owned then by Consolidated Foods and later by Sara Lee. They organized the workers around health issues, working with women who had generically cumulative trauma syndrome, also known as tendonitis or tennis elbow. With the assistance of a union organizer, they brought together a national coalition of faith-based people to dialogue with the corporation. As a result, the Hanes Company did implement ergonomic changes.[12] Sister Imelda went on to earn an MA in the Administration of Long-Term Care Facilities and Retirement Communities from the Applied Gerontology Department of the University of North Texas in Denton in 1999.

When Sister Bernie Galvin went from teaching to advocating for sugar cane workers, the local federal poverty agency supported her work. She also sought encouragement by joining NAWR, the National Assembly of Women Religious, founded in 1969, whose members shared an "avowed commitment to transform the Roman Catholic Church into an institution where women are treated equally, and oppression and racism . . . are not officially condoned." She saved her money for 18 months to attend the national convention in San Francisco in 1975 "to look for hope. Every day I see Sisters and priests buckling under to the economic, political, and social power structure down there. That's the most depressing thing I have to deal with. To see religious people who can and should be courageous go along with racism and oppression is heartbreaking."[13]

Sister Bernie also organized nursing home workers at two mental hospitals in Virginia. With the Congregation's support, she then took a two-year sabbatical at the Graduate Theological Union in Berkeley, California, where she "began to feel this call in my heart to work with homeless people."[14] For two years she was a union organizer with hospital and health care workers in the San Francisco area. The city had 14,000 homeless people with 1,400 shelter beds and an official policy of citing and arresting homeless people for sleeping in parks when there was no other place to sleep. In 1993 under the city's "matrix program" over 136,000 people were arrested or cited for "quality of life" violations. Sister Bernie detected the absence of the united voice of the interfaith community to speak out, so she "organized the interfaith leaders of the Muslim, Buddhist,

---

[11] Sister Imelda Maurer, oral interview, 23 June 2000, CDPA.

[12] See *San Francisco Sentinel*, New Mission News, June, 2002, CDPA.

[13] Article by Lacey Fosburgh, *The New York Times*, Wed., Aug. 27, 1975.

[14] Oral interview, 12 Sept. 2000, CDPA.

Christian, and Jewish communities to publicly demonstrate against the "matrix program."[15]

Arrested several times, notably during the campaign to stop the demolition of Wherry Housing in the Presidio of San Francisco, Sister Bernie was described as a "scrappy and tenacious fighter for the underdog who challenges the policy puppets who so often fail to reflect on their stance. Her tough looks combine with a gentle, yet passionately compassionate, southern voice."[16] On the national level, she organized members of the Religious Leaders' National Call for Action on Housing to endorse the National Affordable Housing Trust Fund campaign.[17]

After Sister Pearl Ceasar and Sister Christine Stephens spent a year at the community center in Houma, Louisiana, their paths separated but came together again when they were employed by the IAF. Sister Pearl became aware through her experiences in Natchitoches how deep racism was because

> the social consciousness of people had not been formed. A football team was more important to them than having religious education, and it was acceptable to let a Catholic school become a school for segregationists. It was also a turning point in my life. I knew I needed to know more if I was going to bring about social change. So I studied at Worden School of Social Service at OLLU for two years and got my MSW. Then I was in Network in Washington D.C. for three years.[18]

While she was in Washington working with Network, Sister Pearl read an article about COPS in San Antonio and immediately resonated with its goals. She returned to San Antonio in 1976 and was hired by Father Bill Davis, OMI, to organize for COPS at St. Alphonsus parish.[19] Further organizing led her to work with The Metropolitan Organization in Houston, El Paso Interreligious Sponsoring Organization, The Metro Alliance in San Antonio, Valley Interfaith

---

[15] Oral interview, 12 Sept. 2000, CDPA. The group called itself the Religious Witness for Homeless People. Its aim was to end municipal abuse of the homeless and to address housing, health, and employment needs of the indigent. Congregational funds helped subsidize Sister Bernie's ministry from 1993 to 1999.

[16] Eric Robertson, *Street Spirit*, 8, 12 (Dec., 2002): 8 and 9.

[17] Sister Bernie received numerous awards for her services and was praised by Andrew Cuomo, National Secretary of Housing and Urban Development, for her efforts.

[18] Oral interview, 18 Aug. 2000, CDPA. Network, founded in 1971 by Catholic Sisters, is a national Catholic social justice lobby.

[19] Disastrous floods on the west side of San Antonio in 1972 contributed to the birth of COPS. Newer neighborhoods had adequate drainage while those on the west side of town, despite repeated efforts, could not get the city to construct adequate drains.

in the Rio Grande Valley, and Dallas Area Interfaith. "Through organizing with IAF in Churches and Congregations, people learn what the possibilities are and develop a sense of hope. I wanted to organize because I saw how people changed in relationship to themselves, their families, their community, and their Church. To me, faith is about the transformation of people. That is what organizing does."[20]

After working in Houma, Sister Christine Stephens returned to her hometown of Houston, where she did social work at St. Theresa's parish and became active in the ecumenical group of ministers, priests, laypeople, and women religious who raised money and support for an IAF organizing drive in Houston. Sister Christine became the chair of the interfaith sponsorship committee, which raised enough funds to sustain for three years the group that evolved into The Metropolitan Organization (TMO).

> TMO is an inter-faith and interracial coalition of congregations and schools in the metro Houston area. . . . Its work is nonpartisan. . . . TMO teaches its members how to reclaim their birthright as active citizens of a democratic country who can work together for the common good. The issues TMO members address come out of hundreds of individual and small-group conversations conducted by its leaders. It is definitely a "bottom-up" approach to activism.[21]

Sixty-five Church organizations from many denominations became members.[22] When Peter Martínez from Chicago asked Sister Christine to become a leader in IAF in 1978, she was ready to step into this more central role. She credits organizer Ernesto Cortés of IAF for empowering her and providing a framework at a time in her life when she felt confused.[23]

Sister Christine said, "We are not as proud of the projects that get done as we are of the people who come alive because of their activity in these organizations, such as organizing to get water and sewers for the poor communities of the border *colonias*." She discovered unrecognized talent in these communities and was convinced that "if we identify them and invest in them, they can do

---

[20] Sister Pearl Ceasar, oral interview, 18 Aug. 2000; and "Profiles of Faith," *Texas Catholic* (Dallas), 15 Aug. 2003, CDPA. Sister Rose Ann Blair was also active in Valley Interfaith in the area of housing and drainage. This organization helped bring a sewer system and pavement of the streets in Sebastian, Texas (Sister Rose Ann Blair, oral interview, 19 June 2000, CDPA).

[21] *SCJ News* (a publication of the Priests of the Sacred Heart, Hales Corners, WI), 24, 3 (June 2003): 3.

[22] *CDP Times*, 1, 4 (Jan. 1981): 1, CDPA. Around this time Sister Bernadette Bezner was President of the ecumenical Ministerial Alliance in Harlingen, Texas.

[23] Oral interview, 18 June 2000, CDPA.

extraordinary things. The monument to our work is mainly the leaders that are in these projects."[24]

Both Sister Pearl and Sister Christine, with the support of the Congregation, became successful organizers for IAF, which is present in most Texas dioceses and has 53 organizations throughout the U.S. As a result, they have had wide experience with racially and economically diverse ecumenical groups that work in a practical way for justice.[25]

Besides the Sisters who tried to integrate schools in Louisiana, other individual Sisters were involved in meeting needs outside the classroom and promoting justice. PHS teacher Sister Marian Maurer, accompanied by Sister Catherine Fuhrmann, helped once a week after school at the Women's Shelter of San Antonio.[26] Sister María Guerra did community organizing with COPS when she, along with two Sisters who also taught full-time at PHS, lived in the Veramendi Housing Project for low income people in San Antonio in the 1970s. Sister María also taught catechism to youth in nearby St. Timothy's parish and worked with the summer remedial reading program at Guadalupe Recreation Center. Sister Margit Nagy worked with Senior Community Services to provide programs for senior citizens at the Rex Apartments and Villa Hermosa. In the summer of 1968 she taught for six weeks with four Presentation Sisters in Project REACH on the East side of San Antonio, offering special help in reading and arithmetic to African-American children in grades one to six.[27] During the racial tensions in Crystal City, Texas, in 1969, she was part of a team of teachers led by State Senator Joe J. Bernal who went there over the Christmas holidays to help public school students make up for instruction they had missed.[28]

Sister Madlyn Pape, who also resided in Veramendi, felt:

> We should be and need to be involved in a wider world, elbow to elbow with all kinds of people, especially people struggling with family and economic problems. We are to be a part of others' lives, and they should be comfortable being around us in a variety of settings and situations. It always bothered me when people were afraid to

---

[24] Oral interview, 18 June 2000, CDPA.

[25] In 1977 Sister Christine was offered an opportunity for graduate study, but she turned it down "because of the important work she had become involved with in connection with the farm worker movement for unionization" (GC minutes, 30 Mar. 1977, CDPA). She did participate in training by the Management by Design Institute (MDI) offered through the Congregation in 1977, but she preferred IAF's emphasis on action to MDI's approach to leadership training skills (Sister Christine Stephens, communication to the author, 24 Feb. 2003).

[26] *CDP Times*, 1, 4 (Jan. 1981): 4, CDPA.

[27] "CDP Summer News Bulletin," 16 June 1969: 5, CDPA.

[28] Sister Margit Maria Nagy, communication to the author, 29 July 2004.

talk to me because they might offend me rather than trusting me as an individual who cared.[29]

Sister Margaret Rose Warburton during decades as a librarian at OLLU expressed her concern for justice issues by recommending reading material. In her 60s she concretized her sympathy for the disadvantaged by moving into the Mirasol Housing Project for low income families, and upon retiring from the University she moved to Houston to do hands-on service of the poor. Sisters Paulette Celis and María Cristina Ruelas had a definite sense of improving life for the disadvantaged by preparing meals at a shelter for battered women and their children in San Antonio.[30] Sister Mary Bordelon, as Director of Catholic Community Services for the diocese of Beaumont, Texas, published a monthly newsletter and gave workshops on justice education. She noticed that "some Sisters are into recycling cans or things like that, which aren't great, big, colossal world-changing events, but they are making their difference in their own way."[31] Sister Cora Machacek, for example, collected more than 115,000 aluminum cans on the convent and college campus during a four-year period. "I'm just a housekeeper," she insisted. "It is good to know that I have been of some use."[32] Sister Mary pointed out: "Many Sisters have a commitment to peace and justice even if they do not want to be pegged as a peace and justice person. And I think they are probably doing more than they realize. They are somehow contributing to systemic change by writing a letter to their Senator on some issue or correcting sexist language."[33]

Individual Sisters with conviction and vigor protested, marched, boycotted, wrote letters, and signed petitions for a variety of causes they found worth supporting. The United Farm Workers, the sanctuary movement for Central American Refugees, anti-abortion efforts, opposition to the death penalty, Habitat for Humanity, Bread for the World, Food for the Poor, and the Nature Conservancy are among groups that have found advocates among CDP individual Sisters and groups. While former Sister Evelyn (Mary Teresa) Thibeaux was studying at the Graduate Theological Union in Berkeley, California, in the 1980s, she met activists like Martin Sheen and Jessie Jackson and protested several times at the Livermore Lab.[34] Seven Sisters and a novice made the Pilgrimage of Peace to

---

[29] Oral interview, 21 Dec. 2000, CDPA.

[30] Sister Paulette Celis, oral interview, 29 July 2001.

[31] Oral interview, 20 June 2000, CDPA.

[32] *San Antonio Light*, June 27, 1982. She sold these cans at 20 cents a pound, donating $1,014 to the Sisters' retirement fund.

[33] Oral interview, 20 June 2000, CDPA.

[34] Oral interview, 15 June 2002, CDPA. Sister Alexia Vinklarek lobbied in Washington, D.C. against the MX missile when she was on sabbatical there in 1983 (oral interview, 21 Jan. 2000, CDPA).

Pantex in Amarillo, Texas, in 1984 to protest the manufacture of nuclear weapons. Sister Ayleson Maxwell succeeded in getting a lawyer for a woman in Noel, Missouri, who was jailed for feeding stray dogs. Her bond was set at $25,000, the same amount set for another prisoner who admitted shooting someone point blank. The lawyer uncovered corruption in the system.[35] Sister Assunta Labrado enabled people in the small West Texas town of Sierra Blanca to march in protest of nuclear waste coming through their community from New York.[36]

Sister Dianne Heinrich summarized her efforts on behalf of the marginalized in society. "I try to be quite sensitive to people who are left out and excluded. In my everyday dealings, whenever there is a least person, I make a special effort to include or help that person. I'm aware of them, and I try to take the steps necessary for someone to help them if I can't do so myself."[37] Similarly, Sister Barbara Lynn Hyzak said, "I deliberately treat the women I work with or those I care for who are at the low end of the totem pole with respect. I give them positive feedback to help them realize their work and care is important and meaningful. I try to help them feel that they have a gift they are giving."[38]

Women's Issues

Sister Angelina Breaux, along with a number of CDPs, did not think of advocacy for women as a "new" role. "We were founded to work for justice for marginalized women, and all through the years this spirit has permeated our individual members and our Congregation as a whole. We were always looking to help the sad child, the underdog, those who did not feel they were equal to the rest." She added, "We looked for the marginalized though we did not use this word at the time."[39] But most of the Sisters also came from families and communities where, in the words of Sister Annalee Prather, "the father was the father and the mother was the mother, and certain roles were delegated to each one."[40] It took a while to realize that often some roles, along with the people who held them and the rewards they received, were considered superior to others. The feminist movement in the U.S. sparked new insights into the basic equality of all human beings.

Some Sisters admitted they were not in favor of the women's movement when they first heard about it. Sister Antoinette Billeaud "thought they were

---

[35] Sister Bertina Maxwell, Sister Ayleson's older sister, oral interview, 23 June 2000, CDPA.

[36] Sister Assunta Labrado, oral interview, 29 May 2000, CDPA.

[37] Oral interview, 20 June 2000, CDPA.

[38] Oral interview, 18 Jan. 2001, CDPA.

[39] Oral interview, 20 Oct. 2000, CDPA.

[40] Oral interview, 14 Mar. 2000, CDPA.

making a mountain out of a mole hill."[41] To Sister Jane Coles they "seemed to be so extreme, so hammering at it, that at first I was turned off."[42] Sister Lora Ann Quiñonez credited an LCWR assignment to give a paper linking celibacy and the women's movement for her own awakening to women's oppression. In 1974

> what I knew about the women's movement was how to spell the two words. But I literally put myself through the equivalent of an 18-hour course on the women's movement. After reading George Tavard's *Women and the Christian Tradition* and Elizabeth' Janeway's *Man's World, Woman's Place* and other books, I was in a totally different place. I began to recognize the effect that sexism had had on me.

> After giving the paper in Bogotá, I experienced hostility, but some of the Latinas linked it with liberation theology and got on board fast. That experience radicalized me, so I continued to study and read and bring up the topic at meetings with the Bishops and in Rome, getting horrendous reactions. Later I got involved in pro-ERA activities, learning all the ways in which U.S. laws discriminate against women.[43]

Sister Rosalie Karstedt acknowledged that she thought the women's movement

> was not really very Christian because there was such anger. It seemed like the feminists were always putting God and the Church down, so I did not like the feminist movement when it first started. But I think it had to happen, and it has moved us on to other issues and brought things to our attention that maybe we were not aware of. It takes everybody in the Congregation to help us grow. When someone gets passionate about one particular issue, it helps the rest of us to learn and grow.[44]

---

[41] Oral interview, 1 June 2000, CDPA

[42] Oral interview, 17 Jan. 2000, CDPA.

[43] Oral interview, 13 June 2000, CDPA.

[44] Oral interview, 20 June 2000, CDPA. Sister Frances Trochta went to a meeting of the National Organization for Women (NOW) in the late 1970s. "Our Congregation was not part of that; I didn't see another CDP there. What bothers me is not that we are not in the forefront but that sometimes we give lip service to something and don't support it in our lives. For example, at one time we were proclaiming that the person was our most important concern; but in my community, I didn't feel there was real respect for the person" (oral interview, 20 June 2000, CDPA).

Some Sisters became aware of the unrecognized dignity and power of women from deeper study of the Bible. For example, Sister Genevieve Prochaska remembered that a prayer service at the Convent one summer brought forth many women from Scripture, "their names, what they did, and how they were recognized. It made me aware how many women were mentioned in the Bible and how meaningful they were."[45] Other Sisters became sensitized when they learned of laywomen's experiences. Sister María Carolina remembered a woman who kept coming late to her evening class at OLLU. Finally the woman told her the reason: Every time she got ready to go to class, her husband picked a fight and delayed her. He threatened to leave her if she got a degree. Sister María Carolina said she "had not experienced such things in my family, among my friends, or in the convent. It opened my eyes to the plight of many Latinas."[46]

Discovering the misogyny experienced in patriarchal institutions and sometimes in the Church was enlightening for many Sisters. Sister Lucille Ann Fritsch, for example, said that her eyes began to open when she heard some laywomen tell their stories at gatherings which the Bishop of Victoria, Texas, programmed to discuss women's issues when the U.S. bishops were thinking of writing a letter on the subject. "I saw how laywomen had been treated by clergy, what had been said to them, what was expected of them, how they had been treated or mistreated. I began to be more conscious of the unjust treatment of women within the Church as well as in society."[47] It is noteworthy that the Congregation stood in solidarity with Sister Agnes Mary Mansour, RSM, who, despite Vatican opposition, wished to continue serving the poor in an organization that allowed birth control.[48]

Sister Jane Ann Slater was instrumental in re-organizing the structure of the meetings of the Bishops of Texas with major Superiors of women religious to be more inclusive. She also stood up to Bishop René H. Gracida of Corpus Christi after pedophilia cases were first publicized. He wanted all superiors of women religious in his diocese to become totally responsible for their Sisters' behavior by signing a paper indicating they would know where every Sister was 24 hours every day. The Superiors refused, pointing out that surely he himself did not know what each of his diocesan priests was doing 24 hours of every day. Sister Jane Ann reflected that the Sisters "as a group are very resilient and accepting of reality. We deal with the fact that we are excluded from most of the functions of the Church. But our problem is with individuals in the Church rather than with the Church. The Church is our home, and we are in it for the

---

[45] Oral interview, 15 Sept. 2000, CDPA.

[46] Oral interview, 25 May 2000, CDPA.

[47] Oral interview, 9 Sept. 2000, CDPA.

[48] GC minutes, 15 June 1983, CDPA.

long haul." She is convinced that "we are going to hang in and not let ourselves be thrown out."[49]

Sister Carolyn Pelzel remembered that from childhood she valued women and girls as images of God that were created good. "The Women's Ordination issue was always important in my life because I think there are many women, including myself, who are called to ordained ministry."[50] Although she was not a member of the National Organization of Women (NOW), she did attend the first Women's Ordination Conference. Sister Frances Klinger and Sister Charlotte Kitowski earned Master of Divinity degrees with the intention of being qualified should women be admitted to ordination in the Roman Catholic Church.

The Sisters' growing experience of making more decisions for themselves probably increased their awareness of women who lacked freedom and were not given their just deserts. Many, like Sister Julian Honza, attributed their support of women's equality to the simple consideration that women "have a right to equal pay when they are doing the same kind of work that men do."[51] Former Sister Evelyn Thibeaux stated that what she gained most from the Congregation was a sense of her own dignity and power in a real inner sense.

> In the world outside the Congregation, you find out pretty quickly that it is very much a man's world. When you work in the Church like I have, you realize that lay people almost automatically look up to the men. But there is a sense of very deep spiritual authority that I have always seen in the Sisters, and I think it has grown through recent years.[52]

Sister Assunta Labrado thought "women have an obligation to share who we are. If we can share, then we can work together."[53]

---

[49] Oral interview, 25 May 2000, CDPA.

[50] Oral interview, 21 June 2000, CDPA. Interviewed at age 85, Sister Josepha Regan said, "I would not like to see women ordained to the priesthood. I think women have their job, and they have enough to do without being ordained priests. But maybe the day will come; and if it does, I'll accept it" (oral interview, 2 Jan. 2000, CDPA).

[51] Oral interview, 28 Feb. 2000, CDPA.

[52] Oral interview, 15 June 2002, CDPA. Sister Ann Regina Ross recalled an incident that showed her sensitivity to women's issues. "I was working on an introduction for Father Paul Ceasar, and I wrote 'women and men.' He came and said, 'I think you put this wrong; you are supposed to say men and women.' I said, 'I want to say women and men because it makes people think'" (oral interview, 18 June 2000, CDPA).

[53] Oral interview, 29 May 2000, CDPA. Sister Rose Frances Rodgers said, "I personally think that it is not a matter of women being ahead of the church. I feel that we should walk side by side, particularly with the clergy. They have their work to do, and we have our work to do" (oral interview, 25 Feb. 2000, CDPA).

Reflection on Scripture, on women's experiences of violation of their basic human right to equality, and on their own worth and power fueled support of feminist issues. Many Sisters also said their awakening to women's oppression began when they became aware of the pervasiveness of exclusive and sexist language. Sister Charlotte Kitowski remarked, "The very fact that men will fight to keep that 'she' language out, especially in the Church, tells me something. Language does affect the way we perceive ourselves."[54] Sister Annalee Prather remembered that her "views changed as we began to use inclusive language more. I saw what words can do to our understanding and our attitudes, and I began to change my own views." For her, this was more than a theoretical exercise. "The more I heard about how women live in situations that are abusive, the more I realized that we can keep them in that relationship unless we are more proactive in promoting use of words that are more inclusive for women."[55]

Sister Sharon Rohde at one time felt that she "was being asked to worship a language rather than God. I didn't believe prayer is a time to use as a teachable moment. But once I came to terms within myself, I found that I am very much a person who uses inclusive language."[56] Sister Regina Decker "was as shocked as anybody the first time I heard somebody call God 'Mother.' But when you stop and use logic, you say, 'How could we ever have thought God is male? God is more than man and more than woman and more than the two put together.'"[57]

Some CDPs commend Sister Lora Ann Quiñonez for sensitizing them to the important role of language in shaping attitudes and values. Sister Lora Ann herself insisted that although more precise verbal expression is needed for full recognition of women's gifts and talents, it is not enough. Women need humility to dialogue and search for a better future. "We women must not be willing to settle for the gains we have made if they have not touched our deepest identity with regard to God." Finding their own deepest identity is for women a step to become clearer about God's identity. "Shared attentiveness in God's presence will show us where God wants us to go."[58]

The Center for Women in Church and Society at Our Lady of the Lake University was a concrete Congregation-supported response to perceived discrimination against women. While former Sister Jane Shafer was director of the Center, she started the volunteer Family Assistance Crisis Training (FACT) program to advocate for women living in abusive situations as well as Women's

---

[54] Oral interview, 13 March 2000, CDPA.

[55] Oral interview, 14 March 2000, CDPA.

[56] Oral interview, 20 June 2000, CDPA.

[57] Oral interview, 8 Nov. 2000, CDPA.

[58] Videotaped interview, CDPA.

World Banking, which is now run by the YWCA. Later she became coordinator of the Family Assistance Crisis Team Program for the city of San Antonio,[59] and after she left the Congregation in 1996 she headed the Victim's Assistant Unit of the San Antonio Police Department.[60] She also coordinated the first celebration at a San Antonio university of women's history month and the bestowal of a women's history award. Among the award recipients were Emma Tenayuca, organizer of the pecan shellers' union; Hattie Briscoe, the first African American to graduate from the law school at St. Mary's University; and María Antonietta Berriozabal, a graduate of PHS in San Antonio, an elected member of the San Antonio City Council, and the founder of an enterprise that increased amounts of money awarded to women to start businesses.

Two Sisters directed their efforts to securing women's rights in the legal and political spheres. Sister Patrice Sullivan became an attorney out of concern for women. She was coordinating social services at an upper middle-class parish when she realized people who came for emergency assistance "didn't need money for a tank of gasoline but some legal protection to escape an abusive spouse." When she tried to find lawyers in the parish, she became aware that they worked for corporations and "didn't know anything about family law and protecting children." She decided she had to help. "My most creative approach was to go to law school." When as an attorney she was doing legal work for low income people, women with children were about 98% of her clients. She was gratified whenever

> the sexism predominant in our society and our world was named and dealt with. Women were actually coming forth and talking about their experience of being raped. Until the women's movement, they were isolated and not supported.
>
> All women can identify with the lack of creditability, oppressions, abuse, and disrespect that for centuries women have experienced. I see the Women's Movement as a very important expression of the sacredness of all human beings and respect for their dignity.[61]

Sister Deborah Ann Fuchs had opportunities to promote the welfare of women in the health care field. As a representative for the Coalition of Texas Certified Nurse-Midwives, she influenced the rules and regulations for Advanced Practice Nurses. She explained how this involved her in the work of social justice:

---

[59] GC minutes, 8-11 Sept. 1992, CDPA.

[60] Jane Shafer, oral interview, 3 March 2003.

[61] Oral interview, 27 June 2000, CDPA.

Physicians stand in the way of Advanced Practice Nurses working to the fullest of their scope and education. These doctors have power, prestige and money they sometimes do not want to share, even for the improving or enhancing of health care and health care education of patients. My work on the political action committee for Advanced Practice in Texas has broadened my horizons and given me real insight into power, the political system, and ways to influence change.[62]

Many Sisters sympathized with feminist activists though they did not consider themselves activists. Sister Agnes Marie Marusak, for example, said, "Sometimes the way women pushed ahead might be objectionable, but for the most part I admire the women who were not afraid to stick their necks out to bring about the idea that women are equal to the male of the species. I think there has been tremendous progress, but there is still a tremendous distance to go."[63] Sister Angelina Breaux's response to her college students who disapproved of the feminist movement was: "You should be thankful for those who choose to be revolutionaries, who do outrageous things to capture the attention needed to correct inequities. Some day you'll recognize that they have done you a favor."[64]

The Congregation as an Agent of Social Change

Sister Lora Ann Quiñonez, a General Councilor from 1973 to 1979 and Superior General from 1993 to 1999, was of the opinion that "many of the Sisters who took up the peace and justice cause in the 60s were very angry women. They were often fighting against the Congregation, and they delighted in making everybody else feel guilty, so they didn't change any hearts. The same thing happened in the larger society." She noticed that "all U.S. congregations of religious speak about peace and justice as if it were a separate agenda," but it is not a project or "an activist's agenda but part of the way one lives her life. What undergirds peace and justice is right relationships." Peace and justice is "largesse of hospitality toward everybody, regardless of how different he or she is. The Blessed Trinity provides the best model for relationships between persons."[65]

CDPs do not see the Congregation as a strong agent of social change, but the Sisters thought the greatest progress made in the area of social justice was

---

[62] Oral interview, 23 June 2000, CDPA.

[63] Oral interview, 16 Aug. 2000, CDPA.

[64] Oral interview, 20 Oct. 2000, CDPA.

[65] Oral interview, 13 June 2000.

when Sister Theresa Anne Billeaud was director of the Congregation's Office of Social Justice from 1981 to 1984. She encouraged the Sisters to analyze the groups in, with, and to which they ministered in terms of structures and operative systems, which were sometimes hidden. Who held the real power in various situations? How could the Sisters and their pupils or clients promote equality? Having maintained an institution for many years was not a sufficient reason for continuing it if it was not contributing to a more just society. In deploying personnel and investing its funds, the Congregation began to give more priority to helping the poor and disenfranchised. Ministry was seen more as making a difference in society rather than as continuing a tradition.

While she was director of the CDP Social Justice Office, Sister Theresa Anne worked with other religious in the area to found the Texas Coalition for Responsible Investment (Texas CRI), to help individuals and groups balance their economic policies and practices with their faith and social concerns. A member of the national Interfaith Center on Corporate Responsibility (ICCR), the coalition later changed its name to Socially Responsible Investment Coalition (SRIC). With the help of SRIC membership, the CDP, along with other members, filed and voted on shareholder resolutions involving social issues.[66]

As Sister Imelda (Charles André) González explained, "Social responsibility is broader than just our investments. We have responsibilities as consumers on where we buy and what we buy. As employers, we are responsible for the benefits we offer and the working conditions we maintain."[67] In 1983, for example, plans were made to file a stockholder resolution with Consolidated Foods Corporation and Hanes Hosiery on tendonitis and repetitive motion diseases.[68] The Congregation began to divest itself of stocks in companies on the U.S. Defense Department's list of top 100 military contract holders.[69] It co-filed with American Baptists a resolution with the Texaco Corporation asking that they withdraw their operations in racist South Africa.[70] The General Council destroyed all of its Exxon credit cards and closed that account, advising the company this was due to their "slow and irresponsible response" to the Exxon Valdez Alaska oil spill in Spring 1989.[71] The Congregation also raised questions

---

[66] GC minutes, 11 Nov. 1985, CDPA. In 1986 an Investment Advisory Committee composed of Sisters and later also of laypeople was formed, and a policy on socially responsible investments was approved in 1990 (GC minutes, 2 Nov. 1990, CDPA).

[67] Oral interview, 15 June 2000, CDPA.

[68] GC minutes, 21 May 1983, CDPA.

[69] GC minutes, 18 Dec. 1985, CDPA.

[70] GC minutes, 8 Dec. 1983, CDPA.

[71] GC minutes, 30-31 Oct. 1989, CDPA.

of social concern with the Chevron Corporation, Eastman Kodak, Chesebrough Pond's, Wendy's, and Houston Industries, to name a few.[72]

A review of General Chapter decisions also reveals a growing awareness and involvement. After the General Chapters of renewal after Vatican Council II held in 1967 and 1968, the subsequent Chapter of 1973 turned its attention to apostolates or ministries, as they were beginning to be called. The General Chapter of 1973, in harmony with a number of U.S. Congregations of religious, expressed its cognizance of the oppression of women, planet Earth, and all who are excluded from benefits. The five goals formulated at this Chapter concerned uniting with others to promote human liberation, apostolic spirituality, life issues, peace, global consciousness, families, support for girls and women, care of the earth, and responsible use of technology. These goals raised the Sisters' consciousness of the need to use water and other natural resources responsibly and to recycle paper, aluminum cans, and glass.

The General Chapter of 1981 followed the assassination of Archbishop Oscar Romero and four women catechists in El Salvador as well as the Jonestown murders and suicides and the Three Mile Island nuclear accident. It took place during the rise of Poland's Solidarity movement under Lech Walesa and the Iraq-Iran War. John Paul II was the new Pope and Patricio Flores the first Mexican-American archbishop of San Antonio. The year of the Chapter, San Antonio elected its first Mexican-American mayor in modern times, Henry Cisneros; and Sandra Day O'Connor became the first woman on the U.S. Supreme Court. Despite disasters, social change seemed possible as the Chapter re-formulated a goal of the 1977 general Chapter: "We form ourselves and others in justice, concretely furthering the transformation of oppressive systems. We actively unite with others, especially minorities and Third World peoples struggling to liberate themselves from the bondage of economic deprivation, racism, and ignorance."[73] The General Chapter of 1993 made a formal commitment to promote the welfare of women and girls, the Earth, and the excluded that formalized long-standing practices and served as reminders that work for justice is important and never-ending.

The topics of women and liberation were addressed by a number of speakers at the annual summer gatherings of the Congregation in the 1970s and 1980s. The theme for the summer of 1979, for example, was "Women Sharing a

---

[72] GC minutes, 13-17 Nov. 1989, CDPA.

[73] A goal of the 1981 General Chapter, CDPA. See Appendix V for synopses of chapter acts after Vatican Council II.

Steps to cooperate on justice issues included the assignment in 1978 of Sister Patrice Sullivan to "Texas Impact, an inter-religious network sponsored by national Protestant, Roman Catholic, and Jewish agencies . . . designed to educate members of Texas religious communities regarding issues of racial, economical, and social justice and to influence public policy on behalf of all people" GC minutes, 8 May 1987, CDPA.

Destiny." At the turn of the century, many Sisters were involved in doing what they could to stop the worldwide trafficking of girls and women.

Movements for peace, laborers' rights, and affordable housing also received support. A Peace Pole was planted at the Motherhouse in the summer of 1989, and the Convent Center was removed from the list of Civil Defense Shelters and declared a Nuclear Free Zone.[74] Sister Lourdes Leal pointed out that "some Congregations had to make big environmental decisions because of a crisis or pollution or because they had to move a building. We've symbolically planted trees, but as a Congregation we've never really had to put our money where our mouth is, to take a corporate stand on the environment."[75] The Congregation endorsed Cesar Chavez's United Farm Workers and boycotts of Campbell soups and California grapes.[76] It was one of nine religious Congregations to make long-term commitments to Merced Housing Texas, which was founded in 1995 to respond to the need for housing justice for the economically poor. Merced was a subsidiary of Mercy Housing, Inc. of Denver, Colorado, until it became an independent San-Antonio based organization in 1999.[77]

In 1970 former Sister Helen Rose Fuchs asked for social action by the Congregation with regard to the war in Cambodia; but Sister Elizabeth McCullough, the Superior General, told her, "Each individual must adopt her own position, which cannot be dictated by the Congregation." More than a decade later, at the request of a Congregational working committee, the RA approved a process for taking a corporate stand in July 1984.[78] Cluster 6 of Oklahoma immediately spearheaded a campaign to declare the Congregation a sanctuary for Central American refugees. Proposals were outlined, recommended, discussed, and debated. The Social Justice Committee explained the Immigration Reform and Control Act and provided an integrative prayer experience for spring cluster meetings in 1990. The process demanded 100% endorsement rather than a consensus, and a corporate stand was not achieved. The closest approximation to a corporate stand on this issue came in the spring of 1991 when the clusters reported that the majority of their members supported assisting refugees and CDPs who supported them. One such person was Sister Margarita Sánchez, who worked from 1994 to 2000 in Casa Providencia, an inter-Congregational

---

[74] GC minutes, 10-11, 15-17 April 1991, CDPA.

[75] Oral interview, 8 Aug. 2000, CDPA.

[76] GC minutes, 6 Feb. and 26 Sept. 1985, CDPA. Sister Assunta Labrado, among others, remembered that the stands and fasts of César Chavez changed her way of thinking about the bracero movement (oral interview, 29 May 2000, CDPA).

[77] CDPA, GC minutes, 1-4 Nov. 1994. Sister Anne Michele Berry for a time was employed by Mercy Management Services in Denver, Colorado, assisting families to obtain affordable housing (GC minutes, 22 June 1989, CDPA).

[78] The 10-page process was employed at the spring cluster meetings in 1984 and revised in 1988 (See GC minutes, 4 Feb. 1985, CDPA.

project in San Benito, Texas, to help refugees from all over the world who were in the legal process of entering the U.S. They were offered training in life and language skills as well as spiritual and psychological support.[79]

When Sister Theresa Anne Billeaud in 1984 closed the Congregation's Office of Social Justice, her CDP Advisory Board was designated a congregational working committee.[80] In 1992 the CDP RA officially dissolved the CDP Social Justice Committee at its own request. "Our awareness of justice issues has deepened, and justice is becoming integral to who we are."[81] Since fewer Sisters were willing to serve on the committee, the work of the committee was to become the responsibility of every individual and continue through local communities and cluster structures. Individuals and groups were to share news of their efforts with all the Sisters.[82] Some corporate efforts continued, however. For example, the Congregation established a "Special Needs Committee" which annually disburses a set amount of money to organizations that work with and for marginalized people. Also, the RA urged the U.N. Earth Summit meeting in Brazil in June 1992 to adopt principles that would assure future generations a healthy planet Earth.

Why was there resistance within the Congregation to taking a firm, public stand on a controversial issue? Lack of interest or information, fear or human respect, strong individualism, and absence of a sense of common mission have been named as possible factors. Some Sisters might have been negatively influenced by the particular person or group inside or outside the Congregation that was promoting the issue. Sister Lucille Ann Fritsch cited fear as well as hesitancy to dictate to others as factors possibly accounting for the lack of communal stands on justice issues.

> Sometimes I leave the General Assembly disappointed that we haven't decided as a group on one particular action. We just leave it open to do what you want to do however you want to do it. I don't feel that this is as effective as 'We're all going to do this,' or 'We're going to do X, and you have a choice of one of these three ways to do it.' I have a feeling that we're afraid as a community to *all* jump in together, so we haven't been as effective as we could have been.[83]

---

[79] Sister Margarita Sánchez, oral interview, 23 June 2000, CDPA.

[80] GC minutes, 15 Nov. 1984, CDPA. Sister Ann Petrus, who was for a time on the board of Camino a la Paz, thought that "many efforts to promote peace and justice have become systemic. They've become part of our ordinary way of thinking and ordinary acting, and we don't call as much attention to them" (oral interview, 30 June 2000, CDPA).

[81] GC minutes, 11, 13-16 Nov. 1991, CDPA.

[82] GC minutes, 11, 13-16 Nov. 1991, and RA minutes, 3-5 Jan. 1992, CDPA.

[83] Oral interview, 9 Sept. 2000, CDPA

Some believed that because the Sisters had accepted certain prevalent societal values such as materialism or individualism, it was difficult to persuade the group to be prophetic or counter-cultural. Those who are materially prosperous benefit from the prevalent status quo and are loathe to alter it. Sister Lora Ann Quiñonez deplored

> the huge emphasis after Vatican Council II on me, my happiness, my fulfillment, my discernment, my needs, etc. We ended up cultivating a narcissism that is not compatible with religious life. The behavior says, 'I am the center of the universe, and everyone else is charged with my happiness, especially if I have been a victim of any sort.' The more individualistic we have become, the less possible it is for us to take any kind of corporate position.[84]

Father Bill Morell, OMI, added that the trend away from common projects to more isolated and individual ministries made it more difficult to take a corporate stand.

> I do not perceive you as a Congregation with a tight focus or sense of common mission. You do have a mission held *in* common. You clearly identify with people in need and commit to helping the marginalized. Individual Sisters are doing very good work. They are connected personally to one another, but they are often not connected ministerially. You are not seen as a group that is associated for a common endeavor or a common mission.[85]

As this chapter has shown, all of the Sisters have become more aware of social injustice; and some Sisters in particular responded with both passion and effectiveness. Dr. Albert Griffith thought that the Congregation "was very responsive to all the social movements of the 60s and 70s" like anti-war, women's liberation, free speech, ecological and world justice. "In fact, some of the mission statements that the Congregation produced during that period almost read like

---

[84] Oral interview, 13 June 2000, CDPA. She added, "We did not become polarized as a result of Vatican Council II because we did not develop mistrust of one another's motives. Also, we didn't fall into the ideological trap of thinking that because Sister X thought a certain way, I have to think that way." Sister Rose Kruppa thought that because "we are real individuals, we have a hard time agreeing. From my experience, we tend to focus on 'What is this going to cost me?'" Oral interview, 27 July 2000, CDPA

[85] Oral interview, 8 Apr. 2003, CDPA.

a manifesto of liberal causes from that period."[86] Sister Jacqualine Kingsbury's view was a bit less sanguine:

> As far as putting high priority of personnel, energy, money, or concerted effort on justice issues, I feel that the Congregation has wobbled. The effort has been sporadic. Besides Congregational statements and workshops, individual CDPs and their work impact and challenge us and move us all along as a whole group. We are not jet-propelled, but we are getting there.[87]

---

[86] Oral interview, 3 September 2002. The Congregation was not involved, however, in the gay and lesbian movement nor the free love movement, he noted.

[87] Oral interview, 20 June 2000, CDPA.

CHAPTER 10

MEETING NEIGHBORHOOD NEEDS

Sister Frances Klinger remembered that in the 1940s

> the College and Convent grounds were beautiful, but the
> neighborhood was poorly kept. We were isolated from our
> neighbors, and we didn't seem to be thinking about doing anything
> to make them different. We built fences and hired people to patrol
> the area so we would be safe from any invasion. We were very
> parochial, not thinking that we had something more we could
> offer to everybody.[1]

Sister Elizabeth Dale Van Gossen "knew that the housing project was behind us.
It was a very poor neighborhood, but we never really had anything to do with
it. It was just there."[2] Sister Assunta Labrado remembered, "We were divided
from the people in the housing project by a fence, and my heart always went
out to them. We did not integrate with them."[3]

Most CDPs worked outside San Antonio and returned to the motherhouse
for only a few weeks each summer, but the Congregation opened four institutions
that provided significant services to the impoverished west side of the city.
Previous chapters detailed the impact of Our Lady of the Lake University and
Stella Maris Clinic. The Worden School of Social Service and Madonna Center
were also important influences. The MCDPs also located their motherhouse on
the west side. Sister Frances Klinger at the turn of the 21st century could say,

---

[1] Oral interview, 20 June 2000, CDPA.

[2] Sister Elizabeth Dale Van Gossen, oral interview, 21 July 2000, CDPA.

[3] Oral interview, 29 May 2000, CDPA.

"I'm happy we have grown into a new understanding that we are a resource for this side of San Antonio."[4]

A brief survey of San Antonio demographics illuminates the neighborhood's needs, which the Sisters gradually learned to address in a more systematic way with more permanent solutions. In 2000 Hispanics comprised more than half of the population of San Antonio, Texas; but this was not always the case. German speakers outnumbered Hispanics and other Anglos in San Antonio, Texas, from about 1860 until after 1877; and in 1880 one-third of San Antonio's population of 20,550 was German.[5] Wealthy German immigrants built elegant homes on the city's near south side beyond the Irish flats neighborhood. Poor immigrants from Mexico settled on the near west side. Farther west toward Medina Valley stretched fields and mesquite brush. The three-story OLL convent begun in 1896 when the motherhouse was moved from Castroville to San Antonio resembled a skyscraper rising out of the prairie. Large fields of Belgian truck farms stretched toward Castroville to the west; but soon scattered, humble dwellings of recent immigrants from Mexico nibbled away the farmland as they crept closer from the east and south, surrounding the Convent and spreading rapidly westward. Mexican Americans soon became the majority ethnic group in the city.

Mexican American families dwelling in tiny, poor houses that often lacked electricity and indoor plumbing multiplied not far from the motherhouse doorstep during and shortly after the Great Depression of the 1930s. Some needy people came directly to the convent for help. When Sister Margarita Sánchez was a candidate she was "assigned to feed the poor people who came. We'd go to the academy and bring the food that was left over, and we packed it in gallon cans. Sometimes they would come to us with their health and family problems. We listened and prayed with them."[6] Sister Muriel Bodin recalled that in 1944 "the poor gathered on certain mornings with their buckets or gallon cans by the kitchen to be fed. It just touched me how they would come. There were so many. Sister Benitia and a Catechist taught some religion in Spanish, too."[7] Sister Lourdes Leal, who was a novice in 1960-61, recounted:

---

[4] Oral interview, 20 June 2000, CDPA.

[5] "San Antonio, Texas," *Handbook of Texas on Line.* http://www.tsha.utexas.edu/handbook/online/articles/view/SS/hds2html. Louis C. Ellsworth claims that two-thirds of the San Antonio population was German (*San Antonio During the Civil War*, Austin, Texas: University of Texas, 1938: 11-12).

[6] Sister Margarita Sánchez, oral interview, 13 Jan. 2001, CDPA.

[7] Sister Muriel Bodin, oral interview, 23 Feb. 2000, CDPA. Sister Kathryn Marie Rieger supplied details, "The Sisters would put oatmeal or some leftover food in the cans, and they put wax paper in between the different foods" (oral interview, 21 Feb. 2000, CDPA).

In the old days we'd had a food line, but by the time we were in the novitiate we were told we couldn't help them. Poor people would ring the doorbell of the novitiate and ask for food, and we would tell them we didn't have it; they could go to Madonna Center. One time we did prepare food for a family while they waited in the car. I used to think it was terrible that we couldn't help them.[8]

While individual Sisters did try to meet immediate needs where they were stationed, the Congregation also impacted larger groups, influenced policy-makers, and altered systems by training social workers at OLLU.

The Worden School of Social Service

The inception of the graduate school of social service dates back to March 1936 when Most Rev. Robert E. Lucey, bishop of Amarillo, Texas, spoke at a session of the Catholic Association for International Peace held at OLLU. He was convinced "that many social problems were related to the lack of professional social workers."[9] In 1941 he wrote to Mother Philothea saying that he intended to establish a school of social work in one of the San Antonio colleges.[10] Mr. Val M. Keating recalled:

Archbishop Lucey arranged a meeting at his office attended by Mother Angelique of Our Lady of the Lake College, Mother Columkille of Incarnate Word College, and me. The two "Mothers" were strong, wise representatives of their respective orders and Catholic educational institutions. Each believed it timely to establish a Graduate School of Social Work in Texas where none existed at that time and each of these determined women wished to set it up at her college. . . . .

No matter what obstacles I presented as to funds, qualifications and standards, Mother Angelique, always undaunted, smiled enigmatically and said softly, "We will meet all requirements and Divine Providence will provide."[11]

---

[8] Sister Lourdes Leal, oral interview, 5 Aug. 2000, CDPA.

[9] *The Southern Messenger*, 12 March 1936. During his tenure, 1941-1969, San Antonio grew from fewer than 200,000 to about 533,000 Roman Catholics and became nationally known for its programs for the poor.

[10] Archbishop Lucey to Mother M. Philothea, 25 Nov. 1941, CDPA.

[11] Val M. Keating to Mr. C. J. Collins, 14 Oct. 1977, OLLUA, Mother Angelique personal file, OLLUA. From 1942 to 1943 Mr. Keating was an instructor in Public Welfare Administration at the Worden School. Mrs. Val M. Keating was on

Her peaceful perseverance must have been persuasive, for OLL was chosen. The Archbishop "selected the first board members for the new school, and it was his expertise that saw the school safely launched and solidly established."[12] Beginning with a co-ed one-year program of professional training for social workers in October 1942, the school soon initiated a two-year program leading to a Master's degree in social work. The American Association of Schools of Social Work provisionally approved it in 1945.[13]

Sister Immaculate Gentemann, who taught at the Worden School from 1943 to 1970, recalled that it was the first graduate school of social work to be accredited in Texas and was the only *Catholic* school of social work in the Southwest, i.e., between the Mississippi River and California and between the Mexican border and St. Louis and Denver.[14] The state department of public welfare sent many of its employees, who already had field experience, to the school. Students could choose to concentrate on casework, group work, or community organization.[15] Worden School "was the first program in the country to adopt an innovative 'block plan' that allowed students to devote one semester to full-time field work, so their on-site experience was not restricted to several hours a week in San Antonio but could be distributed throughout Texas."[16]

Archbishop Lucey expressed his pleasure at the embodiment of his dream in a letter to Mother Angelique. "Enthusiastic congratulations on the honor which has come to your School of Social Work in being given membership in the National Association of Schools of Social Work! I am not surprised because Our Lady of the Lake College does all things well and this approval was inevitable."[17] As a personal gift, he provided a scholarship. Mrs. A. H. (Mary) Worden and her family later made a significant donation to the school, which was named the Worden School of Social Service in 1949.[18]

Sister Rachel Moreno while working toward a certificate in social work at the Worden School in 1946 also supervised a day nursery at Providence House in downtown San Antonio. The nursery was started in 1943 for children aged

---

the Worden School Advisory Council from 1946 to 1955.

[12] Privett, *The Pastoral Vision*, 142. The author notes that Lucey, who "had no professional qualifications to direct a social welfare program, became a strong proponent of professional preparation for those involved in such efforts," Privett, *The Pastoral Vision* 7.

[13] Callahan, *History* 278.

[14] *OLLU Magazine*, vol. 4, no. 4:1-3, OLLUA. The only other program of this kind in the region was at the University of Texas in Austin.

[15] Sister Immaculate Gentemann, videotaped interview, CDPA.

[16] Privett, *The Pastoral Vision* 143.

[17] Archbishop Lucey to Mother Angelique, 31 Jan.1945, CDPA.

[18] *San Antonio Express*, 10 Feb. 1960: C, 3-B.

four and five whose parents were either in the military or employed in wartime factories. When in 1943 it received a temporary license (temporary because the Sisters were planning to erect a new building) for 10 children, Mrs. Violet S. Greenhill, Chief of the State Division of Child Welfare, wrote to Archbishop Lucey

> Miss Hoskins told us, upon her return to Austin, that she had seldom seen a better-planned building. . . . Sister Rachel will do an excellent piece of work since she has spent time in New York [at Columbia University, 1941-1942], giving special emphasis to work with young children in a group situation. . . . This program should be a model for other day care projects in San Antonio and in the state. The Sisters are to be congratulated upon their new venture.[19]

The War Production Board gave a Preference Rating Order for the addition to the nursery on 1 April 1943. The General Council also decided to complete plans for an annex to house some Missionary Catechists of Divine Providence who had moved from Houston to catechize in the area.[20] By 1949 they were teaching nearly 500 children in 10 different centers and had rectified more than 80 marital cases.[21] Providence House was the hub for aid on all levels to the disadvantaged who resided on San Antonio's near west side.

After receiving an MSW degree from Catholic University in 1947, Sister Rachel continued to do social work on the west side for 10 years.[22] She was ready to cooperate when Mother Angelique "conceived the idea of establishing a home for the Spanish-speaking working girls" who were excluded from other residences in San Antonio. Providence House was renovated to accommodate the new residents of the Girls' Club, one of whom was blind.

Meanwhile the School of Social Work was getting established and poised to extend and multiply services like those of Providence House. Its first director, Miss Rita M. Fleming, had been working for Catholic Charities in New York City and was recommended by the New York School of Social Work. She immediately attracted qualified faculty as well as funds. Three members of the faculty were elected to offices in the San Antonio Social Workers' Association in 1943.[23] The Rockefeller Foundation granted the school $25,000 to be spent

---

[19] Violet S. Greenhill to Archbishop Lucey, 9 March 1943, CDPA.

[20] GC minutes, 6 May 1943, CDPA.

[21] FC, March 1949:131, CDPA.

[22] Sister Rachel recalled "Mother Angelique decided to send me to Washington to study. I wasn't very certain in my English yet, but I did it. She sent me, so I went" (Oral interview, 7 Nov. 2000, CDPA).

[23] *Alamo Messenger*, 28 May 1943, p. 4.

on teachers' salaries over a three-year period.[24] The school continued to flourish under Miss Fleming's successor, Mr. George Miles, who was hired in 1948. That same year at a meeting of the Texas Commission on Children and Youth Ms. "Catherine Lenroot, Chief of the U.S. Children's Bureau, highly praised the school and the Superiors of the Congregation for the pioneer work done in the field of social work in Texas."[25]

The Worden School of Social Service awarded its first MSW degree to a Mexican American in 1951 and to an African American in 1952. Professor Lorece Williams, the first full-time African American teacher at OLLU, taught at the Worden School from 1969 to 1992. Although the number of Sister social workers was always small compared to the number of classroom teachers, the influence of the Congregation through the Worden School of Social Service at OLLU has been significant.

Madonna Neighborhood Center

The Girls' Club initiated in 1939 at 403 Dwyer in San Antonio was the precursor to Madonna Center on Castroville Road. Offering programs similar to those at a nearby Boys' Club, the Girls' Club opened its doors to 38 girls from the area just west of the downtown Katy Railroad Station. Over 500 eligible girls ages 7-17 lived within walking distance of the center. Enrollment increased to more than 100 in the first month and to more than 390 by December 1939.[26] The girls came for job training as well as personal and social development, taking classes in typing, cooking, and sewing. Although the Homemaking Project was very successful, the Sisters "grew increasingly concerned about the exploitation of their trainees; they knew the young women were incredibly underpaid." At a special meeting, the Sisters decided this tiny salary "was in direct contradiction to a living wage in the light of Christian principles relating to social justice" and discontinued the project.[27]

The Girls' Club emphasized the value of a total "family" approach. Recreational, social, and cultural activities sponsored for this broadly-based membership had no restriction with regard to nationality, background, color

---

[24] GC minutes, 8 June 1945, CDPA.

[25] FC, March, 1948:134, CDPA.

[26] FC, Dec. 1939:166, CDPA.

[27] Roberto R. Treviño, "Facing Jim Crow: Catholic Sisters and the 'Mexican Problem' in Texas," *Western Historical Quarterly* 34 (Summer 2003): 151. Dr. Treviño thought that this experience, as well as the fact that the Sisters were exposed "to new ideas when they trained for social work in universities outside of Texas" helped to "explain the thrust behind the founding of the Worden School," p. 153.

or creed. Qualified professional leadership, ably assisted by volunteers, was a hallmark of the agency from the beginning.[28] By 1941 the Girls' Club was accepted as a member of the Community Chest, later known as the United Way. From that time it was always supported primarily by funds of this sort, not by the Archdiocese or the Congregation. By 1944 the Girls' Club had set up five extension units, one in the "Las Colonias" area on the west side of San Antonio, where 15,000 residents lived in "a city wilderness of unbelievable destitution and degradation . . . [with] juvenile delinquency, gang wars, chronic tavern brawling, school truancy, marijuana peddling, lack of water and sewers, high infant mortality, and high incidence of tuberculosis."[29]

Social workers from the Girls' Club began to address these problems and needs in a dance hall, which was not used during the day, located on the old Castroville Road. Soon they moved a few blocks farther west to a former dairy barn. In 1956 the name was changed to Madonna Center when it occupied a new building. Sister Immaculate, the first Executive Director, was convinced that for lasting results "the better method of approach is to help the people themselves to understand the causes of their needs and then do something about them cooperatively—in other words, to testify in their own behalf. Social action on the part of the people in their neighborhood is encouraged."[30]

The agency called Madonna Center "was the first in the neighborhood to have sewers, electricity, and water. Many people came in to keep warm and to take showers."[31] Its founders "challenged people to improve themselves personally and to extend this positive development to their families and their neighborhood."[32]

How did Madonna Center serve the neighborhood? Primarily in three ways: (1) comprehensive emergency assistance by providing basic household items as well as assistance from caseworkers in resolving crises and stresses, completing documents, and making referrals, (2) social development programs ranging from supervised recreation for children to care for senior citizens, and (3) day care.[33] Services to low income families and families on welfare were completely free of charge.

---

[28] Letter of Sr. Jane Ann Slater, Superior General, in "The Madonna Neighborhood Centers, Fifty Years of Service, 1939-1989," CDPA.

[29] "The Madonna Neighborhood Centers, Fifty Years of Service, 1939-1989," 8, CDPA.

[30] Sister M. Immaculate Gentemann, "Self-Help through Group Work," *Catholic Charities Review*, 36 (May 1952): 105. Sister Immaculate served as director of Madonna Center from 1946 to 1957.

[31] Interview of Mrs. Soledad Assiz, staff member, 17 Sept 1962, in "History of Madonna Neighborhood Centers," CDPA.

[32] "History of Madonna" 9, CDPA.

[33] "The Madonna Neighborhood Centers, Fifty Years of Service" 10, CDPA.

Sister Mary of Mercy Cunningham, director of the center from 1957 to 1963, recalled starting a kindergarten before the existence of Head Start, the federally-funded program to meet development needs of pre-school children from low income families.

> Our first kindergarten had 12 five-year olds who paid 25 cents a month. It soon grew to 140 children with four teachers and a supervisor. Those children spoke no English whatsoever but were thrown into an English-speaking first grade. Most of them dropped out in the second grade because they did not know what was going on. When Head Start came, we were able to spend more time on after school programs. We also had as many as 300 children coming on Saturday mornings.[34]

A board member became convinced of the need of a program for mothers to earn some money, not just now but for the future.

> Along with a very able staff member who taught sewing, she made patterns for the uniforms which volunteers wore at Santa Rosa Hospital, pink in the adult hospital and yellow in the children's hospital. The women at Madonna Center were taught to sew and finish the uniforms. Then she sold them to the people who ran the volunteer programs. The women who sewed the uniforms were very, very proud to have earned some money.[35]

In 1961 the Congregation relinquished control of Madonna Center to a governing board of 30 members. Two or three members of this board have always been CDPs.

While Sister Marian Angela Aguilar was Dean of the Worden School, she described the close relationship between Madonna Center and the Worden School:

> In many ways, the Worden School owes its existence to Madonna. . . . Perhaps without the firsthand experience of providing social services, the motivation to embark upon an educational venture of training social workers would not have reached fruition. . . . Your organization has provided a fertile training ground for generations of our students. The dedication, perseverance, and courage of the Madonna Center

---

[34] Oral interview, 6 Dec. 1999, CDPA.

[35] Sister Mary of Mercy, oral interview, 6 Dec. 1999, CDPA.

staff have served as an inspiration to numerous young social workers and have shown them what it means to truly care.[36]

In 1971 the Madonna Center Board considered merging with nearby Guadalupe Center. After meeting with people in the area who "were willing to work hard and bring the center back up to its original standards," the Board decided against the merger.[37] A few months later as a part of President Lyndon B. Johnson's "war on poverty" a Model Cities Day Care program started at the agency.[38]

That Madonna Center was needed is indicated by the fact that it was located in the Edgewood Independent School District, which had the highest percentage (31%) in the city of families below the poverty level in 1980. This district also had the highest rate (5.5%) of births to girls under the age of 17. While the infant mortality rate was declining in the nation as well as in Bexar County, after 1980 it increased 11% for those living in poor areas of the county.[39]

By 1975 Sister James Elizabeth González, director of the center from 1975 to 1981, employed a fulltime staff of 20 besides work-study students from Our Lady of the Lake University and St. Mary's University and two Worden School caseworkers under the supervision of a faculty member. Former Sister Micheleen Barragy of the OLLU faculty and volunteers kept the food pantry stocked for emergency cases. Sister James Elizabeth said, "I am just sorry we have to eat and sleep. When I see people in need, it tears out my very heart and drives me relentlessly. We are working to expand our programs. Our main deterrent is lack of money—the eternal struggle for money."[40] In 1994 the Board approved the use of $40,000 in surplus funds for scholarships for parents whose income was slightly above the amount that would qualify them for state assistance for children. The Center also provided scholarships for its day care teachers to obtain their teaching credentials. Among its material acquisitions were computers, equipment for athletic field, and five playgrounds as well as four 15-passenger vans and a panel truck.[41]

Madonna Center in 2000 offered a state-licensed Day Care/After School program for 198 children ages 6 months to 13 years and a full-day summer

---

[36] Sister Marian Angela Aguilar to the Board of Directors of Madonna Neighborhood Center, 10 Oct. 1980, CDPA.

[37] Minutes of Madonna Center Board of Directors, 12 Feb. 1971, and 14 April 1971, CDPA.

[38] Minutes of Madonna Center Board of Directors, 23 Aug. 1971, CDPA. The Model Cities program was designed to solve a number of physical and social problems in blighted inner city neighborhoods.

[39] See "Pride and Poverty: A Report on San Antonio," San Antonio, Texas: Partnership for Hope, Aug. 13, 1991, especially p. 10 and Table 4, p. 41; Table 7, p. 44; Table 9, p. 47; and Table 10, p. 49, CDPA.

[40] Article by Sister Angelina Murphy in *Today's Catholic*, 11 Nov. 1975, CDPA.

[41] "The Madonna Neighborhood Centers, Sixty Years of Service, 1939-1999," pp. 13-14, CDPA.

recreation program. New programs included Saturday morning arts and education for children ages 8-14, evening meals Monday through Friday for the homeless or people in crisis, the Madonna Private Daycare Program, Thrift Store, and Clothes Closet. In 2003 the budget for Madonna Center was $905,000. Its 23 full-time employees included social workers, counselors, certified teachers, and a sports coordinator. In addition, four college work-study students and five or six volunteers, who donated four hours of service daily, assisted at the Center.

Norma Funari, Director of Madonna Center since 1979, proudly reported that it became completely automated in 1991, ahead of the Edgewood Independent School District in which it is located. She accepted a grant offered by the Levi Strauss Company to promote computer literacy and started with 72 children in the Saturday morning education and art program. After a field trip, she asked the children to write thank-you notes to Sea World for 50 free tickets. A while later she went into the computer room and found Greg González, who was about eight years old, typing his letter on the computer. She watched his dexterity with amazement and finally asked him, "Greg, where did you learn so much about computers?" He looked at her, also with surprise. "Right here," he answered. In 2003 Greg graduated from the program for gifted and talented students at nearby Kennedy High School and joined the Navy, expecting to be sent either to the Massachusetts Institute of Technology or to a nuclear technology school. Ms. Funari predicted that he, like many other "alumni" (notably a sheriff and a number of teachers), would continue to return to the neighborhood center to report successes.[42]

In 2002 the Edgewood Independent School district began to provide kindergartens for three- and four-year-olds, so Madonna Center closed that part of its program. However, it offered day care for infants whose teen-age mothers were finishing high school. Nineteen young mothers used the service. The Center employed one such mother of two babies who was a college work-study student. She attended college in the mornings and worked at the Center in the afternoons. This was one example of how the agency continually adjusted. It was also preparing to construct a multi-purpose building and a senior citizens' activity center.

Area citizens did make good on their promise to "work hard," and Madonna employees continued their dedicated service. In assiduously pursuing grant prospects, they were also continuing a practice recommended by Father John Martin Moye, the founder of the Congregation of Divine Providence:

> Since you will be poor yourselves, I know you will hardly be able to
> help the destitute with your resources. If, however, you share with

---

[42] Oral interview, 2 Apr. 2003, CDPA.

them the little you have, your charity will be more pleasing to God than that of the rich who give out of their abundance. The means you will use to help the poor will be to speak of their needs to those who could help them and beg from the rich what you need to relieve them.[43]

By speaking of their needs in 2001, for example, Madonna Center obtained $10,000 from the San Antonio Area Foundation and $50,000 from the UPS Foundation "Neighbor to Neighbor" fund to improve its baseball and soccer fields used by more than 500 children.[44]

Speaking for the poor today in most societies involves speaking against some system, whether it is welfare, criminal justice, immigration, or medical insurance. When she lived in public housing by choice, Sister Cathy Parent learned "how unjust the housing authority system is. If people get a raise, their rent automatically goes up. They never get ahead; they just live from paycheck to paycheck. Many systems we create to assist people actually imprison them."[45] When she developed a social services program in a San Antonio parish, Sister Cathy learned to educate the parishioners who were economically well-off and who didn't know there were poor people in their parish to volunteer their services and share their wealth. When later she directed Catholic Charities in Beaumont, Texas, she advocated and supported a Children's Advocacy Center which brought together Child Protective Services and the District Attorney's investigators in an advocacy program for abused children. The program which set out to lessen the child's trauma was even able to effect change in the court system.

The seed planted by the Sisters at Madonna Center on Castroville Road almost 50 years before had grown by the turn of the century to a large tree that continued to nourish and shelter the needy. The founder's advice had again borne fruit: Do not neglect "those poor ones who, being badly dressed and having a slovenly appearance, cause disgust and aversion. . . [T]hese are the ones who should be preferred to the others because well-regulated charity always reaches out to the most urgent needs."[46]

---

[43] *Directory* 98.

[44] *San Antonio Express/News*, 19 July 2001.

[45] Oral interview, 7 May 2000, CDPA.

[46] *Directory* 114. "[T]ake greater pains with those who have nothing attractive, who are stubborn, who have uncouth manners and appearance, who are poor, badly dressed, dirty . . . For God often chooses the weak, the refuse of the world, to make of them vessels of election, and also what shines in the eyes of men is often rejected in the eyes of God." Directory 143.

The Model Cities Program

In 1965 Worden School moved to its own new building on the OLL campus.[47] Soon it was involved in the first major program of the U.S. Department of Housing and Urban Development, which was given cabinet-level status that same year. The 1966 Demonstration Cities and Metropolitan Development Act, known as the Model Cities Program, "called for a comprehensive, coordinated, carefully-planned attack on a wide variety of physical and social problems within designated inner city neighborhoods."[48] San Antonio was one of five cities originally selected as demonstration cities under the Omnibus Housing Act of 1965. In 1967 it was chosen to participate in the Model Cities venture.[49]

According to former San Antonio Mayor Walter McAllister, Archbishop Lucey "single-handedly" engineered

> the insertion of a welfare clause in the city's charter, which up to that time had been prohibited by statute from allocating any funds for public assistance programs. The 1952 charter at least made city welfare programs a possibility if not a reality; it was this same "welfare clause" that served as the channel through which "Great Society" funds flowed into San Antonio during the administration of President Lyndon Johnson.[50]

The archbishop used his friendship with the president to bring Model City funds to San Antonio, and OLLC was one of 12 institutions chosen by the Bureau of Social Science Research in Washington, D.C. "to be part of a nationwide study of university involvement in the urban crisis."[51] Nine Model City committees with 10 neighborhood residents and five professionals on each committee held their meetings, which were open to all citizens, on the OLL campus. The fact that the headquarters at the College were located some distance from other city offices was considered a disadvantage.[52] Nevertheless, the participants were soon publishing a newsletter, "Voz del Barrio." By 1969 they produced a three-volume

---

[47] Among members of the board who raised funds for the building were Rev. David Jacobson, a Jewish Rabbi, and Mr. Albert Steves, a Protestant (Sister Immaculate Gentemann, videotaped interview, CDPA).

[48] Paul E. Peterson, "The Changing Fiscal Place of Big Cities in the Federal System," in *Interwoven Destinies: Cities and the Nation*, ed. Henry G. Cisneros (New York: W.W. Norton and Co., 1993) 199.

[49] Sister Frances Jerome Woods, CDP, "The Model Cities Program in Perspective: The San Antonio, Texas Experience," (U.S. Govt. Printing Office, 1982) 71, 75.

[50] Privett, *The Pastoral Vision* 144.

[51] "Happenings," 16-22 Nov. 1969, OLLUA.

[52] Woods, "The Model Cities Program" 91.

planning document which included a five-year forecast and an action program for the first year. President Richard Nixon, however, terminated the Model Cities Program when he came into office that year. The Community Development Block Grant established by Congress in 1974 "consolidated model cities, urban renewal, decent housing, [and] suitable environmental and economic opportunities for community residents, particularly residents of low and moderate income."[53]

Sister Frances Jerome Woods was designated by the national Subcommittee on Housing and Community Development to write the evaluative report on the Model Cities Program because of her sociological research interests.[54] Ten years after its termination, she had the advantage of hindsight, which permits a longer, wider perspective.

The Model Cities venture in general was deemed to be unsuccessful. "Since budgets were far below what was needed for effective results, the program had little or no permanent positive changes in its cities—and it was generally viewed as a misfire."[55] It failed because "of an over-ambitious and contradictory legislative design, diluted funding, and default by cooperating Federal agencies."[56] In addition, "the program became bogged down in bureaucratic and intergovernmental fighting."[57] Sister Frances Jerome identified two additional factors that contributed to the demise of Model Cities in San Antonio. In 1979 San Antonio City Manager Gerald C. Henckel acknowledged that City Hall was afraid of the program. Also, "non-cohesive resident groups whose members were not generally politically integrated gave the staff the impression of lacking both a client group and a constituency."[58]

Most of the funds from the Model Cities Project went to education, buildings such as schools, and improvements such as bridges, storm drains, streets, sidewalks, and playgrounds. Its impact on improved housing and small businesses was not so great as expected. "What emerged from the San Antonio Model Cities experience was a cluster of buildings and physical improvements, as well as a multitude of `people programs,' some of which were short-lived, but others of which are continuing into the present time." HUD ranked the San Antonio Model Cities Program the best in the country.[59]

---

[53] Peterson, "The Changing Fiscal Face" 201.

[54] In 1948 Sister wrote her dissertation on Alonso S. Perales, a local politician, "Are We Good Neighbors?" later published as *Mexican-American Leadership in San Antonio, Texas* (New York: Arno Press, 1976).

[55] Paul C. Brophy, "Emerging Approaches to Community Development," in *Interwoven Destinies* 225.

[56] Paul Dudley, "A Requiem for Model Cities," *New Republic*, 168 (April 14, 1973): 13-15, quoted in Woods, "Model Cities" 109.

[57] Peterson, "The Changing Fiscal Face" 199, 225.

[58] Woods, "The Model Cities Program" 89, 95.

[59] Woods, "The Model Cities Program" 251, 295.

Sister Frances Jerome noted that in San Antonio the venture developed leadership as citizens accustomed to being passive began to participate, attend meetings, and become vocal. It promoted "a greater sense of community awareness and less fragmentation, based on the feeling of belonging to one of the quadrants of the city." Moreover, it created a climate where groups such as Communities Organized for Public Service could be successful.[60]

Among the active, involved participants in Model Cities was SANYO, the San Antonio Neighborhood Youth Organization led by Rev. John Yanta, which had about 30 neighborhood centers and an extensive job-training program. The Equal Opportunities Development Corporation (EODC) "was supposed to be the umbrella agency for implementing the War on Poverty, but SANYO had preempted EODC in securing federal funds directly from Washington for its own programs."[61] From 1965-67, for example, this group received $9,000,000, which was more than one-third of federal money sent to San Antonio for poverty programs.[62] Among the pressure groups supported by SANYO was the Brown Berets, a militant Chicano organization allied with vociferous members of MAYO (Mexican-American Youth Organization)[63] whose "tactics were to disrupt, appeal to the emotions, and 'pack,' that is, mobilize many citizens." They were able to marshal support quickly from neighbors for their projects. Sister Frances Jerome concluded that by late 1971 the Chicano activists had succeeded in consciousness-raising to the extent that "anyone who was not a Chicano was not quite acceptable as a leader."[64]

On 25 September 1969, for example, the President of the Board of Madonna Center, Mr. Joe Nicholson, presented at a Board meeting ten demands he had received from activities of another group, La Raza Unida.[65] This group perceived that predominantly white officials in neighborhood

---

[60] Woods, "The Model Cities Program" 279. With 32 chapters, 29 of them headquartered in churches, by 1980 COPS was considered "one of the most important citizen groups in the country" (Woods, "The Model Cities Program" 284).

[61] Woods, "The Model Cities Program" 116. Father Yanta later became the bishop of Amarillo, Texas.

[62] Privett, *The Pastoral Vision* 195, Note 171. "Undoubtedly the magnitude of SANYO and its cohesiveness were factors in some of the failures" to adopt certain plans (Woods, "The Model Cities Program" 124).

[63] Established in 1967 by six young Chicano students, local MAYO chapters helped organize over 50 high school walkouts in Texas and three school confrontations in San Antonio "demanding an up-graded college-bound curriculum as well as greater representation of the Chicano community's contribution to this nation in the history and civics curriculum," Rodolfo Rosales, *The Illusion of Inclusion: the Untold Political Story of San Antonio* (Austin: University of Texas Press, 2000): 108. They were involved in the student protests at OLLU which were discussed in a previous chapter.

[64] Woods, "The Model Cities Program" 123, 124.

[65] La Raza Unida political party was "based more on ethnicity, as opposed to partisanship . . . [and] represented more of a social movement than just a partisan political party," Rosales, *The Illusion*: 117.

centers as well as churches were imposing their decisions rather than eliciting suggestions and empowering the people they were to serve. In a preface to the demands, the authors denounced "the so-called Christian approach used by the Church-supported settlement houses," charging that the governing boards "impose programs." The first demand was "that all settlement house Boards be turned over to Chicano control." The group went on to demand that staffs and boards represent the predominant ethnic group in their areas and "abide by the principal [sic] of self determination and be free from any dictation from the board or the Church." All "supportive services that come to the settlement house" were to be fully staffed "by chicanos, such as Federal, state or local EODC, SANYO, Mental Health Educational Health Services"; and "no retaliation" was to "be taken against the Chicano staff and directors," who were "not responsible for the problem but have been tied down by their gringo board and structures." The next statement after the demands was: "If Christians are sincere when they talk about meeting the need they must listen to the Chicano voice or take the title of *hypocrite*. . . . We are tired of the paternalistic approach and now we want to serve our own."[66]

At a Board meeting on 20 November 1969, members present approved a resolution endorsing the self-determination concept presented by La Raza Unida as "legitimate and proper for the effectiveness" of the Center's philosophy and purposes. They pointed out that 95% of the budget came from the United Fund of San Antonio and Bexar County. Finally, they resolved that in May the board would make "every effort . . . to insure that the composition" of the Board would be "a majority of the predominant ethnic group served by the Madonna Neighborhood Centers with emphasis placed on `barrio' residents."[67] The Board did revise its Constitutions and By-laws at this time.

The Centro del Barrio

While the Worden School, Madonna Center, and indeed the entire OLLU community became involved in the Model Cities Project, a young man from the west side first encountered Sisters of Divine Providence when he enrolled in the Project Teacher Excellence (PTE) program at OLL in 1968. That encounter led to results no one could call a failure or a misfire. His efforts dramatically furthered the mission of the Congregation. The 13th of 14 children and the only one to graduate from college, Ernesto Gómez grew up on the Corner of Leona and El Paso Streets "several blocks from the red light district and in the

---

[66] La Raza Demands, Madonna Center files, CDPA.

[67] Madonna Center files, CDPA.

thick of the drug district of San Antonio."[68] While enrolled in PTE, he was working part-time at a community center; and instead of going on to graduate, he took a full-time job at Wesley Community Center. In 1971 the Worden School, having received four grants totaling $191,000 from federal agencies, recruited him to work on a project funded by the National Institute of Mental Health (NIMH).

Sister Immaculate remembered that in the early days both faculty and students of the Worden School were from different parts of the United States. They brought new ideas and a broader perspective. However, she could not "feature anybody in that early period who was Hispanic."[69] To remedy this lack, the two objectives of the NIMH grant for which Ernesto Gómez was engaged were to recruit Mexican American students and to develop a curriculum to train all Worden students to work with Mexican American clients in poverty, taking their language and culture into account. He continued to work on other NIMH grants as well as on his doctorate from the University of Texas at Austin. He achieved this goal in 1982, producing a dissertation on a test of effectiveness of psychosocial intervention with Mexican American clients at a mental health center.

This dissertation topic grew out of the initial NIMH project under which he was an assistant to Worden School's Professor Guadalupe Gibson. Before the project could be completed, however, President Nixon impounded the funds for the social work education component. Congress objected that the President had no authority to do this, but Professor Gibson was told she had six months to close the project, dispose of the equipment and assets, and terminate the assistant's stipend. Dr. Gómez was working with interns at the Centro del Barrio Teaching/Learning Center, an extension of the Worden School, in a leased building in South San Antonio. Being dependent on the grant funds, it was slated to close. Along with the students, neighbors, and project committee, he wanted to keep the Center open. His requests for grants were not successful until he applied to the San Antonio City Council for general revenue sharing funds, which the federal government gave to cities. Dr. José San Martín, a City Councilor who was also a trustee at OLLU and a member of the Advisory Committee for the NIMH project, helped him obtain a promise of $75,000.

Dr. Gómez was ecstatic. He raced to the office of OLL President John McMahon, who was very pleased with the news. The next day, however, Dr. McMahon informed him that OLL was an institute of higher learning, not a social service agency; therefore, it could not accept the money destined for direct services to low income families. Dr. Daniel Jennings, Dean of the Worden School,

---

[68] Oral interview, 11 Mar. 2003, CDPA. The rest of this section, except where otherwise indicated, is based on information from this interview.

[69] Oral interview, 25 Feb. 2000, CDPA.

who was also on the Advisory Committee for the grant, could not dissuade Dr. McMahon, so the Centro del Barrio incorporated as a non-profit organization separate from the school in 1973 so as to be able to receive the funds from the city. Unexpectedly, at the same time the impounded funds were released, so instead of being asked to leave, Dr. Gómez was asked to submit a five-year plan for using them. Dr. Jennings then devised a creative both/and or win/win solution: the College would administer a project for teaching, curriculum development, and research while the Centro would provide direct services. As a result of this cooperation, Worden students conducted many surveys that quantified many needs of the community. These studies supplied bases for more grant requests. Dr. Gómez estimated that these grants brought close to two million dollars to the College. They contributed to a re-statement of the school's mission to serve minorities—the oppressed, disenfranchised, and mentally ill. OLL developed both graduate and undergraduate courses on understanding and serving Mexican Americans and African Americans.

While appreciating his association with Sisters who taught at the Worden School, Dr. Gómez recalled the special contributions of Sister Marian Angela Aguilar during her six years on the faculty. She contributed greatly to the Centro del Barrio by teaching in seminars and supervising students. She had very good relationships with clients and students. Her "strong convictions, sincerity, dedication to Christian values, and passionate desire to help the underprivileged were noteworthy and very visible. It was not hard to work under her when she was the Dean from 1987 to 1990."[70]

Sister Marian Angela reported that while she was Dean she "worked 60 to 70 hours a week trying to complete a self-study, change the curriculum, and get the school up to par."[71] A founding member of Sisters in Social Service in the 1970s,[72] Sister had also been an acting director and researcher at the Immigration Counseling Center in Houston in 1978. After leaving the Worden School, she went on to teach in the Social Work School at the University of Texas in Austin. In 2001 she became the first Chair of the Department of Psychology, Sociology, and Social Work at Texas A & M International University (TAMIU) in Laredo, Texas.

Thirty years after the initial budget of $75,000, which allowed Centro del Barrio to hire 1.5 social workers and a secretary and pay the utilities, the annual budget had increased to over $18,000,000. In 1980 the Center began receiving around $430,000 per year from the United Way agency. In 2002 it reached over 35,000 patients in three nearby counties as well as in San Antonio and made over

---

[70] Dr. Ernesto Gómez, oral interview, 11 Mar. 2003, CDPA.

[71] Oral interview, 21 June 2000, CDPA.

[72] Initiated by Sister Catherine Swilley, CVI, of Houston, this group of women religious in social work supported one another in efforts to further social action causes.

115,000 visits. Its 290 employees in 17 different locations continued to embrace clients and patients that no one else wanted, filling in gaps in various services such as medical services to abused children and HIV positive adults as well as physical and mental health services for the elderly. To enable the frail elderly to remain in their own homes in the evenings and at night, the Center offered them day activities, respite care, and medical supervision. Approximately 6,000 homeless persons per year received medical, social, mental health, substance abuse, and dental services. The medically uninsured were an object of special concern.

Mindful that women comprise 68% of the population in need of medical help, Centro del Barrio employees went to battered women in shelters to give medical and dental care as well as counseling. They also worked with the WIC program and educated mothers in child-care. One program taught parents how to stimulate brain development in children from birth until the age of three. Nineteen physicians were full-time employees at the Centro, including four obstetrics-gynecology specialists who delivered about 95 babies every month. They were also required to do in-patient services and conduct after-hours classes. In partnership with the San Antonio Independent School District, the Center gave medical and dental care to children referred by school nurses and staffed a clinic at Lanier High School. Other employees included nine full-time dentists and two dental hygienists, around 50 registered nurses, and one full-time psychiatrist besides pharmacists and laboratory technicians.

Ninety-percent of approximately 40 social workers employed by the Centro del Barrio were graduates of the Worden School. The Centro contributed to OLL by providing stipends for interns and social work trainees. When Sister Elizabeth Anne Sueltenfuss was President of OLLU, she informed Dr. Gómez, who continued to head the Center and teach at the Worden School, that OLLU had made the "right investment" in extending educational opportunities to him. She encouraged him to continue using his talents to assist people from his community to better their situation. Dr. Gómez in turn admitted that he could not have achieved the levels of education he has reached if "the Lake" had not afforded him the opportunity. He affirmed taking very seriously Sister's expectation that he do some good. He had already learned to survive in the midst of violence, and he credited Sister with teaching him to use his energy in positive ways and giving him a sense of mission and of social work as a ministry.

> She doesn't have to be physically present to keep me reminded and keep me on my toes. She is forever in my mind. I understand clearly that we can't do everything or solve every problem, but there are some things we can do. I sincerely believe that I was placed here for a reason and have enjoyed a wonderful tenure here among the people on this campus. Inspiration from the Sisters gives me the energy to do the work that I do. When you place yourself among and surround

yourself with good, you'll be able to see things much more clearly and make better use of whatever talents you have.[73]

Dorcas Mladenka, a former CDP, was one of many interviewed for this history who said the Congregation's strongest contribution was the witness of lives dedicated to helping the disenfranchised, the poor, and the underserved—those who because of circumstances or prejudice have been denied equal access to goods and services.[74] Dr. Roberto R. Treviño averred that the witness of Mexican-American Sisters carried additional weight.

> Sisters Mary Rachel and Mary Nelda both devoted their careers to service in Mexican American communities in San Antonio and Houston. They were not educated elites isolated from the Mexican parishioners who needed their expertise and understanding. Rather, as influential role models and culture-brokers, *tejana* nuns contributed significantly to the viability of Mexican American culture. As religious mentors and social work professionals, they provided Mexican Americans both spiritual sustenance and access to material aid, fulfilling in this way an important community-building role wherever they ministered.[75]

Although classroom teaching was the Congregation's primary ministry, the Sisters have always taken seriously the responsibility of leaders to empower more leaders. Where Sisters can no longer be present, people trained by them and inspired by their dedication continue their work. The Sisters try to make sure that the leaders who succeed them will maintain the same concern for the underserved and continue their undertakings.

---

[73] Oral interview, 11 Mar. 2003, CDPA.

[74] Oral interview, 18 July 2001, CDPA.

[75] Treviño, "Facing Jim Crow," 155.

CHAPTER 11

RELINQUISHING CONTROL
WITH HOPE

> At San Juan de los Lagos in the Valley, I had a guitar, but I could only pluck three chords, and I couldn't get people to come and cooperate with me in the church. So one Sunday I decided to play on my own. After Mass, a number of volunteers came saying, "Sister, I think we can do better than you can." And from then on, we had a wonderful choir there.[1]

Sister Marian Angela Aguilar experienced what the Sisters like to call a "Providence moment" when the results far exceeded the input, when one's little gift was multiplied as others offered their gifts also.

Discerning when to let others come in to make a work succeed and when it is time to relinquish control is another example of searching for what would make God's Providence more present here and now. The Sisters invited their companions in ministry into the CDP world of values and empowered them to carry on with confidence in God's help even if the Sisters left. The Sisters who retired kept their interest in the people to whom and with whom they had ministered and continued to support them in prayer.

Memorable Co-Laborers and CDP Associates

In every school, hospital, clinic, or other institution the contribution of lay employees, especially those who served for long periods, was indispensable.

---

[1] Sister Marian Angela Aguilar, oral interview, 21 June 2000, CDPA.

Being Roman Catholic was not a condition for employment, and the Sisters were not known as aggressive proselytizers. Employees were regarded and treated as colleagues rather than as servants even though the Sisters in many cases were very dependent on their help. They accepted the Sisters' view of the meaning and purpose of work and became invaluable collaborators. Employees assimilated this view more from the example than from instructions of the Sisters. Many already ascribed to this philosophy and found themselves very much at home in a CDP workplace. Their loyalty and dedication in turn supported and inspired the Sisters. A few persons whose work at the Motherhouse and the University touched all the Sisters illustrate this co-ministry.

Dr. John L. McMahon, second President of Our Lady of the Lake College (1941-1973), understood its mission and guided it through a period of expansion as well as some dissension in the 1960s. He was able to raise funds, officiate at functions, and attend meetings, and represent the institution in ways that would have been difficult for the Sisters, whose life was still somewhat cloistered during most of those years. He exhibited an international and ecumenical outlook as well as skills in fund-raising and dealing with Church and state issues.[2] He strongly supported free speech and always gave a permit to controversial groups for presentations on campus.[3]

Dr. Albert J. Griffith, who served as Academic Dean and taught in the OLL English department for 45 years, admired the Sisters "for believing enough to do things that common sense would forbid."[4] As a result, he said, OLLU impacted the west side of San Antonio, especially in the area of women's rights and autonomy, even though the Congregation had no focused large-scale impact. In the 1970s when pastors were implementing Vatican Council II reforms in disparate ways and some priests in San Antonio were asking Vatican officials to remove their archbishop, the Sisters introduced Dr. Griffith to vibrant Catholic faith communities outside the hierarchical Church. After he retired, Dr. Griffith stated that "those who know the Congregation must certainly be impressed by the adroit adaptation by which they have been able to maintain so much of the original charism in the formidable conditions of the world of 2004." He singled out the practice of the virtue of simplicity as possibly the Sisters' most relevant contribution.

Unfortunately, today hardly anything seems simple; *everything* seems unbelievably complicated—and thus also totally intimidating,

---

[2] In 1947, for example, he was one of 60 university representatives that the U.S. government sent to Germany to study methods of teaching and education.

[3] Dr. Albert Griffith, oral interview, 3 Sept. 2002, CDPA.

[4] Dr. Albert Griffith, oral interview, 3 Sept. 2002, CDPA.

unfathomable, and unmanageable. . . . Maybe the serenity that true simplicity can bring is what our new century will consider the hallmark of "heroic sanctity." If so, it won't take a Vatican tribunal to tell us that many of our own loved CDPs are a new class of "people's saints."[5]

Dr. Howard Benoist taught in the English department and also served as Academic Dean of OLLU. He characterized the "providential spirit" that he found and approved at OLLU as including the belief "that not everything the Congregation did *had* to succeed; not every new idea was a good idea." But the Sisters were willing to change and communicated that willingness to their lay colleagues.

> Some initiatives at the University died out, but I would rather be in a place that tries things than in one that does things the same old way because it doesn't want to fail or always wants to do the sure thing. There are times when, we knew by hindsight, we should have followed through more strongly or done things in a different way. Still, we are here, against all odds.[6]

Dr. Robert Gibbons, who was also both a teacher and administrator at OLLU, admitted that it was a challenge to meet the standards of his Sister-colleagues who were "serious, purposeful professional educators." He noted that generations of students who never had a Sister as their teacher nevertheless interacted three times a day with Sister Ann Bernadette Laubert in the school cafeteria and formed their impressions of women religious from this contact. Even after she retired, Sister would warmly greet college students whom she met in the corridors of the University and gently advise them, for example, to be sure to use an umbrella because it was raining outside. When fewer Sisters were at the University, Dr. Gibbons continued to appreciate and support Sister-student contacts. He helped his students conduct interviews with retired CDPs, which "created a bond between students and individual Sisters, giving a different personality to what CDP meant for these students."[7] All three laymen who started in the English department at OLL came to relate to Sisters not only as mentors and models but also as true friends.

---

[5] "Reflection" given at the 50th anniversary celebration of the beatification of John Martin Moye, OLLC, Sacred Heart Chapel, 4 May 2004.

[6] Dr. Howard Benoist, oral interview, 11 Aug. 2003, CDPA.

[7] Dr. Robert Gibbons, oral interview, 29 Jan. 2003. When Sister Ann Bernadette Laubert, affectionately known as "Sister Annie B," retired after 57 years of service, the main students' dining room was officially named "The Sister Annie B Dining Room."

Loretta Schlegel, against the wishes of her Baptist father, enrolled at OLL after graduating from neighboring Edgewood High School at age 17. Working while a student with Sister Anunciata Sanchez and Sister Adelaide Marie Heyman in the registrar's office, her organizational abilities were quickly recognized. Shortly after she graduated, President McMahon asked her to become the Registrar, a position she filled for 35 years. The Registrar's work is never done, so she appreciated more and more the humor of Sister Adelaide Marie's never-fulfilled promise, "When we get all caught up, we'll have a martini." Sister did reward her helpers, who also cleaned the office before they left each day, with hard candies. "The files of current students fit into a single four-drawer file cabinet when I came. When I left, we needed 18 or 20 file cabinets," Loretta recalled. Collaborating with numerous Sisters in her office as well as on councils and committees, she was inspired by their care for people, involvement in justice and peace issues, and readiness to step out in faith and became a CDP Associate. She said reliance on Divine Providence made her a stronger Christian, and Providence has taken on a richer meaning for her over the years as she learned to recognize "Providential moments," especially in unexpected or surprising positive events. She credited her special friendship with Sister Marilyn Molloy for making her "a better person. The years Sister Marilyn and her mother, a stroke victim, lived with me I experienced true community and unconditional love." She also remarked that while they were "alike in belief," she was able to introduce Sister Marilyn during their daily prayer periods to the greater variety of prayer styles and services experienced by Protestants.[8]

Like all congregations of women religious, CDPs have numerous stories of loyal alumni who were not only supporters but friends. Jennita Goodman Poston and all her children attended St. Martin Hall, and she organized the first phonathon when she was President of the OLL Alumni Association. Graciela Gutierrez donated her large collection of folk music instruments to the OLLU music department. Parents who served on various committees and boards lengthened the Sisters' outreach into surrounding communities.

The Sisters learned how to leave familiar places and succeed in new locations from persons who came from foreign countries to the United States to start a new life. Until he retired "from active duty" in 1964 after several decades of service, Peter Lagutchik, originally from Russia, was on call night and day at the Motherhouse to chauffeur the Sisters before they were allowed to drive automobiles.[9] John Brusniak fled from the Ukraine to Poland because of religious persecution and then came to the U.S. by way of Germany. He and his wife Bernice resided on the OLL campus in the early 1950s in a converted

---

[8] Loretta Schlegel, oral interview, 2 Sept. 2003, CDPA.

[9] GC minutes, 12 Mar. 1964, CDPA.

garage without a kitchen. Soon many-talented John took on responsibilities at OLLU such as maintaining the boiler and swimming pool, winding the clock in the chapel steeple, upholstering furniture, and re-stringing window blinds. He was also a musician and cobbler. Bernice accepted night duty in the Sisters' infirmary so that during the day she could be with the couple's three sons, all of whom later had successful careers in law, business, and music. "Providence is our guide, especially in difficulties and when we can't see ahead," John stated. Even though their hard work was not always noticed, appreciated, or remunerated fairly, "We have felt at home here and love the Sisters."[10]

Abigail Valencia was born in Michoacán, Mexico, and began more than 50 years of service with the Sisters by helping Sister George Marie Pekar in the laundry. Then she was a housekeeper under Sister Lucretia Wolf in St. Joseph Hall before returning to OLLU. She was particularly devoted to Sister Bernadette Marie Gremillion, but all the Sisters experienced her services with a smile. Widowed at a young age, Abigail raised two sons in Veramendi Homes near the campus and eventually was able to buy her own house; but she always considered OLLU her "second home." She said, "I guess I'm a kind of artist. I like to make things look nice."[11]

Bill Laux supervised maintenance on the OLLU campus while his wife, Katie, worked in the bookbindery. They lived in a house on campus. Bill knew every inch of the College buildings and remained concerned about their upkeep from the 1940s until he retired off campus. He moved to a nursing home in 1982. In 1987 Gilbert Moreno, Sr., retired after 30 years as head of maintenance at OLL Convent and was succeeded by his son, Gilbert Moreno, Jr. The Congregation paid for courses Gilbert Jr. took on various aspects of maintenance, and he earned a master's degree in business at OLLU. Keeping the buildings safe and functional under numerous successive administrators, he particularly appreciated the "kindness, understanding, and patience" of the Sisters, while they marveled at how he could diagnose and solve all kinds of problems. Gilbert Jr. said that his view of Providence changed after he began to work at OLLCC, and he started to read the Bible regularly. Having experienced the "care and love" of the Sisters, he came to view God's Providence as concern for "the well-being of all. We are all connected in kindness, love, and compassion."[12]

Preceded by her mother, Josephine Hurón, and her aunt, Antonia San Román, Rose Peña started as a housekeeper at OLL Convent in 1973. In 1996 she began as an independent contractor to provide hair care for the retired Sisters. Two of her sisters were also employed at the motherhouse, one of them (Carolyn

---

[10] John and Bernice Brusniak, oral interview, 8 Aug. 2001, CDPA.

[11] Abigail Valencia, communication to the author, 12 Nov. 2004.

[12] Gilbert Moreno, Jr., oral interview, 26 March 2002, CDPA.

Chavarría) for over 30 years. Carolyn particularly enjoyed "learning something new every day that you don't learn outside here."[13] This included not only how to clean well but how to make ice sculptures and decorations for the dining room and how to use a computer. The Sisters allowed her to take time off to care for her children and helped her through five deaths in her family. Sister Emelene Matocha played the violin for her daughter's *"Quinceañera"* (debut). Carol had very little formal religious instruction as a child, but she learned about religion from the Sisters, who taught her to pray and believe that God would see her through any difficulty. As supervisor of housekeeping services, Carol trained her lay staff as she herself had been trained by the Sisters.

Mel Johnson came to work at the Motherhouse "from the unemployment line" and stayed for decades. She had gone to a Sisters' school in Louisiana only for the first grade and remembered "the Sisters were tough." When she knocked on the convent door and said she was looking for work, Sister Pauline Narendorf, the portress, said, "Come on in. We need a housekeeper." Not knowing what to expect, Mel was afraid at first. But soon she felt at home and became known for her solicitude in serving the Sisters in their dining room and for her ability to give and take teasing. Asked why she stayed at this job, she replied, "Because I love the Sisters, and I know they love me. And I would really miss their teasing." Mel also enrolled in courses at the Sophia Women's Learning Center, which offered a program for women who wanted to finish high school while working full-time. She would bring her scored tests to the Sisters to show them how well she had done and to thank them for their prayers for her success.[14]

Frances McCarty was hired as a bookkeeper for the CDP Generalate in 1985 and also kept accounts for several other areas. She took the job because it would diminish her commute time, but she stayed on to serve under four General Treasurers because she enjoyed the camaraderie of people with a positive outlook on life. She was most impressed by the Sisters' intelligence and habit of preparing for their tasks and devoting tremendous energy to accomplishing them. Over the years she noted that the Sisters became more "civilian-ized," that is, they began to enjoy more things and events that "people in the world" enjoy. She thought they still showed the influence of earlier training in that sometimes they didn't know people as people and tended to hold others at a distance. In her opinion, the Sisters' greatest impact has been on individuals in rural settings, largely because they interacted with them after hours and became part of their families.[15]

---

[13] Carolyn Chavarría, oral interview, 5 Aug. 2004, CDPA.

[14] Mel Johnson, communication to the author, 3 Aug. 2004.

[15] Frances D. McCarty, oral interview, 8 Sept. 2004, CDPA.

When Sisters who had left the Congregation expressed a desire to maintain ties with it, the General Council began to consider "some sort of affiliate program in which they can be included."[16] As more people collaborated with them in ministry, the Sisters began to receive numerous requests from these co-workers, as well as from alumni of its institutions, for a deeper way to share in the CDP charism. Since 1974 women and men interested in a closer spiritual relationship with the Sisters have been invited to become Associates (ACDPs). Associates, who are not necessarily Roman Catholics, share in the goals, values, and ideals of the CDPs. They manifest the charism and mission of the Congregation in their life and work and express their association in one of two forms, (1) prayer and community, or (2) prayer, community, service, and leadership. A formation process precedes their admission and commitment, which can be renewed annually. Nineteen members of the Associates' Board met to articulate bylaws and chose a distinctive membership pin in 1991.[17] By 2000 there were over 100 ACDPs in the U.S. and over 80 in Mexico.

Janet Quillian was a doctoral student in international public health when she became an Associate in Houston in 1981. She had known CDPs for only a short time but was impressed by their openness, hospitality, and involvement in current events. Ethel Winchester-Didsbury after she raised her four children became an Associate in 1989 because she admired the Sisters' commitment and welcoming stance and wanted to share in and support their ministry. Soon afterwards she did a short-term ministry with two CDPs in El Salvador. She also participated in several General Chapters of the Congregation as an observer. Ethel felt strongly that the wisdom of the Congregation needs to be shared with the wider community.[18] Sister Sharon Rohde, also one of the first Associates, said, "I don't think that our charism is something that the Sisters gave me. I think it is something that I had within me that was part of my own life, and they helped to bring it out in me in gentle ways."[19] Similarly, Frances McCarty felt that as a mother she always knew Providence, but being an Associate deepened her understanding.[20]

Florence Carvajal, who became the first lay Director of CDP Associates in 2000, insisted, "Numbers are not what is most important. Commitment is what counts." She considered the Associate Program to be like an extended family, with opportunities to form closer relationships with the Sisters and learn from them a greater trust in Providence. She personally experienced

---

[16] GC minutes, 2 Dec.1974, CDPA.

[17] GC minutes, 18-22 Mar. 1991, CDPA.

[18] Oral interview, 11 Aug. 2001, CDPA.

[19] Oral interview, 20 June 2000, CDPA.

[20] Oral interview, 8 Sept. 2004.

growing confidence in God and consequent serenity and greater patience in waiting for the movements of Providence to become manifest. As Director, she oversaw a one-year formation program of eight sessions on spirituality and the four fundamental virtues and sent out a newsletter every six weeks. Every year on May 4, the Feast of Blessed John Martin Moye, Associates renewed their commitment at a Eucharistic liturgy, followed by a reception. There are no dues or fees, but Associates are asked to serve on ad hoc committees to plan retreats, publish a yearly calendar containing the birthdays of all Sisters and Associates, and volunteer their services as much as they are able in their parish, community, or in the Congregation.[21]

Relinquishment of Institutions

Every CDP learns the art of "letting go and letting God," by striving to live "entirely dependent on Providence."[22] Indeed, every religious who takes the vow of celibacy manifests a deep trust in God since choosing to remain unmarried entails letting go of more than projects or people. Sister Marlene Rose Quesenberry told the story of her discernment and oblation in capsule form:

> I always wanted to give some kind of service. I liked what I saw in the CDPs and thought, "Why not give it a try?" Then my first year in nursing school when I saw the new moms holding their babies, it was hard. Something in my heart would just kind of twitch. Then I thought, "I know I could be a good mother and wife, but that's not all there is." It was not so much giving up. It was just a different kind of life that I chose, and I'm glad I did.[23]

Being abandoned to the care of a Provident God takes many forms. For example, Sister Berenice Trachta's trust in God was really tested when, after teaching in grade schools for several years, she got three weeks' notice that she was to teach shorthand and typing in high school. A Sister who was teaching business in another school gave her a 30-minute lesson that consisted of showing her the typewriter keys, giving her a typewriting book, and telling her to follow directions. She had no assurance beforehand of a happy ending, but she was willing to be vulnerable. Sister Berenice insisted, "That was one of the greatest classes I ever had. Those students did so well! And it was one of the best things

---

[21] Florence Carvajal, oral interview, 26 Feb. 2002, CDPA.

[22] *Directory* 82.

[23] Oral interview, 21 June 2000, CDPA.

that ever happened to me because when I went to graduate school I had to type my own notes and dissertation. Without having to teach that class, I wouldn't have learned." This early experience strengthened her belief in Divine Providence and influenced her future behavior. "I have never opposed accepting assignments to something I know nothing about. I just say, 'I will work at it, for God knows why he did it.'"[24]

Colleagues have noted the characteristic way the Sisters respond and witness to their deepest beliefs. Monsignor Balthasar Janacek gave his impressions:

> To me the charism of the Sisters of Divine Providence is very evident in their willingness to start something from scratch without necessarily seeing or being fully prepared for its end. They are courageous and willing to back away when they are no longer needed. Part of abandonment to Divine Providence is that it is not *ad aeternitatem* [for eternity].[25]

During many years of association with CDPs, he observed a freedom and personal detachment from having to succeed that also permitted the Sisters to pack up and move on without regret or turn a cherished project over to others.

Sister Leola Ann Doerfler's experience during five years as a youth minister among poor people in the mountains of West Texas and New Mexico is an example of not being certain of the end when she began a project. She planted a seed without guarantee that it would grow. "It was my greatest learning experience to sit under a tree on the ground teaching the children. Then the parents started coming because they realized they didn't know basic religion. When the dads started coming when they got off work, before they cleaned up, I said 'This is where I need to be.'" Years later she returned for a visit and found that her original twelve groups were still functioning. The adults had trained their children to be the leaders.[26]

Sister Mary Margaret Hughes recalled the 1970s as "a sad kind of period."

> I used to shed tears thinking about what all the closures were doing to us, and especially to Sister Elizabeth McCullough as Superior General.

---

[24] Oral interview, 9 Feb. 2000, CDPA.

[25] Msgr. Balthasar Janacek, oral interview, 18 Sept. 2001, CDPA. Similarly, Rev. Ben Mazurkiewicz, pastor for many years at St. John's Church in Fayetteville, Texas, found the Sisters to be pioneers, enthusiastic in service, and very adaptable (oral interview, 9 Feb. 2002, CDPA).

[26] Oral interview, 21 Jan. 2000, CDPA.

She was right there doing her best, but it was just the times. She had to deal with pastors who were upset and sometimes angry with us, and yet we didn't have any alternative. The people were just despairing because the Sisters were leaving them. Yet it just had to be.[27]

The Sisters themselves did not despair because they knew they had done their best; they were sure the seeds they had planted would germinate and bear fruit. Whoever their pupils were, the Sisters agreed with Mother Angelique's assertion: "Every Alumna or ex-student is cooperating with the work of the Congregation of the Sisters of Divine Providence every day of her life when she consciously or habitually puts into her daily actions the ideals and motives and endeavors that her Alma Mater has tried to give her."[28]

But were Catholic schools essential for imparting values? U.S. Roman Catholics as a group became wealthier in the 1970s; their income level exceeded that of their forebears "who were willing to sacrifice to support their schools." The decline in Catholic schools was not primarily due to fiscal pressure, but to "a loss of widely-shared sense of purpose and agreement about the importance, indeed indispensability, of Catholic schools, on the part of Catholics, clerical as well as lay. . . . It is this change in attitude which in the main accounted for the decline in Catholic school attendance from 1965 on."[29] Many Catholics were uncertain whether Catholic schools were necessary or even important.

Why did so many schools and institutions close around 1970? Sometimes the reason was due to adherence to principles. As discussed in previous chapters, the Congregation departed from the school in Pecos, New Mexico, when religious instruction became impossible there. It closed schools in Louisiana because they were not furthering the civil rights of African Americans. When the trend to relinquish schools began, their programs were good and enrollments were usually satisfactory, though traditionally smaller than in public schools. Conditions in U.S. society, in the Church, and in the Congregation, however, contributed to their demise.

Enrollment in small private and parochial schools nationwide declined as it became more convenient to attend larger, better equipped public schools. This was particularly true in rural areas where the trend to move to urban areas that began during World War II continued.

At mid-century requests for Sisters still outnumbered the available personnel and funds, raising hopes that expansion would continue if enough young women responded to the call to religious life. The 1940s and 1950s had indeed

---

[27] Oral interview, 18 June 2000, CDPA.

[28] Mother Angelique Ayres to Mrs. Katherine Randall Staley, 1 Oct. 1943, CDPA.

[29] See Grant and Hunt, *Catholic School Education*, 2.

witnessed a surge of enrollment in schools where the Sisters taught, part of the 118% overall increase in enrollment in U.S. nonpublic schools during this period.[30] The number of women entering the Congregation, however, was not great enough to keep pace with the increase of students.[31]

Sometimes it was impossible to find enough qualified teachers. This situation prevailed in Lawton, Oklahoma.

> The State Inspector on his visit expressed satisfaction for what is being done, but had many suggestions especially regarding short-time teachers, the only kind of lay help we are able to recruit. Monsignor has tried to get volunteers from the East, but it seems the schools nearer the center of the diocese get the first—and last—numbers. . . . The high school could be doubled, if there were rooms in which to house the children, and certified teachers to teach them.[32]

To pay lay teachers' salaries, tuition had to be raised. Often parents were unable or unwilling to pay, so parishes became unable to support a school.

A survey of Catholic dioceses in 1958 revealed that the majority had a statute that required Catholic parents to send their children to a Catholic school. Parents in 38 dioceses were required to apply formally for permission to send their children to a public school, and in 55 dioceses parents who defied the regulation committed a "reserved sin," a sin reserved to the bishop for forgiveness.[33] Neither church sanctions nor the growing affluence of Catholic families, however, boosted Catholic school enrollments in the 1960s. Reasons for the continuing decline—besides those already mentioned—included "challenges from lay and clerical Catholics to the Church's teaching on birth control and abortion, . . . departure of priests and nuns in large numbers . . . [and a] loss of consensus on the nature and purpose of Catholic schools."[34]

Between its arrival in Texas in 1866 and 1976, the Congregation made 180 foundations: in Texas (118), Louisiana (32), Oklahoma (23),[35] New Mexico (2), Missouri (2), Arkansas (1), California (1), and one house of

---

[30] Grant and Hunt, *Catholic School Education*, 127.

[31] Twelve young women pronounced their first vows in 1951. After that, each year the numbers steadily dwindled. In 1961 no one was professed in Texas, but four made their first vows in Mexico. In 1968 and 1970 there were no first professions at all. See Appendix III for statistics on departures from the Congregation.

[32] "News Flashes," First Edition, 1961: 9a-10, CDPA.

[33] Grant and Hunt, *Catholic School Education* 128.

[34] Grant and Hunt, *Catholic School Education* 2.

[35] More than 850 CDPs served in Oklahoma between 1900 and 1983. See James D. White, *The Souls of the Just: A Necrology of the Catholic Church in Oklahoma* (Tulsa, OK: The Sarto Press, 1983) 468. In terms of numbers of responsibilities,

studies for Sisters in Washington, D.C. During the same period of 110 years, 86 foundations were closed. From 1866 to 1924, the Congregation started 133 schools and either closed or departed from 46 of them for various reasons. True, many of these were small, short-lived rural schools; however, there was a sense of continual expansion to meet growing needs. Between 1925 and 1950, 29 foundations were made (most of them schools but also some hospitals and clinics) while 28 were closed or relinquished, usually because of declining populations or lack of Sisters.[36] While the Congregation staffed 76 grade schools and 32 high schools in 1951, by 1966 it had only 64 elementary schools and 26 high schools.[37]

Between 1949 and 1969 the number of Sisters of Divine Providence of Texas remained constant (between 694 and 725); the number of their institutions did not. For the first time in its history, closures (86) outnumbered openings (18). The period of most closures was the seven-year period between 1965 and 1972 when the Sisters withdrew from 41 institutions. This decline coincided with national figures. Between 1966 and 1968, 147 U.S. Catholic elementary schools opened and 420 closed while 60 high schools opened and 217 closed. Between 1965 and 1988, enrollment in U.S. Catholic schools from kindergarten to 12th grade decreased 55%.[38] Between 1967 and 1980 CDPs departed from eight schools started in the 1880s. In some cases, others continued the work the Sisters had begun; but in many instances, closures were permanent. As Sister Patricia Kimball observed,

> It was hard to see all these Sisters shifting away from classrooms, and they were such fantastic teachers. But they did what they had to do; now their vision is somewhere else. If that's what they can do and they do it well, they are still doing God's work. It doesn't have to be teaching per se although the Sisters are teaching no matter what they do. It's just a different outlet.[39]

---

of all religious communities the CDP had the largest commitment in the state during the first century of Catholic presence in Oklahoma.

[36] This number includes the high schools consolidated into Providence High School in San Antonio. Rev. Ben Mazurkiewicz, who had a number of relatives in the Congregation, is convinced that the Church survived in small rural communities because of the Sisters who taught without a salary in a spirit of voluntary sacrifice (Oral interview, 9 Feb. 2002).

[37] "Alumnae News," XXIV, 1 (Jan. 1966): 5, OLLUA. In addition, at this time the Congregation also staffed clinics, catechetical centers, and an orphanage.

[38] Grant and Hunt, *Catholic School Education* 1 and 167.

[39] Oral interview, 21 July 2000, CDPA. Sister Alexia Vinklarek found it difficult as principal of a school to have to solicit Sisters to come teach. Vacancies were no longer filled by the superiors; the principals had to make the effort to attract teachers to their schools (oral interview, 21 Jan. 2000, CDPA).

In 2000, only two high schools staffed by the Sisters were still open: Providence High School of San Antonio and Holy Savior Menard Central High School in Alexandria, Louisiana (the diocesan school which succeeded Providence Central High School). Two others—Bishop Kelley High School in Tulsa, Oklahoma; and St. Augustine's High school in Laredo, Texas—remained open, but the Sisters were no longer on their staffs.

By 1996 only 45 CDP Sisters taught full-time in Catholic schools—29 in elementary and 16 in high schools. Five were principals in elementary schools, and Sister Helen Marie Miksch was principal in Holy Rosary Student Center, Lafayette, Louisiana. Thirteen Sisters were employed in public schools, ten as teachers, one as a teacher assistant, one as a librarian, and one as a school nurse.[40]

Sisters, pupils, and their parents were not the only people affected by the closing of schools. Sometimes lack of personnel meant that a long, harmonious collaboration with a supportive pastor had to be reluctantly terminated. Holy Guardian Angels School in Wallis, Texas, was a typical example. Rev. Aloysius W. Nesvadba in 1945 asked for a "competent Superior to handle good and willing to learn, but restless and very alive, boys that we happen to have in the sixth and seventh grades." He also requested "a Sister to know music, both in English and Czech, like we've had in the past, as we have a very fine choir and we'd hate to see it without a head."[41] Sister Rogata Kalina became the school choir director "when Sister Alcantara Hybner became ill and had to return to San Antonio. She even directed the school choir when they had to sing once a month for a Czech radio program."[42] Father Nesvadba happily reported in 1954, "We have never had an enrollment as high as this time, especially of course in the first two grades, reaching to 60 in the number of pupils [in that room]."[43] But a larger enrollment called for more Sisters. Three years later he wrote to Rev. Mother Amata.

> For 35 years, every year of these, I have had the Sisters of Divine Providence teaching in our Schools, always pleased in every way: at West, Frydek (almost 10 years), Fayetteville (5 years), and here in Wallis, the 16th year. We'd hate to eliminate two grades. But what can we do?
>
> I am going to hope and pray more, that you, dear Reverend Mother, will send us the fourth Sister.[44]

---

[40] *CDP Times*, 16, 6 (Feb., 1996): 12, CDPA.

[41] Rev. A. W. Nesvadba to Mother Angelique, 5 June 1945, CDPA.

[42] *CDP Times*, 15, 8 (April, 1995):10, CDPA.

[43] Rev. A. W. Nesvadba to Mother Amata, 14 July 1954, CDPA.

[44] Rev. A. W. Nesvadba to Mother Amata, 31 July 1957, CDPA.

Four teachers were stationed in Wallis that school year, and the school prospered. Twelve years later, however, another Superior General congratulated the pastor for releasing it. "I believe you showed great foresight in agreeing to merge the two schools in Wallis and in offering the Catholic school facilities to the public school."[45] Two months later, she informed him that "it will be necessary to withdraw one Sister because of the urgent need to retire Sisters and balance the remaining personnel. Since the stressing condition of the present time forces these decisions, I can offer no other apology. I do ask, however, your understanding." The letter ended with a request: "Please join us in prayer for an increase of vocations."[46] In fact, no Sisters taught in Wallis after 1969.

Many parishes in small towns could not provide adequate financing for their schools, which often had a history of going back and forth between Congregational, parish, and state sponsorship and support. For example, the enrollment in St. Joseph's School in Alice, Texas, whose students were predominantly Mexican American, diminished in 1948. The parishioners' contributions were being diverted to the construction of a new church; and the town had two new public elementary schools that were free, modern, and conveniently located. The School Sisters of Notre Dame were planning to open a new, up-to-date Anglo-American School in St. Elizabeth's parish in the same small town.[47] St. Joseph's closed in 1949.

St. Thomas Elementary School in Pilot Point, northeast Texas, began in 1900 and had a new building in 1951. While it was being built, the pastor reported to the Superior General that teachers and students "were under the public school system. They [public school officials] never interfered or suggested anything. The two lay teachers paid by the state go to daily Mass and are fine persons."[48] The Sisters received textbooks from the public school and kept attendance and grade records for each child for the public school in order to retain bus service for all the children.[49] The parish kept the little school open for twenty more years. When it became evident that the Sisters could no longer staff it, the Superior of the Eastern Region wrote to the pastor, "It is our understanding that the public school will be able to absorb the pupils for St. Thomas School beginning with the year 1972-73."[50]

In the metropolis of San Antonio mergers with public schools were not an option. St. Anthony's Elementary School in San Antonio was started by the

---

[45] Sister Elizabeth McCullough to Very Rev. Msgr. A. W. Nesvadba, 27 Jan. 1969, CDPA.

[46] Sister Elizabeth McCullough to Rev. A. W. Nesvadba, 20 March 1969, CDPA.

[47] FC, Dec. 1948:5, CDPA.

[48] Rev. Paul Charcut to Mother Angelique, 11 May 1951, CDPA.

[49] FC, Dec. 1948:5, CDPA.

[50] Sister Henrietta Schroeder to Rev. Severinus Blank, 2 April 1971, CDPA.

CDPs in 1907 at the request of several families living in the Laurel Heights neighborhood. Early in the fall of 1983, the General Council began looking for a Sister-Principal who would serve for three years and organize a lay board to take responsibility for the school. No Sister was available; so a letter to parents of the students announced that beginning in fall 1984, the Principal for the first time would be a layperson. To pay salaries and meet expenses, the tuition was continually raised. Still there was a "lack of cooperation on the part of many parents" and a continued deficit. On 25 March 1985, the parents received a letter saying the school would be closed on 31 May 1985.[51] Two weeks before it closed, Mr. Tom Toudouze and Mr. Dan Dupre, representatives of the parents, offered to rent the school buildings and their contents. After proposing some conditions (none of which concerned the continuation of the charism of Providence), the Sisters agreed to $2,000 per month rent for two years, with later increases. Sister Mary Margaret Hughes, the Superior General, stated that "other schools from which the Sisters have withdrawn have been successfully continued with the leadership of the laity and the Council trusted that this might also be realized in their case."[52] Two years later, however, the Congregation sold St. Anthony's School and all property covered by the lease for $523,000 cash.[53]

Closings made a few Sisters available for new projects, but most of these did not last long, either because the institution closed or the Sisters withdrew, for example: St. Joseph's Elementary School in Bellmead, Texas (1960-1967); St. Benedict's Junior High School in Houston, Texas (1967-1970); St. Cletus School of Religion in Gretna, Louisiana (1967-1972); and St. Joseph's Elementary School in Killeen, Texas (1967-1978). More Sisters began to work outside of church institutions. While in 1970 only three Sisters were holding salaried jobs outside of the traditional Congregational works, in 1986 there were 13 receiving public salaries.[54]

A new challenge to the Sisters' resiliency was the necessity of re-assignment because a school was closing. For example, Sister Imelda Maurer, who made her first vows in 1958, was assigned to three high schools which closed in quick succession between 1967 and 1970. Sacred Heart High School, El Reno, Oklahoma, which moved to a new high school and gymnasium in 1962, closed in 1967 because of low enrollment and a large debt. St. Joseph's High School in Enid, Oklahoma, closed in 1968 in an atmosphere of bitterness.[55] Sister Imelda

---

[51] GC minutes, 13 Mar. 1985, CDPA.

[52] GC minutes, 15 May 1985, CDPA. Later St. Anthony's became affiliated with the University of the Incarnate Word.

[53] GC minutes, 4 May 1987, CDPA.

[54] GC minutes, 19 April 1970 and 25 Feb. 1986, CDPA.

[55] Sister Imelda González recalled that "parents, including the brother of Sister Theresa Joseph Powers, came to physical blows. He lost his teeth at a meeting over whether the school should close or not" (Oral interview, 15 June 2000, CDPA).

was teaching in St. Joseph High School, Yoakum, Texas, in 1970 when it also closed. Closures not only aroused emotions but could weaken self-esteem. In the summer of 1968 Sister Madeleine Zimmerer had the experience of losing three jobs before she actually started them. She expected to return to teach the first grade in Sacred Heart Elementary School in El Reno, Oklahoma; but the grade school closed for lack of finances. Right away she was assigned to St. Louis School in Castroville, Texas; but the school board closed it before she got there. Then she was sent to St. Francis Elementary School in Alexandria, Louisiana; but at the urging of the diocesan school office, the school closed in August before classes began because of low enrollment. Sister Madeleine remarked, "By then, I felt that no one wanted me."[56]

A shortage of Sister-teachers was a factor in school closings, and soon school closings became one cause of the shortage of Sisters. Women who might have been attracted to the religious life because of the example of dynamic, happy teachers had no opportunity to meet such women. When a Sister reached retirement age, no Sister was available to replace her. Martha Pack Brinkmann's tribute to Sister Elizabeth Anne Sueltenfuss, president of OLLU from 1978 to 1997, applies to a large number of CDPs who worked in schools.

> She did great things to improve the appearance and public image of the school. I think she attended and participated in every civic, religious and social event during that time. She served—and served with great dignity and intelligence—on many civic boards and committees. Yet she had time to send notes of congratulations when your name appeared in the paper or you achieved some honor. I admired the way she backed away from the University and let the new President reign when her time was over as she traveled and moved on to new things in her life.[57]

When the number of Sister-students as well as faculty at OLLU decreased in the 1980s, Sister Elizabeth Anne was a key to maintaining the Congregation's presence. When non-CDP Presidents replaced her, concern about perpetuating the values of the Congregation increased. That continued concern was expressed in the University's strategic plan for the twenty-first century:

> For three-quarters of a century the University mission was broadly perceived to be an extension of CDP ministry, and the Sisters themselves were the visible embodiment of CDP values on the

---

[56] Oral interview, 10 July 2000, CDPA).

[57] Martha Pack Brinkmann, oral interview, 7 Sept. 2001, CDPA.

campus. The diminution of CDPs in the faculty and staff, however, requires that the perpetuation of their mission and values in the present and future at the University be a collaborative effort.[58]

One way to perpetuate the CDP mission in schools with few or no Sister-faculty was to assign a former Sister-Administrator to be in charge of "mission effectiveness." Sister Michael Rose Stanzel was the first Sister to undertake this ministry at Providence High School in San Antonio. Sister Cecile Clare Vanderlick, as president of Holy Savior Menard Central High School in Alexandria, Louisiana, saw two aspects to her work, Catholic identity and public relations. She offered daily voluntary prayer services for the faculty, planned school Masses with the campus minister, and recruited new students. She also spoke at civic clubs to raise money for scholarships and for the school.[59] These new positions showed the Sisters' awareness of their own diminishment and call to concretize their abandonment to Divine Providence. They believed that the Congregation's good works could survive and thrive by closer collaboration with laypersons rather than by pioneer and maintenance efforts of the Sisters alone.[60]

The Congregation's hospitals flourished in the 1950s, and new entrants were increasingly attracted to nursing ministry; but circumstances in the communities where the hospitals were located forced a re-evaluation of the need for the institutions. St. Ann's Hospital in Abilene, Texas, closed in 1969 due to "building deterioration, income depletion, increased government aid to non-parochial hospitals, shortage of personnel, and the fact that hospitals are asked not to duplicate services."[61] A few years later doctors on the staff of Madonna Hospital in Denison, Texas, decided to build their own hospital. Madonna Hospital could not compete with the institution they were planning; therefore, Mr. Frank Silverwise, the Administrator, suggested amalgamation. The doctors were not interested, so the Sisters sold Madonna Hospital in 1974 for $400,000.

Joan Laskowski recalled being "devastated" when she learned that the Sisters would no longer administer the hospital in Floresville, Texas. She continued in the accounting and admissions area for over 30 years. She never forgot that when she was being treated for cancer and lost her appetite, Sister Jo Marie Toudouze would sit on her bed and feed her. Shortly afterwards, Sister herself was diagnosed with cancer of the brain and soon died. Joan said,

---

[58] "Moving Forward Together, the Strategic Plan," Fall, 2002, 26, OLLUA.

[59] Sister Cecile Clare Vanderlick, oral interview, 21 July 2000, CDPA.

[60] "Even when our efforts fail, we continue trusting in the God who brings life from death and creates out of nothingness" (Constitution, # 15).

[61] Announcement by Sister Elizabeth McCullough, Superior General, "CDP Summer News Bulletin," 16 June 1969: 2, CDPA.

the Sisters never, never preached except by example. When Sister Laverne Mettlach was the administrator, she had to deal with some harsh criticism; but she continued to do what was right and assured the employees, "Trust God. Things will be OK." Sometimes there was not enough money for the payroll, and Sister Aline Hrncir would say, "Just pray; it will come."[62]

And it did come. Joan considered her connection with the Sisters over the years a personal gift, and she thought the Sisters were a gift to the Floresville community. She believed that even Sisters from this hospital who had died were still interested in the people and in the effectiveness of the hospital.[63]

Armando Castellanos, who was employed in the x-ray department in Floresville for over 29 years, attested that the Sisters set the standard of excellent health care which the lay employees accepted and adhered to even after the Sisters left. "They passed on the spirit, and we continued it." He insisted that he stayed on at the hospital because of his esteem for the Sisters and also because he wanted "to have them on my side when I die."[64]

More than 20 years after the inception of Stella Maris Clinic, the Congregation's General Administration had ongoing concerns about bookkeeping, accountability and the expense of maintaining it even though they were pleased that it was meeting great needs. In 1989 Sister Barbara Lynn Hyzak, the Administrator, faced problems different from those of her pioneer predecessor, Sister Nelda González. The neighborhood population had different occupations and challenges after almost 40 years; and new health needs had arisen for which Bexar County officials were ready to take responsibility. The Stella Maris Clinic building was leased to the Bexar County Health District in July 1992.

After Sister Mary Walter Gutowski, founder and administrator of Our Lady of Guadalupe Clinic in Rosenberg, died suddenly in 1993, the Congregation was unable to provide a successor. The clinic closed, but services to the needy continued with the helpers Sister Mary Walter had trained. In 1994 the Scanlan Foundation conveyed ownership of the clinic property to the Galveston-Houston diocese, which turned over the responsibility of the clinic to Our Lady of Grace parish.[65] The building was converted into Our Lady of Guadalupe Pastoral Center where counseling takes place for teens and families.

---

[62] Joan Laskowski, oral interview, 4 Aug. 2004, CDPA.

[63] Oral interview, 4 Aug. 2004, CDPA.

[64] Oral interview, 4 Aug. 2004, CDPA.

[65] Rosenberg newspaper, May, 1994, CDPA.

Retirement, CDP Style

The formation of women in religious life was geared to instill a spirit of serving others, so little attention was paid to how one would carry on when one could no longer serve actively. CDPs have never exhibited a strong sense that retirement is a right or reward. Accustomed to organizing, managing, and constantly meeting people's needs, the Sisters found the tables turned. They were invited to trust in God by turning over their projects to others and accepting help. Sisters who made this transition were supported by a spirituality of accepting what happens as coming from God and a sense of being dependent on Divine Providence. The road faithfully traveled seemed to have reached a dead end and the road ahead seemed unclear. The impasse could easily lead to discouragement, but not if the journey is seen as a cooperative venture with a caring divine companion.

To let go as well as to accept help require a certain kind of trust that God's work will be done even though one personally cannot do it all. It also entails prioritizing and deciding what is most worthwhile in life. The values of wealth, success, growth, acumen, strength, and popularity may eventually become unattainable. Yet other values remain: hope, love for others, and joy along with gratitude and appreciation of life as a gift from God. Witness to these enduring values may be needed more than ever in the twenty-first century in the northern hemisphere where populations are increasing in mobility as well as in age. Sisters who accept change and diminishment with faith in God thus can continue to perform a needed ministry.

Sister Ermelinda Cannady illustrated gradual detachment when after 15 years of parish ministry in Enid, Oklahoma, at age 81 she retired to the Motherhouse in San Antonio.

> What I find very interesting is that as soon as there is a mishap in a family in Enid, they write to me, mostly it's the men. If they lose their wife, they write. If I get a letter I'll answer it, and very shortly I'll get another one and answer it. Then the period in between letters gets longer, and finally it stops. The letters taper off as soon as they can handle it.[66]

Retired CDPs valued time to do what they had put off before—visit with friends, re-connect with family, explore genealogy, pray and read more. Sister Vera Schad appreciated the TV set in her room as her vision deteriorated. "I love to get the news in the evening. And any services in Annunciation chapel

---

[66] Oral interview, 9 Dec. 1999, CDPA.

are broadcast [by closed circuit TV] right into our rooms at McCullough Hall. I can't go to church now, so I look at the closed circuit TV for Mass and other functions."[67] Church feasts and birthdays were celebrated with special parties or meals. On monthly retreat Sunday and other days, speakers made presentations on Scripture, theology, health, and current events.

When Sister Olga Zotz began to work with the retired Sisters, she had some interesting insights. "I used to wonder why lay people found it so hard to go to nursing homes. Then I began to realize they give up their home and live with strangers. When we retire, we don't give up a home, and we don't live with strangers." Personally she found it easy "to let things go," probably because she was four-and-a-half years old when her mother died. "Your mom dies, and you give up your home. You come to the convent, and you give up things. It's no different, really, as far as I'm concerned." However, she added that she understood that Sisters who had different experiences found divestiture difficult, "especially if retirement was their first experience at really giving up."[68]

Health permitting, CDPs who had been active all their lives tried to stay active when they retired whether "on the mission" or in the Congregation's retirement center. Why? A number of reasons can be given, among them are: (1) They were attracted to the Congregation because it offered opportunities for serving people, so their identity is entwined with active service. (2) They considered health a gift and wanted to use their energies for others as long as they could. Sister Ermelinda Cannady, for example, in her 90s carried on e-mail correspondence and taught computer skills to lay employees as well as to the Sisters. (3) They were raised in middle or lower socioeconomic class families in which retirement was not a custom or even an option. (4) Their habits of daily, active work were so strong that they enjoyed being active and even felt guilty sitting still for long periods. Interviewed when she was 92 years old, Sister Thérèse Pousson said,

> I read the *National Catholic Reporter* thoroughly every week and *Time* magazine, take my hour a day answering the telephone, visit the sick, go for a little exercise, distribute the mail, and spend a lot of time playing games on the computer.
>
> I think the call to holiness is different for different people. For some people it is staying in front of the tabernacle. That's not for me, but I admire anybody who can spend all that time with the Lord. I spend most of my time with people. I like change; I am easily bored.[69]

---

[67] Oral interview, 15 Mar. 2000, CDPA.

[68] Oral interview, 23 Feb. 2000.

[69] Oral interview, 10 Dec. 1999, CDPA.

The Sisters' fun times resembled those of other retired U.S. seniors—conversations with one another, especially reminiscing about earlier days, doing fancywork, or making small items for sale at fairs and bazaars, playing dominoes, or cards.[70] Crossword puzzles and Scrabble were popular games. Sister Rita Fritz was famous for telling jokes. Sisters Ann Linda (Angele) Bell, Clemence Ribitzki and Margeta Krchnak were noted for their great devotion to jigsaw puzzles. Sisters who were avid sports fans continued to watch sports and root for their favorite teams and players. Sisters Martha and Dorothy Ann Vrba as well as Sister Clair (M. Gerald) Osborn cheered for the San Antonio Spurs basketball team. The Dallas Cowboys and the Notre Dame University football teams had loyal supporters among the Sisters. Feltin Center was a well-stocked gathering place for cooking, baking, useful sewing, or fancywork, as well as for a variety of socials. Picnics and excursions to nearby attractions were frequently scheduled.

For CDPs work is not primarily a means of earning something in this world or in the next but is an expression of one's self and a way to co-create with the Creator throughout life. The best "job" for each person is the one where the person's talents, whatever they may be, contribute to the good of the community. The happiness of other workers is valued above mere efficiency. Work undertaken as a means to bring about God's Reign has a distinct flavor lacking in work undertaken for profit or fame. When life is regarded as a gift and accomplishments as ultimately due to the Giver of life, one's satisfaction is measured in more than dollars and cents.

A few examples show how Sisters took opportunities for service even when their age and frailty entitled them to be the recipients of healing care. Sister Floriana Galvin volunteered her services at St. Ann's Hospital in Abilene for several weeks, and Sister Roche Sakowsky did the same at the school in Mansura, Louisiana.[71] Sister Mary Paul Valdez worked at Margil House of Studies in Houston gathering materials and publicizing the cause of Venerable Antonio Margil, OFM, founder of Texas missions in the seventeenth and eighteenth centuries. In San Antonio, Sister Redempta Galvin taught music and singing once a week to the MCDPs in formation at St. Andrew's Convent, and Sister Christiana Freitag spent several weeks as a substitute teacher of German at Providence High School. Sister Serena Brom and Sister Georgia Samland taught children songs and crafts as well as prayers at Mirasol Homes, the federal housing project adjacent to the convent.[72] In the mid-1970s Cenizio Park Elementary

---

[70] When she was 89, Sister Vera Schad recalled that when she was in the first grade Sister Victorine Klein taught her how to tat during the fancywork period on Fridays (Oral interview, 15 Mar. 2000,CDPA).

[71] "CDP Newsletter," 1 Nov. 1969: 8, CDPA.

[72] "CDP Newsletter," 3, 5 (5 Jan. 1976): 134, CDPA.

School appreciated the services of volunteer Sister Dolores Cárdenas, who taught moral values to about 30 pupils weekly as well as English to adults seeking citizenship. Sister Katherine Ann Hays found she could "still teach indirectly by handing out reading materials—magazines, papers, whatever I had—to the lay employees. I figure if you're reading, you're learning. That's how I feel I'm still teaching indirectly. I also tutor."[73]

Among the numerous retired Sisters who tutored were: Francisca Lott and Euphrosine Honc (St. Martin Hall), Corona Hill (Oasis Senior Center), Sister Mary Elizabeth Jupe (OASIS in the public schools), and María Cristina Ruelas (HOSTS [Helping One Student to Succeed]).[74] Sister Anna Marie Kaeberle offered free piano lessons for employees during the lunch hour. Sister Margarita Sánchez counseled some of the lay employees, and a number of Sisters helped the children of these employees with homework assignments. Sister Hubert Lavan and Sister Juliette Lange also assisted in arts and crafts classes.[75]

Life-long habits of responding to needs were exemplified by Sister Evangelista Karlik, who when she retired to Regan Hall sent postcards to Sisters who lived alone, giving them the daily news from the Motherhouse. Sister Mary Martin Haidusek continued to serve as presiding judge for the Democratic Party at local polling places while Sisters Mary Elizabeth Jupe and Ann Carmel Maggio worked as volunteers at polling places near the Motherhouse during elections. Sister Anselma Weselski used her artistic talents to make corsages, table favors, and other items, which she sold through a local variety store.[76] Sister Marcia Havlak crocheted thousands of placemats out of colorful yarn. Sister Juliette Lange and years later her niece, Sister Martha Rose (Mary Melania) Lange, joyfully gardened and landscaped the Convent grounds.

After her term as Superior General, Sister Amata Regan spent six years ministering to the aged at Our Lady of Prompt Succor parish in Alexandria, Louisiana. The pastor, Msgr. Frederick Lyons, described her impact:

> The elderly loved her very much. First of all, she was elderly like them, and then she was French, as many of them were. As they get older, they revert to French. She was good to talk to, so we miss her very much.
>
> After the last Sunday Mass she would pick up the notes I made for my homilies and relay the message to patients in the nursing

---

[73] Oral interview, 26 Jan. 2000, CDPA.

[74] Sister María Cristina Ruelas, oral interview, 27 March 2000.

[75] *Movements*, 3, 1 (Fall/Winter, 1999): 8-9, CDPA.

[76] Sister Anselma also molded figures for a crèche that won first prize in the Fredericksburg Garden Club's Christmas exhibit (FC, March 1949: 126, CDPA).

homes the coming week. She organized the Eucharistic ministers and anybody else who wanted to work with the elderly. She also organized the preparation of baskets and gifts for them on different occasions, and these would be delivered to them.

She was a spiritual person who was always interested in growing in the spiritual life. She had a dignity and a presence that were very impressive. She was dignified herself and she treated people with dignity.[77]

Sister Helen Margaret Schad, who had served as the principal at Prompt Succor, went back years later "to take care of the aging group. I've never had a sabbatical, but working with that aging group was the best sabbatical I ever could have had. Saints of God they were!"[78]

The Sisters encouraged their students to become life-long learners, and those whose health permitted it continued setting good example when they retired. Sister Athanasius Schad, when she was 92 years old, never missed an Audubon movie on campus and kept her daily Hour of Adoration before the Blessed Sacrament. Accepting an invitation at this age to go on a fishing trip near Floresville, Texas, she caught a 2.5-pound fish, the only member of the party to catch one.[79] Sister Dolores Cárdenas was a perpetual teacher and learner.

I am an octogenarian still working and achieving outstanding results. This year I appeared twice on a TV program in Houston to invite the public to come forward and take an active part in the interests and progress of Our Lady of Guadalupe School and parish. It was an exciting experience to face the camera and speak. However, it was more rewarding to observe the response from old and young alike. . . . The media are now an important means used to propagate God's kingdom on earth.

Visiting the poor and lonely, and counseling the young who fail to see the hidden conflicts of the married life is another phase of this apostolate that requires much attention.[80]

Sister Mary Clare Metz began to teach at OLL in 1934 and was the Academic Dean of the University when she retired in 1972. She stayed at the University

---

[77] Oral interview of Msgr. Frederick Lyons by Sister Angelina Murphy, 1983, CDPA.

[78] Oral interview, 19 Feb. 2000, CDPA.

[79] "CDP News Notes," 1 April 1971, CDPA.

[80] *Nunspeak*, Summer, 1972:12, CDPA.

as the Director of the Alumni Office for four more years and at the same time moved to a smaller off-campus community. Learning to cook and to interact with a group of younger Sisters who had as one of their goals to engage in more intimate mutual communication were among her new experiences. Despite chronic and often severe back pain, which she endured for many years, Sister Mary Clare was almost as active during her retirement as she had always been before. She served on several local boards, participated in a charismatic prayer group, and taught in the parish RCIA program. She also instructed candidates for Confirmation and offered Scripture courses in the parish. Sister Mary Clare did not drive, but she maintained her cherished independence by taking advantage of city bus service so she could fulfill all of her obligations. Sister Laetitia Hill and Sister Henry Ehlen spent several years after they retired from the university with the CDP community in Querétaro, Mexico. Sister Laetitia also lived for a year with the Sisters on the Navajo reservation in Tuba City, Arizona. Sister Bernadette Bezner remembered her as "very accepting of the Navajo and very prayerful." When they were drinking coffee in the afternoon, sometimes Sister Laetitia would suddenly start reciting Shakespeare by heart.[81]

Sister Emelene Matocha even after she no longer taught courses at OLLU continued instructing a full load of private violin and piano pupils, playing the violin in a local string quartet, and providing organ music for Sunday services at military bases and retirement centers until she suffered a massive stroke at the age of 83. After 55 years of teaching and administration, Sister Frances (Edmunda) McMann proofread the San Antonio archdiocesan newspaper, *Today's Catholic*, from 1992 until her "early retirement" on her 90th birthday in 2002. Sister Angelina Murphy wrote a weekly column for this paper when she was the Secretary to the Superior General of the Congregation in the 1970s and continued writing articles, books, poems, and essays into her 90s.[82] Sister Mary Nora Herrera learned librarianship "on the job" at St. Mary's School in downtown San Antonio with the help of a library specialist from the Catholic school office. When she retired in 1990, she volunteered at the Westside Catholic School in San Antonio all day Monday through Thursday. Sister Mary Teresa Cullen, CSB, principal, testified, "She was absolutely a godsend. We couldn't afford a librarian, and I was concerned that the children were not able to use the library. Sister Mary Nora made that possible. She gave of herself 100%. I admire her ability to keep going."[83] After being in active ministry for 52 years,

---

[81] Oral interview, 17 Sept., 2000, CDPA.

[82] Sister Angelina was also pleased that she gave Eugene (Gene) Curtsinger the good foundation at St. Joseph's School in Dallas which enabled him to become a Professor of English at the University of Dallas. He authored five novels as well as scholarly studies of Moby Dick and Henry James.

[83] *CDP Times*, 14, 7 (Mar. 1994): 11, CDPA.

Sister Inéz Terán lived at the retirement center but served in nearby St. Jude's parish as a daily Eucharistic minister, distributor of commodities, animator of the parish prayer group, and advocate for senior citizens.[84]

Sister Frances Theresa Schellang, who was never a music teacher even though she had music training before she entered the convent, enjoyed playing the organ for Mass and Benediction in Annunciation Chapel in Regan Hall when she retired.[85] Sister Victorine Klein played her harmonica, and Sister Florida Hruzek played the piano for many sing-alongs. Reading to or writing for the blind or bedridden Sisters was another ministry. The chapel was the venue for sacristans such as Sisters Geraldine Bourg, Rita Rose Bily, and Jacinta Berger and for numerous Eucharistic ministers and lectors as well as organists and song leaders. Of course, answering the doorbell and the telephone, distributing mail, sewing, mending, and caring for potted plants were always needed; and Sisters performed these services as long as they were able.

The retired Sisters tried to stay active, but they understood and accepted that their main ministry in retirement was to pray. They participated joyfully in opportunities for communal prayer. Each had her daily hour before the Blessed Sacrament and a long list of intentions, which were also posted on bulletin boards. Prayer requests came from relatives, former students, employees, and even strangers who telephoned asking the Sisters to intercede with God for someone who was ill or in trouble. Sister Firmina Anders' cousin, Astronaut William Anders, the pilot of Apollo 8, the first human flight around the moon, "frequently wrote to Sister asking prayers for the success of the moon venture."[86] The injustice of capital punishment was a concern. Sister Miriam (Miriam Joseph) Kettermann said, "Now we're trying to do away with the death penalty, trying to get persons to sign petitions. In fact, I carry my slip around to get signatures. And that's justice."[87] Special prayers were offered for prisoners on death row on the day of their execution. Sister Martha (Reginald) Kuban corresponded with a prisoner on death row.

> Javier's correspondence with me was an inspiration. He said I was like a spiritual director, and his last sentence was, "If we don't meet on earth, then we'll meet in heaven." I happened to be there when his

---

[84] *Signs of Providence*, 7, 3 (Jan. 2003): 9, CDPA.

[85] *CDP Times*, 14, 4 (Dec. 1993): 11, CDPA.

[86] *Nunspeak*, summer, 1972:18, CDPA. He took the famous color photo of earthrise from the moon on the Apollo 8 mission on Christmas Eve, 1968. He and his two companions in the spacecraft also read the first verses from Genesis during this flight.

[87] Oral interview, 30 Jan. 2000, CDPA.

body was brought to San Antonio. I attended the funeral and rosary and met his mother. I feel like I have a big friend in heaven now.[88]

Some Sisters responded to a request to continue giving even after death by donating their bodies or parts of their bodies to science. This option was part of a 1985 presentation on "Living Wills," in which the Sisters named a person to whom they gave Power of Attorney and specified the medical care they wanted when they were nearing death. The first cremains buried in a special section of the Convent cemetery were those of Sister Annella Foelker.[89]

At the beginning of the twenty-first century, the number of retired Sisters continued to grow; and they continued to find ways to manifest the compassionate face of God even when they became limited to dealing with one another and with the staff of the retirement center. The General Council developed a handbook outlining the levels of retirement and the ways in which a Sister could know when she was ready for one of them. Three-day pre-retirement retreats were also offered for Sisters who were considering this option.

Retirement security was assured because of social security, teachers' retirement pensions, and the generosity of benefactors. A 15-year projection by the Arthur Anderson Company helped the Congregation forecast its financial future. A fund for retirement needs was initiated in 1971 and the Providence Trust fund was established in 1989. Administered by an appointed board of CDP Sisters, its earnings have been supplemented annually by the National Religious Retirement Office, which in 2003 cited the Congregation for its prudent retirement preparations.

When they were no longer able to staff institutions fully, the Sisters took on the role of sponsors. Presently the Congregation sponsors Our Lady of the Lake University and Providence High School in San Antonio and Moye Retreat Center in Castroville. Sponsorship means assuring that the institution exemplifies and is operated according to the deepest values espoused by the Congregation.[90]

Today CDPs provide occasions for others to meet the Sisters' needs and to practice generosity, mercy, and charity as well as gratitude and sometimes forgiveness. Accepting this reversal graciously was a challenge. Priorities had to be reconsidered and plans re-assessed. The steps of discernment—see needs, judge, enlist help, act—came into play again. As they drew closer to the final passage to the Home of the God whom they loved above all, they found peace

---

[88] Oral interview, 20 Feb. 2000, CDPA.

[89] GC minutes, 5 Feb. 1985, and 17 May 1985, CDPA.

[90] Efforts included sponsoring retreats for the various boards.

in testifying to lasting values. They met death with the conviction that it led to resurrection and new life. Death is a beginning, not an ending.[91]

Monsignor Balthasar Janacek summarized the Sisters' efforts:

> In many ways you Sisters kept the Church alive over the years in the areas where it had schools. You did it for nothing and with nothing. You continued with a smaller number of Sisters to do things that are very helpful to the Church in general. You filled key positions in parishes. Your charism is something that continues to be needed.[92]

Even if their survival as a Congregation became questionable, the Sisters believed that the charism of trust in Providence would continue to exist in others. Part of their understanding of Providence is: "Together with God and with humanity, we are bringing about the New Creation which is the glory of God shared by us."[93] Regardless of major changes, they continued to pass on to their own Sisters and whomever they contacted the conviction that those who are confident in God will be more secure than if they had all the money in the world.[94] Manifested in diminishment as well as in growth, confidence in a Provident God is their chief, highly cherished legacy.

The period of more than 50 years covered by this history manifested obvious changes in the Sisters' institutions as well as in their own awareness of problems and the way in which they might be solved. Accompanying these more visible changes was a profound inner transformation of the structures and customs of the Congregation. Impelled by Vatican Council II directives, the Sisters combed their history and mined their own recent experiences to take their life together in new directions.

---

[91] See Appendix III for the census of CDPs, 1943 to 2003. Hospice workers often expressed approval of the Sisters' positive attitude toward death. For example, Mother Angelica O'Neill, 86, survived several near-death episodes. On the day she actually died, Sister Melissa Maurer joyfully announced to the Sisters as she met them in the convent corridors, "Mother Angelica is going up! She is *really* going this time!" For mortality statistics of CDPs, see Appendix III.

[92] Oral interview, 18 Sept. 2001, CDPA.

[93] Constituion # 8.

[94] See *Directory* 79.

CHAPTER 12

LIVING TOGETHER IN NEW WAYS

A solicitous pastor in 1955 expressed succinctly the prevalent view that women religious should live separated from lay people and a "dirty" world: "Their religious life puts them in [an] entirely different world, and with all the protection which may be given them they will encounter from time to time the filth of the world."[1] Fifty years later Dr. Albert Griffith—who had been around Sisters all his life, had relatives who were Sisters, and worked as a teacher and administrator with CDPs at OLLU for more than 50 years—expressed approval of changes he had observed. The Sisters' semi-cloistered communities had given way to ways of living that promoted not only more numerous and varied friendships but deeper influence.

> Many men in our generation never had women as friends. We had women acquaintances and wives and men friends that we associated with, but we didn't have that kind of just Platonic bonding that women often have. But I feel that it became possible to be really great friends with the Sisters. Then you could be influenced by them to your own advantage.[2]

Changes in the type and scope of CDP service chronicled in previous chapters were accompanied and often required by dramatic but less visible changes in the Congregation's community life and government structure. During the last half of the twentieth century the map of the world altered; communication and trade across national borders accelerated; and the U.S. became the dominant world

---

[1] Rev. James T. Lockwood to Mother M. Angelique, 17 March 1955, CDPA.

[2] Dr. Albert Griffith, oral interview, 3 Sept. 2002, CDPA.

power. The state of Texas located in the Sunbelt saw a surge of population and increased industrialization along with a greater awareness and appreciation of ethnic diversity. The Roman Catholic Church elected Pope John XXIII, who unexpectedly called for *aggiornamento* and dramatic alterations to update the Church. "Challenged to look at both the church and their calling from an entirely new vantage point—the mission of the church in the world—sisters had to alter radically their ways of seeing, judging, acting, and relating."[3]

The second Vatican Council mandated a thorough self-examination by all religious congregations. They were to return to the main insights of their founders but were also given permission to experiment with structures and practices so as to adapt positively and realistically to the contemporary world. Sister Barbara Lynn Hyzak felt that reforms suggested by the Council led to changes "across the board" rather than in just one dimension. "Only now are we finding ourselves catching up with the full impact of what really was intended."[4]

Why were the Sisters able to cope with change more easily than some other groups? Perhaps because at this time they often interpreted the vow of obedience as following orders without questioning. As teachers, they were also accustomed to finding reasons so as to elicit more voluntary cooperation with instructions. More significantly, however, in practicing their characteristic trust in Divine Providence, they were sure the future was in God's hands and they could rely on divine help when they embarked on an unfamiliar new path. Sister Jane Coles, who served as a General Councilor 1979-1981 and later as Director of Communications for the Congregation, believed that "the beauty of our Congregation is that we have made changes as they were called for in the signs of the times. We didn't just change suddenly or get on bandwagons. We did this, I think, gradually and graciously, starting with Mother Angelique."[5]

The Sisters had a useful tool to obtain data that facilitated the updating mandated by the second Vatican Council. An extensive survey prepared by the research committee of the Conference of Major Superiors of Women (CMSW) supervised by Sister Marie Augusta Neal, SNDdeN, was administered to all the Sisters in the Congregation, along with many other women religious in the U.S. Data from this survey began to be used in the Congregation's Renewal Chapter held in 1967 and 1968. Of the many experiments that followed, the ones dealing with forms of community life and government were the most profound and lasting. This chapter will detail how the Sisters outgrew their matriarchal communities, which resembled the patriarchal families from which most of them had come to religious life.

---

[3] Quiñonez and Turner, *The Transformation*: 118.

[4] Sister Barbara Lynn Hyzak, oral interview, 17 Jan. 2001, CDPA.

[5] Sister Jane Coles, oral interview, 17 Jan. 2000, CDPA.

Structure of Local Communities

An ideal religious community "gives us an experience of community with persons not related by blood and gives us a special help to understand and share this experience with others and encourage its growth among them."[6] Religious vows are meant to be supports in constructing and promoting such an alternate "world" modeled on the inclusive community of Jesus and his disciples. Living together in this way in today's individualistic and materialistic society often means being counter-cultural.

Communal living was the first area where the Congregation began to consider change after Vatican Council II. The goal was to improve ministry by encouraging more responsible individual choices, deeper sharing, and healthier relationships among the Sisters as well as with persons outside the Congregation. The Sisters were accustomed to living in groups ranging from two to around 80 members. Most local communities were small, with three to six members. The groups were not monolithic but differed both within and from each other even though their members held basic common values and ideals, dressed alike, followed similar schedules, and observed the same customs regarding prayer and other components of religious life.

Sister Rosalie Karstedt recounted that in the 1960s she resided "in a community with a superior. Then we moved into communities with coordinators, and then we moved into the understanding of community as Congregation, and then to the cluster. I think the way we have lived out community and moved community along has been very significant."[7] After experimenting for almost 30 years, the Sisters did not return to the time-honored structure of religious community, i.e., a group of Sisters assigned to live together under the leadership of one Sister appointed by the Congregation's general administrators.

When the local superior had great power over individuals, her behavior impacted the whole community for good or ill. For example, Sister Elizabeth Anne Sueltenfuss reported not having enough to eat during World War II in Norman, Oklahoma. "The Superior didn't eat anything; the cook counted out the beans; and we had colds all winter."[8] Sister Elizabeth McCullough was stationed with a parsimonious superior on a mission where the Sisters "were always hungry." On Easter Sunday, 1943, the superior locked the kitchen after

---

[6] Sister Redempta Bradley, *Nunspeak*, June, 1971:19, CDPA.

[7] Sister Rosalie Karstedt, oral interview, 20 June 2000, CDPA. On the local level, the superior had virtually absolute power. Sister Mary Lou (Mathilde) Becerra remembered, however, that Sister Bonaventure Jordan was "ahead of her times" in her practice of delegating a job and never questioning or bothering to find out how it was accomplished (Oral interview, 26 Dec. 2000, CDPA).

[8] Oral interview, 20 Oct. 2000, CDPA.

supper. Two of the young Sisters were so hungry they somehow found carrots and bread on which to "feast." Also, one summer Sister Elizabeth was told to study art but not given the necessary supplies. She had to ask to go to the bookstore for each sheet of paper. Sometimes she borrowed from her lay classmates; at other times her mother brought her watercolors and other supplies.[9]

Other difficulties in living together were due to age differences, psychological problems, and the formation of various types of sub-groups. Sister Alexia Vinklarek recalled that her "interaction with the Sisters on my first mission wasn't so good because I was 22, and they were in their 60s and 70s. It was a little bit difficult for me to communicate on their level. And I guess for them it was the same thing. I really didn't have any outlets except study, school, and prayer."[10] Community life also could be difficult if a member had psychological problems, was doing work that was unsuitable and/or unsatisfying for her, or was lacking in social skills. Sister Madlyn Pape remembered a community "where one of the less healthy persons went on a rampage, and it ruined Christmas for us. Nobody talked about it. That was difficult for me, but I belonged to a kind of sub-group of younger Sisters in the house, and that helped me keep a balance."[11] Congregational leaders usually addressed placement problems by providing counseling and/or moving Sisters to other communities or changing their work. To detect potential problems earlier, Mother Amata shortly after the convening of Vatican Council II announced that if a Sister wanted a change "for personal reasons or for the common good," she was to write to her, giving reasons.[12]

Before the second Vatican Council, usually a Sister would be appointed a local superior when her administrative skills, including responsibility and creativity, were noticed and called to the attention of the central administration by someone who was herself a superior. There was no formal leadership training until 1973. Sister Rose Corrine remembered, "We were given tasks that unknowingly trained us for leadership positions later on, tasks that made us come out of our shells and be able to do something."[13] Although local superiors communicated with the general superiors and implemented their decisions and advice, they alone were responsible for the local community "out on the mission" where the Sisters spent most of each year. During this period of most intense experimentation, the General Council decided that the term "superior"

---

[9] Sister Elizabeth McCullough, oral interview, 17 April 2000, CDPA.

[10] Oral interview, 21 Jan. 2000, CDPA.

[11] Oral interview, 21 Dec. 2000, CDPA.

[12] Mother Amata Regan, Circular Letter, 23 Apr. 1963, CDPA.

[13] Sister Rose Corrine Medica, oral interview, 16 June 2000, CDPA. She admitted "it was the first time I got an inkling of what some of our Superiors General have to go through, which they seldom share with us."

would be replaced by the term "coordinator," and for flexibility in government all coordinators would be appointed for one year only.[14]

Three or four different motives for experiments with community structures were revealed in a panel on experimental communities that took place in the summer of 1970. Sister Kathryn (Mary Michael) Keefe and former Sister Judy Elder said they chose to leave the large college community to live together for the main purpose of building community. Former Sister Clara Ann Langley reported that in her group the type of work (nursing and teaching remedial reading) was the determining factor for living communally. Sister Margaret Rose Warburton with several other Sisters lived in Mirasol Homes, a federal housing project for low income families adjacent to the OLL campus. "We came together as a result of wanting to live off campus in a small community in a low income bracket. Even though we belong to the residents' association, we do not attempt to work among the people but continue with our usual jobs."[15] Some Sisters teaching in the Edgewood School district wanted to experience the neighborhood from which their students came, so they rented a house in a neighborhood where crime and gang activities were not unusual.

Most invitations to experiment with ways of living together came from the general administration. For example, Sister Elizabeth McCullough sent a letter of invitation in May 1969 to the college community, which was comprised of about 100 Sisters. She asked them to experiment in styles of living in order "to respond to the signs of the times, especially to society's cry for people who can live community and not just talk about it. The General Council knew, and many of the Sisters there knew, that something had to change." But among the large number of Sisters were some who were content with the status quo. "Some Sisters were digging in their heels, so we finally had to say, 'This is what we are going to do. You can sign up freely.' There was no negotiation possible, but it worked."[16] Sister Elizabeth asked that the Sisters choose not the persons with whom to live but the type of group they preferred: (1) a large community on campus with an appointed coordinator, (2) a large, flexible but structured community on campus in which the group would decide the form of authority, or (3) several small communities on or off campus.

Some Sisters chose the first option. Those who chose the second option moved to the upper stories of Moye Hall, a student residence hall on campus. They had no coordinator or executive board but elected four representatives to

---

[14] GC minutes, 9 May 1969, CDPA.

[15] "CDP Newsletter," 1 July 1970: 3, CDPA.

[16] Sister Elizabeth McCullough, oral interview, 17 Apr. 2000, CDPA. She added that there was no pressure from Rome to do this, and she wrote a letter to the Archbishop informing him of the Sisters' new addresses in various parishes of San Antonio.

deal with finances and living areas. All the members attended a weekly meeting. They were "aware of the challenges of adjustment; yet this awareness seems to be leading to a very contemporary expression of trust in Divine Providence."[17]

Within two years, eight Sisters from this group chose the third option and moved off campus. They took up residence at St. John Berchmans Convent but still considered themselves a sub-group of Moye Hall.[18] Sister Lourdes Leal, a founding member of this community, recalled "We were going to talk about everything, so we really had to express ourselves. We might start a community meeting at 7 o'clock and go on until 10 o'clock. We might be crying, passing the Kleenex around, or really sharing our souls."[19] Soon this community was asking hard questions of the central administration: How does a Sister get assigned to a community? Who initiates the request to change housing, a Sister or the administration? To whom is the request directed? The General Council decided to produce a policy on "admitting new community members to all the different College communities."[20]

Sister Jacqualine Kingsbury detailed another experiment.

> Sister Emily Rabalais and Sister Irma Jean Van Gossen were closing the short-lived junior high school at St. Benedict's parish in Houston, and the leadership of the Congregation asked four of us who had proposed an experimental community, "Would you like to go to St. Benedict's and do parish work?" We readily accepted and while forming community really dug into the meaning of renewal according to Vatican Council II. We were reading *Sisters Today* and determined to use our experience of community to avoid what we knew didn't work well in communities.[21]

Other contemporary publications in the relatively new field of psychology also influenced the re-evaluation of community life. Erving Goffman's *Asylums: Essays in the Social Situations of Mental Patients and Other Inmates* (1959) suggested that convents resemble "total institutions" such as prisons and military establishments, which strip persons of individuality in order to produce conforming behavior. Carl Rogers and Abraham H. Maslow, founders of humanistic psychology, emphasized respect for uniqueness. Rogers' *On*

---

[17] "Summer News Bulletin," 2 July 1969, CDPA.

[18] GC minutes, 3 Jan. 1972, CDPA.

[19] Oral interview, 8 Aug. 2000, CDPA. This community at first had no superior but later elected three members to serve as a kind of house council.

[20] GC minutes, 14 Apr. 1972, CDPA.

[21] Sister Jackie Kingsbury, oral interview, 20 June 2000, CDPA.

Becoming a Person (1961) explained his client-centered therapy. Clients who were understood and valued by their therapists would take responsibility for themselves, promoting their healing. Maslow's *Motivation and Personality* (1954) stated the primary goal of psychotherapy was the integration of the self; self-actualization is the highest human drive.

An anonymous article "Reflection on Community Living" from St. Benedict's parish written in 1970 gives a sense of a rather euphoric spirit that began to appear at this time. The individual self's relationship with the Spirit predominated.

> Life and life in oneness of spirit are actualities that defy examination, analyzing, introspection, and planned patterns.
>
> Life is and you are—NOW. Life flows and you must bend flexibly with it. Tragedies come; tensions of adjustment irritate—you live it in oneness with your community.
>
> Your ideals, hopes, and dreams for your year resolve themselves into the reality of NOW, and you re-learn that there is no way to impose a rigid structure—even one built by your ideals—on life together without cramping the Spirit's free movement in life—theirs and yours.
>
> You breathe in the atmosphere of understanding, of deep penetration into the "you" as you really are, and loving acceptance of that you. Your spirit slowly comes erect and you throw out your arms—free to look outside yourself and your religious community to "where it's at"—God's world with its Spirit presence. And you reaffirm your dedication to that God and you are restless to grow yet more, but still you are at peace.[22]

Another anonymous CDP author concluded that "resolving tensions through communication demands total openness, which is often difficult. But the joy and peace we experience through shared prayer, living together, and working in the apostolate far outweigh the suffering."[23]

Sister Jackie Kingsbury considered her seven years at St. Benedict's to be "a powerful experience in every way. It was a large program with a huge number of volunteers. Three of us were on the parish team with two priests, and [former] Sister Wilma Zalezak was at Ben Taub County Hospital; but she was involved as much as her schedule allowed. We were really united and did much creative programming." Sister Jackie felt that personal growth was enhanced as the

---

[22] "CDP Newsletter," Northern Region, Nov., 1970 n.p., CDPA.

[23] *Nunspeak*, Summer 1972:14, CDPA.

Sisters "shared profoundly with team members, honed their skills of teaching, and developed new skills in counseling and supervising through in-service training for transitional deacons and seminarians. Interaction with the parish community was fabulous."[24]

In another experiment, the Northern Region Council invited the Sisters stationed at Bishop Kelley High School in Tulsa, Oklahoma, in 1970-1971 to form two separate communities, one off campus. Each group was to choose its form of government from among four options: (1) a local coordinator appointed by the General Council, (2) a coordinator elected for one year, (3) coordinators elected to rotate for one to three months, or (4) a team-type government in which community members determined areas of responsibility and members volunteered for different jobs. Within a few years, choosing from these types of community coordinators was available to all the Sisters with the added nuance that the General Council could appoint as a local coordinator either a Sister who lived within the community or one who lived outside the community she coordinated.

Some attempts were made to form "self-chosen" communities. Former Sisters Sylvia Cárdenas and Elaine Marie Newman were allowed to work in distant Starr County, but the "Councilors expressed concern that these two Sisters will remain in the mainstream of CDP life and favored a community of more than two Sisters."[25] More than six months later "after much difficulty they found a house in poor condition to rent for $60 a month."[26] This experimental community lasted only one year.[27] Former Sister Linda Beach said that the "main difficulty in establishing the community in Brownsville was that each Sister assigned there had to go find her own employment."[28]

The last self-chosen community was inaugurated in 1994. One of its members, Sister Anita Brenek, related that in the 1970s she found life in community with Sisters teaching in the same elementary school "was a good experience the first years. It got progressively harder as the community got smaller, and then we were the same people in the school and in the house. I just felt like I was living the school day over again while eating dinner in the evening." She and four other CDPs, each in a different ministry, planned for several years before they actually formed the "Naciendo" community in Tyler, Texas. They chose to minister in a town where each Sister could apply her professional skills as a midwife, teacher, lawyer, chaplain, and social worker. Sister Anita remembered:

---

[24] Sister Jackie Kingsbury, oral interview, 20 June 2000, CDPA.

[25] GC minutes, 27 Nov. 1972, CDPA.

[26] GC minutes, 22 June 1973, CDPA.

[27] GC minutes, 4 June 1974, CDPA.

[28] Panel on experimental communities, summer 1970, CDPA.

"Coming home and table sharing was great. We would process our days and go on with our evening and community together."[29]

The General Council was responsible for assigning each Sister and insisted that new community members not be simply invited to join by those already living in the house. However, in at least two cases, Sisters tried but did not find any community that would accept them as members. The Superior General told one of these Sisters that the only option left was to live with her family. Since there was no room for her in her blood sister's house, this Sister decided to take a leave of absence.[30] As community life became less regimented, some Sisters began to spend less time with their companions and excessive amounts of time on a hobby or visiting relatives or friends outside the Congregation. On the other hand, more open communication between the Sisters helped in identifying two or three who were addicted to alcohol. They returned to full participation in community life after spending time in treatment centers

The ideal in forming communities modeled more on friendship than on the military model of a group responding uniformly to a commander was that "each person in the group must assume the responsibility of group decisions and actions."[31] Sister Regina Decker was in a community in 1973, the first year that it did not have an assigned coordinator.

> We were ten Sisters there, and nobody wanted to open the mail from the Generalate because nobody wanted to take the responsibility of carrying through any requests it might contain. The Sister-principal stayed away from leading the community because she did not want to go back to that dual role. Nobody else in the house wanted to be superior. Because so many decisions revolved around money, they would turn to me, the bookkeeper, when they wanted something. I would say, "I don't decide; the community decides," and then I would simply say whether we had the money or not.[32]

Sister Regina greatly appreciated that "there came a point in our history where we began to treat Sisters more as adults and not as children."[33] But she also felt that

---

[29] Sister Anita Brenek, oral interview, 4 Aug. 2000, CDPA.

[30] GC minutes, 17and 24 June 1975, CDPA. Eventually she returned to the Congregation.

[31] "CDP Newsletter," 1 July 1970: 4, CDPA.

[32] Sister Regina Decker, oral interview, 8 Nov. 2000, CDPA. Sister Blandina Paul who was in the same community, remembered: "We were all from the same energy space on the Enneagram; we were all number six. Number six will follow a leader, and we had no leader. So we were assigned a Sister who came periodically, and we had sessions with her" (oral interview, 26 June 2000, CDPA).

[33] Sister Rosalie Karstedt, oral interview, 20 June 2000, CDPA.

for a time the pendulum swung far out because "the desire for independence is really fed by our American culture. It is very easy to get to the point of approving of something only if it is right for me. That is too individual. Now we have achieved more balance in this area."[34] Sister Rose Kruppa expressed a similar opinion. "After years of formation we became so much a member of the group that at times we were even asked to give up self. But now many have found a sense of self and don't want to lose it. It's almost like a fear of re-commitment or re-investment in the group."[35]

Sometimes community living was easier if Sisters were *not* from the same Congregation. Sister Jackie Kingsbury and Sister Frances Klinger, for example, lived in a community that included a Sister of the Holy Spirit, several Mount Carmel Sisters, and several Blessed Sacrament Sisters in Crowley, Louisiana. "It was great because we had to talk to each other. We couldn't assume community life structures. It was good, though hard, because we were all involved with the same youth at the high school. It was enriching because everyone brought the experience of her own religious Congregation. We learned from each other."[36]

Sister Rosalie Karstedt at different times lived with Sisters of six distinct Congregations. "I began to make connections and see differences. Sometimes you don't know what you have until you are able to contrast it with something you don't have. Only then do you appreciate what you do have."[37] Sister Margarita Sánchez after living with Sisters from a number of different congregations realized she became more appreciative of CDP simplicity, hospitality, and readiness to celebrate.[38]

Sister Fran Trochta said that when she was in her mid-30s she

> had a tremendous experience at Prompt Succor in Alexandria of linking not just with lay people but also with a group of priests. It was probably the first time as an adult that I really had interactions with people of the other sex. We would stay up at night and maybe even have a drink over the kitchen table as we were discussing changes in the Church. To me it was a different experience of community and certainly a broadening of my relationships to men at a very personal level, not just as functionaries celebrating Mass or the Sacraments.[39]

---

[34] Sister Regina Decker, oral interview, 8 Nov. 2000, CDPA.

[35] Sister Rose Kruppa, oral interview, 27 July 2000, CDPA. She also detected "a strong desire to leave something for the next generations and a lack of knowledge on what to leave."

[36] Oral interview, 20 June 2000, CDPA.

[37] Oral interview, 20 June 2000, CDPA.

[38] Oral interview, 23 June 2000, CDPA.

[39] Oral interview, 20 June 2000, CDPA.

Before long the general administration's concern about how Sisters got along with each other in a house was overshadowed by concern about Sisters living singly because of their work. Sister Madeleine Zimmerer discovered that in living by herself, "I really have to be true to my vows and really belong to the Congregation. If I didn't find prayer life and community valuable, I could just be working all the time and forget about going to Mass or praying the Office, which is a connection through the Liturgy of the Hours with the rest of the community."[40]

Sister Bernadette Bezner recalled, "I had never lived alone. I had never set up an apartment and didn't even know how to look for one. I had never had to get electricity turned on or set up a bank account. I had never had a car for which I was responsible. I really had to grow up."[41] Sister Margaret Ann (M. Gregory) Verzwyvelt said:

> I personally think everybody should live in an apartment for a year for the experience. You really learn how to live the Congregational vow of poverty when you know that you are responsible for the use of money allotted to you. In time you learn to budget. If you need something, you watch for a sale. You may want something better, but you ask yourself, "Do I really need that?" Most of the time, the answer is "No. What I have is sufficient."[42]

Sister Bernadette and Sister Margaret Ann enjoyed the new challenges of living by themselves. Sister Lourdes Leal, however, found that she missed a former practice of the Congregation. The Mother General "would come visit you every once in a while and find out about you personally." In the 1980s Sister Lourdes' contact councilor "didn't have any individual conferences, and she didn't really want to hear what I was going through. It was a rude awakening. When you live where there aren't many of you, if someone coming on an official visit doesn't want to hear what you're doing, whom do you really tell?" She concluded that such experiences might be why some Sisters say "We don't care enough about each other."[43]

The advantage of "apartment living" was "the freedom to give all of your energy to your ministry. Then you could have some time to get away from it and just let your hair down, just be quiet to recoup and get your rest, pray, or

---

[40] Oral interview, 10 July 2000, CDPA.

[41] Oral interview, 17 Sept. 2000, CDPA.

[42] Oral interview, 20 July 2000, CDPA.

[43] Oral interview, 8 Aug 2000, CDPA.

play."[44] On the other hand, Sisters living alone in apartments lacked opportunities for daily close interaction with other Sisters, which had always facilitated the formation of friendships, helped identify talent and leadership potential, promoted a united focus on a common project, and aided the development of a CDP *esprit de corps*. Rubbing shoulders in close quarters could also lead to growth in consideration and sensitivity to the neighbor's feelings, needs, and problems. The General Council decided that Sisters living by themselves or in houses where there was room for more Sisters "need to be confronted about placing their own needs before the needs of the corporate body, their accountability regarding housing, and the way to practice obedience today."[45] In 1982 the General Council formulated "Guidelines for local communities," "Ten Beliefs about Community," and procedures and processes for community and ministry placement.[46]

Many Sisters living singly began to look on the cluster, a group of five to twenty Sisters which met in the fall and in the spring and was comprised of members named by the General Council, as their "local community."[47] Sister Dianne Heinrich, who did not have everyday contact with CDPs, summarized how she stayed bonded:

> I take the initiative to stay in touch with members of the Congregation through e-mail, the phone, and written notes. I definitely try to read whatever comes to us through the community, and I make it a point to attend cluster meetings. I belong to one of the Congregational committees. I try to be aware of my identity as a Sister of Divine Providence in my ministry and keep that identity foremost in being present to people.[48]

Sister Evelyn Marie (Mary Felix) Rischner pointed out the tie between cluster and community spirit. "Cluster gives us a forum and a sense of ownership of the family, and that's what makes us at home. Each of us is

---

[44] Sister Barbara Lynn Hyzak, oral interview, 18 Jan. 2001, CDPA. Sister Barbara Fry pointed out some concerns avoided when one lives alone. "In religious communities there was always commotion about who would drive this car or wash the dishes or do the shopping. There are so many things more important than these petty ordinary, everyday items" (oral interview, 27 Oct. 2000, CDPA).

[45] GC minutes, 5 Sept. 1979, CDPA.

[46] GC minutes, 3 Sept. 1982 and 4 Jan. 1983, CDPA.

[47] The Constitution, # 68f, p. 48, designated the local community as the basic unit of government. However, "for those Sisters not living in communities large enough to have a Local Coordinator, the basic unit of government is the Cluster."

[48] Oral interview, 2 Sept. 2000, CDPA.

a heartbeat of the Congregation and responsible for its spirit."[49] Sister Virginia Huser appreciated the cluster as a support group and saw the value of cluster meetings. "Different issues are brought to us at the cluster that we might not have thought about individually, or at least not discussed together. I think the cluster stretches us to become more involved in the general CDP community."[50] Sister Diane Langford "learned that you don't have to live with Sisters to be in community. Living in community is a state of mind; it is not a housing arrangement."[51]

When the Sisters began to live singly or chose which community to join, they discovered that good human relationships are not automatic but have to be sustained by personal effort. They realized they were actually members of many communities—Congregational, familial, ministerial, professional or even recreational and needed to prioritize them to stay spiritually and psychologically healthy. Some found they lacked the energy to sustain strong ties in all these communities and chose one which was not Congregational as their primary affective community.[52]

More than ever, the shape of community was being dictated by ministry as an increasing number of Sisters found employment in the public arena rather than in Church-sponsored institutions or works. Sister Jackie Kingsbury found that she began to consider herself more as a representative of God than as an envoy of a religious congregation.

> I deliberately chose not to identify myself publicly as a Sister, and that left room for people to see just me as a caring presence. I didn't have to deal with people's misconceptions of religious life and have long discussions about it. Some of my clients know that I am a Sister and others do not. I found myself acquiring a really strong sense of being a presence of God through what I do, through my caring, listening, and my particular way of being. I need to connect with people who are on some kind of spiritual path, and frequently that is outside of Church structures. I am connected to people of all faiths and no

---

[49] Oral interview, 9 June 2000, CDPA.

[50] Oral interview, 2 Sept. 2000. Sister Agnes Marie Marusak held that "we have an obligation to bring something to the cluster meeting to share with people. There is something about sharing in a group that you never will get from reading a document" (oral interview, 16 Aug. 2000, CDPA).

[51] Oral interview, 4 Nov. 2000, CDPA.

[52] Speaking of the importance of choosing the Congregation as one's primary affective community, Sister Lora Ann Quinónez stated, "I feel very strongly that each community has its own identity, and I don't think it's honest to belong to a particular religious community but have all your primary relationships outside the community" (oral interview, 13 June 2000, CDPA).

faiths. We minister to one another, and it is very enlivening to share that quest with people.[53]

She continued: "Currently I live with a Holy Cross Sister, and I feel very connected to the Congregation even though I'm not living in a CDP community. I feel part of the vital life of the community. I consider myself a mainstream person in the Congregation."[54] Sister Barbara Fry stated, "I've never missed being in Church-related work since I got into social work. In Church work there is so much petty bickering."[55] Her experience was that after ten years in religious life her superiors trusted her judgment and just wanted to be informed where she was living and working.

The 1970s brought dramatic and sometimes traumatic changes in the official or formal community structures of the Congregation, and the Sisters negotiated or adapted with varied degrees of success. By the turn of the 21st century, most of the Congregation's active members selected their own living arrangements as well as their employment in dialogue with a General Councilor designated as their Contact Councilor.

Sub-groups within the Congregation

Even when communities were highly structured and their members were very dependent on appointed superiors, there were always various sub-groups within the Congregation. A Sister's experience or conflict with such groups colored her ability to adapt to different styles of group living.

Differences between Sisters who were highly educated professionals and those assigned to household tasks could lead to friction. Of about 70 Sisters assigned in 1943-1944 to the College community,[34] were teachers and 20 were housekeepers;[56] the rest were administrators or teachers at St. Martin Hall grade school. Sister Sarah Kainer, whose ministry was housekeeping, remembered developing a kind of "sub-culture" during her years at the College. "We all slept in St. Ann's Hall and ate with the prefects, who took their meals earlier than the rest of the Sisters. We met in the bakery to plan the menus while the teachers were having teachers' meetings on Sunday evening."[57] The Sister-cooks at the College prepared daily meals for boarders,

---

[53] Oral interview, 20 June 2000, CDPA.

[54] Oral interview, 20 June 2000, CDPA.

[55] Oral interview, 27 Oct. 2000, CDPA.

[56] This number included Sister Ventura Rollwitz, a self-taught expert bookbinder.

[57] Oral interview, 19 May 2000, CDPA.

Sisters, and priests (and some laymen on the faculty) who had a separate dining room and tableware.

Sister Sarah insisted:

> But we had fun, too! Sister Balbina Pekar, who was in charge of the kitchen, found out that Sister William and I could skate, so she saved coupons and got each of us a pair of skates. We used to lock the doors and skate there in the kitchen after Sunday dinner for a couple of hours. We made rings around the stove, and fortunately we never had an accident. Sister Jane Marie Barbour and Sister Amabilis Hanley even lent us records to play while we skated.[58]

Differences between Sisters stationed at the college and those on the missions were also real. The College community tended to be stable while mission communities were more mobile. Sisters at the College usually worked year-round, so they did not feel they had a break in the summer. College teachers who did not teach in the summer term, however, had "from three to four months of vacation every year, a luxury which very few people can have."[59] Sisters on the mission, on the other hand, spent the summer at the Motherhouse away from their usual workplace; so even though they usually took classes, their stay could be considered a kind of vacation. Sister Margaret Ann Verzwyvelt had a memorable insight that had behavioral consequences.

> The college community for me was always kind of aloof, and I guess it was because I really didn't know the Sisters there. As I got to know more of them and took courses at the College, I became more aware that the college belonged to me also. I can remember going out behind the grotto and looking at all those buildings and saying to myself, "That is mine. As a member of the Congregation it belongs to me, too." I guess that thought has made me more aware of helping to economize and be a better steward of everything that belongs to the Congregation.[60]

Another recognized distinction within the Congregation was between "household" Sisters on the one hand and teachers or nurses on the other. Superiors and formation personnel were aware of various positions in the Congregation's ministries and kept their needs in mind as they monitored the

---

[58] Oral interview, 19 May 2000, CDPA.

[59] GC minutes, 18 Dec. 1981, CDPA.

[60] Oral interview, 20 July 2000, CDPA.

studies of new recruits. Difficulty with studies was not in itself a sign that a candidate lacked a religious vocation. Someone who had problems with oral communication or multi-tasking might have other valuable skills, so she might be advised to become a "little Mary."[61]

Sister Martha Rose Lange, who was a housekeeper most of her religious life, stated that she always "felt inferior," but a favorite saying of Mother Angelique, "It doesn't matter what you do but who you are" always "kept me going. Also, I found God in nature wherever I went, enjoyed arts and crafts, and especially making personal contact with people."[62] Sister Margaret Ann Verzwyvelt admitted,

> It took me a while really to realize that food service was a ministry. A little elderly lady making a retreat helped me. I was making biscuits for breakfast, and she just stood in the door of the kitchen. I turned and asked if she needed something, and she said, "No. The way you do this work as service has been such an inspiration to me." When the people enjoyed the food, I realized that to have food for the soul it is important to have food for the body.[63]

This Congregation of French origin never had a distinction between "lay" and "choir" Sisters. When it branched out into the United States in the nineteenth century, all the Sisters as well as those in formation did some household chores. This was considered integral to contributing to order in the house and the well being of its inhabitants and was also a way to practice simplicity and humility. It led to financial savings as well since lay employees were not needed for these tasks. In 1969 in the entire Congregation 44 Sisters performed household services full-time; 39 did so in 1973. The reason for hiring more lay housekeepers beginning in the 1980s was not primarily to give the Sisters time for more important work. The chief consideration was that there were fewer "little Marys" and most of the Sisters were becoming old and frail.

As communities diminished in size and more lay people came to be employed, the "household Sisters" sometimes went into new occupations that demonstrated their resourcefulness and superior managerial skills. After cooking for over 20 years, Sister Rita Rose Bily took on the community financial account and then a sixth grade catechism class. Next she became the sacristan in Sacred Heart Conventual Chapel and for over 15 years helped about 800 couples

---

[61] This was an intra-Congregational term for Sisters whose full-time assignment was work such as housekeeping, cooking, or sewing.

[62] Oral interview, 16 Feb. 2000, CDPA.

[63] Oral interview, 20 July 2000, CDPA.

with their weddings. In addition to calming nervous brides, she sometimes instructed clerics. "If the priest doesn't come for the rehearsal, then I have to do the rehearsal. When the priest comes the next day, I have to tell him how to do everything; and he follows my directions."[64] Sister Paulette Celis held a variety of posts in more than 50 years of religious life—cooking, sewing, providing day care for children, and supervising a maintenance crew. She said, "My present ministry, cooking in a shelter for abused women and children, came to me as an overwhelming gift. All along but without my knowledge, God has been preparing me for ministry to battered women and children. I feel rewarded by their love and deep appreciation for my service. God has indeed kept the best for last."[65]

After serving as housekeeper, laundress, and seamstress, Sister Emily Bolcerek went to help with three-year-olds at Providence Day Care Center in Alexandria, Louisiana, where she earned her GED and her driver's license. Next she taught for 10 years in a Title I after school program for Hispanic children in Houston, Texas, going on to cook at a Montessori School with over 500 pupils for 14 years. Her last ministry before retiring was to take care of babies aged six weeks to six months in an infant center. She said she was "very grateful that the Congregation accepted me and gave me all these privileges to do what I did in my life to enrich my life."[66]

The distinction between teachers and "others" was not hard and fast, nor did Sisters necessarily stay in the same type of work all their lives. Similarly, the title of superior was not permanent. Not to be re-appointed or re-elected to leadership was not considered a disgrace. After 40 years Sister Relindis Barthel left teaching to become supervisor of housekeeping at Floresville Memorial Hospital and then at OLLC retirement center. Sister Mary Ann (Dolorita) Hoelscher began to teach in 1955, went into food service and housekeeping in the 1980s, and returned to teaching in the 1990s. Sister Theophane Hladik also taught for over 40 years before she became a volunteer at Guadalupe Clinic in Rosenberg, Texas, and then supervisor of housekeeping at McCullough Hall.[67]

Were the Constitutions accurate in stating "The members of the Institute form but one class, all having the same rights and the same duties"?[68] Sister Martha Rose Lange felt that "peace and justice could have started sooner in the Congregation; the oppression of the working Sisters was still there."

---

[64] Oral interview, 11 Feb. 2000, CDPA.

[65] Oral interview, 29 July 2001, CDPA.

[66] Oral interview, 23 June 2000, CDPA.

[67] Oral interview, 3 May 2000, CDPA.

[68] Constitutions, # 4.

At the College I had four floors of girls' rooms to clean three times a week, and once a week we had to clean all their bathrooms. We went to the laundry every week to fold all their sheets. We had to clean the downstairs classrooms, and over the noon hour I always had to help in the serving line and cashier line in the day students' cafeteria. I also had to take switchboard duty for people on their lunch hour.[69]

Later Sister Martha Rose spent three years at an orphanage in Oklahoma City that was "a very hard place to be" because she had no days off and the children were "very neglected" and needed much attention. An effort to equalize or "democratize" membership might be detected in the decision by the General Chapter of 1961 to list Sisters assigned to household work according to seniority rather than at the end of the annual assignment lists. To enable household Sisters to participate in the summer General Assembly, in 1977 the meals were catered during the meetings. In the 1980s household Sisters were urged to rise later than 4 a.m., but Sister Rita Fritz resisted. "I know Sister Mary Margaret Hughes was looking out for us, but roast has to have its time to bake. If you want it ready for noon, you have to put it on early."[70]

Two other sub-groups that could potentially have a negative impact on community life were based on ethnicity and blood relationship. During their initial formation, the Sisters were told to speak only in English and to avoid conversations about their families. Sister Frances Trochta remembered that in the 1950s, however, "it was not unusual for there to be clusters of ethnic groups. For the most part these groups cut those not of their ethnicity out of community interactions, and they were very isolated. I coped by keeping busy in school and not dwelling on how unpleasant the community situation might be."[71] Sister Rose Ann Blair, who did not know German, was stationed in New Braunfels in the 1970s. "The atmosphere in the school was fine. Community life was difficult, though, because several of the Sisters who were in their late 70s and early 80s spoke German at home in the convent and at meals. German took priority over English, and I found that a challenge." Sister Rose Ann found that she "became angry and in my heart separated from the group. I was not

---

[69] Oral interview, 16 Feb. 2000, CDPA. She added, "The girls were very nice, and I always had a good rapport with them." She also remembered that "many of the girls wanted to take care of their own rooms, but we were told to do it. In those days you did what you were told."

[70] Oral interview, 19 May 2000, CDPA.

[71] Oral interview, 20 June 2000, CDPA. Sister also said, "What I didn't feel in the Sister community I felt in the parish community. I never felt a disconnect with community as such. It was just that a different group of people provided that."

bold enough to speak to them about it." Her way of coping was to "go out with my tennis racquet and ball and bounce the ball off the school wall to get rid of my anger."[72]

Ethnic heritages were not celebrated. Even though this policy was supposed to promote unity through greater uniformity, its negative impact—especially on Hispanics—has been indicated in previous chapters. Sister Charlene Wedelich, Superior General from 1973 to 1981, became concerned about ethnic diversity and invited Rev. Anthony Bellagamba one summer to sensitize the Sisters to the Hispanic population. Unexpectedly, the speaker helped to reveal the great cultural diversity within the Congregation itself. Some Sisters who were not Hispanic admitted that they felt inferior because of their ethnicity. One Sister thanked Sister Charlene for the program and said, "I feel like for the first time I have permission to be Czech."[73] During the U.S. bicentennial summer of 1976, the Sisters staged an ethnic festival featuring 13 cultures to which CDPs belonged: Belgian, Czech, Dutch, English, French, Irish, German, Hungarian, Italian, Mexican, Polish, Scotch, and Lebanese.[74] They dressed in native costumes, carried flags in a campus parade, and served special ethnic foods. Ethnicity gradually came to be regarded as something to be celebrated rather than hidden.

Sisters who came from Germany and Ireland just before and after the turn of the twentieth century knew they might never return to their birthplaces. Great was the rejoicing of six CDPs who went to visit relatives in Ireland in 1954 after 25 to 40 years of absence.[75] In 1966, there were still 65 native Irish Sisters in the Congregation, mostly from County Clare and County Kerry, and 48 from Germany, mostly from East Prussia. In 2000, Sister Miriam Teresa Fenlon, the last Sister to enter from Ireland, explained:

> The mission spirit of St. Patrick captivated Irish girls. They all wanted to go to foreign countries, and they went in groups to imitate St. Patrick in the spreading of the faith. My intention was to go to a foreign country, but my three aunts—Sisters Norbert, James, and Roseline—invited me to come to the foreign land, the U.S. A., where they were already professed.[76]

---

[72] Oral interview, 19 June 2000, CDPA.

[73] Sister Charlene Wedelich, oral interview, 9 May 2000, CDPA. Sisters Julianna Kozuch, Bernadette Hajovsky, and Anna Marie (Eugene Marie) Vrazel have been very active in Czech organizations.

[74] "CDP Newsletter," 3, 9, (1 May 1976): 159.

[75] "OLL Summer-News," vol. 1, 1 (July 4, 1954): 2, CDPA.

[76] Oral interview, 8 Mar. 2000, CDPA. Sister added "I made my first vows in 1930, and I have been happy all my religious life."

Sisters from the large German and Irish as well as Alsatian ethnic groups were elected to posts in the general administration from the Congregation's earliest days in Texas, but ability rather than ethnicity was the chief reason these Europeans were selected. Sisters from other groups with a smaller representation were chosen in more recent years: Sisters Amata Regan and Bernadette Marie Gremillion (French from Louisiana, 1955) Lora Ann Quiñonez (Hispanic from Honduras, 1973), Irene (Amelia Clare) Ceasar (Lebanese, 1977), Madonna Sangalli (Italian, 1981) Lourdes Leal (Mexican American, 1993) and Rose Kruppa (Czech, 1993).

The solid (and often large) Catholic families served by the Sisters since 1866 sometimes sent more than one daughter to the convent. A large number of Sisters were siblings to other Sisters.[77] Naturally, these blood sisters would have more in common with each other and would take advantage of opportunities to be together during the summer. Sharing family joys as well as sorrows provided support, and more than once someone tempted to leave the Congregation was persuaded by her sibling Sister to persevere.[78] After the death of her sister, Sister Silverius Karnowski, Sister Anicetus Karnowski recounted "I took it so hard. That's when my shingles broke out. Oh, they're so painful. They will not leave; I have them almost four years now. No matter how many Masses I've had offered, no matter how much I pray, those shingles just stay there."[79] When Sister Bernadine Leonards died in 1986, her sister, Sister Mildred Leonards, said "It was like half my heart was taken away."[80] Sister Elizabeth Dale Van Gossen remembered that when her sibling left the Congregation

> it was a difficult time because she left with hard feelings. Yet these Sisters that she had hard feelings about were women that I admired. I just tried to understand that this was something personal that she was going through, but at the same time I could not condemn those Sisters. Eventually, my sister got over that. I have to admire her for doing what she felt she needed to do.[81]

---

[77] See Appendix VI for names of siblings in the CDP.

[78] Sister Vera Schad reported that Sister Fortunata Zimmerer and her nine nieces would gather several times in the summer "just to talk and go walking" (Sister Vera Schad, oral interview, 15 Mar. 2000, CDPA). Sister Dorothy Ann Vrba said she felt that "she was coming from one family and going into another family" when she entered the convent because "Sister Marie Podsednik was my first cousin, Sister Mary Elizabeth Jupe was my second cousin, and Sister Angelene Holzer was my third cousin" (Sister Dorothy Ann Vrba, oral interview, 25 Oct. 2000, CDPA). Sister Madeleine Zimmerer was "the sixteenth relative of her family to enter the CDP" (oral interview, 10 July 2000, CDPA).

[79] Oral interview, 2 Jan. 2000, CDPA.

[80] Oral interview, 1 Sept. 2000, CDPA.

[81] Oral interview, 21 July 2000, CDPA.

During the school year siblings were very rarely stationed in the same place. When she was over 90 years old, Sister Thérèse Pousson recalled how she could not continue a very significant friendship:

> Mother Amata Regan was my first cousin and the person to whom I was the closest. We spent every weekend at home together, and we came to the convent together. Our parents hired a sleeper on the train for us, but we never went to sleep. We sat on the lower berth all night long and talked. That was the last time we ever had a long talk. In the postulate and novitiate we couldn't, and we were never on the mission together. When she became Superior General, she was much too busy. That's just how life went.[82]

How to acquire skills in relating to people and forming friendships was not part of the formation curriculum although such skills were considered valuable in ministry. Friendships within the Congregation always seemed to be based more on common interests and experiences together on the mission rather than on blood ties. During the summer, it was customary to "make a date" with a Sister to converse with her during the evening recreation hour. It was expected that such "dates" would be with a number of different Sisters. To recreate with one's novitiate group or with Sisters with whom one had been stationed was encouraged, but exclusive friendships were not tolerated.

From their earliest training, the Sisters heard every kind of intimacy characterized as dangerous if not evil. True, there was danger of divisive cliques, but homophobia was undoubtedly another reason for insisting that closeness be avoided. Socializing repeatedly with the same Sister, or obviously enjoying the company of one Sister more than of others was labeled a "particular friendship." Sister Angelina Breaux remembered, "We were not encouraged to develop relationships with anyone. There was such a fear of 'particular friendships' that relationships were discouraged. We were like professionals, not sisters or even friends. We also were not supposed to keep up with students nor their parents when we left a place." She testified, however, that "many Sisters disregarded this injunction, and all of this changed after Vatican Council II."[83]

---

[82] Oral interview, 10 Dec. 1999, CDPA.

[83] Oral interview, 20 Oct. 2000, CDPA. Although the term "gay" or "homosexual" was not used until the 1990s, any evidence of a tendency to form very intimate relationships was an unquestioned reason for dismissal in all congregations of women religious.

Evaluations of Changes in Community Life

Sociologist Sister Frances Jerome Woods was concerned about the changes in community life in the Congregation discussed in this chapter.

> We are changing in a way that's going to cause us problems later. There used to be systemic rewards for being a good Sister of Divine Providence, for example, being made a local superior or a principal, or being sent off for a higher degree. Now we don't have any systemic rewards, so people get no sense of being rewarded and being recognized for service to the corporate body. An organization cannot live and be itself and fulfill its purpose when there is no structure, no system. We have totally dismantled an old system and put no system in its place.[84]

Sister Bernadette Bezner felt that since she made her first vows in 1967. "Everything has been experiment. That was very positive because everything is possible; we learn from doing. However, the down side is that we never really got to rest."[85] Sister Leola Ann Doerfler thought that "we lost an opportunity when so many Sisters began to live in private apartments. Even though I lived in communities where everybody had a different job, we were still living together. I miss that we don't have times together." Besides the availability for companionship, Sister thought that "living and praying together helped me become more concerned about what was happening in other people's lives and not just my own."[86]

Sister Anne Michele Berry expressed the feelings of a number of Sisters when they looked back on the dramatic changes in community structures. "What I miss the most is a focused kind of work that we were doing together. There was a spirit that we all brought to it. I miss being able to work together toward a common focus where everyone brings her different gifts. This is part of our struggle with what is our identity as religious today." When she was alone in a parish, she found she had to make greater efforts to build and maintain relationships. "I felt that formerly we were ministering in the heart of the parish community, but now sometimes I can feel excluded within a parish, so I have to make constant efforts to reach out. But change has freed us to be more present to people and develop our gifts in diverse ways."[87]

---

[84] Sister Lora Ann Quiñonez, oral interview, section recalling Sister Frances Jerome's words, 13 June 2000, CDPA.

[85] Oral interview, 17 Sept. 2000, CDPA.

[86] Oral interview, 21 Jan. 2000, CDPA.

[87] Sister Anne Michele Berry, oral interview, 20 June 2000, CDPA.

Sister Teresa Pauline Hereford believed the hardest change for her was "the feeling of isolation as a result of being in smaller and smaller communities or even living alone." She also missed "the bonding that occurred with being part of a common ministerial effort. Even if we're living with another CDP, very often we're not in the same ministry and therefore don't feel that we're working together for a particular goal. We are, but it's not as evident now."[88] Sister Bernadette Bezner came to a greater appreciation of community even when she lived and worked alone.

> I think we have always respected the importance of the individual Sister and the importance of the resource that she is. We have always put people first, both within our own Congregation and within our ministry. Maybe we have gotten to be career women and independent rather than making sacrifices to make community happen. I believe that community is very important because for me religious life can't make sense if we are not witnessing to more than a career.[89]

During the monumental changes in religious life during the last half-century the Sisters' appreciation of life in community seems to have grown rather than diminished. A desire to escape some discomforts of living closely with a group of other women might have been one motive for experimentation with community structures, but the chief motive was always a yearning to be more available to a larger community not limited to CDPs. Earlier, apostolic service shaped the formation of institutions and the communities that staffed them; and it continued to be the determining factor for where, how, and with whom the Sisters lived. In just a few decades, religious community life passed from a very hierarchical organization through an emphasis on democracy and assertion of individuality to an appreciation of community as a free association of women united by common ideals as well as friendship to concretize God's love. Separation and less frequent interaction with other CDPs indeed seemed to make "the heart grow fonder." Disconnection in space has led to greater appreciation for treasured times of being together.

---

[88] Oral interview, 9 Sept. 2000, CDPA.

[89] Oral interview, 17 Sept. 2000, CDPA.

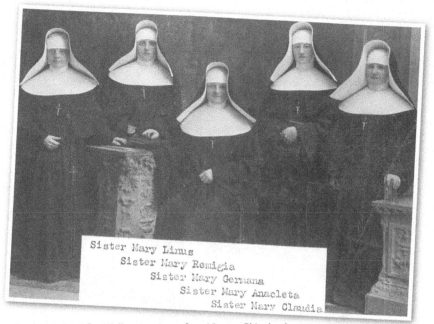

Sister Mary Linus
　Sister Mary Remigia
　　Sister Mary Germana
　　　Sister Mary Anacleta
　　　　Sister Mary Claudia

From 1900-1955 five Wollgarten sisters from Viersen, Rhineland, Germany served a total of 215 years as Sisters of Divine Providence. *(CDP Archives)*

Sisters Rita Fritz, Balbina Pekar, Annie Tepera, Sarah Kainer, and Edgar Hilscher, Our Lady of the Lake College Kitchen Staff, prepare barbeque. *(CDP Archives)*

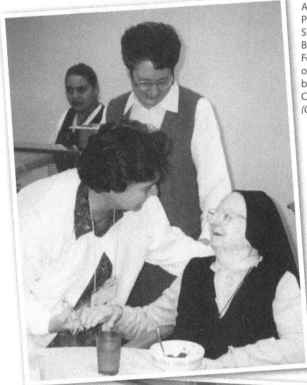

As Sister Annalee Prather looks on, Sister Antoinette Billeaud greets Sister Felicia Beck, who on January 1, 2000 became the eleventh CDP centenarian. *(CDP Archives)*

Benefactor Al Russomono and Sister Elizabeth McCullough at the dedication of McCullough Hall, Our Lady of the Lake Convent, 1976 *(CDP Archives)*

Sisters Mary Margaret Hughes and Jane Ann Slater chat at "A Celebration of   Providence," a 1999 gala honoring five living CDP Superior Generals.
(CDP Archives)

Dr. Janet Quillian, first CDP Associate, and Sister Frances Klinger visit in Houston, 1985.
(CDP Associate Office)

1957 Profession Ceremonies at Sacred Heart Conventual Chapel:
final vow group returning to pews; first vow group in pews
(CDP Archives)

CHAPTER 13

PRACTICING COLLEGIALITY AND SUBSIDIARITY

Experimentation in community forms was accompanied by experimentation with the Congregation's government structures during this period. Sister Teresa Pauline Hereford remembered:

> I came back from my leave of absence, and it seemed like the whole Congregation had changed overnight. I left in 1969 and came back in 1971 to find the Congregation in the midst of trying to govern ourselves in a more collegial manner. . . . I was more excited about the process than the eventual decision because we were practicing a new form of government.[1]

The process was not always smooth, but the resilient Sisters not only changed but also earned commendation from skilled observers for their distinctive "tradition of both strong, visionary leadership and high levels of membership involvement and participation. They have a highly participative governance structure that includes clusters and representative assembly" and "facilitates member participation and education. Many of the initiatives of the Congregation have come up through the grassroots."[2]

Since 1973 the Sisters have understood "authority" in the Scriptural sense of power to be exercised in the service of others in three different ways:

---

[1] Oral interview, 9 Sept. 2000, CDPA.

[2] CARA report, 2003, 252 and 359.

administration, education, and mediation in furthering the life of the group.[3] Government is "the structures by which authority is formally exercised in the Congregation," based on four interrelated principles: participation, interdependence, accountability, and subsidiarity.[4]

Government Structures

The Second Vatican Council approved and promoted collegiality and subsidiarity. CDPs defined these terms as follows and tried to implement these concepts:

> *Collegiality:* "shared responsibility by all of the sisters in the local community for examining common problems and attempting to arrive at a workable solution through dialogue with one another. Once consensus is reached, the coordinator then makes the final decision as to the course of action to be followed."
>
> *Subsidiarity:* as Pius XI said in *Quadragesimo Ano*, "authority is never exercised at a higher level than is truly necessary for the common good"[5]

The General Chapter, the highest governing body of the Congregation, throughout its history convened periodically to enact general decrees and elect top administrators. Different ways to elect Chapter delegates were tried in the last half of the twentieth century. In 1973 and 1977 the central administrators' terms of office were changed from six to four years, and a variety of ways to receive input from the Sisters was devised. Sister Dianne Heinrich, who has been a delegate at every General Chapter since 1967 when she represented the annual professed Sisters, recalled how "General Chapters changed drastically these last 35 years. Everything used to be so extremely formal. I felt there was a hierarchy of older and wiser Sisters who alone would be spokespersons and knew answers. Later there was more freedom, but the election of delegates continued to be a source of conflict." Reasons for the variance included a concern that retired Sisters be fairly represented. "Some Sisters felt they could never get elected and wanted to be part of that decision-making group. I am very grateful that now anyone who wants to be a delegate can be elected. This takes away a lot of unnecessary energy that went into issues like who would be elected." Sister

---

[3] "Refounding Our Communion," booklet compiled after the General Chapters of 1973 and 1977, p. 19.

[4] Constitution and Norms, approved in 1989, # 67a, p. 41.

[5] Constitutions, Norms and Commentary, 1968, p. 27.

Dianne also observed that discussion of Chapter proposals or ideas was always high-quality theological discussion. "I saw the evolution of our thinking about proposals and the learning taking place inside of us as we discussed them. In the process, people were always changed."[6]

Since the Congregation's early days in Texas, the elected general or central administration (the Superior General and her four Councilors) was installed after each General Chapter and charged to implement its decisions. The General Council was also responsible for the common good of the Congregation. In 1971, for example, it amended the Articles of Incorporation. In 1989 it secured state approval for changes to these Articles which made the Congregation a corporation with no members and changed its legal title to "Congregation of Divine Providence, Inc."[7]

While regularly meeting to advise the Superior General, the Councilors sometimes also held other posts such as Superior of the Motherhouse community or Mistress of Studies. Early in this period, Chapter delegates also made sure the Council was comprised of Sisters with experience in the chief ministries of the Congregation at that time—college, high schools, elementary schools, and hospitals. Delegates usually assured continuity in government by electing at least one General Councilor who had previous experience on the central administration, but this pattern was broken in 1967 and 1999 when all members of the general administration were new to their positions.[8] In 1967, however, one elected councilor had served the previous administration as the appointed secretary general; and in 1999 the same appointed general treasurer continued to serve the new administration. From 1967 to 1999, seven Sisters provided a thread of continuity by serving from 12 to 18 years on several administrations as Superior General or Councilor.[9]

In 1963 each Councilor was given specific responsibilities,[10] and in 1967 each had specific areas of concern such as planning and development, personnel, or finance.[11] A dozen years later, a new configuration placed one Councilor in charge of professional development (especially elementary education) and the retired, another in charge of temporalities, and another in charge of parish, high school, and

---

[6] Oral interview, 20 June 2000, CDPA.

[7] GC minutes of the Corporation, 31 Aug. 1971, 13 Dec. 1988, CDPA.

[8] See Appendix VII.

[9] See Appendix VIII.

[10] The responsibilities were: dean of studies; caretaker of the sick, aged and infirm; communicator with houses of the Congregation; and supervisor of physical expansion and maintenance of the college campus (considered a temporary position), GC minutes, 24 Apr.1963, CDPA.

[11] Sister Elizabeth McCullough, oral interview, 17 Apr. 2000, CDPA.

hospital ministry.[12] In 1976 the Councilors re-wrote their job descriptions[13] and began to concern themselves with setting measurable goals, cultivating leadership among the Sisters, and working with the new development team that was given charge of initial and ongoing formation as well as retirement.[14]

The general administration that was elected in 1981 decided that the Superior General should no longer be considered a personal counselor. The General Councilors would deal with a certain number of Sisters in a geographical area and have more authority to make decisions concerning all aspects of their lives.[15] Sister Madonna, a General Councilor from 1981 to 1987, recalled that as more Sisters began to serve outside of the Congregation's institutions, "it was good to go out and see what influence the Sisters were having in their new settings, how the people appreciated them, and how the people learned from them and gave back to them. Association was much freer, and the Sisters began to develop real friendships with laity."[16] At the turn of the 21st century, Councilors continued to make decisions on major Congregational matters, serve on various boards, chair committees of Sisters that were implementing Chapter decisions, and act as liaisons to various entities within the Congregation.

Sister Madonna Sangalli indicated how serving on the team of the General Council differed from serving on other teams.

> Councilors have a lot of common information, and they are responsible for decisions concerning Sisters and situations that matter to the Congregation. Dealing with individual Sisters took longer because the situations were more serious or more complex. Sometimes it was hard to see things differently as a team and reach a decision that we knew was not the response the Sister hoped for. And we had to continue working on our relationship with the Sister concerned. Although we were comfortable with one another as a team and could speak freely knowing confidences would be kept, we didn't always agree.[17]

Sometimes the rest of the Sisters did not agree with the General Councilors. In one instance, for example, "the Council decided to focus on serving in rural ministries and helping the Sisters learn Spanish. We were excited about this

---

[12] GC minutes, 3 Sept. 1975, CDPA.

[13] GC minutes, 18 Feb. 1976, CDPA.

[14] GC minutes, 12 July 1977, CDPA.

[15] GC minutes, 17 Feb. 1982, and Sister Jane Ann Slater, oral interview, 25 May 2000, CDPA.

[16] Oral interview, 31 Mar. 2000, CDPA.

[17] Oral interview, 31 Mar. 2000, CDPA.

and brought it to the General Assembly [GA] in the summer, but the Sisters let us know 'That's *your* focus and *your* plan, but it's not ours.' That's the way the team worked; we had to give and take."[18]

When the Congregation grew to more than 700 members, the Vatican advised preparing for possible division into provinces. In 1964 four regions, each with a regional superior and four regional councilors appointed by the General Administration, were inaugurated. From 1965 to 1970 the headquarters of the Northern Region was in Bethany, Oklahoma. The Eastern region included the Houston area and all of Louisiana. San Antonio and surrounding towns belonged to the San Antonio region while the Central region included the motherhouse, the college, the MCDPs, and the Sisters in Mexico. As a liaison between the Sisters on the local level and the central administration, an advisory board called the Sisters' Advisory Council and comprised of 12 Sisters, three elected from each region, was formed. One of the advisory board's duties was to study reports of four standing commissions created by the General Chapter of 1967: Planning and Development, Finance, Personnel, and Public Relations. A Council of Regional Committees (CRC) succeeded the advisory council in 1973; it also served as a grievance board.

Sister Cecile Clare Vanderlick, superior of the Eastern Region from 1970 to 1971, summarized the results of the Congregation's nine-year experimentation with regions:

> The advantage of regions was that they promoted unity among the Sisters in the area and gave them a chance to contact a delegated person more regularly and have their needs addressed. Most of the Sisters worked on committees and thus were involved in specific work. Everybody agreed that the weakness of the regions was that there was no real authority for the regional superior; she made no major decisions. For instance, when a Sister wanted to be changed for a personal reason, she had to reveal the reasons to the regional superior and again to the Sisters who were members of the ministry committee.[19]

Regional superiors were replaced in 1973 by a development team comprised of four Sisters who visited communities in a given area to facilitate communication between them and the Generalate and encourage spiritual development. Sister Elizabeth Anne Sueltenfuss felt that her time on this team "prepared me for the presidency of OLL because we had workshops and good lectures and training in

---

[18] Oral interview, 31 Mar. 2000, CDPA.

[19] Oral interview by Sister Angelina Murphy, 1983, CDPA.

communication and conflict resolution."[20] Sister Marian Frances Margo, who was a member of the team later, recalled that sometimes it "was difficult because some of the Sisters really did not need what we were trying to do, namely share what we got from the Generalate and give them an idea of what was going on. There were other ways of learning that."[21] The development team was dissolved in 1977 when its functions were divided among the leaders of the initial and ongoing formation programs.[22]

The CRC, whose members nominated themselves for election, functioned during the time of regional superiors as well as of the development team. The CRC took on the role of sifting out input from the Sisters and making recommendations to the central administration, which sometimes returned them because "the CRC needs to make proposals to themselves rather than to the administration. They have their own responsibility and authority, and they should take this upon themselves. They have to be able to spark the Sisters in their regions to new life."[23]

The annual GA also became much more participative as committees planned the agendas in detail and the Sisters voiced their views at "open mike" sessions.

> Often we began with some big disagreement as to how things should operate or what techniques to use. The consensus method seemed so time-consuming; but when we came to the solution together, we could all own it more. We could see why certain positions had been rejected and others adopted. We could very much value each Sister's gifts and know her better because of being able to witness those gifts. Through discussions and voting gradually as time went on we came to a position, and even to wording, of which we could be proud.[24]

The change from passive reception to active participation was dramatically symbolized in the summer of 1979. Instead of occupying wooden folding chairs fixed in rows or gathering at rectangular cafeteria tables, the Sisters sat on padded chairs at movable round tables where they faced each other to discuss and share. Collegiality was concretized. Most Sisters agreed with Sister Dianne Heinrich that the GA "always makes me aware of the fact that I'm not in this alone, that

---

[20] Oral interview, 20 Oct. 2000, CDPA.

[21] Oral interview, 3 May 2000, CDPA.

[22] GC minutes, 12 July 1977, CDPA.

[23] GC minutes, 30 Mar. 1977 and 3 Sept.1975, CDPA.

[24] Sister Teresa Pauline Hereford, oral interview, 9 Sept. 2000, CDPA.

I am in this with a group of people who have the same values, the same kinds of desires for spirituality and for sharing the Gospel with others."[25]

The summer of 1979 also saw an experiment of using the annual GA to replace the CRC "for better communication, participation in decision making, involvement of all the Sisters."[26] The CRC evolved into the Representative Assembly (RA). Sister Rosalie Karstedt, its first President, thought that "the RA forced us as Sisters on the grass roots level to do some thinking and really to take responsibility for what was happening within the Congregation and not always just to blame the administration or blame those elected." As a result of participation in the RA, "we came to a much greater appreciation of who we were as women religious and women religious in the Church."[27] The RA had the potential to become the mid-level government of the Congregation; however, its nature changed when the General Chapter of 1981 decided it would be an advisory body.

In 1982 "clusters," small groups of Sisters usually from the same geographical area, replaced communities as the basic units of government.[28] A designated General Councilor then became the contact between each Sister in the cluster and the General Council.

Continuing to search for ways to improve governance, in 1993 the general administration undertook another study of the roles and functions of those involved in the Congregation's "decision-making loop." Information and decisions were to flow from the General Council to the GA, to the RA, to the clusters, and then back to the General Council.[29] The General Council also asked the RA, the "consultative body," to communicate what the members of the RA, rather than cluster members, were thinking.[30] Sister Theresa Gossen experienced this as a challenge "to be assemblywomen, not just representatives, to represent not only our clusters but ourselves by virtue of having been elected. We were challenged to take on the role of leader in a much bigger way than in the past."[31]

As the Sisters' daily work became more disparate, periodic meetings of each local community (or group of Sisters from several houses in a geographical area) assumed greater importance. Monthly community meetings replaced the daily gathering for spiritual reading and weekly gathering for teachers' meeting. The

---

[25] Oral interview, 20 June 2000, CDPA.

[26] GC minutes, 9 Feb. 1979, CDPA.

[27] Oral interview, 20 June 2000, CDPA.

[28] GC minutes, 9-11 Mar. 1982, CDPA.

[29] GC minutes, 2-22, 19-31 Aug. 1993 and 10-11, 17-19 Jan. 1996, CDPA.

[30] GC minutes, 22-23 Nov. 1993, CDPA.

[31] Oral interview, 20 Feb. 2000, CDPA.

General Council began to provide materials for these meetings, which came to be called monthly community discussions.[32]

As they tried different ways to organize themselves, the Sisters grew in their communication skills and desire to stay in contact. Newsletters, which usually originated from Congregational administrators, were discontinued in 1979 when a committee that evaluated communication in the Congregation recommended the establishment of an Office of Communications. Sister Margaret Ellen Gallatin was its first director.[33] This office published the newsletter *CDP Times* and furnished each Sister a copy of the annual Congregational "Directory" containing the names and addresses of all the Sisters, arranged by community location.

Learning to communicate also led to better collaboration with persons outside the Congregation. Sister Barbara Fry observed, "The Sisters hooked on to Vatican Council II and ran with it. We had workshops and we not only studied the documents; we applied them. We became a kind of leaven for the clergy, the hierarchy, and the laity. We showed them how to work as a team because we were really collaborating."[34] Closer collaboration with laypeople revealed a need for deeper faith formation. Sister Thadine Hyzak summarized the challenges of motivating a group composed predominantly of lay people.

> When the Sisters were the leaders and administrators, we all had the same kind of formation and the same goal. It was much easier to move or to promote projects. Now the members of the staff have varied formation; and that diversity challenges us to dialogue, improve awareness, give time for transitions, and accept the fact that some do not have much background. They may not be able to connect right away with goals or move together in the desired direction. I notice that I am feeling much more strongly the importance of empowering people so they can pass on faith or knowledge or the spirit of things.[35]

With more interaction in and with "the world," the Sisters learned to utilize whatever resources were available to improve efficient collaboration.

Earlier in this period, superiors tended to rely on Church officials or trusted individuals for advice. Mother Angelique in many cases followed the lead of

---

[32] GC minutes, 1 and 3 Sept. 1982; 8-10, 16-17 Nov. 1995; 15-16, 22-23 May 1996, CDPA.

[33] GC minutes, 17 Sept. 1979 and 18 Sept. 1980, CDPA. In recognition of her communications skills, Sister Margaret Ellen was named to the San Antonio Woman's Hall of Fame.

[34] Oral interview, 27 Oct. 2000, CDPA.

[35] Oral interview, 18 May 2000, CDPA.

Archbishop Lucey. Her successor, Mother Amata, invited Rev. Charles Schleck, CSC, to make presentations and retreats on spiritual renewal and engaged Rev. Anthony Falanga, CM, as critic and advisor "to study and refine the general and specific objectives of the General Council in terms of the general and specific objectives of the Congregation."[36] Sister Charlene Wedelich often took counsel with Rev. Quentin Hakenewerth, provincial of the Society of Mary, who like herself had also been in formation ministry.

After several years of very rapid changes that increased leadership responsibilities and complicated the governance of the Congregation, the General Chapter of 1973 proposed hiring a placement consultant. The newly elected General Council, however, took a bolder step, deciding to "make a concrete effort to find a person or persons who could help us make a complete plan for an integrated apostolic spirituality." They hired the Management Design Institute (MDI) not only to revise structures but also to train 40 Sisters who would train others in leadership skills.[37] MDI consultants—especially Sister Catherine Harmer, A Medical Missionary Sister, and Mr. John Sherwood—attended General Council meetings and advised various groups how to articulate definite, measurable goals before developing programs. They revised structures and devised procedures for personnel placement in comprehensive planning from 1975 to 1982. A leadership skills workshop was held in 1980. In 1982 Sister Catherine led a planning session for every aspect of the Congregation—General Assembly, Representative Assembly, Office of Social Advocacy, *CDP Times*, vocation recruitment, formation, retirement, and Associates.[38] The corps of Sisters trained in organization and management employed their skills not only in their ministries but also at meetings and planning sessions both inside and outside the Congregation.

Another group, Dini Associates, was contracted in 1994 to prepare "a comprehensive program related to development, communications, design of materials for use in new membership work, and/or the immediate efforts to consolidate CDP external and internal communications programs."[39]

---

[36] GC minutes, 25 Nov. 1962, CDPA.

[37] GC minutes, 7 Jan.1975 and 19 Dec. 1975, CDPA. Of 29 MDI trainees in 1977, only three later left the Congregation (GC minutes, 12 July 1977, CDPA). In 1979 the Congregation joined "Journey," the MDI association (GC minutes, 7 Mar.1979).

[38] CDPA, GC minutes 7 Jan., 18 Feb., and 17 June 1976; 12 July and 20 Dec. 1977; 9-11 Mar. and 24-28 May 1982. Sister Lora Ann Quiñonez, who was on the General Council during part of this time (1973-1979), considered working with MDI "one of the best things that the council decided to do. They really taught us how to be administrators, how to make policy and administrative decisions. They worked with the Myers-Briggs personality inventory and the way in which each person's type would impact decision making" (oral interview, 13 June 2000, CDPA).

[39] GC minutes, 22-24 Aug. 1994, CDPA. See GC minutes of 7 June 1994, CDPA.

Following Dini recommendations resulted in decisions to reorganize offices, select a Congregational logo, and raise three million dollars for the restoration of Sacred Heart Chapel.[40] Sister Regina Decker found this restoration to be a unifying project "to which we were really committed. We did it in fine style and in three years time. If we set a goal, pray about it, and do all our homework and groundwork, then when we go for it, God's Providence gets us there."[41]

Leadership in the Congregation tended to be seen primarily as governing and organizing, but the concept also included planning for the future. Themes and activities of the annual General Assemblies of the Congregation often encouraged looking forward. The 1989 GA asked all the Sisters present to estimate where they would be in 10, 20 or 30 years: employed, semi-retired, retired, or deceased. The large number in the retired category was a wake-up call to anticipate and prognosticate the Congregation's future. In 1996 the general administration scheduled special meetings with all the Sisters under 50 years of age to determine their unique needs and urge them to exercise leadership.

Major financial decisions made by General Councils after the Second Vatican Council included investing in the stock market (1968) and giving a monthly allowance to each Sister (1971). To prepare for retirement, $25 (later $50) of the monthly salary of each Sister was set aside for her retirement and education. The interest from an account established with the National Bank of Commerce was to be used for retirement (1972). The Congregation, along with many other congregations in the U.S., entered the Social Security System in 1973 when it became available to non-salaried religious with a vow of poverty. Despite some Sisters' feeling that they were not being trusted, central financing was initiated (1973). Pastors were informed that the annual salary increase would be 5% instead of being negotiated each year (1974). In 1980 the Congregation began to use the Religious Communities' Trust (RCT), a cash management service of the Christian Brothers Investment Service, Inc. (CBIS) for student accounts. A few years later, the use of RCT was made available to all the Sisters. Income from investment began to be re-invested rather than used for current expenses (1985). The National Association of Treasurers of Religious Institutes (NATRI) was hired for consultation (1986, 1993-94). A development office for fund raising was established with Sister Virginia Clare Duncan as its first director (1987),[42] and major capital campaigns were conducted to enhance CDP retirement funds (1991) and to finance the renovation of Sacred Heart Chapel (1995) and St. Joseph Hall (2000). Recognizing that some Sisters would

---

[40] GC minutes of 16-18 Aug. 1995 and 12-13, 24-25 Jan. 1995, CDPA.

[41] Oral interview, 8 Nov. 2000, CDPA.

[42] This became a permanent office that came to be called "mission support" and published an annual report intended primarily for donors.

qualify for Supplementary Security income (SSI), the General Council invited them to apply in 1989.

Sister Imelda González, General Treasurer from 1987 to 1996, remembered three unrelated events of 1985-1986 which "changed the way we do finances in religious institutions": (1) Priests' misconduct cases came to light in Louisiana, which led to measures to protect Congregational assets. (2) Public figures such as movie star Rock Hudson acknowledged they had AIDS, which prompted arrangements for risk management. (3) The press revealed that unfounded past service liability for religious was in the billions, which emphasized the need to have adequate funds for retirement.

> We made a massive effort to increase our compensation and our assets through investments. We secured professional management for our financial assets, generated many financial policies, and critically evaluated insurance programs. We provided our employees with benefits and retirement plans. At the same time we began to use computers and automated our accounting system.[43]

The wisdom of the Congregation's leadership and the expertise of its treasurers led to its being commended by the U.S. Commission on Religious Life and Ministry for its good practices concerning planning for retirement in the light of its mission. It was considered to be "distinctive" for its "early recognition of the financial crisis" regarding retirement of religious and its "decisive action to address it." It was one of seven Congregations selected for comprehensive site visits in 2002. The researchers found the Congregation to be "relatively unique" with regard to the priorities which the Sisters surveyed considered to be "most important" in planning for the future: recruiting new members (24%), meeting the needs of retired members (23%), planning for the future (19%), and passing on the mission of the Congregation to others (13%). With regard to priorities in providing for retirement, 62% of the respondents chose providing quality care for members. One of the three most important priorities was "having our own retirement facilities (58%)."[44]

While the General Treasurers handled the finances of the Congregation, individual Sisters often assumed the role of fund-raisers for institutions or projects dear to them. Sister Jane Marie Barbour and Sister Catherine Walker solicited

---

[43] Oral interview, 15 June 2000, CDPA. "The tenure of Sister Imelda González as treasurer was a significant turning point for the congregation" (CARA report, p. 253). She set up charts of accounts and recommended consulting an investment manager and establishing an investment advisory committee.

[44] CARA reports 252, 244, and 246. A large number of those queried also considered these priorities to be second and third most important.

funds for the library and counseling departments of OLLU. Numerous local superiors, such as Sister Alma Marty, cultivated donors for their schools and their projects. The Sisters' good deeds as well as good sales pitches made people happy to contribute to their causes.

Membership in national organizations was always valued in the Congregation. Sister Elizabeth McCullough served in 1971 on the Board of Directors of the National Conference of Major Superiors of Women, which changed its name to the Leadership Conference of Women Religious (LCWR) that year.[45] Sister Lora Ann Quiñonez delivered a paper at the LCWR Inter-American Conference in Bogotá, Colombia in 1974 and was an observer for the LCWR at the third Inter-American Conference of Religious held in Montreal in 1977. During her second term on the General Council, she resigned to become the Associate Director of LCWR. From 1981 to 1986 she was its Executive Director. In 1995 she was one of three delegates elected by the U.S. superiors general to represent them in the General Assembly of the International Union of Superiors General (IUSG) in Rome.[46]

Some Sisters were officers in other national organizations for women religious. Sister Frances Klinger was one of 15 members on the steering committee of the national board of the National Assembly of Women Religious (NAWR), an organization that "linked religious identity and social activism."[47] She also chaired a committee that researched the changing roles of women in the Church, which Sister Catherine Pinkerton, CSJ, foundress of NAWR, had called "'the multinational corporation that could make the difference in the world' if it would change its social and economic policies."[48] Former Sister Jane Shafer was chosen to attend the 1974 NAWR gathering and helped to host the group's convention in San Antonio in 1979.[49] Sister Imelda González, who became the Associate Director of the National Association of Treasurers of Religious Institutes (NATRI) in 1997,[50] had authored a major paper on Scriptural foundations for a theology of stewardship while on sabbatical at the Graduate Theological Union in Berkeley, California.

While most of the structural changes in the Congregation can be traced to initiatives from the Vatican, two are the result of the maturation and resulting desire for more independence on the part of the MCDPs and the native Mexican Sisters. These were discussed in Chapter 5.

---

[45] *Nunspeak*, June, 1971:10, CDPA.

[46] *CDP Times*, 15, 9 (May, 1995):17, CDPA.

[47] Lora Ann Quiñonez, CDP, and Mary Daniel Turner, SNDdeN, *The Transformation*, 142.

[48] Lacey Fosburgh, *New York Times*, Aug. 17, 1975.

[49] GC minutes, 12 June 1974 and 23 June 1979, CDPA.

[50] GC minutes, 21-24, 29 Jan. 1996, CDPA. Sister Imelda also directed the installation of the first computer at the Generalate (oral interview, 15 June 2000, CDPA).

Taking Responsibility for Decisions

Coming from a formation program that featured a rigorous schedule with little free time, Sister Phyllis Ann Bunnell observed that "the most difficult part about my first mission in 1960 was getting used to being in charge of my own life and making more decisions." The community on the mission had a schedule too; "but because of the school schedule, the day was a great deal different. I learned more than ever that I was responsible for my own time. I had to get my work done, and it was up to me to see that it got done."[51] After the second Vatican Council even more decisions were left up to individual Sisters.

Sister Regina Decker, who left the novitiate in 1962 for health reasons and returned in 1972, called "gut-wrenching" the changes that happened right after Vatican Council II as religious took renewal seriously. She also pinpointed the flexibility that facilitated the traumatic transitions. Sisters

> were not only given more opportunities but were put into situations where they had to make some responsible choices or decisions for themselves. Working later with the retired Sisters, I realized that those who survived best and were the happiest were those who had to a certain extent done that all along. The ones who managed to come through with flying colors and be happy were the ones who didn't take all of the rules too seriously. Even though the changes were hard, those who were more flexible found them easier.[52]

Sister Ida Marie Deville thought the most important change for the Congregation was being able to voice one's opinion and accept others' opinions because gradually it made the whole group more democratic and inclusive. "Not that our opinion would necessarily make others change, but our opinions were heard. We felt that we were worth something, and sometimes actions resulted."[53] Sister Antoinette Billeaud thought an important change was the autonomy Sisters were given "to experience their own gifts, develop those gifts, and go out and share those gifts with others. I think the individuation of professions and service was necessary to make us more mature women and not little girls doing as mother told us to do."[54]

---

[51] Sister Phyllis Bunnell, oral interview, 17 May 2000, CDPA.

[52] Oral interview, 8 Nov. 2000, CDPA.

[53] Oral interview, 20 June 2000, CDPA. Sister Miriam Dorothy Lueb expressed a similar opinion. "We were used to being told where to go and what to do. But now we can make plans or suggestions and explain them to the administration. With a discussion, it can be done" (oral interview, 13 Feb. 2000, CDPA).

[54] Oral interview, 1 June 2000, CDPA.

Former Sister Evelyn Thibeaux said the years of experimentation were the most exciting and rewarding years for her,

> especially when we started having open General Chapters. I attended every meeting I possibly could, listening and contributing and having the sense of wonderment that all of the things that had always been secret were now open. We were all part of it. We were making decisions that had to do with our own lives instead of, it seems to me, following what someone else said we should do.[55]

Sister Lucille Ann Fritsch was used to doing what she was told, willingly following the crowd and not questioning. When many choices were left to her, she noticed, "I didn't know who I was. I could express my individuality in dress, for example, but I wasn't sure what it was. It was a hard time for me emotionally."[56]

Sister Alexandrine Gienec was among those who felt that she learned to be more responsible and charitable as a result of being allowed to budget for a monthly allowance to be spent at her own discretion. Sometimes she would buy food for a hungry street person or a treat for Mrs. Varkonyi, aged 98, who lived across the street. "It was a wonderful opportunity not only for sharing but also for depriving myself so that somebody else could have something."[57] In rare cases, Sisters did not seem ready to accept new responsibilities. The General Council decided that a certain community "is very independent and does not meet the requirements set down for all CDP communities as far as finances are concerned. Two members are not self-supporting . . . [and] are not being faced by the community to support themselves. It is difficult to get this community to face its obligation to the Congregation."[58]

In the 1970s offering Sisters a sabbatical opportunity became more common. Sister Mary Margaret Hughes articulated what many Sisters experienced during sabbaticals.

> My year at Berkeley, California, in 1977 was so freeing. The climate was just perfect—the blue sky, the cool breeze, the bay. When I walked into that class of 43 lay people, priests, and Sisters from all over the world dressed however we pleased, I felt so happy. For the first time in a long, long time I was free from responsibilities

---

[55] Oral interview, 15 June 2002, CDPA.

[56] Oral interview, 9 Sept. 2000, CDPA.

[57] Oral interview, 8 June 2000, CDPA.

[58] GC minutes, 30 Apr. 1975, CDPA.

as the dean of students and from two terms on the Congregational general administration where you served everybody day and night. The latest theology, wonderful professors, interesting students—it was a real gift!

Ten years later, she had a sabbatical in Washington, D.C., with a different flavor.

> I spent much time getting in touch with what it means to be getting old, to be in the winter of my life. God has given me so much. Now it was time to surrender, give it back, accept who I am and where I am. It was a rather dark time, and we had much snow. But when spring came, I resurrected. I got out of the darkness and have been out of it ever since. I realized that I'm not getting ready for the end. It's going to be a new beginning![59]

During graduate studies at the University of Michigan in Ann Arbor from 1965 to 1970, Sister Lora Ann Quiñonez observed some change factors that came from outside the Congregation. She became aware of the goals of Gray Panthers, Black Panthers, Students for a Democratic Society, and feminist movements as well as "new ideas of Church as the People of God and of religious life as profoundly ecclesial." The notion that spirituality is a private matter or that the Church is a perfect society did not escape scrutiny. She began to see that "vows were not just a relationship between God and me but also values with mystical, social, and even political meaning. Later I also came to realize that the Church was profoundly flawed when I understood more clearly the use and abuse of power."[60]

Superiors shared more power as they began to see the Sisters more as co-laborers than subjects and to view their responsibility more as calling forth talents to further God's Reign than as filling empty slots. At mid-century, the vow of obedience was interpreted primarily as following orders, conforming not only one's behavior but one's "heart and mind" to what superiors proposed. The yearly assignment, probably the greatest manifestation of the power of superiors, was even called "an obedience." Sisters professed after 1965 did not experience the days when Sisters discovered their assignment only when their name appeared on a certain blackboard or was read aloud to the whole assembled community. In 1970 assignments were sent by mail for the last time to all the Sisters at once. By the 1980s when it was time for a change, instead of

---

[59] Sister Mary Margaret Hughes, oral interview, 18 June 2000, CDPA.

[60] Videotaped interview, CDPA.

"assigning" the Superiors asked each Sister to take initiative and explore more than one possibility. The choice was made in continuing dialogue between the Sister and the Superior.

Later the Sisters were expected to consult their contact Councilors and, between 1988 and 1996, the Sister in charge of the Congregation's ministry office.[61] Sister Miriam Fidelis Mellein at age 84 said, "I think it's good that we have to pick our own place of service. The responsibility is ours and makes us appreciate what lay people have to go through."[62]

Sister Frances Trochta also had a positive view of job-hunting. "I thought it was a very growing-up experience to be told you go, you find, you interview, and you don't fall back on somebody to tell you what your next job is going to be. I thought that was a dramatic step in the Congregation." She felt that administrators "looked at a Sister and tried to find out what she needed rather than asking her to fill a need they had. Being granted a sabbatical was one example of my needs being recognized."[63]

Some Sisters went into areas where no CDP had gone before. The first CDP attorney, midwife, union organizer, and occupational therapist have already been mentioned. In addition, Sister Imelda González, for example, was supported by the Congregation in her (unsuccessful) bid for a seat on the City Council in Alexandria, Louisiana.[64] Sister Eva Rollwitz found a job in the serving line at Luby's Cafeteria on Bandera Road in San Antonio.[65] Sister Elsa Bennett taught beginners' swimming and was a tennis instructor at the YWCA. She became known for her popular course "Swimming for People Who are Terrified of Water." Sister Mary Ruth Kotula became the hairdresser for many retired Sisters who opted to uncover their hair when they adopted different styles of clothing. When Sister Delia Ruelas realized after brain surgery in 1976 that her activities would be limited, she asked to study cosmetology so she could provide the same service. The General Council instructed her "to take a battery of tests to find out if this is really something that she would be interested in."[66] Sister Elise Bengfort became Associate Director of Maryhill Retreat Center in Pineville, Louisiana.[67]

---

[61] Sister Ramona Bezner was the first director of this office (GC minutes, 19-22-23, 25 Feb. 1988, CDPA).

[62] Oral interview, 13 June 2000, CDPA.

[63] Oral interview, 20 June 2000, CDPA.

[64] GC minutes, 5 Jan. 1977, CDPA. Sister Imelda centered her campaign speeches on "quality of life." It needed to improve because open ditches in some parts of the city made it possible for diseases to be transmitted (oral interview, 15 June 2000, CDPA).

[65] GC minutes, 5 Sept. 1974, CDPA.

[66] GC minutes, 18 June 1978, CDPA.

[67] GC minutes, 24 Apr.1979, CDPA. Sister Barbara Fry headed a retreat center in Moline, Illinois, from 1987-1988. Sisters Ramona Bezner, Lucille Ann Fritsch Jane Ann Slater, and Ann Umscheid were later among the Sisters active in the

Sister Delia Ruelas and Sister Clemence Ribitzki worked for "Sister Care of San Antonio," which provided services for the elderly and sick in their homes.[68] Sister Roberta Haby became a licensed occupational therapist.[69]

Not all experiences of looking for jobs were pleasant, however. Sometimes searches and negotiations for employment dragged on as Sisters on the "Unassigned List" tried "to find a place for themselves with the help of the ministries office."[70] Some excellent teachers who had to leave the parochial school system because schools were closing found no welcome in public employment because they were older and overqualified. When Sister Paulette Celis and Sister María Cristina Ruelas left St. Augustine School in Laredo, they came to San Antonio.

> Nobody seemed to care what we would do, so we looked in the newspapers for jobs. We considered taking a course in working with senior citizens or working in a meat packing plant but finally settled for a nursing course at a private school. We were disillusioned during our internship when we saw how roughly they expected us to treat patients in the nursing home.[71]

Finally they found their niche taking care of the children at Providence Home for Children with AIDS.

Contracts for the Sisters' services were a long-standing practice of the Congregation since contracts stabilize a specified salary for a given time. Mother Angelique, for example, sent annual contracts to 53 pastors in 10 dioceses as well as agreements to bishops for parish schools for their signatures. She did "not believe that the Sisters can subsist upon less than is called for by the agreement."[72] Sister Madonna Sangalli, General Treasurer from 1968 to 1981, credited Sister Elizabeth McCulllough and her Council (1967-1973) with "much financial planning. They began to formalize the contracts for Sisters, talking with other Congregations about a base stipend and benefits for all Sisters. Then we were able to budget better."[73] In 1973 pastors were asked to raise each Sister's salary to $3,000 plus an amount for social security, and a 5% increase was requested in

---

ACTS retreat movement.

[68] GC minutes, 17-21 Jan. 1994, CDPA.

[69] GC minutes, 21-25 Feb. 1994, CDPA.

[70] GC minutes, 4 June 1974, CDPA.

[71] Sister María Cristina Ruelas, oral interview, 27 Mar. 2000, CDPA.

[72] Mother Angelique Ayres, Circular Letter, 8 Sept. 1943, CDPA.

[73] Sister Madonna also credited her successor, Sister John Martin Ebrom, with "really modernizing the generalate financial office" (oral interview, 31 Mar. 2000, CDPA).

1974 and subsequent years.[74] In the 1990s, 3% was the expected annual increase. As mentioned in a previous chapter, Sisters were invited to apply for positions in the public schools because of the higher salaries there. Sister Charlotte Kitowski resigned as head of the English department at OLLU in 1987 when the Sisters were told they could no longer be housed on the campus. She found employment as a librarian in Sinclair Elementary School in San Antonio. Her salary was more than three times what it had been after the University, following a standard procedure, deducted an amount for contributed services.[75]

The Congregation has always subsidized OLL University, Providence High School, and other Congregational enterprises. Sometimes it also subsidized, completely or partially, worthwhile ministries for which no other compensation was available. In 1975, for example, five Sisters were subsidized, and the practice continues to this day.[76] Sister Pearl Ceasar served at Network.[77] The employment of Sister Imelda Maurer and Sister Bernie Galvin with the SMHA, as detailed in a previous chapter of this book, and Sister Cathy Parent's social work at Hope House in New Orleans were partially subsidized by the Congregation.[78] The Congregation contributed a third of Sister Lora Ann Quiñonez's salary to LCWR when she became its Executive Director.[79]

Corporate decisions in the Congregation which had the greatest impact on individuals had to do with types of ministry and contracts for services. A survey of 1974 showed the Sisters in general had a positive attitude toward placement; however, in the opinion of the General Council, "The Sisters as a whole are not able yet to get and hold outside jobs. A Sister should also be responsible not only for herself but also for the Congregation—her Sisters. . . . Corporate responsibility is sadly lacking in many cases."[80] Some Sisters did not know how to apply for jobs in a competitive market. Others were content with employment that did not utilize their full potential or they underestimated the worth of their skills. An evaluation of placement procedures enacted by the General Chapter of 1977 found two years later that of the 50 Sisters who asked the ministry team for help, only 12 found it "not too effective." Some respondents suggested a

---

[74] GC minutes, 26 Jan.1973, and 4 Jan. 1974, CDPA.

[75] Oral interview, 13 Mar. 2000, CDPA.

[76] GC minutes, 5 Sept. 1975, CDPA.

[77] GC minutes, 2 Apr. 1974, CDPA.

[78] GC minutes, 3 July 1974 and 7 Feb.1979, CDPA.

[79] GC minutes, 9 July 1980, CDPA. At times the General Council declined to give monetary donations to justice-oriented groups in cases where it was "furnishing the more valuable asset, actual personnel which we subsidize" (GC minutes, 18 Feb. 1976, CDPA).

[80] GC minutes, 5 Dec. 1974, CDPA.

better way should be found to connect decisions about ministry with decisions about community.[81]

While changes in community forms and government structures had a bearing on individuals and the membership as a whole, the departure of individual Sisters could also make a big difference to their companions and to the Congregation's ministries. In this period—more than in any other period in the Congregation's history—many Sisters discerned whether or not to remain in the Congregation. A large number departed. Changing cultural mores such as reevaluation of traditional forms of the family, women's rights, and increased emphasis on self-fulfillment and self-understanding impacted religious Congregations. Sister Elizabeth McCullough, Superior General from 1967 to 1973, recalled:

> As each Sister reflected on her life, on her past choices, some felt their original, youthful choice no longer fit them as adults. They made a new decision, the decision to withdraw. . . . Saying "goodbye" to Sisters whom I loved and worked with tore at the very fabric of my soul. Those scars are still with me. I honored the choices of my Sisters, but the turmoil caused by their decisions was emotionally scarring.[82]

Sister Madonna Sangalli concurred that after the Chapter of Renewal "we lost some key people. They were not the new ones but Sisters who had so much to offer anywhere (and are still offering it where they are today). They were the up and coming Sisters, and we knew they had a lot of potential. They made their choices to leave, and that was hard for all of us."[83] Six Sisters who left the Congregation later re-entered.[84]

The main reasons for leaving can be grouped into personal or psychological and dissatisfaction with the community or, for some Sisters, both. Personal reasons given for leaving included a sense of calling to ministry in a wider world with more varied opportunities or an attraction to the married life. Other reasons were difficulties in ministry or in family of origin, a tendency to scrupulosity, fear of permanent commitment, and problems with practicing the vow of

---

[81] GC minutes, 26 June 1979, CDPA.

[82] *Movements*, 4, 1 (Fall/Winter 2000): 13, CDPA. Sister Elizabeth thought that some who left had been struggling with life choices for a long time; others "probably always wanted a husband or a companion" (oral interview, 17 Apr. 2000, CDPA).

[83] Oral interview, 3 Mar. 2000, CDPA.

[84] *CDP Times*, 15, 8 (Apr. 1995): 8 and 9, CDPA. Sister Rose Marie Uhlig said: "The times I was not in the convent, I still kept in touch with many of the Sisters. There seems to be a bond with Sisters you have lived with, and Sister friendships are more stable and meaningful, probably because they have a spiritual basis" (oral interview, 29 Feb. 2000, CDPA).

poverty. Strongly drawn to Church service while they were very young, some later became aware of other more appealing service opportunities. Sister Sylvia Schmidt, for example, while teaching religion at Bishop Kelley High School in Tulsa, Oklahoma, felt that her help was essential to keep the diocesan youth program, in which she was also involved, from disintegrating. She left BKHS and moved into a smaller convent when she went to work full-time for the diocese. Soon she learned about an ecumenical secular institute, the Sisters for Christian Community, whose "profile matched her understanding of the living out of the vows in contemporary society."[85] She withdrew from the Congregation to join this institute.

Some found community life to be psychologically unhealthy for themselves and felt that Congregational rights sometimes overrode individual personal rights. Others were irritated by secrecy, especially about departures, or by the penchant of authorities to skirt rather than address controversial issues. For some, change was too rapid; they thought the priority of the spiritual life was slipping and detected some hypocrisy and spitefulness. Captivated by high ideals of sanctity and pious practices, they felt anchorless when certain devotions were dropped or disillusioned when Sisters they admired decided no longer to observe them. For others, change was too slow. Superiors did not recognize or financially support, for example, the travel and entertainment expected of professional women. Some also became disheartened by the lack of recognition and promotion of women in Church ministries. Former Sister Micheleen Barragy said that out of honesty she had to leave the Congregation, which she loved, because she no longer found the Catholic Church credible.[86] While 28 Sisters left in the decade 1940-50 and 22 in 1950-60, the largest exit was 63 between 1960 and 1970.[87]

Most of those who departed did feel that they were supported in their decision to leave. Sister Elizabeth McCullough remembered that during her time in leadership she "learned to be a discriminating listener. I learned that trusting the Sisters in this time of transition and transformation was most important. I learned that the Holy Spirit speaks to and works through people everywhere. The Spirit knows no hierarchy."[88] She was "at peace with the way things were going. Those who objected let me know they were criticizing, but they stayed with us. The majority of the Sisters were seeking to understand, and they were

---

[85] Oral interview, 3 Feb. 2003, CDPA.

[86] Reasons for departures are culled from oral interviews with former members. See Appendix III for statistics on departures.

[87] Sister Helen Louise Rivas recalled that a large number of MCDPs also left between 1962 and 1965 "because there was so much uncertainty" (oral interview, 17 Oct. 2000, CDPA).

[88] *Movements*, 4, 1 (Fall/Winter 2000):14, CDPA.

going out of their way to learn about Vatican Council II. They might have been searching, but they were not unhappy."[89]

Mary Catherine Franz-Eide, formerly Sister M. Loyola, reported

> I had a significant dream when I was preparing to leave the Congregation. I was preparing to cross over a small footbridge, but I was afraid and hesitated. A number of Sisters were standing around, and one said to her, "Don't be afraid if you want to go. If you fall down, it's not that far."
>
> This dream is consistent with the encouragement, spirit of adventure, and assurance of being accepted I have always experienced with the Sisters. I do find that they are more open to all vocations and accept that a person can be capable of more than one vocation in a lifetime.[90]

The fact that many members left in the 1960s and 1970s can be regarded either as an Exodus to the "Promised Land" outside of religious life or as a diaspora, a wider sowing of the seeds of trust in Providence. Those who remained did feel pride in former members who shared their talents with more audiences than those available to them prior to their departure from the Congregation. For example, Mary Catherine Villagómez, the former Sister Delphine Marie, helped compile information for a year-long exhibit, *Los Tejanos—Sus Huellas en Esta Tierra*," at the LBJ Library in Austin, Texas. Elizabeth Carrow Woolfolk, the former Sister Mary Arthur, devised test instruments for language competency and authored books on language theory and disorders as well as a genealogical history of the family of her husband, a descendant of George Washington. Former Sister Helen Rose Fuchs Ebaugh became an authority in the field of sociology of religion and published numerous articles and books.

Women who left the Congregation stayed in touch and attended reunions of the Sisters with former members, which were held every five or six years after the first one in 1979. Helen Rose Fuchs Ebaugh said she felt no bitterness toward the Congregation, and her husband remarked, "You know how to produce good wives."[91] Mary Catherine Franz-Eide noted, "Our husbands always feel very welcome among the Sisters."[92]

As CDPs adjusted to the post-Vatican Council II changes, trusting that these were part of God's Providential plan, how they organized and regulated their

---

[89] Oral interview, 17 Apr. 2000, CDPA.

[90] Oral interview, 20 Feb. 2003, CDPA. Most of the material in the next paragraph comes from oral interviews.

[91] Oral interview, 16 Feb. 2003, CDPA.

[92] Oral interview, 20 Feb. 2003, CDPA.

communal life affected not only each Sister's work but the very components of her religious identity. Instead of living in closed, self-sufficient communities controlled by a Superior, CDPs often lived singly and rather independently, consulting with a member of the General Council on major decisions. The General Council spent less time assigning Sisters or supervising Congregational institutions and more time on long-range planning, managing Congregational assets, and devising means to animate and motivate the Sisters in their ministries. The General Councilors had more contacts with individual Sisters and were also in closer contact with their peers in other religious Congregations. They were more aware of the impact of events in the Church and the world on the Sisters' lives. More collaboration with persons outside the Congregation was not only a necessity but also a welcome reality.

While community and government forms changed, they were accompanied by gradual alterations in the formation of new members, customary exercises and devotions, and ways of making decisions on all levels. Change of clothing was visible; other changes were less visible but more profound.

CHAPTER 14

TRANSITIONING WITH TRUST

> I always think my novitiate group was really in the "in between" state. Between 1963 and 1969, everything blew up. Thirty of us were postulants together; 22 entered the novitiate in 1962, were invested in the wool serge habit, and were assigned new names. Eighteen made first vows, and by the time eight of us made final vows in 1969, we were no longer in the habit, we had gone back to our baptismal names, and we were beginning to do different ministries.[1]

Sister Ann Umscheid (Anthony Marie) viewed her group as the "bridge" because it experienced the old but was ready for the new. The novices learned to recite the Little Office of the Blessed Virgin Mary and spent most of their day in silence, speaking "only in case of necessity, and in low or at least quiet tones, and briefly."[2] Thirty years later, the mainstay of communal prayer was a version of the Divine Office, and the Sisters were constantly looking for ways to be more articulate and improve their communication skills.

Previous chapters showed changes in ministries, living arrangements, and governance that were visible to the public during a half-century of dramatic transformation. This chapter details changes usually known only to the Sisters that caused or were caused by exterior alterations, particularly in the areas of formation, prayer life, customs, manner of making decisions, appreciation of the founder, understanding of the charism of Providence, and written documents.

---

[1] Sister Ann Umscheid, oral interview, 19 May 2000, CDPA. Sister Dianne Jean Heinrich, who entered the novitiate in 1965, considered her group to be "at the cutting edge; we were always at the beginning of new things. We never really got into the old convent way of doing things. We were the new breed" (oral interview, 20 June, 2000, CDPA).

[2] Constitutions (1928) # 93.

The Second Ecumenical Vatican Council, 1962-1965, which called for a return to foundations as well as reforms, accelerated changes that had already been initiated in Sisterhoods. Social and economic factors were also important contributors to unprecedented changes. World War II drew many women to work outside the home. Suburbs grew and inner cities declined. The Civil Rights Movement weakened racial barriers and strengthened efforts for equality and social justice. President Kennedy's Peace Corps initiative and the peace movement of the Vietnam era made people aware that individuals have some power as well as the right to make their voices heard. Economic inflation and deflation as well as an aging population led to greater participation in social security and more investment in the stock market. Economic globalization and wars in Vietnam, Central America, and the Middle East along with space exploration spurred technological development and expanded self-knowledge as well as widened geographical horizons. The changes were truly radical; the Congregation in 2000 differed greatly from the Congregation in 1950. In the opinion of a former member, who was a sociologist, it changed from a "total institution par excellence to a contemporary form of voluntary organization committed to providing resources to members."[3]

How did the Congregation maintain its identity and purpose in the midst of such constant upheaval? One factor was that to be effective in teaching and health care, the Sisters were accustomed to being flexible. Not only were they regularly welcoming new students, clients, or patients, they were also trying new methods and following new regulations. The Congregation's leadership often anticipated and helped the members prepare for various changes. Sister L. Suzanne Dancer, a younger member, noted "Because I entered the Congregation in the late 1960s, I've never known the Congregation when it was not in the midst of change. Change has been a constant, and therefore in and of itself has been rather unremarkable."[4]

Common interests and problems in forming new members led U.S. Sisters by 1953 to establish the Sister Formation Conference (SFC) as a committee of the National Catholic Education Association (NCEA). The Sister Formation Movement (SFM) is considered "the single most critical ground for the radical transformative process following Vatican Council II." It is credited with raising the education level of U.S. Sisters, providing a vehicle to transmit common ideas about change in religious life, and effecting "the first mass shift in the worldview of American sisters."[5] Mother Angelique fully supported this movement on the national as well as regional level, writing: "May I congratulate you on the splendid work done recently at the Southern Sister Formation Committee held

---

[3] Helen Rose Fuchs Ebaugh, *Becoming an Ex: the Process of Role Exit* (University of Chicago Press, 1988) 44.

[4] Written interview, 15 Nov. 2003, CDPA.

[5] Quiñonez and Turner, *The Transformation* 6.

in New Orleans. God grant that the movement may progress with His blessing for the need of Sisters is great."[6]

Mother Amata Regan also strongly supported the SFM, serving as vice-chair of its West Central Region and chair of its Catechetical Committee.[7] She engaged Sister M. Emil Penet, IHM, to speak to Sisters from Congregations in the San Antonio area and cooperated with the efforts of Bishop Stephen Leven, auxiliary bishop of San Antonio from 1956 to1969, to improve communication and cooperation among the major superiors of the archdiocese. She scheduled special speakers, workshops, and retreats for local superiors, and promoted ongoing spiritual formation.[8] Sister Ann Linda Bell thought that Mother Amata

> changed our Congregation from European to American. Mother Angelique would have liked to do it, and she did it as far as academics were concerned; but she changed very minute things slowly. Mother Amata had gone away to study hospital administration, so when she came back she noticed a number of things we were doing that were not very healthful. For example, washing our dishes at the table in a cup or using the same cloth napkin for a week. So she did away with those kinds of customs.[9]

Sister Frances McMann recalled that Mother Amata "got the teachers' desks out of the community room and had them put into their own bedrooms. Then the Sisters would have more room during recreation and an incentive to do something besides preparing lessons and checking papers."[10] There was little resistance to the changes proposed by Mother Amata because they were already being suggested by some of the Sisters.

Sister Elizabeth McCullough thought that the most important change was "we have become more person-oriented. We are interested in the person and try to really listen and help when possible."[11] While daily life altered gradually,

---

[6] Mother Angelique to Sister Mary Peter, OP, 15 Sept. 1954, CDPA.

[7] GC minutes, 8 Sept. 1962, CDPA.

[8] Mother Amata Regan, Circular Letters, 3 Dec. 1956; 28 Nov. 1962; and 2 Dec. 1963, CDPA. For example, a second workshop for superiors was held 28-31 Dec. 1963, on "Basic Means of Spiritual Development." A Canon Law Institute was given 15-17 July 1966, by Rev. Joseph Gallen, SJ, who then stayed to preach the annual retreat. In 1956 Mother Amata sent a Sister to St. Louis University to enter a doctoral program for Sister-Formators being initiated there.

[9] Oral interview, 11 Apr. 2000, CDPA.

[10] Oral interview, 20 Jan. 2000, CDPA.

[11] Sister Elizabeth McCullough, oral interview, 14 Apr. 2000, CDPA. In the opinion of Sister Miriam Dorothy Lueb, "We became more people-conscious. We became more aware of people rather than what we were doing for or with people"

motivation for service, dedication to people, and adherence to professional excellence remained steady. Still, Sister Ann Umscheid detected continuity in the continuous alterations.

> I think that what first attracted us to religious life in this Congregation is still here. We are still interested in meeting the needs of people and also having God as the center of our lives. We have always valued and worked on these two things. Both of them, not one or the other. I think people look to us for these things, and that gives us life.[12]

Formation

The manner of socializing and training new recruits in the last half of the twentieth century changed from being quasi-military or "total institution" to being highly individualized under the direction of Sisters educated in psychology and spirituality. At the same time, cooperation and exchange with formators in other Congregations increased.

Returning a questionnaire with a contribution to the Regina Mundi Institute, an international house of studies for women religious in Rome, Mother Angelique wrote, "We are making a strenuous effort to increase vocations by the erection of a Juniorate [called an Aspirancy after 1957]. . . . There is everywhere in the United States a shortage of vocations, but we are painfully aware of our own."[13] Although at least 11 women from the village of West, Texas, had entered the Congregation, almost a decade earlier she had already written to the pastor: "If you must have another teacher, I suggest that you employ a lay person. Perhaps you might encourage some of your good girls to enter our Congregation and help supply the sad deficiency."[14]

Most women who entered before the 1960s were in their teens or twenties, had been raised in rural areas or small-town, ethnically identifiable Catholic communities (usually German, Czech, Polish, or Louisiana French), and were already formed in Catholic beliefs and practices in their homes. A vocation to the priesthood or religious life was a regular topic in their religion classes, retreats, or parish missions. Sister Bernadette (Charles Frances) Hajovsky's experience was typical:

(oral interview, 13 Feb. 2000, CDPA).

[12] Oral interview, 19 May 2000, CDPA.

[13] Mother Angelique to Rev. Mother Marie de St. Jean Martin, 25 March 1955, CDPA.

[14] Mother Angelique to Rev. E. J. Polcak, 10 Aug. 1946, CDPA.

I thought of becoming a Sister for many years. When I was a junior in high school, there was a parish mission and Father Joseph Ryan, OMI, gave a special talk to the high school students. I remember he asked, "I wonder how many of you would be willing to make the sacrifice to be priests, brothers, or sisters?" I tried to think of names of my classmates, and then it hit me! I knew from then on that is what God wanted me to do.[15]

Assured that most recruits already had a basic religious formation, Sisters in charge of formation in the Congregation looked mostly for whether they had good health and ability to teach or provide support services. The convent was unfamiliar, and leaving home was difficult for many; but they were familiar with God and attracted to a group that confided in God. Sister Clair Osborn recalled her entrance day.

The thing that struck me most was the eye within the triangle carved in the cream-colored stone over the front porch and repeated in gold, blue, and brown against a deep red background in that stained glass window above the doorway. I was ready to run back and get in the car with Mom and Daddy. Then I looked up there, and it said, *Providentiae tuae me committo* [I entrust myself to your Providence], and that is the only thing that kept me on the course.[16]

Religious symbols and the ideal of dedicated service helped to sustain new members like Sister Clair, strengthening their motivation and willingness to endure hardships and inconveniences.

Sister Lora Ann Quiñonez observed that "Our sense of calling and of being called in those days did not have the huge individualistic thrust that it has today when anything and everything is considered a call."[17] To be formed was primarily to learn to behave according to the traditions and customs of the Congregation motivated by love and a desire to serve people. The first step or test was to adhere to a routine and follow directions. When candidates were not taking a course in a college classroom, they studied at their desks in a large room called the postulate, took their meals in a large dining room, and slept in large dorms on the fourth floor where conditions were Spartan. In the postulate they heard the clock in the chapel steeple chiming every quarter hour. On the hour, it played the Lourdes hymn, "Immaculate Mary," and everyone paused to recite some

---

[15] Oral interview, 23 Mar. 2000, CDPA.

[16] Oral interview, 23 Nov. 2002, CDPA.

[17] Videotaped interview, CDPA.

prayers aloud. In the dormitories straight-backed chairs separated the iron beds from each other, and the cotton pallet mattresses had to be flipped over when the bed was re-made every morning before prayers at 5:25 a.m. Morning and evening ablutions were done with cold water in metal washbasins. All their clothing fit into a 3' x 7' x 1.5' closet which was called a "press."

Everyone in formation was assigned a chore called an "office" to be done after each meal. These offices were tasks such as weeding a flowerbed, mopping and dusting a corridor, cleaning bathrooms, or sweeping flights of stairs. On most days before supper the mistress of postulants gave "spiritual reading," consisting of passages from books about virtues or prayer. The women in formation took turns reading aloud Thomas à Kempis' *The Imitation of Christ* during breakfast and lives of saints or books by contemporary spiritual writers during dinner at noon and supper.

Important characteristics of Sisters chosen to be formators were exemplary observance of the Rule, ability to judge human character, and willingness to spend 24-hours a day with their charges. The formation philosophy of Sister Ann Joseph Wagner, mistress of postulants during the 40s and 50s, was to learn to "do the right thing at the right time because it is the right thing to do." Formators—indeed all the Sisters—measured their success by their faithfulness to the Constitutions and traditions and not by how many of the women they formed persevered. Sister Mary John Stehling, mistress of postulants and novices from 1937 to 1961, stated: "I don't give myself credit for those who stay and for the work they do, so I don't blame myself for those who leave."[18] Nevertheless, in her last years she would sometimes ask pardon of Sisters with whom she remembered having been strict.

The Sister Formation movement urged thorough preparation for Sister-formators as well as quality education of entrants at all levels. During the following decades the Sisters in charge of formation were prepared for their work in a variety of ways and implemented different programs.

Applicants of high school age desiring to become Sisters of Divine Providence of Texas had always been accepted into the CDP Motherhouse as candidates and given a high school education. If they were to become teachers, they then completed two years of college (a Congregational requirement since 1937) before entering the novitiate. In 1954, there were 49 girls of high school age in the postulate, and the General Council decided they needed a more distinctive formation. They were to be called "juniors" instead of "candidates"[19] and wear beige skirts and blouses instead of black uniforms. They began to reside in a separate section of the convent. By 1959 the number of aspirants had grown to the point where the general administration considered constructing a new

---

[18] *CDP Times*, 1, 4 (Jan., 1981): 8, CDPA.

[19] Soon they began to be called "aspirants," and the term "juniors" was reserved for Sisters with annual vows.

building on campus for them, but the needs of the retired Sisters had to take precedence. In a bold move, the superiors closed the prosperous Moye Military School in Castroville, Texas, in the summer of 1959 and moved the aspirancy there to the site of the first motherhouse. Local superiors and principals of grammar schools vied with one another to bring their eighth grade graduates to one-week intensive immersion summer workshops, hoping that at least some would choose to enter the aspirancy.[20] Although always enrolling fewer than 100 aspirants, Moye High School was fully accredited by the Texas Education Association in November 1960; its graduates, many of whom entered the convent, performed very well in college.

Sister Barbara Lynn Hyzak entered the convent after completing the eighth grade in Granger, Texas. She saw the aspirancy as

> a wonderful opportunity and luxury of being in a setting to focus on whether this was the kind of life that I might want to live. If we do this kind of experience only because we want the end result to be entrance into religious life, then we don't have a very good record. But as far as just being an experience in life, I think it was a worthwhile experience.[21]

From the viewpoint of a formator, Sister Joan Michele Rake expressed a similar opinion: "I didn't expect all of the aspirants to become Sisters, but we always need good, highly educated Catholic and morally good women to become professionals and mothers in our world. And that is what many have become because they got a good foundation from the excellent teachers we had."[22] The aspirancy program continued to flourish, and additional sites were opened in Oklahoma and Louisiana in 1964; but they lasted only a few years.

The aspirancy faculty and students engaged in community outreach such as literacy tutoring for local residents and helping a French immigrant earn her citizenship papers; but the aspirants did not mingle with the students of the parish high school located a block away until the two schools later merged.

In 1966, for the first time in its history, the Congregation asked women to finish college or complete some professional training prior to applying for entrance. No new aspirants were admitted, and Moye-St. Louis High School closed in 1968. In the 1970s three Sisters moved to a house close to the Motherhouse in San Antonio with the purpose of "inviting girls who were interested in becoming

---

[20] For example, 60 girls attended the workshop May 31-June 6, 1958 and were asked to contribute $12.50 for the week. Often the Sisters on the mission paid this fee (Mother Amata Regan, Circular Letter, 11 Apr. 1958, CDPA).

[21] Oral interview, 18 Jan. 2001, CDPA.

[22] Oral interview, 23 June 2000, CDPA.

Sisters to come live with us. We had a little room in the back, and two good girls lived there for a year, but neither entered the convent."[23]

Two younger Sisters who had taken advantage of opportunities arranged through the SFM were put in charge of formation. Sister Joan Michele Rake, in 1959 received an MA from St. Mary's College of Notre Dame Indiana, the first college in the country to offer a graduate program in theology for women. She specialized in vocation work and spirituality and felt well prepared in the areas of dogmatic and moral theology as well as Scripture when she was appointed mistress of novices.[24] Sister Denise Billeaud, who received the same degree in 1962, became mistress of postulants. She recalled the excitement of the second Vatican Council. "The postulants and I read, watched what was happening, and talked about the documents as they appeared. We took Hans Küng's *The Council, Reform and Reunion*, outlined it, and tore it apart."[25] Rigid boundaries separating the sacred from the secular were questioned. Sister Barbara Fry recalled that hers was the first group allowed to listen to popular records of Peter, Paul and Mary, Al Hirt, and the Tijuana Brass in the postulate.[26]

Instructions on the vows of poverty, chastity, and obedience changed after the documents of Vatican Council II pointed out that God's Spirit permeated the world and "secular" was not to be equated with "bad." The vows began to be seen less in terms of what to avoid and more in terms of what to initiate. The "Commentary" that accompanied the interim Constitutions described the vow of chastity as a response to the love of Christ, a "free choice of celibacy" signifying "a love without reservations; it stimulates to a charity which is open to all."[27] Holiness depended on properly building relationships, rather than on fleeing them. The "Commentary" averred that Father Moye, the founder, associated poverty

> with dependence on God, on sharing things rather than with possessing nothing. For, to be poor in the Gospel sense is to be personally dispossessed for the sake of showing that generosity which foreshadows the sharing by all in the Kingdom of Heaven. . . . Zeal for a proportionate distribution of wealth to all people shows that one has a proper view of the value of material goods.[28]

---

[23] Sister Tiolinda Marotta, oral interview,13 June 2000, CDPA.

[24] Oral interview, 23 June 2000, CDPA.

[25] Oral interview, 5 July 2000, CDPA. The book was translated into English by Cecily Hastings in 1962 (New York, Sheed and Ward).

[26] Oral interview, 27 Oct. 2000, CDPA.

[27] "Constitutions, Norms and Commentary," 1967-1968, pp. 35-36. This section is quoting from Pope Paul VI's "Sacerdotales Caelibatus," 12:291-319.

[28] "Commentary," p. 39.

Thus the vow of poverty came to be seen primarily as "communal sharing." The vow of obedience began to be explained in terms of listening and dialogue. "The freedom God gives to each sister is restricted only when necessary for attaining a corporately chosen goal." The Sisters were to be "alert to contemporary movements and together continually ask themselves what the spirit of God is suggesting for a solution."[29]

Theologians began to write more on the vows, and Sisters reflected on their own experiences. As renewal accelerated, the vows were interpreted in various ways from diverse angles. Poverty was sometimes tied to liberation of the economically oppressed and the role of religious as witnesses to "gift economics," a sense that ownership is rather arbitrary since all is gift. Discoveries in astronomy made possible by more powerful telescopes led to situating the vowed life in the cosmos by emphasizing human responsibility for ongoing creation. Scriptural studies also led to more profound reflection on communities described in the New Testament and how they could be emulated.

Sister Joan Michele Rake stated that she

> did not believe these young women should just be memorizing the catechism of vows and the Holy Rule. I had them organize seminars, work in the library, and do outside reading. I taught the novitiate in units, and we wrote plays in the style of melodramas, pageants for Advent, and a shadow show relating the plight of the Negroes in the U.S. with the plight of the Israelites in bondage.[30]

Considering it a privilege to be among the 100 out of 400 Congregations of women religious in the U.S. that had their own college in which to educate their Sisters,[31] Mother Amata sent Sisters Mary Clare Metz, Marietta Fischer, and Irma Jean Van Gossen to courses offered by the SFC at Marquette University on the role of a college faculty in Sister Formation.

---

[29] "Commentary," pp. 42 and 45. Sister Margaret Ann Verzwyvelt noted "we have really learned to be a listening Congregation, not just intellectually but also compassionately. We listen with our heart as well as with our heads" (oral interview, 20 July 2000, CDPA).

[30] Oral interview, 23 June 2000, CDPA. Sister Patricia Regan, the only novice at the start of the new millennium, said "each day is different. I have class with the novice director three times a week. We listen to tapes, and I meet with different groups of Sisters to discuss topics such as prayer. Tuesday I go to various sites for off-campus ministry, and Friday is integration day. There is a great deal of reading, and I am also taking a class at Oblate School of Theology once a week. During the second year, I expect to spend time working with various Sisters in their places of ministry" (oral interview, 12 Nov. 2000, CDPA).

[31] Mother Amata Regan, Circular Letter, 11 Feb. 1956, CDPA.

Some of the Sisters assigned to formation work were given little time to prepare. Sister Marie Cecile (Cassiana) Dumesnil, who had been teaching Spanish at OLL High School, listened to tapes on formation before she became the mistress of MCDP novices. She and Sister Marian Frances Margo, who replaced Sister Theodore Mary Von Elm as mistress of MCDP aspirants and postulants in 1954, did however attend a workshop on formation given in Winona, Minnesota, by Father Elio Gambari, SMM, staff member of the Vatican Congregation for Religious.[32] Sister Huberta Gallatin had been in charge of the annual professed Sisters while she was principal and teacher in several elementary schools. From 1958 to 1962 she came to the Motherhouse as the first full-time mistress of the juniorate, a program of college courses and continued formation for newly professed Sisters. She was "completely miserable," largely because the Sisters who lived at the Motherhouse and the College criticized her formation methods.[33] These older Sisters were themselves undergoing great adjustments, which were made more difficult when they considered the novices to be "too free."

Sister Catherine Fuhrmann was appointed mistress of CDP Novices in 1963 and considered it her "hardest mission. I wasn't accustomed to working with the older girls because I was used to the elementary grades. I didn't feel that I was prepared for that task at all. Mother Amata assured me that I was, so we went forth." She remembered that "the novices were very vocal about what they wanted and they didn't want. Many times they did not understand a rule and wanted to know why we had it. Sometimes it was difficult to explain it to them. In my formation we did not question the rules, but for them rules were no longer 'the Gospel truth.'"[34] She also observed that the women in formation found it very difficult to be away from people and saw no value in enclosure or cloister. Sister Imelda González corroborated that observation:

> Some rules just didn't make sense. I had gone to school on this campus since kindergarten. All of a sudden I went to classes with students I knew but was reprimanded for having conversations with them. If there hadn't been some evidence of change, the Sisters who were chomping at the bit would have left because of the restrictions and inhumanness.[35]

---

[32] *CDP Times*, 12, 6 (Feb., 1992): 12-13, CDPA.

[33] Sister Huberta Gallatin, interview with Sister Angelina Murphy, 17 Nov. 1982, CDPA.

[34] Oral interview, 14 June 2000, CDPA. Sister Anna Marie Vrazel recalled, "When we were preparing for final vows in 1967, the novices wanted guitars, and we wanted the Sisters' choir. We went to the Sister in charge in tears, saying we didn't want those novices ruining everything. We had the Sisters' choir, and I think most of them eventually left" (oral interview, 15 Feb. 2000, CDPA).

[35] Oral interview, 15 June 2000, CDPA.

In 1964 Sister Dorothy Hunter was put in charge of the juniors. Although she had more experience with young Sisters, she admitted that

> the Sisters became progressively harder to handle. They were victims of rebellion against authority much as secular students were. It was difficult to teach and give instructions. They were anti-authoritarian and revolted against institutionalism. The Rule was being changed, and there was much insecurity. They asked such difficult questions and made so many demands, it was hard to deal with them. I think they resented missing what was going on in the world, and their anger was put onto me.[36]

Enthusiastic, well-informed young women who also wanted to be involved in world-saving presented more challenges for the Sisters in charge of their formation. Sister María Carolina Flores recalled "We tried to do some things at 100 miles an hour, and the people in charge wanted to do them at about 15 miles an hour. Then when they were gung-ho, we had already been there; and we said, 'So what?' 'Who cares?'"[37]

Sister Anita Brenek recalled that even though her parents' deep faith influenced her, some of her friends were anti-institution and anti-Church. "Religious life looked like a way that I could live what I believed without being different. I saw it somewhat as an escape from the directions in which I saw many of my friends going. But when I entered, I was surprised to find an anti-structure and anti-Church attitude in some of the girls here."[38]

Pope John XXIII proposed for the whole Church the plea for updating or *aggiornamento* of religious life that had been voiced by Pope Pius XII. Sister Ann Petrus, a novice in 1962, recalled

> I remember the readings at meals. We would hear all about the Council and what was happening. It was really, incredibly exciting. It was a wonderful breath of fresh air. We were hearing about all the liturgical changes that were going to happen, the view of the Church as the People of God, and the ecumenical spirit. The Council brought us out of the ghetto and gave us a more global consciousness.[39]

---

[36] Oral interview with Sister Angelina Murphy, 1982. General Council minutes, 9 Jan. 1968, CDPA, noted "a destructive element of criticism which appears prevalent among the annual professed at this time."

[37] Oral interview, 25 May 2000, CDPA.

[38] Oral interview, 4 Aug. 2000, CDPA.

[39] Oral interview, 30 June 2000, CDPA. It is noteworthy that even before Vatican Council II Sister Tharsilla Fuchs and Sister Providencia Srader of OLLC attended six or seven regional and national liturgical conferences (Sister Tharsilla Fuchs,

Sister Jackie Kingsbury, a member of the same novitiate, liked the sense of a powerful spiritual energy that accompanied "gathering in the back of the room and having all those 'save the world' conversations."[40]

Being able to adhere to schedules, instructions, and duties was no longer considered the major indicator of fitness for religious life. Qualities such as willingness to grow spiritually, leadership potential, initiative, and ability to relate with warmth were more highly valued. Psychological considerations carried more weight, and individual talents and tastes were respected. With a decreasing number of young women entering, the formation program was moved from the motherhouse in San Antonio to Castroville and placed under the direction of a team of three Sisters.[41] They emphasized psychological health and invited psychologists like Dr. Robert Cortner and Rev. Quentin Hakenewerth, SM, to give workshops for the annual professed during the Christmas holidays. Sister Suzanne Dancer recalled:

> Our days of formation were tumultuous. This was, after all, the 1970s—Vietnam War protests, drugs, defiance, excessive cultural unrest—and you can be sure these forces exerted their energies in our houses of formation. I don't look fondly on my days in formation not because I thought the program was poor or lacking but because there was no peace to be had anywhere in American culture in the '70s. *Everything* was being tried, protested against, and redefined.[42]

Influenced by George Aschenbrenner, SJ, in 1978 the formators extended the novitiate to two years because "one year just wasn't enough time to do the things we felt were really important."[43] A Mission Statement for Moye Formation Center was formulated in 1979.[44] Increasingly, older women entered.[45] Sister Roberta Haby explained: "I was a single woman. I had built a house and was doing a lot of work with the Church like religious education or CCD. I had a Master's degree in Education, but I was still looking for something in my life. I was not content. Something seemed to be missing." She came into contact with young Sisters at

---

videotaped interview).

[40] Oral interview, 20 June 2000, CDPA.

[41] Sisters Charlene Wedelich, Patrice Sullivan, and Bernadine Leonards. Sisters Anne Michele Berry, Dianne Heinrich, Nicole Bunnell, and Ann Petrus later served on this team.

[42] Written interview, 15 Nov. 2003, CDPA.

[43] Sister Dianne Heinrich, oral interview, 20 June 2000., CDPA.

[44] GC minutes, 6 June 1979, CDPA.

[45] A 40-year-old woman, for example, asked to enter in 1967 (GC minutes, 4 Sept. 1967, CDPA).

Moye Formation Center and was impressed with "their liveliness and concern for each other and their dedication. Their community impressed me."[46] Sister Diane Langford, who left the Congregation in 1969 but re-entered in 1976 remembered that during her first novitiate "There was no Constitution to study; everything was in change; support from the administration seemed to be absent. Every month one of the novices left, so emotionally it was very hard on everybody." Her second novitiate was a "very creative time" and "like a treasure chest."[47]

Sister Sharon Rohde, the first accepted candidate who had been married and had children and grandchildren, entered in 1990. She said, "My experience had been of parent-child relationships. I had to learn community as an adult to an adult."[48] The initiation of professional women who had headed households or lived alone included having to divest themselves of their homes and cars and sometimes having to overcome habits of smoking or drinking.

Sister Ramona Bezner, who was on the formation team from 1983 to 1988, indicated one reason why there were few entrants.

> We women in the Church looked very seriously at our rules, at our whole Congregation, and changed, anticipating all kinds of wonderful things. And wonderful things have happened, but what we didn't anticipate was that it would take away so many of our Congregational members and no new ones would come. We thought, "How wonderful it's going to be for these young women to come to these congregations. They are going to have all these opportunities!" But they saw opportunities outside the congregations.[49]

Sister Anita Brenek felt that in the early 1990s men and women again began to show interest in religious life. "My personal perception is that our whole Church needed to comprehend the role of the laity better. It took about 20 years to work out what this would look like. Now we religious can return to a leadership role not necessarily as the workforce but possibly as prophetic leaders."[50]

Sister Elise Bengfort, who was on the formation team from 1987 to 1993, felt that she received good preparation at the Institute of Religious Formation in St. Louis, Missouri, as well as peer encouragement.

---

[46] Oral interview, 26 July 2000, CDPA.

[47] Oral interview, 4 Nov. 2000, CDPA.

[48] Oral interview, 20 June 2000, CDPA.

[49] Oral interview, 4 Nov. 2000, CDPA. Sister Marlene Rose Quesenberry pointed out "families were smaller. Times were changing. Some people thought they were missing out on life and missing out on things. In my family, we were only two daughters, so 50% went into the convent" (oral interview, 21 June 2000, CDPA).

[50] Oral interview, 4 Aug. 2000, CDPA.

One of the enriching things in formation work, other than self-knowledge, materials that we read, and discussions that we had, was the very active inter-community pre-novitiate and novitiate program in San Antonio. All the directors in town met periodically to plan our days together. We gathered to pray, discuss, or just have fun. That was a very good supportive experience.[51]

As communication with formation personnel of other Congregations improved, they shared the experience of trying to form women who were often from non-traditional families, more outspoken, and less instructed in the Catholic faith. Some recruits were incest survivors; others battled anorexia or other disorders. In 1993 formation was revamped again. The director no longer lived in the formation house, but the women being formed came to her office for conferences. The Sisters in formation lived in a "regular community" which operated collegially without a named superior and met regularly with men and women in formation in nearby Congregations. Sister Karen Kudlac, however, said she "didn't remember anything in particular that we did that stood out. I didn't develop any relationships with any of those people."[52]

At all levels of their formation, the women had much more contact with their families, fellow-students or parishioners, and Sisters of the Congregation who before the 1960s had been discouraged from communicating with them. While the formation team gave retreats for women of the parish in Castroville, for example, the novices would baby-sit their children.[53] Women in formation went out of the residence to teach catechism or visit the sick. Since they had little experience of the daily life and work of women religious, periods of time to stay with the Sisters at various locations along with immersion experiences in Mexico and clinical CPE in a San Antonio hospital were built into their formation program.

Elaborate investiture ceremonies in the large conventual chapel every June 21st ceased in the later 1960s. Gone was the pageantry of young women with curled hair filing into the chapel sanctuary dressed as brides, retiring to a nearby room with the bundled habit received at the altar, and returning shortly in a long, flowing habit with a white veil over their newly cropped hair to receive their new names. In keeping with the teaching of Vatican II that religious life was not a clerical state and its members were to be as leaven in the world rather than set apart, investiture became private. On 24 July 1969, for example, six postulants received their white veils in a private ceremony at 6:30 a.m. Later in

[51] Oral interview, 27 Sept. 2000, CDPA.

[52] Oral interview, 14 June 2000, CDPA.

[53] Sister Charlene Wedelich, oral interview, 9 May 2000, CDPA.

the day, however, they did celebrate with their families and the community at a "song-filled" late morning Mass in the Main Chapel.[54] Sisters also began to pronounce their final vows in their home parishes.

No CDP record, written or oral, of the last half-century states that the Congregation had sufficient vocations and did not need more Sisters. There was always more work than there were hands to do it. Sister Margaret Rose Warburton identified prospective candidates among the college students in the 1940s and invited them to join the "Glorious Glees." Sister Reparata Glenn started the SSS (Secret Society of Sisters) at Providence High School for girls interested in becoming Sisters. Individual Sisters used various ways to encourage young women to enter the convent, but the main motivator was example. Sister Marcella Marie Frazier's only contact with CDPs, for example, was in religious vacation school in Jourdanton near her hometown of Goliad, Texas.[55] Their conduct and obvious satisfaction with their way of life drew her to imitate them. A movie called "Those Convent Walls," featuring Betty Lou Bezner as a new entrant, was circulated in the early 1950s in an effort to provide information about steps in becoming a CDP.[56] The General Chapter of 1961 decided the Sisters could make more frequent visits to their families as a vocations recruitment strategy. Brochures were published from time to time, and Sisters often gave vocation talks or provided exhibits on various occasions.

Former Sister Jane Shafer was appointed Vocation Director of the Congregation in 1978 and received a purpose statement on vocation direction and recruiting from the General Council to guide her in this re-established position.[57] She was followed by other directors and teams until at the beginning of the twenty-first century the General Council assigned four Sisters to full-time vocation/formation work.

Transfers from other Congregations were a source of new members also utilized for the past thirty years. Five MCDPs became CDPs: Sisters Marian Angela Aguilar, Sarah Ann Morales, Helen Louise Rivas, Ann Regina Ross, and Mary Paul Valdez. Four Sisters from other Congregations, one a Sister Mary Nguyen from Vietnam, asked to transfer, completed a trial period, and then decided against the move. Three CDPs also left for discernment periods with other Congregations. Two of them returned and the third Sister returned but later departed.

---

[54] "CDP Newsletter," Nov. 1, 1969: 3, CDPA. Other long-standing customs that ceased at this time were the June 22 Mass during which Sisters made first vows or final vows and the renewal of annual vows after Vespers on the previous four days.

[55] Oral interview, 20 Feb. 2000, CDPA.

[56] FC, Nov. 1951: 24, CDPA. Similarly, in 2002 the CDPs in Mexico produced a video following a young woman's process of discerning her religious vocation.

[57] GC minutes, 7 Feb. 1979, CDPA.

Sister María Carolina Flores asked, "Why after all these years that we taught in Oklahoma and Louisiana don't we have African American Sisters or Native American Sisters? And why are there so few Mexican Americans in the Congregation?" She answered her own question. "We have been pretty blind to how we stereotype."[58] Several Mexican American CDPs cited instances when other Sisters automatically concluded they were either laywomen or MCDPs because they were brown-skinned.

Sister Ann Petrus mused:

> We are perhaps closer to each other because we are a smaller number; I think we have more common ground. But we also really have to be careful not to think things have to be the way they are because we are comfortable with one another. If and when God chooses to send us new folks, we're going to have to really challenge ourselves to be very open to them.[59]

While the SFC boosted the education of new recruits, it also urged attention to the continued educational and spiritual needs of older Sisters. At the First National Congress of the Religious of the U.S. in 1952, Archbishop Arcadio Larraona, secretary of the Sacred Congregation of Religious in Rome, recommended "the deepening and strengthening of the religious life throughout the world as an effective antidote against the widespread evils and dangers of these troubled times."[60] Mother Amata Regan avidly implemented the call for renewal. Summer programs of spiritual renewal were offered for the Sisters preparing for silver jubilee as well as for perpetually professed Sisters. Month-long renovation programs were made available at Marycrest, a private residence on over 100 acres of land in the hills north of San Antonio purchased in 1954 to serve as a place of rest for the Sisters. Another popular spot for vacations and recreation weekends was Camp Cayoca outside of Castroville with its large outdoor pool and rustic cabin with a fireplace.

Mother Amata's successors continued the renewal efforts by sending Sisters to workshops and bringing speakers to the OLL campus.[61] In the 1970s renewal programs for CDPs that lasted a full year were offered at Moye Center, and a renewal team of three full-time Sisters traveled to all Congregational houses to promote

---

[58] Oral interview, 25 May 2000, CDPA. Monsignor Balthasar Janacek, long-time friend, confessor, and chaplain, noted that some Sisters could not understand or accept cultural differences easily (oral interview, 18 Sept. 2001, CDPA).

[59] Oral interview, 30 June 2000, CDPA.

[60] Larraona speech at Notre Dame University, August, 1952.

[61] In 1969, for example, four Sisters attended workshops at Notre Dame University on "The Nun in the World of the 70s" and "Continuing Renewal Through Personal Responsibility."

spiritual development. For five summers in the 1980s courses in contemporary liberation and process theology were offered to all religious in the local area. The themes of these courses were: The Human Search for Security, Injustice as the Cause of Poverty, Creativity in Poverty, Liberation from Poverty, and Celebrating Poverty Sacramentally. By the late 1980s, workshops often took a practical turn with topics such as how to apply for jobs; how to cope with mid-life issues; how to prepare for retirement; or how to deal with stress, anger, or addictions. By the 1990s many Sisters who had MA degrees had gone from teaching to other works, so they no longer enrolled in summer courses at OLLU; but the Congregation continued to engage noted speakers for lectures and workshops, which continued to be open to all local religious women and men.

New approaches to initial formation were tried because fewer women were applying for entrance and those who came were not reluctant to question traditional methods and practices. Continuing formation was also extended beyond taking academic courses to studying new theologies and spiritualities, usually from lecturers and workshops, as the Sisters increasingly took on new ministries. This led to new forms of prayer and to discarding some customs either because they no longer seemed helpful or meaningful or because the post-Vatican II church did not encourage them.

Prayer Life and Customs

> We used to pick yellow sunflowers and make chalices and other designs for the annual Corpus Christi procession.[62] Altars were placed in front of the Convent, Main Building, and Moye Hall. We put our designs on the road in front of the altars. The procession went from one altar to the other, and at each station the priest blessed us with the monstrance that he carried. During the procession we sang and prayed as we walked along.[63]

The procession began in majestic Sacred Heart Conventual Chapel in the late afternoon as the stained glass windows above the sanctuary were brilliantly

---

[62] "Mounds of sand would be placed in a pattern on the pavement in front of the door, and then sunflowers and daisies would be placed in the wet sand to make the decoration. It was a work of art!" (Sister Joanne Eustice, oral interview, 20 June 2000, CDPA).

[63] Sister Ermelinda Cannady, oral interview, 9 Dec.1999, CDPA. Marjorie Tuttle Basila who attended a CDP grade school and later served as the nurse at OLLU for 20 years had vivid memories of watching rows of Sisters in flowing habits and listening to the clink of their rosary beads at each step as they prayed the rosary and sang hymns during the procession (oral interview, 12 May 2001, CDPA).

illumined by the sun, their deep blues, reds, and purples contributing to the festive yet reverent atmosphere. The priest in his white richly embroidered cope carried the golden monstrance while thurifiers sent up a continual cloud of aromatic incense. The local Catholic paper published photographs of the event attended by more than 1,000 Sisters of different Congregations and a large number of laity.[64]

Solemn ceremonies like these were the only experience many people had of the prayer life of Sisters, which was largely invisible to lay people. For example, lay people were invited to Midnight Mass in the Conventual chapel for the first time in 1950, and the Sisters paid $155 to have the ceremony broadcast by Col. Joseph B. McShane on radio station KTSA.[65] Helen Hillbig Pickard, who was in the aspirancy for a few months in 1954, relished some additional Congregational practices to which she was exposed.

> I loved the singing of Compline (Night Prayer) and the Gregorian hymns. So often I have missed the singing of the beautiful choir, which really completed the Mass and made us feel like we were almost in heaven. I also missed the peace of just walking on the beautiful grounds with the grotto and the Stations of the Cross and the all-night adoration of the Blessed Sacrament. I was too young to realize the gift.[66]

Because of the shrinking number of Sisters and their increasing age, 24-hour adoration in St. Joseph Hall Chapel was reduced to 10 or 12 hours a day by decision of the 1961 General Chapter.

Even aspirants, however, might not have been aware that each Sister spent about three hours a day in communal prayer. Daily the Sisters attended Mass and prayed aloud the Mass responses, Office, Rosary, morning prayers which included a litany, and night prayers. They meditated in silence for half an hour each morning, generally using a passage read the night before for their reflection; they usually made an examen of conscience at noon.

In addition to reciting prayers together, the Sisters spent a half hour each day together in the community room listening while one Sister read from a spiritual book and the rest mended or folded clothes, sorted papers, or performed other tasks that would not distract them from the reading. This reading, often preceded by announcements or admonitions, was also a means of ongoing formation. The

---

[64] *The Southern Messenger*, July 1, 1943, p. 4.

[65] FC, Feb., 1951: 69, CDPA. The Midnight Mass in this chapel continued until 2001, when it was discontinued largely because there were not enough Sisters for a choir.

[66] Written communication, June 2002, CDPA.

superiors general utilized this forum in the summertime when each weekday evening all the Sisters sang in parts the ethereal "*Ave Maris Stella*" as they gathered in the large auditorium under the chapel after their recreation period. Seating was not according to rank, and the younger Sisters who had spent their recreation in some activity that encouraged perspiration often tried to find a place under a ceiling fan. Personal as well as corporate views and concerns communicated by their leader to the members promoted a sense of knowing what was expected of them as well as where the Congregation was heading.

The choice of texts as well as times for meditation and spiritual reading began to be left up to each Sister in 1955, and soon the number of recited prayers was reduced. Sister Lora Ann Quiñonez would tease Mother Amata,

> You are really the one that caused us to slide down the downward path! The minute each of us began to choose our own spiritual reading, a huge ideological diversity crept in.
>
> It was exhilarating to think we were going to be able to think differently, and we did after reading Hans Küng, Harvey Cox, and Cardinal Suenens. It was mind-boggling to listen to articles from *America* or *Commonweal* instead of the *Imitation of Christ* during breakfast.[67]

Sister Anne Michele Berry remembered reading about Dorothy Day and César Chávez, for "the focus of the Church in those days was the call to be and work with people that were oppressed."[68] Sister Jane Ann Slater recalled a significant incident concerning reading material considered too *avant-garde*:

> A communication from the Benedictine Brothers headed by George Gannon made the rounds like wildfire because we were just itching for new ideas. Mother Amata recalled this paper, and we were supposed to turn in all copies of it. I wanted to keep mine, so I asked my superior at the college, Sister Providentia Srader, to read it. She said she didn't see anything wrong with it. So three of us got an appointment with Mother Amata and told her, "We are adults, and we have final vows. We are old enough to decide for ourselves and form our own judgment."[69]

Mother Amata received them graciously, agreed with their reasoning, and revoked the prohibition.

---

[67] Sister Lora Ann Quiñonez, oral interview, 13 June 2000, CDPA

[68] Oral interview, 20 June 2000, CDPA.

[69] Oral interview, 25 May 2000, CDPA.

Sister Regina Decker recalled "going through a time when no one told you when to pray. Community prayer was there, but it wasn't the same thing as when we all marched over to the big chapel for morning prayer or Vespers."[70] Sister Casilda Hyzak enjoyed the introduction of greater freedom in prayer styles. "I felt like I could not pray if I did not use the words from a prayer book. After Vatican Council II it didn't bother me just to pray from my heart. I felt God heard my prayers both ways, whether I used a book or didn't use a book. Now I go to pray because I want to pray. I don't just follow a routine."[71] Sister Beatrice Ann (David Anton) Kainer was influenced by Sister José Hobday, a Native American, who gave a talk in Houston. "Hers was a simplified prayer, and I liked that. She said she got up early, got her early cup of coffee, and climbed back into bed. She just sat there with God and her cup of coffee and enjoyed it. I thought I could do that."[72] Sister Frances McMann said, "I'm always praying, especially when I drive the car, because I feel that I am under my Guardian Angel's protection. I don't have to be in any particular place to pray; I can pray everywhere."[73]

Sisters learned to adhere to their chosen personal prayer schedule because experience taught them that one's successful influence on the lives of others was impossible without frequent intimate prayer time with God. "Shared prayer," articulating one's own insights or petitions, was difficult for many Sisters who had never been encouraged or given the opportunity to voice to a group what was deep in their hearts. Sister Evangelista Karlik remembered,

> we began to discuss the readings of the Sunday Mass together on Saturdays, and Sister Rafaela Hruzek was one who impressed me. She tried so hard to get the meaning of the Epistle and Gospel and then talk about it in her own way. I really admired her. Another Sister was not that cooperative. She just didn't think it was right for us to be discussing this, but she went there, and she sat in silence during the discussions.[74]

In 1969 the practice of "prayer partners" was introduced. Sisters in the retirement center were "adopted" by Sisters still on the mission who promised to pray for them. This partnership grew to the partners' sharing in each other's prayer intentions.

---

[70] Oral interview, 8 Nov. 20, CDPA.

[71] Oral interview, 18 Mar. 2000, CDPA.

[72] Oral interview, 4 Mar. 2000, CDPA.

[73] Oral interview, 20 June 2000, CDPA.

[74] Oral interview, 16 Feb. 2000, CDPA.

Liturgical renewal was aided by the use of missals with English translations of the Latin prayers of the Mass and the revival of interest in Gregorian chant at mid-century. Before the second Vatican Council, especially in Oklahoma, dialogue Masses with parts recited in English encouraged participation in the Eucharist. By 1970 the majority of Sisters on the missions were appointed extraordinary ministers of Holy Communion.

The Eucharist, meant to be a source and sign of unity among its participants, sometimes became a source of division in the 1980s. Some Sisters were uncomfortable with the use of bread other than round white hosts or with the celebration of Eucharist in homes rather than in church buildings. Others were concerned that folk music with guitars and other instruments would completely replace Gregorian chant and the stately organ.

The Divine Office of Psalms and Scripture readings was intended to be a means of uniting at regular intervals with the prayer of the whole church. In January 1956 the Sisters started to chant the Little Office in English on a lower tone and also began to recite all community prayers in English instead of Latin.[75] Some rubrics were changed in 1961, and in 1965 the Congregation took advantage of permission from the Vatican for members of active religious orders to change to the Roman Breviary in English.[76] Gradually the pattern became to recite the office together in the morning and late afternoon in large communities while in smaller houses the Sisters came together either in the morning or in the evening and often prayed the office silently alone.

Work and prayer were combined in a creative way at St. Henry's School in San Antonio in the mid-1950s. The superior, Sister Huberta Gallatin, decided the school needed painting, but there were no funds for it. The Sisters in the community got paint donated and then stuccoed and painted all the walls in the afternoons after classes were dismissed while Sister Huberta did 30 minutes of spiritual reading, followed by the Office. "We painted the whole school *and* the convent without missing our spiritual exercises."[77]

Sister Lourdes Leal, who experienced communal prayer both north and south of the U.S. border, observed differences due to culture:

> In Mexico we do much shared prayer, but in the U.S., there is no way we're going to adopt anything that's the same. We would have to have a committee, and they wouldn't even agree. I don't think that's bad. It's just where we are. Living religious life is not just the prayer

[75] GC minutes, 3 Dec. 1956, CDPA. It is noteworthy that although the Congregation came from Alsace-Lorraine, it immediately began to receive U.S. novices, so English quickly became the common language.

[76] "News Flashes," 1961: 20, CDPA.

[77] Sister Cecile Clare Vanderlick, oral interview, 21 July 2000, CDPA.

life; it's the choices we make—just like in any other lifestyle. So we have to keep questioning and looking at our life.[78]

The traditional format of monthly retreat Sunday, which always included a preparation for death by private reflection on a series of questions read aloud by the superior, became more flexible. The General Chapter of 1961 allowed a group to experiment with a new method of conducting the monthly Chapter of Faults during which each Sister accused herself of infractions of the Constitutions, but soon afterwards this custom was dropped entirely.

One or more weeklong preached retreats were always offered at the Motherhouse so each Sister could have this annual experience, but their format now began to vary. Some retreats were scheduled for targeted groups—for example, those professed 11-16 years[79]—or on special topics.[80] A Jesuit gave the first directed retreat at the Motherhouse in 1973, and retreats of this type have been offered ever since that time.[81] Sisters were also allowed to make retreats not sponsored by the Congregation. A few years later Sister Frances Lorene Lange and Rev. Bill Morell, OMI, prepared a booklet of retreat opportunities available for all religious in the area.

In addition to prayer life, long-standing customs of the Congregation also changed in the latter half of the twentieth century. Commenting on the Quinquennial report of 1951-1956, the Sacred Congregation for Religious recommended that CDP Superiors "remind their charges of the illicitness of clandestine correspondence and punish them severely according to the gravity of the fault involved."[82] Nevertheless, the General Chapter of 1961 decided that superiors were no longer to read the correspondence between professed Sisters and their families. At least five years earlier, however, some superiors had already decided to ignore this custom. Sister Margaret Ann Verzwyvelt remembered Mother Mercedes Kennedy told her: "'You write to your parents every chance you get.' I don't think she ever read a letter addressed to a Sister either."[83]

---

[78] Oral interview, 8 Aug. 2000, CDPA. Sister Margit Nagy said that some customs and communal prayer affirmed "the fact that we aren't just individuals doing ministry. We belong to a Congregation." (Oral interview, 17 Nov. 2000, CDPA).

[79] Mother Amata Regan, Circular Letter, 30 Nov. 1962, CDPA.

[80] Rev. Charles Schleck, CSC, for example, gave a retreat on "Woman's Role as an Image of the Trinity" (Mother Amata Regan, Circular Letter, 30 Aug. 1961, CDPA).

[81] Sister Esther Habermann recalled hearing Mother Amata announce to all the Sisters in the 1960s that there would now be a variety of retreats. She asked herself, "I wonder who would make that decision?" Within a few decades, it was understood that each Sister made that decision for herself (oral interview, 28 Nov. 2003, CDPA).

[82] GC minutes, 20 July 1958, CDPA.

[83] Oral interview, 20 July 2000, CDPA.

Other examples of interpreting law loosely were recalled by Sister Alma Rose Booty:

> You were supposed to have the Superior General's permission to travel over 50 miles, but that did not bother my first superior, Sister Narcissa Saha. She let me go see my aunt who lived 51 miles away, and in return my uncle would bring her cottonseed hulls for her flowerbeds. Sister let me go to their house for dinner.
>
> One summer she got into trouble with the Superior General because she did not have private conferences every retreat Sunday with about 10 of us annual professed. Evidently someone reported her, and after that she followed the letter of the law. We would all stand in line and go in just to chat, and then she would let us go.[84]

In 1957 with Rome's permission the Sisters who previously maintained silence during meals were allowed "to talk at the evening meal after a short reading of the life of a saint for the following day."[85] The customary half-hour of communal recreation after supper continued, but warnings were issued about not giving the entire time "to the use of the radio and television sets."[86] Mother Amata and her Council studied the television programs viewed in the houses of the Congregation, suggested guidelines, and listed seven types of program considered acceptable. The five types considered undesirable were: Detective and Mystery, Western Shows, Stunts and Varieties, Comedies, and Quiz Shows.[87] Radios were still considered "superfluities" in 1961, and no Sister was to have one in her possession "except for a very special reason, and that with special permission."[88] With the increased freedom came some abuses, which the Superior General periodically addressed. For example, the Sisters were to limit their use of cars and were to wear the habit at all times in public. They

---

[84] Sister Alma Rose Booty, oral interview, 5 Mar. 2003, CDPA.

[85] Mother Amata Regan, Circular Letter, 30 Aug. 1957, CDPA. Normally the Sisters spoke only when necessary except for brief chats during the after-school afternoon snack and conversation during the daily recreation period or on Sunday and feast day afternoons.

[86] Mother Angelique Ayres, Circular Letter, 6 Jan. 1953, CDPA. Sister Mary Elizabeth Shafer said "I was a history teacher as well as an English teacher, so I would try to get information by connecting with someone, listening to someone talk about current events, or finding a magazine" (oral interview, 21 Jan. 2000, CDPA).

[87] GC minutes, 20 July 1958, CDPA. Sister Lora Ann Quiñonez thought that Mother Amata became frightened and cautious in the last years of her term, reminding the Sisters of what they should not be doing, because through the conferences of major superiors she learned about congregations where there was polarization and whole groups exiting (Oral interview, 13 June 2000, CDPA).

[88] Mother Amata Regan, Circular Letter, 2 Feb.1961, CDPA.

could vacation with other Sisters but were to lounge in a robe with their head covered and not wear two-piece bathing suits. They were not to go in rowboats or motorboats on picnics but could ride in a large yacht.[89]

Interaction with laypeople was so proscribed that, for example, in 1964 Brother Bernardine, FSC, the principal at Bishop Kelley High School in Tulsa, Oklahoma, had to request permission from the General Council for Sisters teaching at the school to attend PTA meetings and stay for conversation and refreshments, to eat their noon meal in the cafeteria and help supervise the students, to help prefect mixed groups, and to participate in faculty dinners held on the Kelley campus. When she was principal of the girls' section at BKHS, Sister Angelina Murphy obtained additional permission for the Sisters to chaperone a bus trip for the annual sports tournaments and to go out at night to appropriate educational, civic, and athletic events provided they made a separate request for each event and supplied details. She found a way around another custom that was an obstacle. "The Sisters and Brothers were not supposed to eat in one another's homes, yet they recognized the value of an occasional meal together. So they worked out a solution for which they did not have to ask permission: they served those meals in the home economics building."[90]

The Religious Habit

The "holy habit" was solemnly received at the investiture ceremony in the sanctuary of the convent chapel when a Sister entered the novitiate. It was regarded as a sign of her vows and identity as a woman religious, so it was always worn in public as well as inside the convent. Sister Constance Christopher recalled that she was "miserable in that habit. My dad thought it was the most beautiful thing he'd ever seen. But I was hot, sweaty, uncomfortable, and miserable most of the time."[91] Sister Marie Elise Van Dijk found the habit to be heavy, hard to keep clean, and "a lot of unnecessary work to keep nice."[92] Those who later missed the traditional garb revered its symbolism, not its practicality.

In 1953, following directives from Pope Pius XII concerning better professional preparation and adaptation to modern conditions, the habit was

---

[89] Mother Amata Regan, Circular Letter, 16 Sept. 1963 and GC minutes, 22 May 1963, CDPA.

[90] Sister Angelina Murphy, oral communication. The Constitutions forbade the Sisters to take any nourishment outside the refectory without the Superior's permission (#147).

[91] Oral interview, 7 Nov. 2000, CDPA.

[92] Oral interview, 17 Aug. 2002, CDPA.

noticeably modified after consulting the Sisters, a process which was somewhat rare before Vatican Council II. Under Mother Angelique's supervision, Sisters Ancilla Kneupper and Angelina Breaux made a model of the proposed habit which included a shortened coronet and a white Roman collar instead of the guimpe. The model or a photograph of it was presented to all the Sisters for suggestions or approval. After the majority—716 out of the 722 polled—approved the model, a petition for change was sent to the Sacred Congregation for Religious in Rome.[93] The reaction of lay people was mixed. Most were surprised at the change. Sister Mary Ann Phillipp recalled that at St. Anne's Convent in Houston "Sister Margaret (Mechtilde) Gonzalez's students would always meet us and usher us into the classroom. The morning we appeared in our shortened coronet and no guimpe, those children looked at us, ran back into the classroom, and hid in the cloakroom."[94] Sister Rose Corinne Medica observed that "Some doctors were glad because they felt that healthwise it was actually better for some of us."[95]

The headpiece was slightly modified in 1959 after a period of experimentation "because of Rome's concern for drivers."[96] Two years later Sisters in health care and household work were allowed to wear white uniforms, which were cooler and easier to clean than black wool serge.[97] Still, Sister Sarah Kainer recalled, "It was not easy to cook in that white habit, especially when we cut up the sides of meat in the basement or cooked hundreds of steaks outside for the students. If something would splash or grease would splatter, you would have to change the whole thing. And of course it was hot in the kitchen before we had fans."[98] Permission for nurses and technicians to wear wristwatches was received joyfully after the General Chapter of 1961 by most members as another sign that Sisters were in step with the modern world.[99]

After the Chapter of Renewal of 1967-1968 and some controlled experiments, the Sisters were allowed to choose from certain colors and styles in their apparel.[100] Sister Mary Margaret Hughes recalled going to the Hemisfair

---

[93] GC minutes, 21 Jan. and 27 Jan. 1953, CDPA.

[94] Oral interview, 15 Oct. 2000, CDPA.

[95] Oral interview, 16 June 2000, CDPA. Some Sisters developed ear problems from the constant rubbing of the starched coronet.

[96] Mother Amata Regan, Circular Letter, 14 March 1959, and GC minutes, 28 May 1959, CDPA.

[97] Mother Amata Regan, Circular Letter, 30 Oct. 1961, CDPA.

[98] Oral interview, 19 May 2000, CDPA.

[99] The General Chapter of 1967 extended this permission to all the Sisters.

[100] Sister Florentine Mazurkiewicz appreciated the fact "that we were prepared for the change. We had workshops, and communities helped each other. Speakers came in the summer to talk about how to dress, how to sit, how to get in and out of a car. That was important because we were in long habits before" (oral interview, 18 Feb. 2000, CDPA).

exposition in downtown San Antonio in 1968 when she was a General Councilor. "We from the Generalate went wearing our veils, and we met many Sisters from the College and other places without veils, one frowning on the other. That's what was going on in these days, questioning who was looking like a nun and who wasn't."[101] The oldest cohort of the Congregation adapted to this change more readily than the middle-aged Sisters. For example, Sister Joanne Eustice remembered that elderly Sister Erasma Fitzpatrick was stationed with her in El Reno, Oklahoma, when the Sisters there were asked to be one of the communities that experimented with dress. "It was so upsetting to her that she asked to come back to San Antonio. When I arrived there in the summer, here was Sister Erasma, already wearing a blouse and skirt! At first it was too hard for her, but soon she accepted it."[102]

The gold ring engraved with an eye within a triangle received at the time of perpetual profession became the only visible symbol of membership worn by every member of the Congregation. The triangle is a traditional symbol of the Blessed Trinity, and the eye is a symbol of God's Providential care. Many Sisters wore a plain wooden cross recalling the one Father Moye gave the first Sisters "as a sign of simplicity and poverty, and because a wooden cross has more resemblance to the cross of Jesus Christ."[103]

Sister Barbara (Barbara James) Zimmerer "enjoyed very much the change of habit. In Louisiana we'd come home with that starched headpiece just hanging on our shoulders. Or in New Mexico our skirts would be lined with dirt and sand because it was so dusty out there. I don't think the change made any difference as to how people reacted to us."[104] Sister Elsa Mary Bennett thought the change "was the best thing that ever happened because then we were treated as equal to other people. We weren't put up on a pedestal where everybody had to open the door and bow and curtsy."[105] Sister Marie Elise Van Dijk also noticed that "we don't stand out as much when we dress more simply, and it is easier for people to relate to us. We are not such a mystery to them."[106]

Once the Sisters adopted street clothes, a veil seemed inappropriate and was gradually abandoned. Then more attention was given to hair care and to the face. Sister Deborah Ann Fuchs, who made her first vows in 1966, explained her motivation: "Make-up and ear piercing had nothing to do with actual personal appearance. It had to do with expressing my individuality and

---

[101] Oral interview, 18 June 2000, CDPA.

[102] Oral interview, 7 June 2000, CDPA.

[103] *Directory*, 347.

[104] Oral interview, 3 July 2000, CDPA.

[105] Oral interview, 28 July 2000, CDPA.

[106] Oral interview, 17 August, 2000, CDPA.

being the person I wanted to be. Sisters my age were beginning to realize that we needed to develop our individuality and who God put us on this earth to really be."[107]

Although the Congregation as a whole successfully adapted to changes, the process was not without resistances and hesitations. Sister Viola Lecomte, for example, felt that after Vatican II "many of the ideas that were being circulated seemed to be contrary to those few requirements expressed by Rome." She disapproved of what she considered "the whole departure from the essential elements of religious life,"[108] and to her a habit was essential. Her blood sister, Sister Agnes Celine Lecomte, noted that at this time "many were going their own way, and didn't care what the Holy Father said."[109] Most of the Sisters, however, were convinced it was important to change and thought the changes were improvements. They enjoyed greater freedom from the regimentation suggested by uniform clothing as well as from other forms of pressure and tension. Sister Julie (M. Valeria) Budai, who made her first vows in 1946, said :

> I recall being under a lot of stress trying to do everything just exactly the way it was laid down for us. It was very good later to have the flexibility of taking part in activities like cultural events or entertainment and being free to choose our form of recreation. It was also good to be able to speak and not be called on the carpet for speaking out of time or for not keeping silence. Those things were all good in their time, but the new things were even better.[110]

Spiritual Fruits of Vatican Council II

Sister Elizabeth McCullough, who became Superior General in June 1967, recalled:

> The Vatican Council II document, *Perfectae Caritatis*, called for special Chapters and asked members of religious communities to examine every facet of their lives: to check everything against Gospel values, to renew the founding spirit and charism of the community,

---

[107] Oral interview, 23 June 2000, CDPA.

[108] Oral interview, 17 Feb. 2000, CDPA.

[109] Oral interview, 24 Feb. 2000, CDPA. These two Sisters transferred to the Sisters of Charity of Our Lady Mother of the Church in Baltic, Connecticut in September 1982 but returned in May 1983.

[110] Oral interview, 23 June 2000, CDPA.

to examine living the vows in contemporary times, to study ministries and community structures.[111]

The Sisters responded wholeheartedly and enthusiastically, and they examined thoroughly and in detail. Along with other women in U.S. religious congregations, they led the way in reforming religious life.[112] Sister Madonna Sangalli articulated a prevalent opinion. "The spirit that came out of Vatican II was to me the spirit of Jesus—the spirit of love of neighbor, of accepting, of not judging. Information became available to help us understand and be aware. It is not a spirit that is easily squelched."[113]

A tangible product of the call of the second Vatican Council was a new constitution approved by Rome on 12 December 1989.[114] Its sections on community, mission, ministry, and charism—none of which were even chapter headings in the *Constitutions* of 1927—expressed what the Sisters had learned in their 20 years of experimentation and wanted to continue in the future. In 1961 several committees had made tentative revisions of the 1927 document.[115] After the renewal Chapter of 1967-68, a new interim "Constitutions, Norms, and Commentary" that articulated the ideals of Vatican Council II was assembled by a committee and given to each Sister. The writing of a definitive new constitution got underway with preliminary reflections and a workday inviting input from all the Sisters on 14 June 1978. A committee chaired by Sister Ann Petrus scheduled reflection processes and invited speakers such as Sisters Dianne Fassel, SL, and Dianne Bergant, CSA. In 1981 another committee chaired by former Sister Evelyn Thibeaux collected all the input and began the writing process. Taking as central the mission of showing the loving Providence of God to the world, the group worked for four years "doing really good theology," "looking at what God was saying to our community" and "trying to see 'Who are we?'"[116] Jesus' mission was to bring the Good News of God's love to the world, and the Church in the Spirit carries on this mission. The Sisters' mission is to participate in God's act of continuing creation and redemption. "There is only one call.

---

[111] *Movements*, 4, 1 (Fall/Winter, 2000): 13, CDPA.

[112] Rev. Bill Morell, OMI, believed that most changes in the "patriarchal, hierarchical Church which you love began with women religious, who were 10 years ahead of the men" (oral interview, 8 Apr. 2003, CDPA).

[113] Oral interview, 31 Mar. 2000, CDPA. Sister Elizabeth Dale Van Gossen expressed similar views. "Before Vatican Council II it was like we knew everything and everything was said. That's really not the way it is. There's room for new understanding, new growth, and new expectations of what God is for us and what the church should be" (oral interview, 21 July 2000, CDPA).

[114] This was the same date the MCDP Constitution and their separation from the CDP was approved by Rome.

[115] Mother Amata Regan, Circular Letter, 10 April 1961, CDPA.

[116] Sister Theresa Anne Billeaud, group oral interview of Constitution Committee, 17 June 2001, CDPA.

God not being narcissistic does not call us to sit and contemplate in his sight. Our lives are cheap and shallow unless contemplation and action are united. To be attached to God is to understand that God wants to be paying attention to the needs of human beings through us."[117]

Each section of the new Constitution made a statement about the Church, about Jesus' mission, and about CDP experience. Although the Sacred Congregation for Religious and Secular Institutes (SCRIS) advised including norms in the Constitution, the committee decided to place the juridical items into a separate section titled "Norms."[118] Sister James Aloysius, who taught French at OLLU, had become an expert on Father Moye, so having her as a participant made the committee members feel "like Father Moye was sitting at the table with us."[119] Former Sister Evelyn Thibeaux said her work on this committee

> was a life-changing experience. We truly worked together as equals, truly listened to the voice of "the people" (the whole Congregation). The Constitution is a real expression of the life of this community because of the way it was written. After we had a draft, we would take it to the Sisters for numerous discussions until it had the right words to express the spirit of the community. The fact that it has endured shows that it still expresses well what the community is all about.[120]

All the members of the Constitution writing committee agreed that theirs was an outstanding, meaningful renewing experience resulting in true consensus, a group composition, "like another Scripture that we use." The whole Congregation critiqued their work, and in the end the authors were very satisfied with the document and the process because they sensed that "The Spirit wrote it."[121]

The "Historical Perspective of the Congregation" at the beginning of the new Constitution gives credit to Mother St. Andrew Feltin as the "courageous leader of the pioneer group" of Sisters who came to Texas in 1866.[122] Appreciation for her grew during the last decades of the twentieth century, not so much for

---

[117] Sister Lora Ann Quiñonez, videotaped interview, CDPA.

[118] GC minutes, 16 Jan. 1984, CDPA.

[119] Sister Ann Umscheid, group oral interview of the Constitution Committee, 17 June 2001, CDPA. Sister Jane Coles was also a member of this committee.

[120] Oral interview, 15 June 2002, CDPA.

[121] Evelyn Thibeaux, oral interview, 15 June 2002, CDPA. The revisions of the constitution suggested by the Holy See were sent to all the Sisters in 1989 (GC minutes 16-17, 20-22 Mar. 1989, CDPA).

[122] Sister Mary Diane Langford in 2007 published a fictional biography of Mother St. Andrew titled, *The Tattered Heart.*

her initiation of numerous schools as for her "struggle through the dark night of trial" and willing acceptance of the pain that came because of her clash with Bishop John C. Neraz. The conflict began with accusations by diocesan priests that the Superior threw suspicions on their honor and ended with her forced resignation and departure. Beginning in the 1990s, her intercession began to be requested in prayer services composed by the Sisters for various Congregational celebrations.

In response to post-Vatican Council II instructions, the Sisters looked more closely at the life of their founder, Jean Martin Moye (1730-1793), a parish priest in Lorraine, France, and a missionary in China for 10 years. They appreciated even more the fact that his devotion to the Child Jesus was fueled by a passion to educate. His zeal expressed itself in a project to instruct the underprivileged rural children in France as well as non-Christians in Western China. He chose women of strong character who could live alone in tiny villages, distinguished from their neighbors not by their dress but by their virtuous lives. He consecrated the first Sisters to the Child Jesus and recommended a "singular devotion" to him, so one of the litanies recited weekly was in honor of the Holy Child Jesus. Father Moye also practiced great penance and self-denial. He stated: "The spirit that I would like to instill in you above all is that of Jesus Christ with a great devotion to His sorrowful passion."[123] Imitating his austerity tended to be emphasized in initial formation before 1954.

In anticipation of Father Moye's beatification, a statue of the founder was installed in a circle in front of the new Fine Arts building on the OLL campus in 1948.[124] Sister James Aloysius Landry and Sister Mary Generosa Callahan translated *Shepherd of Untended Sheep, John Martin Moye* by Raoul Plus, SJ, from the French into English.[125] An oil painting was commissioned through Mother Anna Marie Elizabeth, Superior General of the Sisters at St. Jean-de-Bassel.[126] The Texas CDPs gave $10,000 as an initial contribution to the beatification and additional funds to prepare the church at his birthplace in Cutting, France, for the event.[127] He was beatified on 21 November 1954, by Pope Pius XII, who had been taught by the Sisters of Providence of Portieux, France, in an elementary school in Rome. Mother Angelique, Mother Antonina Quinn, and Sister Gabriel Ann Tamayo, MCDP, were present.

---

[123] *Directory* 323.

[124] The statue cost $600 (GC minutes, 12 Jan. 1948, CDPA).

[125] Raoul Plus, SJ, *J.-M. Moÿe, Prêtre de la Societé des Missions Etrangères de Paris, Fondateur des Soeurs de la* Providence (Paris: Beauchesne et ses Fils, 1947). The translated biography was published by New Press, Westminster, Maryland, in 1950.

[126] This painting cost $100 (GC minutes, 22 Sept. 1950, CDPA).

[127] GC minutes, 8 June 1953 and 30 Sept. 1954, CDPA.

Another statue of the new Blessed of white Carrara marble was installed on a side altar in the sanctuary of the Motherhouse chapel.[128] In 1959 the Cardinal Protector granted permission to expose for public veneration a second-class relic of Father Moye, and the Sacred Congregation of Rites gave permission for ten years to offer a special Votive Mass in his honor.[129] Details of his life became more easily available in English with the publication in 1964 of *The Life of Blessed John Martin Moye*, written by Sister Generosa Callahan, with much help from Mother Angelique.[130] Sister Generosa also translated Moye's treatise "The Dogma of Grace" into English in 1979.[131] Sister Elaine Gentemann composed a rousing hymn, "Beate Moye," and a Mass in his honor. Sister James Aloysius Landry, who accompanied Sister Generosa in her archival research, began to give talks on Father Moye; and her appreciation and enthusiasm were contagious. In 1978, for example, she spoke to the General Council and the initial formation staffs on Fr. George Tavard's biography of the founder, *Mission et Mystique*.[132] Sister Mary Huber, CDP, of Kentucky, conducted a retreat for all the Sisters focused on the founder in 1993, the 200th anniversary of his death. This anniversary, May 4, began to be observed with a special Mass and renewal of vows.

The Sisters were always aware that they were called to a distinctive practice of four fundamental virtues identified by their founder. He instructed them to be known for their charity, simplicity, poverty, and abandonment to Divine Providence.[133] Implementing a decision of the General Chapter of 1961, a pamphlet titled "Reflections on the Charism and Spirit of the Sisters of Divine Providence" was written, and in 1979 the General Council formulated objectives regarding the four fundamental virtues and an apostolic spirituality rooted in justice.[134] The Development Team published several articles on the virtues between 1978 and 1980 in connection with area retreats. A member of the formation team, Sister Nicole Bunnell, for example, issued a New Year's letter on poverty from the perspective of being accepted in one's limitations by a crucified Lord.[135]

---

[128] This statue ordered through Mother Honorine, Superior General of the Sisters at Portieux, cost $2,934 (GC minutes, 27 Apr. 1953, CDPA).

[129] CDPA, GC minutes, Feb. 27, 1959 and Feb. 24, 1960.

[130] Milwaukee: Bruce Press, 1964.

[131] Printed by Our Lady of the Lake University Press.

[132] GC minutes, 18 Dec. 1978, CDPA.

[133] Former Sister Georgia Ann Fucik said, "Moye's impact on me is an ongoing process. I find that being immersed in a materialistic society since birth, it is very difficult for me to be detached from it. So much remains unconscious and gradually surfaces in time. Our very concept of security is wrapped up in materialism, insurance policies, military might, retirement nest egg, locked doors, etc., so to rely on God's Providence is hard to come by" (written interview, 26 Jan. 2004, CDPA).

[134] GC minutes, 10 Sept. 1979, CDPA.

[135] "CDP In-Formation," 1979, CDPA.

Prayer services composed especially for Congregational feasts appeared as the Sisters gained experience in shared, less structured prayer. On the 125th anniversary of the Congregation's arrival in Texas, artist G.E. Mullan of San Antonio was commissioned to produce a painting of Our Lady of Providence. Sister Mary Daniel Turner, SNDdeN, gave a retreat on the theme of Providence for the whole Congregation in 1996.

After the founder's beatification, there was more communication among the branches of the Congregations rooted in his spirituality. After the celebration of the 200th anniversary of the Sisters of Providence of Portieux, in 1962 the Daughters of Father Moye headquartered in France (St. Jean-de-Bassel, Portieux, and Gap) and Belgium (Champion) as well as the CDPs and MCDPs of Texas began to schedule regular meetings of their general administrations.[136] After the first gathering at St. Jean-de-Bassel in 1975, the sites of the meetings, usually held every ten years, alternated among the Congregations. The Texas CDP General Administrators hosted their counterparts in 1981, 1991, and 2003. In 1981 Rev. George Tavard, AA, spoke on "Understanding Providence in Our Ministry Today"; in 1991 Sister Mary Christine Morkovsky spoke on "Father Moye as Liberator." Three speakers presented at the 2003 meeting, which featured the theme "Redeemed in Providence." Their themes illustrate attempts to relate the Providence charism to current problems and interests: Sister Anita DeLuna, MCDP, "Spirituality of Oppressed Peoples in Relation to Providence"; Rev. Virgilio Elizondo, "The Feminine Side of God'"; and Sister Mary Christine Morkovsky, CDP, "Cosmic Spirituality and Providence."

Daughters of Father Moye stationed in Latin America have scheduled similar "Encuentros" since the 1980s, and the San Antonio CDPs stationed in Mexico hosted one in Mexico City in 1996. All of these reunions fostered closer personal relationships as well as awareness that the Daughters of Father Moye have been in Manchuria, Vietnam, Brazil, Colombia, Mexico, and Madagascar for over 100 years. During ten years as a missionary in Western China, Father Moye out of concern for children also started another group, the Chinese Virgins, Christian women who lived with their families but dedicated themselves to the education of children, prayer, and good works. Two of these women, Agatha Lin and Lucy Y, were canonized in 2000. Ministry in Father Moye's spirit of trust in Providence takes place on every continent except Australia.

---

[136] Relationships between the Texas Congregation and the group in France from which they were separated by the Texas ordinary continued to be cordial, as indicated by a letter of 1959: "The traditional box of Mexican candies came this week and was received, as ever, with much pleasure. . . . [W]e would like to have some Sister CDP of San Antonio with us each year for a little time." (CDPA, Mother A. Marie-Elisabeth, CDP., Superior General, to Mother M. Angelique, Couvent Saint-Jean-de-Bassel, le 16 janvier 1959), CDPA.

With improved communication and easier travel after the end of World War II, ties between the Motherhouse at St. Jean-de-Bassel and the Sisters in Texas were strengthened as U.S. CDPs spent longer or shorter periods there. Sister Generosa, for example lived at this French Motherhouse while researching and writing on Father Moye. Numerous Sisters have taken advantage of pilgrimages to places in Lorraine and Alsace where the founder lived as well as to Trier, Germany, where he died in 1793.

To prepare for the centennial anniversary of the Congregation in Texas in 1966, the Father Moye Guild was organized to create interest in the works of the Congregation, to promote vocations, to generate funds, and to improve public relations.[137] An English translation of the *Directory of Portieux* containing a brief history of the founding of the group in France, advice of the founder, and letters from the founder became available in 1983. This book gave the Sisters access to the founder's patrimony as they continued to return to the sources of their spirituality. Ten years later each Sister received a boxed set of quotations from this directory for her daily reflection. At the beginning of the 21st century, the rest of Father Moye's writings began to be available on line, thanks to the efforts of Rev. Georges Tavard, AA, a distant relative of Moye from his father's side, and Rev. Dominique Poirot, OCD, a distant relative from his mother's side, with the assistance of Rev. Philippe Lécrivain, SJ, historian of missions in China.

As the Sisters were encouraged to express their experience of living the four virtues, their appreciation for the founder and their distinctive Providence charism increased. Sisters "define" Providence differently, as evident in contemporary responses to the question, "What do you understand by Providence?" Some Sisters, especially those who entered before Vatican Council II, tended to see Providence as God revealed in people, while others enlarged the view to include all creatures, events, and circumstances in detail. Knowing this leads to an enduring experience that "all is well." Those who entered later were more inclined to emphasize that it is incumbent on devotees of Providence to be alert and aware in order to detect "more" possible good, which motivates striving. God's Providence was also experienced as a "force" which grants insight as well as a plan to carry out ongoing projects or initiate new ones. One contemporary expression characterized the Provident God as a loving guide who invites persons, creatures, and events into partnership.[138] Sister Madlyn Pape voiced an

---

[137] General Chapter decisions, 1961. In Westphalia, Texas, for example, four families belonging to the Father Moye Guild worked to form a Perpetual Family Enrollment. In four years they collected over $1,000, which the Generalate used to educate MCDPs ("CDP Newsletter," Central Region, 1 Jan. 1970: 7, CDPA).

[138] Survey by the Club Drive, San Antonio, discussion group, 2001: Sisters Margit Maria Nagy, Madonna Sangalli, Esther Habermann, Eugenia Ann Stell, Ann Petrus, María Carolina Flores, and Sharon Rohde, CDPA.

experience many Sisters have had. "As I look back, I see that every place I have been and everything to which I have been called—even if at the time I didn't know what I was doing or wasn't that well prepared for it—served to develop something in me I didn't even know was there. And that prepared me for what came next."[139] This was an example of Providence at work.

Sister Anita Brenek said that before Vatican Council II she saw God primarily as the provider of rules, requirements, and regulations who is to be followed on a straight and narrow path. In the convent she came to know a loving God. "I came to know Jesus in addition to the Father Provider, the Jesus who asks us to risk in life and to live fully and trust God. The last few years I've been on a journey toward the Spirit, trusting more in the Spirit's guidance."[140]

The words differed; the profound experience was similar; and the people served agreed that they learned much about the provident aspect of God simply from observing the Sisters. Rev. Bill Morell, OMI, who was Provincial of the OMI Southwest Province and then a missionary in Zambia before becoming the President of Oblate School of Theology in San Antonio, after long association with the Sisters, observed that their charism could be considered both an advantage and a disadvantage:

> You are committed both to reading the signs of the times and standing in faith before the future with confidence that Divine Providence will guide the community to build the Kingdom. With you, giving credit to God rather than taking it on yourselves is a habit of the heart; you do not worry much about yourselves or your future. However, this may be why you do not seem eager to advertise the Congregation and urge women to join you. Knowing you well and admiring you, I am surprised that recruits are not lining up eager to enter the Congregation.[141]

Mary Catherine Franz-Eide noticed that the

> Sisters reached out in educating those who lacked opportunity or faith in themselves. They also recognized people with academic ability beyond the usual and supported them to develop that ability to the fullest. They helped people accept that we all contribute by what we do wherever we are. This is God's providential plan.[142]

---

[139] Oral interview, 21 Dec. 2000, CDPA.

[140] Oral interview, 4 Aug. 2000, CDPA.

[141] Oral interview, 8 Apr. 2003, CDPA.

[142] Oral interview, 20 Feb. 2003, CDPA.

Archbishop Patrick Flores believed that the CDPs he knew taught him that "Providence is the reality of God's presence, and we can tune into it and let God be in charge. The Lord will provide; we are just to have faith and confidence."[143] The CARA report described Sisters having the charism of Providence: "They react to difficult situations not with fear, but with a clear eye toward the facts of the situation and a practical attitude about doing what they need to do."[144]

Intensified interest in the charism of Providence did not lead to self-centeredness but rather to awareness that it was shared by other Congregations not founded by Father Moye and was also evident in persons who were not vowed religious. In April 1980, Sisters from eleven Congregations named Providence met in Great Falls, Montana, for the first Providence Symposium. Calling themselves Women of Providence in Collaboration (WPC), this group sponsored regular retreats, colloquia, and symposia dealing with topics of common interest. Theologians from the Congregations reflected, wrote, and published their best insights on that aspect of God called Providence. Sister Mary Christine Morkovsky delivered a key address, "A Process View of Divine Providence," at a Providence Colloquium in Holyoke, Massachusetts, in 1991. Sister Jane Ann Slater and Sister Ann Petrus facilitated WPC "Providence Events" in 1996 and 2003.

Former Sister Evelyn Thibeaux when she was on exclaustration in the late 1980s noticed "the real deepening of the spirituality of the Congregation." She sensed "growth not only spiritually but psychologically in the sense of hope." She also observed some "anxiety because of the growing age of the Congregation and the small number." The Sisters said, "We don't know exactly what is going to happen to us as a religious community far into the future, but we are going to lay the foundation for our work to continue." Along with hope, anxiety, and concern to lay a lasting foundation, she "noticed a new peace and a new openness, which I would describe as a real deepening of faith."[145]

Conclusion

No one anticipated in the middle of the twentieth century all of the changes that were in store for women religious in the Catholic Church. The Congregation's history illustrates the description of historian R. Scott Appleby:

> The combination of change at home and in the universal Church meant that long taken-for-granted patterns of behavior, forms of

---

[143] Oral interview, 8 May 2003, CDPA.

[144] CARA report, 259.

[145] Oral interview, 15 June 2002, CDPA.

the expression of belief and moral attitudes became problematic; to be examined, evaluated, retained, discarded or renewed in terms of contemporary perspectives and needs, a process increasingly personal rather than corporate.[146]

Sister Huberta Gallatin looking back over this period observed:

> It took time and experience and a certain permissiveness along with discernment to make necessary changes. The climate had to be prepared. Had we rushed ahead, there would have been more error than trial. Processes must be carried out by unique individuals with their own human qualities. True, some are more visionary and intuitive than others, but others may think more clearly and demand more practicality. The balance is necessary. I think Divine Providence had a hand in positioning all of us. There was prayerful sincerity in all that we did.[147]

Mary Catherine Franz-Eide, who was a member of the Congregation living through some of the changes to which Sister Huberta referred, believed that "the Sisters worked through major changes in this period because all were encouraged to participate in the changes. No one was forced, and everyone was accepted. Ideas of change were presented, but it was left to individuals if, when, and how they would respond." Because of participation and respect for each individual's pace of adaptation, "we stuck together as a Congregation, counted on one another, and accepted our responsibilities to the Congregation, to one another, and to the Church. We were encouraged not to be afraid, to go ahead, to see and prepare for all aspects of change."[148]

Sister Margaret Ann Verzwyvelt also identified some distinctive reasons CDPs stayed a mid-course during this period of great societal and ecclesial change. "We are a group of women who deep down know our place in the work of the Church. We are not afraid to go forward. That is a tremendous gift of our administrations from years gone by and the legacy of Father Moye."[149]

Priests who have cooperated with the Sisters over the years corroborated this view. Monsignor Roy Rihn, an octogenarian who interacted with the Sisters since his childhood in Castroville, Texas, singled out five characteristics.

---

[146] Address to the assembly of the National Federation of Priests' Councils, May 5, 2003, Kansas City, Missouri, quoted in "Historical Overview: Priests in America, 1930-2002," *Origins* 33, 4 (June 5, 2003): 55.

[147] Oral interview by Sister Angelina Murphy, 1982, CDPA.

[148] Oral interview, 20 Feb. 2003, CDPA.

[149] Oral interview, 20 July 2000, CDPA.

They are real sisters to one another. They don't just believe; they believe *in* the Providence of a loving God. Other characteristics are their openness to change and their loving acceptance of former CDPs. Their hospitality is legendary. And finally, they are not angry, strident feminists. They are gentle Christian feminists. I owe them a debt of gratitude for first opening my eyes to patriarchies of oppression of women, both in society and in the Church.[150]

Father Bill Morell, OMI, also noted that he would not characterize CDPs as angry. "Trust in Providence does not fit with anger, which implies that what I'm doing is exclusively *my job* or that someone let me down. You are dedicated to excellence in everything you do without a hint of arrogance. You do not need to broadcast or put on airs. You let competency be your credentials."[151]

Father Mario Arroyo, former vocation director of the Galveston-Houston diocese, first met CDPs when he was a seminarian and worked closely with a number of them for almost 30 years. He found a good match between his priorities of evangelization and catechesis and the charism of the Congregation. CDPs were not a "flash in the pan" or "fair-weather volunteers who leave when they are bored or not appreciated." They are flexible, but "pull steadily in the same direction, no matter what." The adaptability that enabled them to weather fast-paced change is rooted in a firm sense of what it is to be a woman religious and enables them to resist extremes. They are neither carried away by the latest fads nor stubbornly attached to their own plans.

The Sisters have a very good balance between pragmatism and a stable identity as religious focused on the mission. They are neither overly liberal nor overly conservative. They have been impacted by the world in a positive way. I've always experienced in them a reasoned, Gospel-driven desire to make good judgments within the signs of the times. I've never experienced a CDP having an a priori agenda or giving excessive attention to superficial things such as a traditional habit. I used to want to see clearly the end of a project before I got it started, but I have assimilated from them some of the Providence charism of total commitment to the Gospel without needing to have everything tied down.[152]

---

[150] Written communication, 25 March 2001, CDPA.

[151] Oral interview, 4 Apr. 2003, CDPA. Father Morell's description of CDPs is extremely positive. He sees the Sisters as courageous, honest, fun-loving, collaborative, outstanding educators and ministers.

[152] Oral interview, 17 Feb. 2003, CDPA.

Sister Barbara Zimmerer illustrated Father Arroyo's assessment. She was never in one place longer than six years, but "I never got into a rut. I had to start over so many times that I just learned to create my own things."[153] Sister Madeleine Zimmerer, when she decided to leave a parish after eight years, was not sure where she would go next, but her attitude was very typical of CDPs. "I trust God will put me where I'm supposed to be. There are times my trust in Divine Providence has gotten very thin like a thread, and other times it has been very thick like a rope. But I still keep hanging on and trusting. I have a very peaceful feeling."[154]

At the present time no one can see clearly whether the Congregation itself will continue into the future. Sister Madlyn Pape thought congregations do not need to be "as large as they used to be, partly because we have done such a good job of educating lay people. However, I do think that as there are fewer of us, it is more important for us to be in roles, positions, and ministries where our values can make a difference in the larger setting."[155]

Sister María Carolina Flores thought that being a Congregation of older women was an advantage

> because older women don't have to worry about many things. We could challenge people more and be less afraid to offend. Our past leaders sometimes offended others because they were working not to their advantage but to the advantage of the people they were serving. We have become more cautious as we became more professional and more concerned about our public image. I think we could have a future and be prophetic. If anyone knows the injustices of the Church, we do.[156]

Sister Teresa Pauline Hereford thought that "the second Vatican Council was definitely a turning point in the history of the Church and definitely a turning point in the history of our Congregation." Although all the effects of the Council are not yet known, it helped each Sister see herself "not so much as just a member of a religious congregation but as a member of the total Church." The Sisters began to ask themselves where they "fit in the trends and choices of the total Church. We haven't totally answered that question and probably will have to live through this uncertainty longer to find out just how we as women religious contribute to the life of the Church as a whole."[157]

---

[153] Oral interview, 3 July 2000, CDPA.

[154] Oral interview, 10 July 2000, CDPA.

[155] Oral interview, 21 Dec. 2000, CDPA.

[156] Oral interview, 25 May 2000, CDPA.

[157] Oral interview, 9 Sept. 2000, CDPA.

Sister Mary Margaret Hughes also thought that Sisters needed to grow up and make adult decisions rather than be led like children. However, she was not sure of the Congregation's future. "We religious have certainly served an important role in the world. We lost something by changes we made, but I believe we gained more than we lost. Until we find a new direction, until we really begin to be for people and serve in a more dedicated way, then I can't say that we are as good as we could be."[158] Sister Antoinette Billeaud's opinion was:

> We thought that our congregation would always exist, but we are beginning to understand now that some of us will and some of us won't. We will do the best we can to preserve the mission. If it's to be, then it will be. Maybe there are other ways of doing mission and ministry than what we have done. Maybe there are other organizations that will come to take our place. We have to trust that our Provident God will be a part of all of this transition.[159]

Like the first two Sisters who came to Texas from France, the leaders who went into debt to launch new institutions, the Sisters who stood up against social injustice, the chapter delegates who approved experimentation with basic structures and customs, or the retired Sisters who patiently waited for their final call, the CDPs at the start of the twenty-first century had no blueprints to follow for their next steps. Looking back at their predecessors, they knew they also would have to adjust and change to remain faithful co-creators with a Provident God. Looking forward they remained ready "to follow the promptings of the Spirit in Christ's attitude of self-offering" so as to make "the love of the Father for each person" evident in all their relationships."[160] An unwavering trust in God urged them to continue looking for signs in events and people around them that would indicate where to go and what to do.

---

[158] Oral interview, 18 June 2000, CDPA.

[159] Oral interview, 1 June 2000, CDPA.

[160] "Constitutions, Norms, and Commentary," 1968, p. 56.

APPENDICES

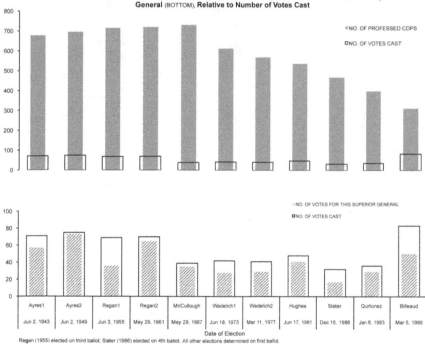

Appendix I.
Number of Professed CDPs on Day of Election (TOP) and Number of Votes for the Sister Elected Superior General (BOTTOM), Relative to Number of Votes Cast

Regan (1955) elected on third ballot; Slater (1986) elected on 4th ballot. All other elections determined on first ballot.

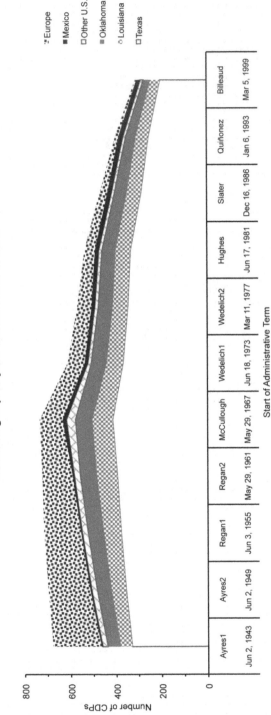

Appendix II.

Geographical Areas from which CDPs Entered the Congregation for All Who Were Professed at the Time of Mother Angelique Ayres' 1943 Election or Later

Legend:
- :' Europe
- ■ Mexico
- □ Other U.S.
- ■ Oklahoma
- ◇ Louisiana
- □ Texas

Y-axis: Number of CDPs (0, 200, 400, 600, 800)

X-axis: Start of Administrative Term

Ayres1	Ayres2	Regan1	Regan2	McCullough	Wedelich1	Wedelich2	Hughes	Slater	Quiñonez	Billeaud
Jun 2, 1943	Jun 2, 1949	Jun 3, 1955	May 29, 1961	May 29, 1967	Jun 18, 1973	Mar 11, 1977	Jun 17, 1981	Dec 16, 1986	Jan 6, 1993	Mar 5, 1999

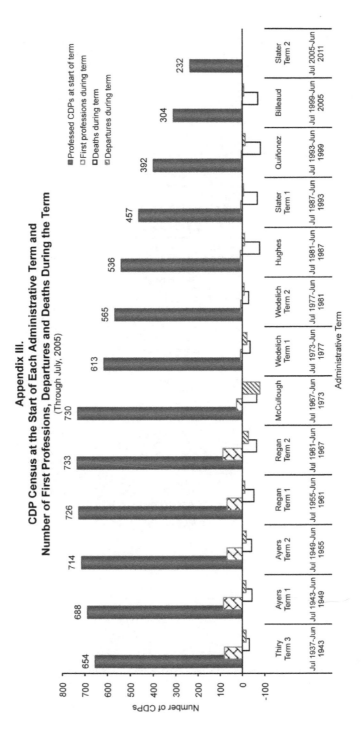

Appendix III.
CDP Census at the Start of Each Administrative Term and
Number of First Professions, Departures and Deaths During the Term
(Through July, 2005)

LS Dancer. Based on data maintained by CDP Archives.

Appendix IV.
Field of Study, University Conferring Degree, and Year Degree Conferred
for CDPs with Earned Doctorates
who Ministered at Our Lady of the Lake University

Field	University Conferring Degree	Sister of Divine Providence
BIOLOGY	Catholic University of America	Mary Clare Metz
	Notre Dame University	Elizabeth Anne Sueltenfuss
	University of Maryland	Hilary Christopher*
CHEMISTRY	Catholic University of America	Clarence Friesenhahn
	Catholic University of America	Mary Grace Doebel
	University of Texas at Austin	Isabel Ball
	University of Colorado	Jane Ann Slater
CLASSICAL LANGUAGES	Catholic University of America	Inviolata Barry
DRAMATIC ART	Northwestern University	Kathryn Keefe
EDUCATION	Catholic University of America	Pia Heinrich
	Catholic University of America	Antonina Quinn
	Northwestern University	Catherine Walker
	George Peabody College	Micheleen Barragy*
	University of Houston	Eugenia Ann Stell
EDUCATIONAL ADMINISTRATION	University of Texas at Austin	Virginia Clare Duncan
EDUCATIONAL PSYCHOLOGY	University of Texas at Austin	L Suzanne Dancer
ENGLISH	Catholic University of America	Angelica O'Neill
	University of Texas at Austin	Generosa Callahan
	Yale University	Callista Carr*
	University of Michigan	Lora Ann Quiñonez
	Michigan State University	Francine Danis*
	University of North Texas	Phyllis Bunnell
ENGLISH EDUCATION	University of Texas at Austin	Charlotte Kitowski
GREEK	Catholic University of America	Agnes Clare Way
HISTORY	Catholic University of America	Paul of the Cross McGrath
	Catholic University of America	Angela Fitzmorris
	St. Louis University	Janet Griffin
	University of Washington	Margit Maria Nagy
	Arizona State University	Maria Carolina Flores
HOME ECONOMICS EDUCATION	Ohio State University	Angelina Breaux
LIBRARY SCIENCE	Columbia University	Lucille McCreedy*
MATHEMATICS	Catholic University of America	Laetitia Hill
	University of Texas at Austin	Marilyn Molloy
	University of Maryland	Matthew Twardowski*
	Tulane University	Ann Petrus
MUSIC THEORY	Indiana University	Jule Adele Espey
PHILOSOPHY	St. Louis University	Mary Christine Morkovsky
PSYCHOLOGY	St. Louis University	Karen Keefe*
SOCIAL WORK	University of Illinois	Marian Angela Aguilar
SOCIOLOGY	Catholic University of America	Frances Jerome Woods
	Columbia University	Helen Rose Fuchs*
SPANISH	Louisiana State University	Maria Christina Quiñonez*
SPEECH PATHOLOGY	Northwestern University	Mary Arthur Carrow*
	Oklahoma University	Lourdes Leal
THEOLOGY	St. Mary's School of Sacred Theology	Berenice Trachta
	Fordham University	Lillian Turney

*Subsequently left the congregation

APPENDIX V

SYNOPSIS OF ACTS OF CDP CHAPTERS
SINCE VATICAN COUNCIL II

Chapter 1967-1968, Renewal Chapter, Constitution Chapter
Formulate a new CDP Constitution in the context of Vatican II decrees and documents
Introduce experimentation in various aspects of community life and in dress
Introduce collegiality and subsidiarity in decision making
Introduce Sisters' participation in meaningful civic and social programs
Permit Sisters to return to baptismal names and to wear wrist watches

Chapter 1973, Renewal Chapter, Direction-setting Chapter
Endorse the *1967-68 Constitution*
Formulate *Refounding our Communion:* principles and beliefs from the *1967-68 Constitution*
    adapted to the times
Change administrative term of office to four years
Establish a Council of Regional Committees, a development team to assist community and
    personal development, and centralized financing
Preserve our heritage by initiating plans for a Congregational archives

Chapter 1977, Renewal Chapter, Direction-setting Chapter
Establish goals: 1) carry out our mission in contemporary society, 2) express concern for all creation,
    3) form ourselves and others in justice, 4) interpret our four fundamental virtues in ways
    significant to the times, 5) discover and articulate our apostolic spirituality
Re-affirm principles and beliefs in *Refounding Our Communion*
Re-emphasize collegiality and subsidiarity in decision making
Study government structures

Chapter 1981, Direction-setting Chapter
Re-state the five goals of Chapter 1977
Declare a corporate commitment to stand with the materially poor
Establish an office of social justice
Return to six-year administrative term of office
Establish clusters as basic units of government
Call for a Constitution-writing Committee
Accept widows and divorcees as candidates for membership
Establish a program for CDP Associates

Chapter 1987, Constitution Chapter, Direction-setting Chapter
Accept the new CDP Constitution and seek Rome's approval
Adopt a mission statement
Suggest a Congregation-wide discernment process to consider international ministry
Develop further the Associates program
Study more deeply the Congregation as community and our apostolic spirituality
Establish a Ministry Office and a Development Office

Chapter 1993, Direction-setting Chapter, Transformational Chapter
Formally adopt a Statement of Commitment: "The transforming power of Providence impels
    us to commit ourselves to the mission of Jesus to bring about the New Creation of justice,
    peace, freedom, and love. At this moment in our history this mission calls us to a particular
    commitment to women, the earth, and the excluded. . . Living out this commitment, we
    will together, with all creation, be transformed."

Chapter 1999, Direction-setting Chapter
Resolve to:
    (1)   live our fundamental virtues as a witness to the transforming power of Providence,
    (2)   build anew community founded on the unity and diversity of the Trinity,
    (3)   practice radical hospitality,
    (4)   determine and act out of a common understanding of authority, power, and
          interrelatedness

APPENDIX VI

Sisters Professed between 1943 and 2000 having more than two CDP Siblings with Dates of Profession

Beyer, Bridget (1888-1954)
Antonia (1887-1898)
Clothilda (1888-1937)

Bell, Ann Linda (1935-
Romaine (1936-
Mary Jane (1941-

Bezner, Anna Rose (1946-
Ramona (1948-
*Kathleen (1952-1972)

Bielski, Barbara (1923-1950)
Laura (1926-1988)
Martha Marie (1940-1994)

Billeaud, Denise (1948-
Antoinette (1959-
Theresa Ann (1965-

Brossman, Alphonsus (1920-1982)
George (1924-1990)
Eugene (1925-1985)

Doebel, Mary Grace (1928-2002)
Marie (1934-2002)
Pauline (1947-2000)

Fenelon, Norbert (1904-1987)
James (1907-1971)
Rosaline (1913-1969)

Fikac, Sylvester (1907-1912)
Prisca (1908-1970)
Dennis (1921-1992)
Mildred (1929-1998)

Fitzpatrick, Crescentia (1906-1918)
Berchmans (1907-1979)
Vivian (1908-1988)
Erasma (1910-1980)

Flusche, Josephine (1899-1961)
Constantia (1904-1963)
Cordula (1904-1960)
Emerita (1904-1960)

Frei, Adela, (1900-1935)
Ludwina (1910-1966)
Florentina (1912-1965)
Perseveranda (1912-1962)

Friesenhahn, Columba (1896-1943)
Clarence (1906-1972)
Hope (1907-1972)
Assumpta (1903-1962)

Fuchs, Tharsilla (1932-2001)
Liliosa (1937-1984)
Audrey (1944-2005)

Gallatin, Huberta (1929-2002)
Margaret Ellen (1946-1999)
Rose Marie (1949-

---

* *left the Congregation*

Gentemann, Lucille (1926-1944)
Immaculate (1927-
Elaine (1929-
Anysia (1932-1983)

Heinrich,Pia (1904-1959)
Romuald (1904-1982
Joan of Arc (1916-1960)

Hruzek, Raphaella (1916-1986)
Flora (1919-1987)
Florida (1925-1997)

Klein, Consortia (1910-1975)
Victorine (1914-1997)
*Adolphine (1914-1941)

Lehman, Cyril (1908-1954)
Fidelis (1911-1991)
Celeste (1912-1984)
Evelyn (1913-1991)

Martinka, Rose Marie (1925-1989)
Kostka (1927-
Elizabeth Marie (1936-1995)

Meyer, Edward (1895-1950)
Cecilia (1900-1973)
Romana (1904-1964)

Okruhlik, Cyprian (1904-1983)
Monica (1905-1973)
Eustacia (1915-1993)

Pekar, Pacifica (1925-1999)
Balbina (1927-1981)
George Marie (1940-1999)

Podesva, Geralda (1916-1986)
Dymphna (1917-1983)
Ruth (1919-1920)

Pousson, Rose (1925-1989)
Thérèse (1927-2006)
Carola (1930-1998)
*Rolanda (1935-1936)

Rodriguez, Julia Marie (1927-1997)
Agnes Rita (1929-1997)
Natalie Jean (1932-2003)

Rolf, Thomas Aquin (1893-1955)
Benedicta (1904-1963)
Leopoldine (1904-1957)

Rollwitz, Ventura (1930-2002)
Adeline (1932-1999)
Eva (1934-1991)
Eulalia (1940-1986)

Samland, Georgia (1907-1981)
Feliciana (1916-1985)
Gertrude Marie (1916-1974)

Schad, Liboria (1923-1997)
Alma Sophie (1929-1999)
Vera (1932-
*Ann Virginia (1941-1944)

Schoech, *Rosalia (1899-1906)
*Anselma (1904-1909)
Perpetua (1920-1962)

Schwenzfeier, Conception (1907-1968)
Pachomius (1908-1915)
Fidelia (1911-1979)
Wendelina (1911-1975)

Sheehan, Basil (1906-1964)
Maxima (1908-1970)
Malachy (1912-1987

Tomczak, Lillian (1926-2000)
Mary (1924-2002)
Simplicius (1924-1956)

Vrba, Theonilla (1932-1994)
Martha (1935-2004)
Dorothy Ann (1938-2007)

Wollgarten, Remigia (1900-1941)
Bermana (1904-1935)
Anacleta (1904-1955)
Linus (1904-1953)
Claudia (1904-1947)

Zimmerer, Mary Rose (1945-
Herman Mary (1946-
Barbara James (1950-

---

* *left the Congregation*

APPENDIX VII

CDP GENERAL ADMINISTRATIONS, 1943-1999

(# did not complete her term of office)

1943   Angelique Ayres
Philothea Thiry #
    Angelica O'Neill, 1946-49
Antonina Quinn
Antoinette Loth
Eugenia Kaiser

1949   Angelique Ayres
Antonina Quinn
Eugenia Kaiser
Angelica O'Neill
Mercedes Kennedy

1955   Amata Regan
Angelique Ayres
Adelaide Marie Heyman
Mercedes Kennedy
Antonina Quinn

1961   Amata Regan
Mercedes Kennedy
Antonina Quinn #
    Marietta Fischer, 1963-67
Bernadette Marie Gremillion
Florence Marie Kubis

1967   Elizabeth McCullough
Frances Jerome Woods #
    Emella Hughes, 1970-73
Theresa Joseph Powers
Michael Rose Stanzel
Thérèse Pousson

1973   Charlene Wedelich
Lora Ann Quiñonez
Emella Hughes
Frances Lorene Lange
LoRayne Hoge #
    Marietta Fischer, 1974-77

1977   Charlene Wedelich
Irene Ceasar
Marietta Fischer
Lora Ann Quiñonez #
    Jane Coles, 1978-81
Frances Lorene Lange

1981   Mary Margaret Hughes
Jane Ann Slater
Anne Michele Berry
Madonna Sangalli
Irene Ceasar

1987   Jane Ann Slater
Frances Lorene Lange
Ann Petrus
Roberta Haby
Madlyn Pape

1993   Lora Ann Quiñonez
Ann Umscheid
Rose Kruppa
Lourdes Leal
Regina Decker

1999   Antoinette Billeaud
Cathy Parent
Mary Christine Morkovsky
Patrice Sullivan
Diane Langford

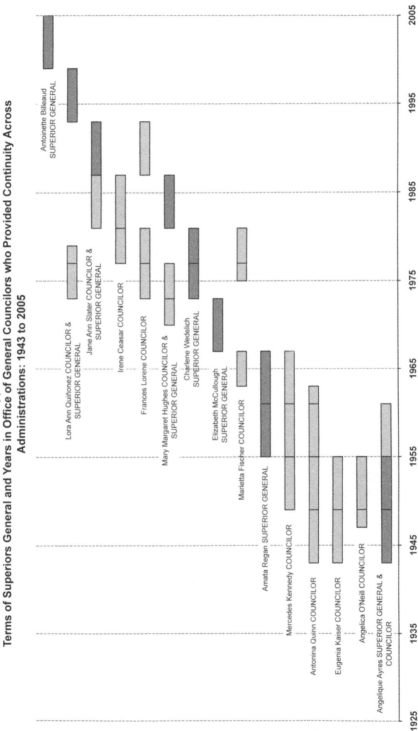

Appendix VIII.
Terms of Superiors General and Years in Office of General Councilors who Provided Continuity Across Administrations: 1943 to 2005

INDEX OF PERSONS

Unless otherwise indicated, all Sisters are members of the Congregation of Divine Providence (CDP).

INDEX OF TOPICS

CPSIA information can be obtained
at www.ICGtesting.com
Printed in the USA
LVHW091613300720
661977LV00001B/57